Mabel Dodge Luhan

New Woman, New Worlds

Lois Palken Rudnick

University of New Mexico Press
Albuquerque

Library of Congress Cataloging in Publication Data

Rudnick, Lois Palken, 1944–
  Mabel Dodge Luhan.

  Bibliography: p.
  Includes index.
  1. Luhan, Mabel Dodge, 1879–1962.   2. United States—
Biography.   I. Title
CT275.L838R83   1984   973.9′092′4 [B]   84-7415
ISBN 0-8263-0763-9, cloth
      0-8263-0995-X, paper

Design by Milenda Nan Ok Lee

© 1984 by the University of New Mexico Press.
First paperbound printing, University of New Mexico Press, 1987

Contents

Acknowledgments

For Steven and Deborah

I owe a great deal of thanks to the following people for their help and advice during the preparation of my manuscript for publication: my colleagues and friends Francis R. Hart, Linda Dittmar, Mary Anne Ferguson; my editors, Beth Hadas and Dana Asbury; and, most of all, my husband, Steven, who has been a constant support and keen critic throughout all the stages of my research and writing. I would also like to thank the following people for taking the time to share with me their memories of Mabel Luhan: Bonnie Evans, Miriam Hapgood DeWitt, Frank Waters, Joseph Foster, Eya Fechin Branham, Rowena Myers Martinez.

Grateful acknowledgment is extended to the following libraries and persons for permission to quote from unpublished letters and manuscripts: David Schoonover, American Literature Collection, the Beinecke Rare Book and Manuscript Library, Yale University; Judith Schiff, Sterling Library, Yale University; Cathy Henderson, Humanities Research Center, the University of Texas at Austin; Irene Moran, the Bancroft Library, University of California, Berkeley; and Miriam Hapgood DeWitt, Marjorie Content Toomer, Grace Collier, Georgia O'Keeffe, Ansel Adams, Harrison Smith, James Kraft, Paul Gitlin, Calman Levin, Donald Gallup, Laurence Pollinger.

Introduction

It is in man and not in woman that it has hitherto been possible for Man to be incarnated. For the individuals who seem to us most outstanding, who are honored with the name of genius, are those who have proposed to enact the fate of all humanity in their personal existences, and no woman has believed herself authorized to do this.
(Simone de Beauvoir, The Second Sex)[1]

Mabel Dodge Luhan tried to enact the fate of humanity through her personal existence. In the early 1920s, a Chicago newspaper reporter claimed she was "the most peculiar common denominator that society, literature, art and radical revolutionaries ever found in New York and Europe."[2] Although one cannot be sure what the reporter meant by "peculiar," Luhan was indeed a "common denominator" whose life connects important social and intellectual issues in late-nineteenth- and early-twentieth-century European and American life. Chief among these was the issue of the "New Woman" and her relationship to modern America's emergence from the Victorian age. Through her own writings and activities and the works of newspaper reporters, painters, poets, and fiction writers, Mabel became a leading symbol of the New Woman: sexually emancipated, self-determining, in control of her own destiny. She seemed free to go where she wanted and do as she pleased. To many she heralded Woman as World Builder.

Born in 1879 to a wealthy Buffalo family, Mabel was schooled in charm and groomed to marry, like most Victorian women of her class. Stultified emotionally and intellectually at home and in school, she yearned for a life ennobled by Poetry and Beauty. After the accidental death of her first husband and the birth of her first and only child, Mabel was sent to Paris by her family. In 1905 she met and married Edwin Dodge. When they moved to Florence, Mabel determined to make a new life that would express her aesthetic impulses. She devoted the next eight years to realizing her dream of the Renaissance. The villa she reconstructed, the clothes she wore, the very consciousness she applied to her daily life—all were materials for her living monument. So too were the artists she collected to grace her salon and share her table: Gertrude and Leo Stein, Paul and Muriel Draper, Eleanor Duse, and Bernard Berenson. Jacques-Émile Blanche, a portrait painter of the socially mighty, was commissioned to immortalize her in her guise as a Renaissance lady.

By 1912, Mabel found this Florentine world aesthetically and emotionally bankrupt. It seemed all form and no content. She returned to America and settled in Greenwich Village, where, for the next three years, she presided over what was perhaps the most famous salon in American history. Her apartment at 23 Fifth Avenue became internationally known as a gathering spot where the "movers and shakers" of the pre–World War I era engaged in a free exchange of avant-garde ideas in art, politics, and society. On Mabel's "Wednesday Evenings," one might find A. A. Brill introducing Freud's latest theory to a roomful of prominent writers and activists, among them Walter Lippmann, Max Eastman, and Lincoln Steffens. Here, Margaret Sanger sought support for her nascent birth-control movement, Hutchins Hapgood debated the virtues of free love, Bill Haywood and Emma Goldman argued the anarchist's view of the struggle of the proletariat. Out of the heady confusion of competing programs and ideals, Mabel predicted, would emerge a brave new world to replace the anomie of twentieth-century life.

The Victorian and *fin de siècle* world Mabel had rejected left as one legacy a generation of men and women who craved and demanded a deeper emotional sustenance, a broader social base, a freer range of expression. The radical innocents of Greenwich Village had the exuberant optimism and the will to experiment that made such a new world seem imminent. Within it, men and women would rejoice in their sexuality and all classes work in harmony for a nonexploitative economic system, while artists, humanists, social scientists, and political activists cooperated to enact change.

Mabel immersed herself in the spirit of her times, supporting, writing, and speaking about the various causes that promised to liberate her and her fellow men and women from the spiritual and psychological shackles of the past. She became vice-president of the Association of Artists and Sculptors that sponsored the Armory Show; a member of the advisory board and a contributor to *The Masses,* the leading left-wing journal of the day; a supporter of the Woman's Peace Party; and one of the early popularizers of Freudian psychology in a weekly column she wrote for the Hearst papers.

During World War I, some of Mabel's friends and associates rushed to Europe as correspondents, while others stayed home to join or fight the Wilsonian war machine. Mabel chose a different course. In Greenwich Village the dynamic of her life had been revolutionary change. By 1916, however, she had begun to feel scattered in so many directions she feared she would never unite the fragments. When her third husband, Maurice Sterne, discovered northern New Mexico as the ideal place for her to find herself, she agreed to move. Among the Pueblo Indians of Taos, New Mexico, Mabel discovered a culture that seemed to offer everything she had lacked in childhood, failed to re-create in Florence, and could not find in Greenwich Village. The Pueblos offered a model of permanence and stability, a 600-year-old community where individual, social, artistic, and religious values were fully integrated.

Taos was the last place Mabel tried to build what she called a "cosmos." Here she became a leading proponent of the primitivist doctrines that attracted many alienated white intellectuals in the 1920s. Soon after her arrival, she met and fell in love with Antonio Luhan, a full-blooded Pueblo Indian who became her fourth and last husband in 1923. Mabel believed that she and Tony would serve as a "bridge between cultures." She dreamed of establishing Taos as the birthplace for a new American civilization, one not based on getting and spending, or on the redistribution of wealth. The Pueblos' lack of interest in material wealth, their devotion to communal values, their healthy respect for human limitation and for the natural environment seemed a sane counterpoint to the frenetic white civilization she saw as heading for self-annihilation. Throughout the 1920s, 1930s, and 1940s, Mabel wrote numerous articles both for the popular press and for literary journals to convince her fellow Americans that salvation lay in the Indian way. She sought support for her messianic mission by attracting talented artists, writers, and reformers to Taos: John Marin, Georgia O'Keeffe, and Andrew Dasburg, to immortalize the beauty of the Taos landscape; Leopold Stokowski, to capture the rhythms of native American music; D. H. Lawrence and Robinson Jeffers, to help write the gospel of her newfound Eden; John Collier, to protect the Pueblos' lands and cultural hegemony.

Of all the worlds that Mabel tried to create, her dream of turning Taos into a paradise regained speaks to us most clearly today, and not just because it was a modern reincarnation of the oldest American myth. She addressed the issues that still challenge us: the possibility of our survival in an individualistic world, in a country where community is rarely found, in a land that slowly chokes itself on the effluence of its industrial processes.

Mabel also speaks to those of us who are seeking to understand the roles of women in the American past and to define them for the future. For while she wished "to justify the universe by changing it, by thinking about it, by revealing it," she was convinced that what Beauvoir calls the   xi desire "to found the world anew" could only be actualized by men. The selves and worlds she tried to build always had to be "authorized" by men.[3] In spite of the many important contributions she made to the people and causes she supported, in spite of her myriad writings that are perceptive documentations of the social and intellectual history of her times, the outstanding fact of Mabel's life is that she never found a clear and coherent direction for herself. The primary reason why she never did was that she believed that women were dependent on men to realize their destinies.

Once we look past the sexually liberated image of the New Woman in the popular press and fiction of her day, we often discover women who are intellectually and emotionally reliant on men. When we examine the role that Mabel played in some of the fiction written about her, we find a woman as old as the Greek hetaira. In *The von Richthofen Sisters,* Martin Green places Mabel alongside Frieda Lawrence, Isadora Duncan, and Alma Mahler as one of the key figures in the revival of the *mutterrecht:* an early-twentieth-century movement that identified the basic creative energies of the life-force with women. The new women of the *mutterrecht* were intended to aid in the regeneration of society by inspiring its great male talents. Mabel cultivated this role assiduously and was duly rewarded: "In the hetaira men's myths find their most seductive embodiment; she is beyond all others flesh and spirit, idol, inspiration, muse; painters and sculptors will want her as model; she will feed the dreams of poets; in her the intellectual will explore the treasure of feminine 'intuition.'"[4]

Many forces in Mabel's life encouraged her to believe that playing the Muse to men of genius was the major route to power and importance for women. She had been trained from childhood in feminine passivity and learned well what Virginia Woolf called women's function "as looking-glasses possessing the magic and delicious power of reflecting the figure of a man at twice its natural size."[5] The male bohemians Mabel associated with in Greenwich Village encouraged her to be what Max Eastman called a "Mother Postulate," so they could be provided with the security and inspiration necessary to transform the world. Her twenty years in Freudian analysis, and her desire to become another Frieda for D. H. Lawrence, intensified her belief.

By allowing the powerful men she collected to draw upon her feminine essence, Mabel expected to control the process and direction of their creative energies. She wanted to be the artist-as-god, but she ended up playing the more traditional female role of the artist-of-life: at times shaping the lives of those about her into interesting patterns and textures, "happenings" that were brilliant but evanescent; at times plotting out the loves and lifelines of poets, painters, and men of action in order to satisfy her will-to-power. If Mabel remained a "child-woman," who never fully developed the "strengths and skills of adult autonomy,"[6] it was in good part because she could never reconcile her belief in women's necessary dependence on men with her strong desire for self-assertion and independence.

In *The Female Imagination,* Patricia Spacks suggests that Mabel's life and prose convey "the essential confusion of the woman whose sense of reality was always vicarious—unable fully to accept herself as a 'finger post' [a model or guide who points the way for other women], unable fully to exist as a separate self." It is just this "essential confusion" that makes Mabel representative of her times in a way that her more accomplished women friends—Emma Goldman, Margaret Sanger, Willa Cather—were not. As June Sochen has shown in her study *The New Woman: Feminism in Greenwich Village,* many of the heroines of feminist fiction suffered from just this kind of confusion.[7]

Mabel deliberately sought to become a heroine in fiction because she could not realize herself. She expected the artists she collected to transform what she called her "undifferentiated flow of vitality" into a coherent personality. By presenting herself as an object for their imaginations, she hoped to be transformed into a "subject." That Mabel looked to the world of art for self-realization and significance is not surprising if we recall Virginia Woolf's sardonic commentary on the conspicuous absence of women from the history texts:

> Not being a historian, one might go even further and say that women
> have burnt like beacons in all the works of all the poets from the
> beginning of time—Clytemnestra, Antigone, Cleopatra . . . Becky
> Sharp, Anna Karenina . . . the names flock to mind, nor do they recall
> women "lacking in personality and character." Indeed, if woman had no
> existence save in the fiction written by men, one would imagine her a
> person of the utmost importance; very various; heroic and mean;
> splendid and sordid; infinitely beautiful and hideous in the extreme; as
> great as a man, some think even greater. But this is woman in fiction.[8]

While Mabel never achieved the stature of a Clytemnestra or of an Anna Karenina in any of the fiction created about her, she was, interestingly enough, portrayed in all the roles that Woolf says one can imagine women in. She was heroic and mean, splendid and sordid, and if not infinitely beautiful, definitely striking and seductive; at times, hideous in the extreme. One of the most fascinating aspects of Mabel's life was the way she served the imaginations of artists engaged in the developing myth of the American character in the twentieth century.

Not long after the American Revolution, Hector St. Jean de Crèvecoeur asked, "What then *is* the American, this new man?" Those who wrote about Mabel seemed to be asking, "Who then is this New Woman?" The answer to the question depended on who was asking it. To Gertrude Stein,   xiii

Carl Van Vechten, and Max Eastman, Mabel's undammable and discontinuous feminine vitality was particularly suited to express the dynamism of modern American life. Mabel became nationally known as "Edith Dale" in the 1920s novels of Van Vechten. She was the woman who smiled and manipulated the vortex of artistic and social life in pre- and postwar America. In Eastman's *Venture* (1927), she is the hetaira, who initiates young rebels of the prewar era into the mysteries and glories of sex, art, and radical politics.

To Jacques-Émile Blanche's horrified and amused Jamesian eye, she was the New World on the make, out to rifle a decaying Europe and destroy what was not to her taste (*Aymeris, 1923*). During her early years in New Mexico, Mabel served Witter Bynner in a similar vein. In his protoabsurdist drama, *Cake* (1926), she is a type of the ugly American whose sexual and cultural appetites drive her to devour the world. For D. H. Lawrence, Mabel was an emblem of what he most loathed and liked about America: the lust for "knowing" that violated the mysteries of man and nature; the questing spirit of the New World, once embodied in the male American, now best represented in the female. In her final literary incarnation, *All of Their Lives* (1941), Myron Brinig embodied Mabel as an American Becky Sharp, a seriocomic symbol of his vision of twentieth-century America's Vanity Fair.

Many of the artists who fictionalized Mabel's life used it as a paradigm of the human condition in twentieth-century America. She was continually mythologized as a figure who had the potential to transform the world. Mabel's life represented what had traditionally been a male heroic quest: the commitment to break new frontiers, the desire to dominate the human and physical environment, the search for some transcendental reality that would give the individual a sense of connection and relatedness. What they felt was dangerous about Mabel was that she had too often merely disguised the worst of the male American's will-to-power with feminine sexual allure. While they saw her as having the potential to take the best in the American national character and improve upon it, she did not seem able to escape the sexual politics of the past.[9]

When Mabel began writing her memoirs in 1924, one of her overriding purposes was to offer her life as a paradigm for the human condition in the twentieth century. She offered the worst of herself on the public altar because she wished to facilitate the destruction of the system that had produced her. Mabel believed that all of her life before New Mexico epitomized the psychological and social destructiveness of the national obsession with "power, prestige, and possession."[10] In the fourth and final volume of her memoirs, she presented herself as redeemed through the grace offered her by Tony Luhan's love. Although she could not internalize them, she had the sensitivity to appreciate the values of Pueblo culture, which did not reward aggression and personal achievement as the highest social goals.

The final self Mabel offered the world, and through which she hoped to restore the world, was more the product of art than of reality. Mabel had attempted what she believed was the task of all true artists, a task that she had been convinced only men could achieve:

> Real art has the man in it, the spirit, the wish, and the courage that spin out of himself those qualities he needs to satisfy the discontent in him, and the artist is the greatest of us all in these divine aesthetics of self-creation.

Patricia Spacks speaks of the long tradition of women writers who have discovered their identities by "manufacturing [them] in prose," women for whom literature becomes a realm in which they achieve a kind of freedom they can not attain in their lives.[11] In this regard, as well as for the perceptive documentation of her times, Mabel's memoirs are an important contribution to the social and intellectual history of the human imagination.

Mabel's published memoirs play an important but limited role, however, in establishing her individual and representative significance as a twentieth-century American. In 1951, she shipped to Yale University 1,500 pounds of papers, including twenty-three volumes of autobiographical manuscripts and letters; seventeen volumes of scrapbooks that contain most of the articles written about her over her lifetime (as well as many about her prominent friends); several unpublished stories, poems, and essays (most of them autobiographical); and two unpublished novels.[12]

Mabel left the evidence of her life so carefully clipped, typed, and bound that one must conclude she was preparing for a postmortem continuation of her search "to be made real." Biography was the final, and perhaps most risky, mode through which she sought to have her identity and place in history established. Since her death in 1962, she has been treated with the lack of seriousness that has traditionally relegated women culture-carriers to footnotes in scholarly texts or to the gossipy accounts of popular biographers. Neither of the two biographical assessments written since then take account of the rich body of sources, her own and others, that establish her important place in American cultural history. Christopher Lasch dismisses Mabel as "another rich and restless woman, a footnote in the cultural history of Bohemia." Emily Hahn's *Mabel* reduces her life to an extended anecdote about her many loves and her headhunting of the famous artists with whom she surrounded herself.[13]

This biography makes use of all the resources that are available. They reveal a complex woman who tried to influence the course of American history and in so doing captured the imaginations of writers and artists who were seeking to come to terms with their own understanding of twentieth-century America. Because the fictional versions of Mabel's life document both the real and legendary roles she played, I take as much account of the literary as of the historical and social events that shaped her. Each biographical section is followed by a close analysis of Mabel's relationships with the writers who used her life to invent their visions of America. By examining Mabel's real and imagined lives, we will increase our understanding of the cultural forces that shaped modern America and of the New Woman who struggled to make her mark upon it.

Chapter 1

Background

The year is 1887, the place New York City. Grandfather Cook stands imposingly at the top of the staircase in his gloomy Fifth Avenue mansion. At the bottom of the stairs, looking up at his six feet some inches with awe, is his eight-year-old granddaughter, Mabel Ganson. To the child, he is "like a noble bird of some kind—the real American eagle." He moves slowly down the staircase, a self-assured Victorian priest of finance capitalism. When he arrives at the bottom of the staircase, he reaches "his bloodless, clawlike hand" into his pocket and withdraws a shining silver coin. "Here . . . Here is a silver dollar for you! Look at it! Now take it and never forget it!"[1]

This memory epitomized the substitution of power for love that Mabel attributed to the American upper classes into which she was born. Her response to her grandfather's votive offering was a mixture of respect and rage: admiration for the weight of the past he symbolized, matched by revulsion for the kind of life and living he stood for. She felt a "deep veneration" for her grandfather, "a glad reverence that he was mine and his words were law . . . a willingness and a submission to this symbol, yes, a desire to be prostrate to it because of that noble man, my lawgiver." Mabel's desire to submit to her grandfather's authority warred with an equally strong desire to ridicule it because of the inferiority of its power base: "So while I almost wanted to kneel down and accept that silver dollar from him like a sacrament, at the same time I wanted to cry out: 'Oh, nonsense! What do I care for your old dollars!'"

Scenes like this one crystallized D. H. Lawrence's view of Mabel's memoirs as "the most serious 'confession' that ever came out of America, and perhaps the most heart-destroying revelation of the American life-process that ever has or will be produced. . . . Life gave America gold and a ghoulish destiny." Mabel became the center of that destiny in Lawrence's American fiction, as her family had been central to it in fact.

1

She could not have chosen a more appropriate set of forebears to provide authentic background for her development as "a twentieth-century type."[2]

Mabel's great-grandparents partook in the founding and building of the American nation. They were pioneers and sturdy yeomen, the kind of people Thomas Jefferson asserted were the backbone of the young republic. Her grandparents belonged to the first generation of wealth created by the burgeoning trade and manufacturing associated with the rise of modern capitalism in the Jacksonian period. By middle age they had achieved the social and economic prominence earned by the financiers of the Industrial Revolution. They were preeminent representatives of the life-styles and values of the upper classes in the "Gilded Age." Mabel's parents' social and economic prominence was based solely on what they inherited. Their unfulfilled lives and unhappy marriage reflected a decaying Victorian gentility.

On Mabel's mother's side, the Cook family were pioneer settlers of western New York whose original ancestors came to America from Dorset, England in the seventeenth century and settled in Rhode Island. Great-grandfather Constant Cook settled in Bath. As Mabel put it, the Cooks "were" the town of Bath. When Cook could no longer "keep his dollars occupied" in his Bath bank, he moved to New York City, where he built his Fifth Avenue mansion.

Mabel's description of her Grandmother Cook's life in Bath is a wonderful evocation of a well-to-do countrywoman's life in mid-nineteenth-century America:

> Grandmother was always superintending the kitchen, helping to prepare
> the splendid country meals, training the young country maids,
> overseeing the preserving, the many complicated puddings and cakes and
> pies, the roasting of the big joints and fowls, and attending to the
> thousand details of a hearty, comfortable living. Besides, she was always
> "bringing up" her four handsome girls while their father, down in the
> village, spun the whole countryside out of himself. Horse-shoeing,
> banking, judging, railroad-building, house-building, town-building![3]

Grandfather spun so well that Grandmother Cook was deprived of her duties after they moved to New York City. There her days were filled by writing minutely detailed instructions to her daughters about how to run their households. Much later, in New Mexico, Mabel tried to re-create her grandmother's way of life in Bath. She hoped to regain the physical and psychological health she associated with the preindustrial America that men like her grandfather helped to destroy.

Great-grandfather Ganson left Scotland in the mid-eighteenth century and settled in Vermont. A captain in the Revolutionary War, he was wounded at the Battle of Bunker Hill. After the war, he settled in Le

Roy, a frontier town in western New York state. Captain Ganson's second son, John, was educated at Harvard, passed the bar, and was elected to the Senate in 1862 as a Democrat. A close friend of Abraham Lincoln's, he supported all of Lincoln's war measures, including emancipation. Mabel was brought up with the rumor that her great-uncle "would have been President if—." John's older brother, James, who was Mabel's grandfather, made his fortune in banking. Mabel remembers him as a "severe, humorless man" who spent most of his days in his downtown bank. The Ganson family was associated with Buffalo from the beginning of its industrial growth.[4]

Buffalo

The Buffalo the Ganson family moved to in the 1830s was a tightly knit, relatively homogeneous community of about eight thousand, with a strong sense of social cohesion. Few people lived on unearned increment. Property owners were usually the managers of their holdings, while the working class was made up mostly of artisans who served a small and well-known clientele. The social classes were not geographically segregated. Until the mid-1840s, Buffalo had only one paid policeman. It was the kind of small-town America that post–Civil War writers would remember with nostalgia.

By the late 1860s, Buffalo had become a major center of trade and commerce in America, second only to Chicago in shipping because of its strategic location at the "foot" of Lake Erie. In one generation, it began its growth from a village into an urban giant, whose flour, steel, and lumber mills, oil and sugar refineries, and breweries brought it both enormous wealth and poverty. According to a recent study, the city began to lose its social cohesion in the 1840s, as class lines solidified with the increasing "power of the ruling elite."[5]

Helping to support the city's wealth and its precipitous growth (the population tripled from 81,000 in 1861 to 244,000 in 1890) was the arrival of thousands of Irish, Italian, Slavic, and Polish immigrants. Alongside native workers, they labored in the mills and railroads, often for as little as ten and twenty cents an hour. Injuries, fatalities, and unemployment were a fact of their daily lives. By the turn of the century, 4,000 workmen a year were injured at the Lackawanna Railroad yards. In 1900, Buffalo had an unemployment rate of 19 percent and a class of chronic indigents who were supported through poor relief. Strikes and wage cuts went hand in hand with the economic recessions that occurred from the 1870s through the 1890s.[6] The Mabel Ganson who grew up in the high noon of the Gilded Age had only the remotest awareness of this "other America" that would become one of her focal points in the radical world she later joined in Greenwich Village.

An 1870 lithograph of Delaware Avenue gives a clear sense of how beautiful and secluded life was in the Buffalo Mabel knew as a child. Looking downtown from North Street, one sees princely estates hidden behind dignified rows of uniform trees. Thin wisps of smoke and blurred matchbox houses in the far background convey the only indications of industry and of the working classes. By the 1890s, there were sixty millionaires in Buffalo. The wealthy owners of the mills and refineries lived only two or three miles from the industries, wharves, row houses, and slums of the inner city. Yet socially and psychologically they were much further removed, for they lived in the city with the baronial splendor of a landed gentry.

In 1869, the same year that Mark Twain moved to Buffalo, America's foremost landscape designer, Frederick Law Olmsted, was commissioned to design a park system for the city. The parks and parkways he created covered one thousand acres. Spacious tree-lined avenues 100 feet across and boulevards 200 feet across, lined with six rows of trees on each side, were the product of his labors. The boulevards were designed to be the spokes of a wheel that would provide access for people from all over the city to a rural park four miles from downtown Buffalo. The park and parkways were, in fact, used primarily by the wealthy whose homes lined them.

Olmsted planned Delaware Avenue as one of the central arteries. Even today one can see remnants of its grandeur in the few remaining mansions that are being renovated and restored. While Mabel was growing up, the street was home to prominent bankers, lawyers, doctors, to the president of Lackawanna Steel and to the founder of Wells Fargo. The mansions built to display their fortunes were a mélange of architectural styles: imitation Tuscan villas stood next to English country houses of stucco and timber. French mansards rubbed shoulders with Queen Anne; Georgian Revival vied with Greek and Tudor. Such prominent architects as Stanford White and H. H. Richardson designed these mansions of marble and gingerbread that housed the splendor and the clutter of the Gilded Age.

In the 1880s and 1890s, most middle- and upper-class Buffalonians would have agreed with an author of *New England Magazine* that "The Queen of the Lakes" had "in store a mighty future." Buffalo was a microcosm of the burgeoning economic power of the nation: not only an important center of commerce, but of political power as well. In these decades, its reform mayor was sent to the White House. Grover Cleveland was the ideal president for the golden age of laissez-faire capitalism. His sound money policies and conservative political philosophy were firmly grounded in a faith that business would take care of the country's needs. In 1901 Buffalo achieved its apotheosis when it hosted the Pan-American

World Exhibition, a lavish and costly symbol of America's coming-of-age as an imperial power after the Spanish-American War.[7]

The street on which Mabel lived housed the social, economic, and political elite of Buffalo. Delaware Avenue was host to four presidents. Here Millard Fillmore built his Tudor Gothic mansion in the 1850s, where Lincoln came to visit as president-elect. In 1901, President McKinley was carried to a Pompeian brick mansion, where he died after having been shot by the anarchist Czoglocz. Theodore Roosevelt was sworn in as president across the street from Mabel's Delaware and North Street home, on the front steps of the Wilcox House, where she played frequently as a child.

The Rumseys and Carys, friends of the Gansons, set the social tone in late-nineteenth-century Buffalo. The Rumseys' lavish estate included a large lake for boating in the summer and skating in the winter. Horse-racing down Delaware Avenue was a favorite sport. There were elaborate costume balls; private theatricals; sleigh rides and strolls around Delaware Circle, lit with ornate gas lamps and banked with flowers; and vacations in the Berkshires, Newport, and Europe in the summers. There were elaborate dinner parties with numerous courses, for which Mabel's mother was famous.

The wealthy were building themselves a civilization: raising funds for music halls, a symphony orchestra, libraries, and a historical society to solidify their culture and their past.[8] The houses of worship they built were as lavish as their homes. As a child, Mabel attended Trinity Episcopal Church, just a few blocks from her home. It is a magnificent example of Gothic Revival, its dark, rich woods and velvet pews illuminated by stained-glass windows representing some of the finest work of America's master craftsmen John La Farge and Louis Tiffany. The rich also died lavishly. Forest Lawn Cemetery was a Delaware Avenue neighborhood, designed as a beautiful park with elaborate funeral statuary graced by lush grass and trees. Here, in 1890, an anonymous lady gave tribute to the earliest occupants of the land by paying $10,000 to have a statue erected of Red Jacket, a famous orator who was chief of the Wolf tribe of the Seneca. The young Mabel Ganson who picnicked in Forest Lawn would have missed the import of the monument's inscription. But it may have impressed upon her an early image of the American Indians whose savior she later tried to become: "When I am gone and my warnings are no longer heeded, the craft and avarice of the white man will prevail. My heart fails me when I think of my people, so soon to be scattered and forgotten."

Delaware Avenue was meant to stay an Anglo-Saxon preserve. When a German immigrant, who had recently made his fortune, moved onto it in the 1890s, his daughters were snubbed. It was whispered that they had not "'come out' like the other girls—they just 'came over.'" Mabel remembered her childhood milieu as a gilded wasteland, whose social rigidity and lavish exteriors often hid barren and empty lives. On Delaware Avenue everybody knew everyone else, but "people never talked to each other except of outward things. . . . There was hardly any real intimacy between friends, and people had no confidence in each other . . . [they] neither showed their feelings nor talked about them to each other."[9]

Childhood

The large, brick Victorian mansion in which Mabel was born on February 26, 1879, was a home that seemed "destined for sorrow." Originally built by a wealthy lumberman, who was found dead one winter night near his place of business, the house was then purchased by Buffalo's wealthiest social leader, Dexter Rumsey, as a wedding present for his daughter. She died within a year of moving into it. Next, James Ganson bought it for his son Charles as a wedding gift, when he married Sara Cook.[10] Though their destinies were not carved out for murder and early death, they certainly did seem programmed for marital misery.

Charles and Sara Ganson's lives were shadows of their parents' vigor and purposeful activity. Mabel's father was trained in law, but because of an extremely nervous and volatile disposition, he never worked at that or any other profession. He was an ineffectual man noted for his violent verbal outbursts and antisocial behavior. His inability to function satisfactorily in either business or private life may well have been compounded by his sense that there was nothing he had to do. Mabel remembered her father spending days in his study, when he wasn't shouting at Mabel's mother because of jealous "fits." While he lavished affection on his thoroughbred dogs, he gave none to Mabel: "I knew with all the prescience of a child that my father had no love for me at all. To him I was something that made a noise sometimes in the house and had to be told to get out of the way."[11]

Charles Ganson's feelings for his wife were summed up in his only recorded exhibition of a sense of humor: whenever Sara returned home from a trip, he would lower the monogrammed flag he flew on his front lawn to half-mast. Mabel's mother had all the "masculine" attributes her father lacked. According to Mabel, she was strong and decisive but also cold, unfeeling, and entirely self-centered. Mrs. Ganson had none of the responsibilities of her busy and capable mother and no creative outlets for her robust energies in a life given over to visiting, hunting, and dinner parties. She seemed indifferent toward her husband as well as toward her child. The only times Mabel remembers sharing any intimacy with her mother were on Sunday mornings when Sara would lie in bed and weep

Charles Ganson.   Sara Cook Ganson.

Grandma Cook (writing to her three daughters every day from her Fifth Avenue and 28th Street home).

Mabel Ganson, around age 5.

Mabel Ganson, around age 16.

Mabel Ganson, age 18, in coming-out dress.

Violette.

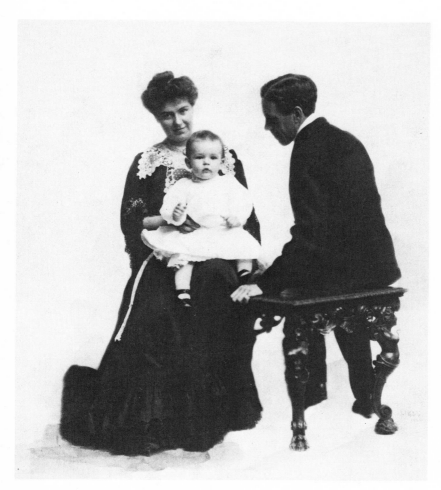

Mabel, Karl Evans, and John Evans.

Villa Curonia, Florence, 1904.

Yellow Salon, Villa Curonia.

Mabel and Edwin Dodge with John Evans, 1905.

Portrait of Mabel Dodge, by Florence Bradley, 1910.

Portrait of Mabel Dodge, by Jacques-Émile Blanche, 1911.

in self-pity about being bored and blue. "I have no recollections," Mabel tells us, "of my mother's ever giving me a kiss or a smile of spontaneous affection, or of any sign from my father except dark looks and angry sound. . . . We all needed to love each other and to express it, but we did not know how."[12]

Mabel's memories affirm Christopher Lasch's observation that the context for identity once provided by a strong family and community life was disappearing among the upper classes in the late nineteenth century. The society Mabel grew up in, with its stress on facade and its lack of purposeful activity (for women in particular), exacerbated the problems of her immediate family life. The child-rearing practices widespread among her class further contributed to her sense of social and personal isolation.[13]

The primary adult caretakers for Mabel and her friends in their formative years were their nursemaids. Often these were young immigrant girls who paid the children little mind except to correct their manners or to see that their physical needs were cared for. The children's relationships with their parents were primarily formal: "It was the custom to have the children after dinner," Mabel notes, in her sardonic description of the "children's hour." In the Ganson social circle, as in the family circle, people seemed to ignore each other's inward lives. All was form without content. Mrs. Ganson's formal tulip bed was Mabel's symbol for a society so petrified that it left no room for the growth of feeling, or for the development of a young person's identity. The garden, like Mabel's life, was "ordered and organized, nothing was left to fortuitous chance, and no life ever arose in it taking its own form."[14]

Two of Mabel's earliest childhood memories stand out as evocative symbols of her emotional and sensory hunger. Watching her nursemaid's friend tease the kitchen help one day by squirting milk across the room from her breast, Mabel stood transfixed. She slept with her nurse that evening, pulling, fondling, and kissing the girl's breast, after she had fallen asleep. When no milk appeared, she began to get rough and tried to injure it. Mabel obviously exaggerates her abuse of the breast, for the girl certainly would have awakened if her description were literally true. But the incident clearly indicates her desperation for maternal nourishment. That she experienced the breast as an object, as a detached symbol of mother love, is significant for understanding her narcissism; for as an adolescent and an adult she often related to women and men as objects for her manipulation.

During the many hours she spent in her nursery, Mabel sought to appease her need for affection by pressing her mouth against the Mother Goose figures that decorated her bedroom walls "until I had aroused in myself some feeling of comfort. . . . I believe if there had been one picture in that house that I could have looked at from which I could have drawn some of the spirit of life, I would have been satisfied by it. . . . Or one

15

face that had real feeling in it for me would have answered. But there was nothing and no one." Mabel's lifelong desire for "thrills" began during those nursery days when she experienced the panic of nonbeing that she so often called by the name of boredom: "Better a real pain, better a danger to life itself, than this negation of living that comes from not having anything to do." Her fear of purposelessness led to her obsession as an adult to be part of everything in her environment, to take up every cause, to experience emotions to their furthest limits. It contributed to her inability to stand still long enough to find herself or to commit herself to any one line of development: "So to escape from that burden became the great problem in the first five years and has remained so ever since, and to escape the *fear* of the pain of idleness has led me in curious deviations away from the true chances of escape into occupation. . . ."[15]

Mabel was given a great deal of freedom, within her limited social environment, once she was old enough to be let out of the house by herself. She spent much of her time doing as she pleased: riding her ponies wildly through her part of town, romping through the cemetery, rough-housing, playing games with the boys and girls in her set. The rigidity that marred the lives of the adults she knew did not affect the lives of their children, at least until they were old enough to be sent away to school: "all the streets and houses of our town were a good deal like a big campus where we could go in and out as we liked and where everything was alike as it is in a family. . . ."[16]

Mabel's neighborhood was, indeed, a good deal like a preserve that she did not have to leave in order to play, go to school, or worship. The church she attended was a few blocks from home, a palace that awed her with its solemn beauty. St. Margaret's Episcopal School for Girls was a Victorian house located conveniently across the street from her. The park in which she and her friends played was a mile away. Sometimes they were tempted to visit the "bad" part of Buffalo, but this was never more than a brief glimpse into an underworld that must have seemed magical to them, so distant was it from the world they knew.

Although Mabel gives us evidence of how active she was as a child, once she was allowed to leave the confines of her nursery on her own, she insists that she was idle, will-less, and doll-like. Because she was a girl, she was not a "self-starter," but always waited for the boys in her group to "take initiative and suggest things." This assertion contradicts her descriptions of herself as a mobilizer of many of the childhood activities and pranks in which she engaged. The virtuous Victorian maidens who sat on piano stools until they fainted were the heroines of her children's books. But they were not the role models she chose to imitate in her play. She enjoyed helping her friends steal all the door numbers on Delaware Avenue and received a severe scolding when she tried to satisfy her anatomical curiosity by soaking her friend's rag doll in water to make it urinate.

Mabel never resolved this contradiction because she could not reconcile her belief in women's derivative powers with her passion to achieve in her own right. Time and again as an adult, she lapsed into neurasthenic depressions during which she claimed she could accomplish nothing without a man to "use" her. These depressions would be followed by her engaging in more activities in a few months' time than most people engage in during a lifetime. While she always insisted that it was a man who energized her into action, she was responsible for most of her creative ideas and she never tolerated direction from any man for very long. In fact, Mabel's desire to control others was at least as strong as her need to submit to direction. The "exhibitions of power, of prowess, and of courage" that she admits to as a child who sought to manipulate friends she could feel no affection for remained an adult strategy that continually warred with her feminine ideology of submissiveness.

Surely Sara Ganson's assertion of "masculine" drive within the confines of a highly conventional feminine role and Charles Ganson's fluctuations between hysteria and passive withdrawal contributed greatly to Mabel's sexual confusion. She admired Sara's beauty and tried to emulate the self-assurance and high-spiritedness that were the marks of her social distinction. Although she recalled that her father could be kind and had moments of fumbling gentleness, there was nothing that Mabel admired about him. When he accused Sara of having "beaux" and went into one of his jealous rages, Mabel immediately sided with her mother.

Sara's face sometimes took on a look of "cold, merciless contempt" that Mabel did her best to imitate. Numbing herself into a state of emotional immobility was one of the survival tactics she learned that she often used as an adult when confronted by emotional traumas she could not handle. The sphinx-like silences with which Sara tormented Charles were repeated by Mabel with devastating effect on her husbands and lovers. When he was particularly aroused to anger by Sara, Charles would threaten to leave her and take Mabel with him. Mabel, of course, knew for what purpose she was being used. Once she recognized, however, that her parents' battles were merely verbal combats that would never result in any disruption of the outer semblance of family life, she had some guarantee of psychic security: "when the cunning watchfulness of childhood made out that the two antagonists were helpless and bound, from that time on I was at liberty, in myself, to find my escape from them both. And all the years I have to tell of are but a record of that search."[17]

In order to minimize the effect of her parents on her, Mabel developed a fantasy that is endemic to American literature. American writers, particularly male writers, have often set off, in their lives and in their works, on real and metamorphic journeys of self-discovery. Like Ben Franklin, Walt Whitman, or F. Scott Fitzgerald, Mabel imagined she was responsible for creating herself: "As a child, I had felt no one in front of me— an unopened space with no paths in it encircled me; my parents had seemed like dim, dull figures far, far behind. I could not make them a part of my journey. I had to set off alone by myself and I was always alone."[18] Mabel's ambition to "make" herself in the traditionally male American way was, however, undercut by a number of factors. The only way she could gain approval in the adult world was by behaving in accordance with proper female norms, which did not encourage either figurative or literal running away.

Middle- and upper-class Victorian women were "routinely socialized to fill a weak, dependent and severely limited social role. They were sharply discouraged from expressing competition or mastery," the effect of which was that they often had "a low evaluation of themselves. . . ." More important was the fact that her parents' failure of love left Mabel with little basis for self-affirmation; thus she looked to others to define her in order to escape her sense of being an orphan "drifting forlornly in the universe." The mirroring effect she learned as a child to gain recognition was a traditional feminine strategy that she refined into an art. As an adult, Mabel was famous for her ability to adapt her mood and personality to those of whomever she happened to be with: "I have always been myself and at the same time . . . always able to be the other person, feel with him, think his thoughts . . . I flowed out to them and identified myself with them, and it always made people want to kiss me, to manifest an actual nearness and union. . . ."[19]

Mabel found few nourishing alternatives in her social or educational milieu. Certainly St. Margaret's Episcopal School for Girls offered little in the way of encouragement for her emotional and intellectual development and independence. Mabel's class motto, "They also serve who only stand and wait," seemed far more in keeping with the school's philosophy of providing upper-class girls with the requisite social skills, and the refinements of drawing and horticulture, than her teachers' vague admonitions that if she would only "work" she could "do anything." Mabel was justifiably puzzled by her teachers' words, since as far as she could see, women of her class did not "do" anything: "I learned, then, early, to say to myself that I was serving by living: by hearing, seeing, smelling, tasting. . . . And all the years through I have said to myself I was serving by waiting. Waiting to work."[20]

In spite of her lack of direction during adolescence, Mabel displayed an instinct for survival and strength of will that were formidable. Watching the play *Iris* in New York City when she was sixteen, she reacted to it the same way she had reacted to the passive Victorian maidens in her children's books. She scorned the weakness of the heroine, who was destroyed by shame when her lover abandoned her. This would *never* happen to Mabel: "'Maybe that Iris will be destroyed, but I never will be.' I registered it right then and there—joyful, certain, strong. No matter what happened to me, I would never go down and I would never be destroyed."[21]

Schooling

Grandma Cook, the iron matriarch who regulated her daughters' lives through her daily letters, disapproved of Mabel's high spirits and strong will. Displeased with the evident lack of discipline at St. Margaret's, she ordered Sara to send Mabel to Miss Graham's School in New York City, where she was enrolled in September 1895. At Miss Graham's, Mabel learned very little discipline. But she did learn a lot about *"la grande vie intérieure,"* a mode of intellectual and emotional self-exploration that she cultivated assiduously during her Florence and New York salon years. Mabel set herself apart from most of the other girls at the school because they seemed "common" to her, and took up the defense of a young American girl who had lived most of her life in France. Mary Shillito was ostracized by the girls because she seemed "queer"; but she attracted Mabel because of her "savor," as many others in Mabel's life would attract her for similar reasons. Mary was one of the first of Mabel's friends whom she used to reach out into new realms of experience and sensation: "I always had something very strongly 'arrivist' in me. I *would* arrive. . . . I would know everything, feel everything, be everything."[22]

A book of poetic quotations Mabel kept throughout the year indicates what that realm of experience and sensation was like. While her notebook displays a wide range of readings in Shakespeare, Socrates, Pope, Milton, and other "classic" authors, the vast majority of it was devoted to excerpts from Romantic and Victorian poets. Mabel's favorite authors were Byron, Tennyson, Browning, Rossetti, and Matthew Arnold. Over and over, she copied lines that long for death and sing of the stale weariness of life and the "faded hopes of earthly love." Her world-weariness is not, of course, an unusual attribute for a sheltered adolescent girl, who had experienced the world chiefly through books. But the despair and the repetitious quest for self-obliteration would pursue Mabel throughout her life. The lines she quotes at age sixteen from Matthew Arnold's "Self-Dependence" would be equally relevant to her life at age forty: "Weary of myself and sick of asking/What I am, and what I ought to be. . . ."

The passages and poems also reveal how much of Mabel's emotional life was invested in romantic longings for an ideal world in which she would not have to suffer the pain of human hurt and loss, for a world in which sensuous fulfillment would compensate her for the actively achieving self her family and her society repressed. She captured her Byronic vision in an excerpt from a story that can stand as a prologue to her adult life:

> She was thinking . . . of that poetic love, which seemed to have a being apart from material life, and which she knew neither suffering nor starvation could kill. It is a grand power, that of endowing, with a sort of objective existence, an ideal love which holds its own against disillusionments. . . . "All my life it has been the same. Nothing—no one—has been *great* enough. People were not strong enough—or not quite true. Music might have always been more glorious, mountains higher, and the sea more vast. There was never *enough*. Nothing filled me quite."

Like Browning's Aurora Leigh, the young girl whose story she ends her notebook with, "She had lived a sorry cage bird life." And like the woman in her short story, she would wait, passively and un-Byronically, to be rescued from it: "But I always felt that there would come something someday which should drag me imperiously from every thing that had gone before, and be a will in me and fill me so that I should be satisfied."[23]

Soon after the completion of her year at Miss Graham's, Mabel met a young woman who fulfilled her romantic requirements. Mary Shillito's sister, Violet (pronounced Veeolette), attended another private girls' school in New York City. A frail, intense, and exotic young woman, she spurned the vulgarity of her bourgeois parents. Violet cultivated herself by learning Italian to read Dante, and Greek in order to study Plato. Mabel met her in June 1896, when Sara took Mabel on her first European tour.

Violet seemed to have stepped out of the pages of Edgar Allan Poe. She initiated Mabel into the rarefied world of *fin de siècle* culture, the temper, attitudes, and poses of which Mabel practiced during her Florentine years. In Paris together, Mabel and she read George Sand and Alfred de Musset. In retrospect, Mabel saw Violet as a symbol of a civilization that was "coming to pieces . . . ; she had reached the last phase" of the old order and was the crest of the wave about to fall "back into dissolution."[24] Violet cultivated in Mabel both a desire for serious literature and a philosophy of the superiority of suffering. Her capacity for it seemed beyond that of anyone Mabel had ever met.

Violet was the first to teach Mabel the blessings of the amoral aesthetic imagination, the lust for "art for life's sake." She "had awakened once for all the strange, ineffable love that no words of mine can name, nor any other love completely submerge or destroy—that has to do with purely spiritual values, though quite unqualified by ethics or morals as we have hitherto perceived them." If Lawrence was later to see Mabel as a modern reincarnation of Ligeia, it was because she had learned her lessons well.

Violet was also the first woman that Mabel consciously used as a model for herself. She trained Mabel to turn her natural genius for "flowing" into a fine art. Violet gave to people her "spirit," a vital, electric, and intense discharge that pierced "one's secret channels like a permeating, sweet elixir."[25] It was the same sort of "discharge" that Mabel later transmitted to the artists whose lives and works she wished to inspire and mold. Violet was like the Kwannon goddess who had forfeited Nirvana to come back to earth in order to help men complete their destinies: "an unaging goddess fresh and unfaded, yet of the most ancient days. . . ."[26]

Mabel described her relationship with Violet Shillito as spiritually intimate and physically "chaste," though they were both stirred by what Mabel called an "exquisite and commendable" sensuality. When they lay together in bed and Mabel shyly touched her breasts, she felt that the "stone room became vital with the overflow of our increased life, for we passed it out of us in rapid, singing waves—an emanation more fine and powerful than that from radium."[27] Mabel achieved with Violet an integration of spiritual and physical passion she would not know again until she met her fourth husband, Antonio Luhan.

When Mabel was sent to the Chevy Chase School in Washington, D.C., for a final year of "finishing" after her return from Europe, she sought out classmates with whom she might establish the same kind of relationship she had with Violet. But the brief relationships she had with two young women were more like a recapitulation of the night she spent with her nursemaid's breast. The girls were passive subjects of Mabel's desire to explore their budding sexuality. Mabel, however, was no longer the desperate child, and she explored them with an almost cold disdain.

Mabel's relationships with men during her late adolescence were equally manipulative. She spent the summer before her "coming out" making conquests: "My interest in men was in discovering my effect upon them, instead of in responding to their feeling in me."[28] The men she had known in her childhood had, of course, contributed both to her desire to conquer and to her inability to love. Her grandfathers were coldly distant symbols of power whom she tried to imitate in the personal and social spheres of her life. Her father's indifference and weakness fed her hostility toward men and a latent contempt for their supposed supremacy. When a boy she was dating the summer before her coming out party grew "rough" with her, it was not the first time Mabel was to feel assaulted by a man.

Given her anger and confusion, it is understandable that Mabel sought to arouse in men the very reactions she feared. This is seen most clearly in a fascinating episode that Henry James could have imagined. Mabel had a young and very beautiful cousin who married a Spanish aristocrat. A man who had lived in Europe solely on beauty and sensuous pleasures, he slowly withered within a few years of his living in the hothouse

Victorian atmosphere of Mabel's family. In a desperate effort to restore his vitality, Mabel tells us, he latched on to her youth. She encouraged her uncle, from whom she received her "first kisses in the world," at age sixteen: "I was beginning to get an anxious feeling mingled with the delicious pleasure of having Uncle Carlos seize me around the waist and press me to him. . . ." The anxiety Mabel felt presaged her future relationships with men whom she wanted to want her, only to withdraw when she felt her identity being absorbed by them:

> I remember now the feeling of the particular type of guile that circumstances had developed in Uncle Carlos, a poisonous, slow deceit, absolutely ruthless and bent upon its own ends, for the replenishment of his unused and diminishing fire. . . . All my own self-guarded energy turned from him when he became too needful. . . .[29]

Coming Out

Mabel's coming-out party was her first opportunity to use her "self-guarded energy" to shape an environment that expressed her aesthetic imagination. The photographic portraits taken of her at the time belie the determination that lay just beneath her conventional feminine image: the plump, girlish face, the luminous, dreaming eyes, and the hourglass figure in "white satin with . . . billowing folds of white net covered all over with hyacinth petals and dewdrops." At Mabel's direction, the usual "refined mediocrity" of the Victorian clubhouse, where her set made their debuts, was turned into a baronial hall, filled with imitation Rembrandts, Velasquez, banners, and coats of arms. As Mabel describes the scene, we can see the foreshadowing of her Florence salon: "The incongruous scene melted together—*fin de siècle* clothes of the nineteenth century blended, with the help of punch and champagne . . . into the background of the Middle Ages."[30]

Within just a few years, Mabel would be playing with the past in earnest, when the adolescent pageantry of her coming-out party evolved into her first serious effort to exploit the past in order to furnish herself with an identity. For the present, however, the only identity for which her debut had prepared her was that of wife, a role she was not yet willing to take on. When Arthur Brisbane, a friend of the Carys, asked her what she wanted to do with her life, she told the famous Hearst publisher that she did not wish to marry or to stay in Buffalo. She wanted "to live and try to understand more and feel life itself." When she asked if she could go to work on his paper, "He laughed a little I suppose, at the idea of this girl trying to leave Buffalo and all the chains holding her back, and coming, unprepared and undisciplined, to work on his paper. Women didn't do that sort of thing then."[31]

At age eighteen, Mabel's only other available option was to continue a more adult form of the play she had engaged in since childhood. Her favorite playmate was Seward Cary, a young man whose untamed wildness attracted her and carried no sexual threat. She spent a great deal of time with him, breaking "green horses," and running off on adventures, such as the evening they spent chasing each other over the rooftops of an old inn where they were staying with a group of friends. When he gave her his whip as a tribute to her daring, she felt she had won it by her own power; that is, until she reminded herself that she had been "galvanized" into action by his "man's force."[32]

Mabel thought she wanted to be the girl he wanted her to be, just as she had with Uncle Carlos: "if one could become *real* to others, then one was *real* to oneself." While this need to shape herself to meet men's needs was rooted in her socialization and in her emotional isolation as a child, it was also related to Mabel's belief that she lacked the one attribute women of her class needed to succeed personally and socially: "I was not much to look at, ever, I am sorry to say. (Really sorry.)"[33]

Marriage

Mabel's relationship with Seward Cary was the first in her adult life to embody the conflict between her desire for autonomy and her belief that she must derive her identity from men. Mabel's first marriage was a model of that conflict. She chose Karl Evans partly because of his resemblance to Seward Cary. Karl was a "light-hearted, thoughtless boy for whom the world was a rabbit to hunt." A man-child, really, he had no sense of adult responsibilities but was a creature who operated purely on impulse. Although he presumably worked for his father's steamship company, he rarely showed up at work. Mabel recalls the fierce protectiveness of his father's employees, for whom Karl served as a symbol of their own dreams to roam unhampered.[34]

Mabel's interest in Karl was initiated by his interest in another girl to whom he was assumed to be engaged. (She was never seriously interested in a man whose affections were not previously "engaged.") Elsie Reinhardt was one of the daughters of the German brewer who had been snubbed when they moved to Delaware Avenue. Mabel felt no compunction about Elsie's prior claim. Because she had been emotionally deprived as a child, she believed she had every right to steal love. Her substitution of power for love, and for personal and moral integrity, was also part of a class-learned ideology. The only principle she held on to was the one that women of her class had to preserve in order to be able to barter themselves into marriage—her virginity. "Surely," she tells us, "no one had ever given me the slightest ethical or moral instruction." Mabel's growing reputation

23

as an outlaw of love testified to her power: "To strengthen it was my dearest, deepest wish, the exercise of it my most profound enjoyment."[35]

Mabel was intent on getting Karl even though he was no more important to her than "a nice dog." She tried to accommodate herself to him by never letting him know she was a woman who lived the life of the mind and loved beautiful things. Mabel wanted Karl to see her as being like himself, interested in hunting and an outdoor life. One night, she called Karl because she knew he was at the house of his "stupid and beautiful" fiancée-to-be. Karl came running, after pushing poor Elsie out of the way. "I want you," Mabel told him, for the first time since they had gone out together. She spoke "in a hard, low voice, without any love, just with power." In that moment, they became engaged: "I had no thought of marrying him, but only of keeping him from Elsie."[36]

Mabel's engagement to Karl was also a weapon she could use against her father. When she cut off her long hair after meeting Seward Cary, the act sent Charles to bed in an "impotent, opposing frenzy." When she announced her engagement to Karl, he went into a towering rage and threatened to lock her up in the house. (Mabel gives no reason for her father's reaction; however, it seems likely to have been due to Karl's irresponsibility, not to his social position.) Her father's opposition energized her and gave her the feeling that she could accomplish anything. This was not the last time that a man's opposition to her aroused and channeled her energies in less-than-constructive directions.

Nor was it the last time that Mabel turned out to be the victim of her own machinations. Her marriage to Karl Evans reads like something James Fenimore Cooper might have invented for the abduction of one of his anemic heroines. "Kidnapped" into marriage, Mabel once again found herself the "passive" victim of a male aggressor.

One Sunday morning in July 1900, Karl took Mabel on what she presumed was an outing to the family country house, Penjerrick, located on the Niagara River. There she was to meet Karl's hunting friend, Jack Piper. Jack was colorful and mindless, but he made up in brute strength and loyalty to Karl what he lacked in brains. Mabel was taken to a little country church where the minister was waiting. With Jack Piper guarding her rear, "I could no more have managed to escape than the casual rabbit . . . ," she tells us. Mabel's commentary on her half hoped for, half feared new status makes clear her strong ambivalence: "when I was twenty-one, I *was married*—the passive, truly female experience!" Her lack of ecstasy at the prospect was reinforced by Jack's warning that she had better be good to Karl. "I belonged to myself only," she felt at the time, "and my own law was the only one I could admit."[37]

Yet Mabel's first few weeks of marriage were not unhappy. She took pleasure in renting and decorating a small house, in secret, of course, since neither set of parents had any idea that she and Karl were married. When her parents did find out, her mother was supportive, insisting on a church wedding to make it official. Karl and Mabel were married on October 3 in Trinity Church, without Mabel's father to give her away. He was at home in bed with an attack of gout precipitated by the news.

Mabel gave in to Karl's sexual demands as a concession to his status as her husband. But her own sexual awakening did not occur until she made love with Karl in her parents' house—in the very room where she had experienced her father's "impotent rages" and her mother's "aloof indifference": "I had never heard of that gentle transformation . . . as though the nerves expressed themselves in the manner of silent, fiery fountains falling on black velvet. My body had burned with high fires but had never penetrated this far, strange other world. No one had ever told me about this definite, so definite and surprising thing." While Mabel's sexual response was a final triumph over her parents, it did not liberate her in any meaningful way. It increased her loathing for her father, although she felt a greater alliance with her mother. And it further separated her from Karl. Mabel felt more than ever that he was too inexperienced and stupid to share the subtleties of her interior life. If she was at last awake "after the long dark sleep" of her youth, Karl was merely the fairy prince "who delivered the sleeping princess."[38]

Mabel's sexual awakening was her first experience with the biological power of being female. When she became pregnant that winter, she realized the fullness of that power. The nine months of pregnancy were the most contented of her life. Sitting tranquilly in her room, with a pot of pansies, dishes of fresh grapes, and her books and sewing basket, Mabel did not have to strive to achieve an identity, nor reflect that of anyone else. She was wholly occupied as a servant of Mother Nature: "Maybe the reason is plain for, biologically, at that moment I myself was of the greatest value to this fruitful earth that I have ever been before or since. . . ."

During her pregnancy, Mabel transcended her partial self and identified with the eternal Feminine: "It was so wonderful to give up—to lose completely my sense of individual life with its hopes and its fears and its weary, weary wishes," Mabel recalls, in her paean to maternity: "Ever after birth there is the tug and pull: but in the reciprocity of the womb, there is unity and peace and the only legitimate contentment we are ever allowed to know in the world. . . . I would give up all of the psychological life for the nine months of the biological claim." Mabel's later pursuit of a variety of mind cures and Eastern philosophies was at least partly based on a desire to match the unselfconscious equipoise she associated with her pregnancy.[39]

With the birth of her child in January 1902, she was brought abruptly back to the agony of individual existence. She was bitter to find her "soul" 25 had returned to her body and with it "that return to knowledge and feeling and the estimations of the psyche." When her baby was laid beside her, Mabel reacted to it with the same frigidity that characterized her reaction to her parents' marital antagonisms: "I saw the pathos and pity of life and I thought, 'I don't like it,' and my heart shut up right then and there. . . . It seemed I didn't want a baby after all."[40]

Marriage and motherhood—the two roles that were supposed to fulfill her as a woman—only created discontent. Soon after her marriage, in fact, Mabel engaged in a clandestine affair with her gynecologist. A family friend of the Gansons whom Mabel had used as a go-between to her parents after her secret marriage, Dr. Parmenter was one of the most prominent physicians in Buffalo society. The fact that Mabel was in love with him and could do nothing about it, and that he may have been the father of the child he delivered, undoubtedly complicated her reactions to her newborn son.[41]

John's birth was followed by a series of traumas over the next year and a half that brought Mabel to a state of nervous collapse. On November 25, 1902, her father died, after a painful illness. Mabel's statement that she felt nothing at his funeral, that she was as "cold as ice," is indicative of the emotional scars he left with her. Within a few weeks of Charles's death, Mabel entered Buffalo General Hospital for an operation she needed as a result of continuing gynecological problems that were related to John's birth. (In 1929, she had a hysterectomy due to problems that had continued to plague her.) While she was recuperating from her first operation, Dr. Parmenter brought her the news that Karl had been shot in a hunting accident. Barely able to stand, Mabel was rushed to his hospital bed: "'Hello, Karl,' I said. He raised up his head a trifle and gasped: 'Peg! Tell Bris it's all right—' and fell back dead."[42]

Karl died on February 25, 1903, the day before Mabel's twenty-fifth birthday. Mabel remembered little of what followed, except that she insisted Bris, who had shot him, be one of the pallbearers. After Karl's death, Mabel's affair with the married and respectable Dr. Parmenter became an open scandal. When his wife threatened to take it to court, Mabel was forced to give up her lover, or see him ruined financially and socially. Sara sent her off to Europe.[43]

All of the social institutions through which Mabel had sought to establish her identity had failed her—her family, her schooling, marriage, and finally motherhood. The Victorian world in which she had been reared had not allowed her any respectable position outside of marriage and motherhood through which she could channel her intelligence and her energies. In Europe, Mabel turned to the supportive structure of a society that had a long-established tradition of women who devoted themselves to the transformation of life into a work of art. This trip was the first of three journeys Mabel would make that profoundly altered her life. She "took up" the European past as the first move in a lifelong search to create a self and a world in which she could be "at home." The imaginative daring with which Mabel pursued her task initiated her legendary status as a "representative" twentieth-century American.

Chapter 2

European Experiences

Mabel left for Paris in July 1904 with John and two trained nurses. She spent most of the voyage in a state of dreamlike passivity, like "a white banner unfolding idly against a blue sky." The deaths of her father and her husband and the forced ending of her turbulent affair with Dr. Parmenter left her without the energy to shape or choose direction for her life. The night before she landed in Paris, she was coaxed into the dining room, where "a nice young man in tweeds" paid her court throughout dinner. Edwin Dodge had been reared in a wealthy Boston family and had studied architecture at the École de Beaux Arts in Paris. His sanguine face, kind blue eyes, and unforced cheeriness seemed just the antidote for Mabel's depression.[1]

Both Mabel and Edwin were staying at the Hotel Meurice. There Edwin began a courtship that did not cease until Mabel agreed to marry him. He did not, however, have an easy road before him in his suit. For waiting to greet Mabel at the train station was Mary Shillito, with the tragic news of Violet's death from typhoid the previous winter in Cannes. Mary had a friend ready to take Violet's place in Mabel's life. Thus began a tug-of-war over Mabel's person that pitted the earnest and dapper Edwin against the Catholic aristocrat, Marcelle, who longed to take up *la vie intérieure* where Violet left off.

Dodge pursued Mabel indefatigably. He arranged for her meals and entertainment and sent her notes demanding her presence at dinners that preempted engagements the Shillitos had arranged. He assumed from the beginning a proprietary interest that Mabel acceded to because it required no decision making on her part. As soon as she was able, Mary whisked Mabel off to her friend Marcelle's chateau in Burgundy. Marcelle appealed to the yearning, mystical side of Mabel's nature. She "had the kind of character that a man is supposed to have. . . . And because I had at that moment no will of my own left, no wishes, even no grief, I was willing to let whoever would detain me and plan for me."[2] Marcelle planned for Mabel a life of asceticism devoted to the pursuit of an intense spirituality. Edwin saw in all this a Catholic plot. The gulf between his bourgeois American Protestantism and Marcelle's medieval French Catholicism was as wide, Mabel ruefully noted, as that between a Methodist and a Hottentot.

Edwin Dodge

Mabel's pragmatism led her away from Marcelle and back to Edwin. He plainly offered her a life far more in keeping with her desire for security and luxury—not to mention the need of a father for John. When she decided to marry Edwin, she says she was in no mood for the *plaisir d'amour* that lasts but for a moment. "Rubbish," she thought, when an orchestra at a small café where she dined with Edwin played this song. Mabel was apparently quite open with Edwin about her lack of feeling for him. She told him that the only desire she felt was to have him about her "to help me, and to enable me to make something new and beautiful." Dodge must have been smitten, indeed, to have married her so soon and under such conditions.[3]

Edwin may have captured her hand in marriage, but Mabel's spirit still belonged to the world of Violet Shillito. She felt within her "talents for living and understanding" that were awaiting a chance to be born. No sooner had she married Edwin in October 1904 then she plunged into a depression that lasted for several months. On their honeymoon in Biarritz, she lived in a state of emotional numbness, unable to respond to anything. Mabel's neurasthenia was the refuge of a person incapable of dealing with inner conflict. She felt as trapped by this marriage as she had by her first. Once again, she was unable to admit that it was the actual state of marriage she was at war with. So she picked on Edwin. She accused him of failing both to fulfill and to appreciate her. She convinced herself that she had married beneath her intelligence and refined sensibility.

Mabel tried to increase her authority over Edwin by maintaining physical as well as emotional distance from him. One day, however, she made the mistake of standing up to greet him when he returned from his daily tennis game. As she teetered toward him on high heels, he exclaimed, "My God, Mabel! You're short! I thought you were tall!"[4] Perhaps Mabel was right in thinking he was not the most perceptive of men.

The Dodges wintered on the Riviera, where Mabel fell into prolonged states of brooding silence, in the tradition of her mother. Her good-natured and befuddled husband responded to her indifference, "Well, if this is marriage, excuse me!" Mabel even resented the fact that Edwin was a wonderful father to John Evans. Watching them roughhouse in the surf, she finally admitted to herself, "Really, I hated men anyway."[5] In retrospect, Mabel recognized that her unhappiness and lack of responsiveness had much to do with her total lack of faith in herself. The French doctor who tended her that winter was allowed to visit only when she was not sick enough to look unattractive. Even in illness, Mabel had to be suitably charming, so concerned was she to engage the interest of men in her vicinity.

When she wrote the record of her European experiences, Mabel recognized that "at that period I was very stupid, & unhappy, indeed quite desperate, & with no heart at all, nor any brains."[6] Throughout the second volume of her memoirs, she emphasized those aspects of her life that exemplified the decadence of late-nineteenth-century European aestheticism. Her loathing for her European past drove her to create an unsympathetic self-portrait, one that often masks the genuine suffering and despair that was responsible for some of her more extreme behavior.

With her need for love unsatisfied, Mabel began to buy "things" as a substitute, to appease her longings for sensuous fulfillment. The aestheticism she had shared with Violet developed into her *raison d'être:* "I had turned to beauty and the pleasures of delicate food and wine for my sustenance, and my thoughts were of a life made up of beautiful things, of art, of color, of noble forms, and of ideas and perceptions about them that had been waiting, asleep, within me, and that now allured me by their untried, uncreated images."[7] The Riviera lacked the nuance and subtlety Mabel felt were necessary to awaken her creative energies. And so the Dodges moved to Switzerland for the summer, where the altitude seemed to restore her physical and psychological well-being.

By the time she and Edwin moved to Florence in the fall of 1905, Mabel was ready to adopt an aesthetic mode of being. Leaning out of the window of her hotel's *salone,* she inhaled the centuries-old night air:

the strange odor of Florence mounted to me—a smell of damp, old stone, of damp box and laurel from dark garden corners where the roots are never dry, and of cypress trees which have known only air and light. And mixed with these, the odor of dust and roses. A queer smell it was, made of strong contrasts and delicious to my senses, but not a part of

31

me. Its unfamiliarity made a kind of arrogant anger rise in my heart,
and I found myself saying to the indifferent old city, lying there . . . "I
will make you mine."

Mabel absorbed the essence of the city by buying small objects, inhaling
their perfumes, exploring their textures. She believed she had at last found
a society that could accommodate her spirit: "I felt that I could sink down
into its past and it would support me." She dreamed of the strange and
beautiful people that had inhabited the ancient villas during the Renaissance and felt diminished when she met the men and women who now
lived in them.[8]

Mabel approached the Renaissance from a purely aesthetic perspective.
She was the godlike artist for whom the realm of fancy was preferable to
the uncontrollable material of human existence: "It was almost inevitable
for one to become seriously involved with *things* over there, emotionally
so, I mean. There is so much thought and feeling given to them. To their
discovery, their attainment, their disposition, in one's house. It's almost
like a love affair, the drama over the antique."[9] A drama, she might have
added, that had no costly moral or psychological consequences.

In Florence, Mabel could live, like Bernard Berenson who had moved
there five years before her, in accordance with Walter Pater's prescription
for success in life. Pater, the theoretician for the Pre-Raphaelites, had
urged his disciples, among them the Rossettis and Oscar Wilde, to account
that life worth living which was devoted to an intense appreciation of
beauty, especially the beauty of great art.[10] His essays on the Renaissance
had profoundly affected Berenson when he was a student at Harvard in
the 1880s. By the time he moved to Florence, Berenson was on his way
to becoming the most highly regarded connoisseur and critic of Renaissance art in the world.

Thus Mabel entered a world whose ambience was devoted to what Pater
called "the love of art for its own sake," a world that incarnated the values
she had learned from Violet and had tested briefly at her coming-out
party. Mabel knew Berenson and shared his epicurean gospel. For a time,
the devotion of her life to art did for her what connoisseurship did for
Berenson: it "healed his breach with life. . . . In the presence of great
art, his self-doubts, guilts, nihilistic philosophy, and jaundiced view of
the world were swept away in a torrent of passionate response."[11]

The Villa Curonia

Mabel found the perfect home for her role as a Renaissance lady in the
Villa Curonia: "I knew quite well the kind of queen I wanted to be and
the type of royal residence in which I would immolate myself. . . . It

would allow one to be both majestic and careless, spontaneous and pic-turesque, and yet always framed and supported by a secure and beautiful authenticity of background."[12] Mabel's home would be the antithesis of everything she had loathed growing up in Victorian Buffalo. Not only had her curious fingers been denied the right to explore art objects, but most of those that filled her home and those of her childhood playmates were, she felt, grotesque displays of drab and deadened sensibilities.

Mabel summed up the tastelessness of this bric-a-brac world in an anecdote about Oscar Wilde's visit to Buffalo during his 1882 tour of America. After a series of talks he gave on interior design, a prominent Buffalonian piloted Wilde about her house to get his opinion of it. Mabel's description of the house is delicious: the woodwork was "twisted and tortured and varnished," the draperies beribboned, jugs shaped "like sau-sages" were scattered about the rooms, oil lamps sported floppy shades, intricately patterned wallpapers "writhed" on the walls, satin chairs and sofas "bulged." At the entrance of the main hall stood a life-sized carved bear, who held out his paws to receive calling cards. After the grand tour, the hostess turned with pride to Wilde and asked, "Now, Mr. Wilde, what do you really think I should do with my house?" "It is reported," Mabel tells us, "that he gazed at her in somber fashion and replied: 'Burn it, madam!' and then seized his hat and fled from the scene."[13]

Mabel lavished years and an enormous amount of her own and Edwin's money in creating her "royal residence." When Carl Van Vechten archly remarked that the heroine of his novel *Peter Whiffle,* Edith Dale (Mabel Dodge), had "done" the last 300 years in three in her Florentine villa, he was not exaggerating by much. Mabel was like Henry James's Christopher Newman in her American impatience to buy a past that would legitimize her wealth and self. To the business of making herself and her surroundings into a work of art she brought a great deal of creative intelligence and energy. She "was possessed," said Enrico Barfucci, who knew her in Flor-ence when he was a young man, "of . . . a rich and joyous imagination which turned her life into something nearing poetry."[14]

The palatial Villa Curonia had been built by the Medici in the fifteenth century to house one of their doctors. It perched on a hill in Arcetri with a view of Florence and the sweeping roll of land that flattened into the plains leading to Pisa: "The villa was like a crown on the gray-green land. . . . The town lay far below in a huddle of pale opal colors." Across to the north were the Apennines, purple-black and gray blue, "a tumbled heap of solid shapes whose summits never lost their mystery. . . ." The villa was surrounded with terraces and gardens and the fragrance of olive trees, roses, jasmine, and gardenias.[15]

A magnificent Brunelleschi-style courtyard, which Edwin had unbu-ried, led to the iron-studded doors of the main entrance hall where large stone columns sported multicolored banners. Like Tennyson's "Palace of

Art," each room in the villa was designed to correspond with a mood in the house of Mabel's emotions. The ninety-foot-long "gran' Salon" was arranged to create a sense of both spaciousness and intimacy. When Berenson saw it, he commented to Mabel, "Ah! No one can build rooms like this any more!" Hung with red damask, silken brocades, and tapestries, its three French windows opened onto a loggia overlooking a formal garden:

> The way the light came in past the full golden red curtains, the way the logs burning behind the grill threw golden light on the dark oak floor, the glimpses of the Italian hills one caught from outside the loggia, framed between the pale stone columns . . . like the backgrounds in early Florentine paintings, firelight flickerings on silver and bronze, somnolent great masses of flowers from the garden, the green dying eastern sky from the high east windows, the crimson glow from the western sky over towards Pisa—and then, in a while, Domenico coming in with a waxen taper to light the oil wicks of the six tall Florentine lamps whose lighted flames brought the whole place into one crimson dusk . . . there was a soothing magic in all this.[16]

It was, she concluded, reassuring, "embracing, and so alive like a womb." The library was a somber room where no one lingered, its solid bookcases filled with classics and decorated in Empire style. The dining room was voluptuously Renaissance, with crimson damask chairs and heavy sideboards that displayed Mabel's collection of Venetian glass and silver dishes.

The only practical room in the house was the kitchen, which Mabel never entered. It was furnished in New England Colonial by her Yankee Aunt Rosa. Mabel's sitting room, the Yellow Salon, was eighteenth-century blue-stocking, light, pale, and brightly French. There she read the poems of Stephen Haweis, "that suited the gay tristesse that always trembled there," and, fittingly enough, the latest Henry James novel.[17] Mabel's bedroom was designed like a medieval chamber, complete with a silken ladder that came through a trapdoor above, meant for the rapid descent of a lover. Her ornately carved bed was covered by a heavy silken brocade spread of a deep midnight blue, chosen, perhaps, to represent the unexplored depths of her emotional life. Edwin, the ever-practical Bostonian, used the silken ladder only once, to see if it would work. The only other evidence of eroticism in the room was a bas-relief that had been cunningly devised to reveal a woman holding her lover's phallus. It infuriated Mabel's romantic sensibility when she discovered it.

Typically, Mabel spent her morning hours in bed, eating her breakfast and inhaling the intermingling odors of the jasmine flowers outside her windows, the coffee on her tray, and the exquisite perfumes that floated through the air of her dressing room. After a leisured choice of the raiments

suited to her day and her mood, she dressed. In the evenings, she wore
Renaissance coats that hung loose from her shoulders, stiff brocades in
the colors of Titian and Tintoretto, and turbans of chiffon. She was, indeed,
a walking work of art. In her memoirs, Mabel evoked the absurd self-
portrait she sometimes struck:

> Sweep the long terrace, making a long line from shoulder to earth. Head
> back and eyebrows so disdainful! (Weltschmerz!)

> Pour the Chianti . . . pour it, Domenico, from the gold Venetian glass
> decanters into tall, gold and white goblets. The dead Florentines are
> thick in the dust all about on nights like these.

> I so deep, so fatal, and so glamorous—and he [Edwin] so ordinary and
> matter of fact! Little does he guess of the layers upon layers of
> perceptions . . . of feeling for things, that I carried locked within me.[18]

Behind the parodic portrait was a woman who suffered from the emptiness and desperation reminiscent of the "Game of Chess" section in T.
S. Eliot's *The Wasteland:* "'Heavens! I can't stand this. I'm going to dress.
I'm going to town. I'm going . . . I'm going . . . Hurry! In an anguish
of haste. Why? To go somewhere. . . .' This is haste. Pure haste without
incentive. Without goal. Haste for its own sake, barren, barren." Mabel
had designed a magnificent set, but the actress who was supposed to hold
center stage could not clearly define her role. The beautiful old door frame
she had placed in the north salon was "a very fair symbol" of herself "at
the time, for it led nowhere. Like the fireplace in the hall, it was only
for effect."[19]

When her villa was at last completed, Mabel celebrated with a Medicean
feast. The servants lit the rooms with flaming torches and "as the pale
green evening sky shown into the *Gran' Salone* from between the columns
on the loggia, and the great white sparkling star popped over the far-
away hill, a beautiful voice arose singing the Evening Star song from
Tannhäuser, and there was a murmur of delight for it was thought very
ben trovato. . . ." The guests were served a cornucopia of sumptuous food
and drink, amid soft candlelight and roses. It was, Mabel tells us, a
"dramatic success."[20]

Lavish food and raiment, elegant surroundings, and artfully arranged
parties were not enough, however, to nourish the growth of Mabel's
identity. When the *objets d'art* she collected failed to substantiate her, she
turned to collecting people, in the hope that they would provide her with
the "materials" she needed to fabricate a self. Mabel brought to her villa
some of the great acting, writing, and musical talent of her day, along
with a variety of emigré socialites and royalty. In Florence, she began her

apprenticeship as a salon hostess. Barfucci remembers her as "one of the most vivid personalities in the Florentine cosmopolitan set, which was one of the most intellectually refined of the last hundred years."[21]

At Mabel's dinner table, always graced with flagons of wine, hot loaves of fresh bread, and flowers from her gardens, one could find at various times and in various combinations, one of the world's greatest actresses, Eleanor Duse; the English actor Robert de la Comandine; the French novelist André Gide; Gertrude and Leo Stein; an Indian swami hired to exorcise a ghost; Arthur Rubinstein; Muriel and Paul Draper—the wife a close friend of Henry James and a leading London salon hostess, the husband a well-known tenor; Lord and Lady Acton, the heads of the international set in Florence; the sculptors Janet Scudder and Jo Davidson; Pen Browning, the son of Robert and Elizabeth; and Jacques-Émile Blanche, a French portrait painter commissioned by Mabel to immortalize her as a Renaissance woman.

Mabel's guests moved through her life like figures in a medieval masque because she trained her consciousness to focus on the textures of pattern recognition:

> All a-making and aping of pictures and talking about them. People
> always being told they had "character," which did not at all mean they
> had virtues—often quite the contrary. But that they had *genre:* strange
> form, or "interesting color," or they were very "period" or picturesque.

She learned to define people in terms of the painters and sculptors she was studying (a trait that followed her to Taos where she dropped it in order to have an "original" relationship to her new world). Her Aunt Rosa was a Memling; her chauffeur, a Maillol; Paul Draper, a Blake drawing; and the flamboyant Gordon Craig (Isadora Duncan's lover and the father of her children), "a Mother Goose as drawn by Arthur Rackham."[22]

The social and artistic circles in which Mabel moved were full of outcasts and tragic figures, whose life stories fostered Mabel's *fin de siècle* mentality. She had inherited a woman named Marguerite from the villa's previous owners. So passionately did this stranger attach herself to Mabel that when Marguerite died she haunted her old room—much to the discomfort of Janet Scudder and Jo Davidson, who stayed there. Mabel called upon a priest, and later a swami, to perform the exorcism rite she hoped would cast off Marguerite's unappeased spirit.

Through Lady Paget, the head of English society in Florence, Mabel met most of the interesting characters who later peopled her villa. Francesca Alexander was one, an American girl who had been brought by her mother to Florence after her sea-captain father died. They transplanted their cozy Salem home to their Florentine palazzio where they lived as recluses. Francesca was never allowed to grow up or go out into society.

The one exception her mother made was for John Ruskin, who had seen some paintings Francesca had done that were hanging in the Uffizi. He took her on a walk in the hills outside Florence, dug up an olive tree which he transplanted for her in her garden at home, and became the one outsider enshrined in the past to which Francesca and her mother devoted their lives.

Mabel met and entertained Gladys Deacon, who had grown up with Consuelo Vanderbilt, and whose young life was ruined by her mother's divorce. Gladys and her mother lived as outlaws in Florence in the luxurious palace given the mother by her lover, a Roman duke. Gladys's one mission was to avenge her mother's social humiliation. This she did by "stealing" Consuelo's husband, the duke of Marlborough, and becoming his duchess. Constance Fletcher was another outcast, one whose story was the basis for Henry James's *Aspern Papers*. Her mother had eloped with her brother's tutor to Venice. Constance's mother lived there like a queen, her lover ensuring that fresh rose petals were scattered down the wide marble staircase of their villa before she descended each morning. Constance went to England and became a successful playwright and book reviewer. There she had the romance of her life with Lord Lovelace, Byron's grandson, who gave her his grandfather's ever-sought-after papers. When the affair was over, Constance retreated to Venice where she enshrined herself in the past, a "middle-aged dreamer."

Not far away from Mabel lived the Queen of Saxony. She, too, had run off with her children's tutor and lived among the others who had found the world well lost for love. Menie Dowie was not so fortunate. A middle-class, married Englishwoman, she had fallen passionately in love with Edward Fitzgerald, the author of the popular Victorian translation of "The Rubáyát of Omar Khayám." She divorced her husband and ran off to Florence with Fitzgerald, only to find him sullen and unhappy in their marriage. Menie trailed "long, romantic muslin skirts . . . broad-brimmed garden hats, . . . shading her faded, disillusioned face."[23]

John Herron and Carrie Rand were hounded out of America by the newspapers. The Reverend Herron had been a minister and professor of religion at Grinnell College, where Carrie served in a position analogous to dean of women. He and Carrie were active in the Socialist party; Herron, in fact, helped to write the 1904 party platform. When they fell in love and he divorced his wife, Herron's careers at the university and in the church were finished. When they fled the country, they settled in Florence with their two children. There, Mabel says, "The house, the clothes they wore, the dinners they gave, the things they said, were all a kind of special pleading for the right to live, love, and to be happy."[24]

There was no tale more filled with tragic and romantic wonder in the Italy of that time than the love affair of Eleanor Duse and Gabriel D'Annunzio. The Duse, as she was known, was the most fluent and expressive

37

actress of her day, idolized worldwide for her great interpretive roles. In her prime, she fell in love with one of the most prolific and controversial writers of the turn of the century. D'Annunzio was a poet, novelist, dramatist, and journalist, known for his dazzling verbal virtuosity and celebration of eroticism. His liaison with Duse began in 1894 and inspired a series of tragic plays that he wrote for her. Like Pygmalion, the Duse seemed to have been created by the poet, who, Mabel says, poured "into her woman's emptiness a noble form" and called it by her name.[25] She was Mabel's first contact with a woman who had sacrified her life for art and love.

During one of the Duse's greatest performances, D'Annunzio entered the theater with a Roman society woman, Carlotta Rudini. The Duse broke out of character when she saw them and was booed off the stage. Arrogant and egomaniacal, D'Annunzio ended their affair and exposed their intimacies in his novel, *il fuoco* (*The Flame of Life,* 1900). In 1909, suffering from ill health, the Duse left the stage. She stayed at Mabel's villa for a time while she was recuperating. Mabel was later to write a very moving story based on the Duse's affair. Like Poe's "The Oval Portrait," it tells of a woman whose personality is destroyed by an artist so intent on making her his creature that she loses any independent power of existence—a theme Mabel became well versed in.[26]

Mabel also entertained Gordon Craig. Actor, director, and one of the most innovative stage designers of the early twentieth century, he talked incessantly of the need for a new world. When Mabel tempted him with "taking up" Florence and re-creating the Renaissance, Craig offered to give up his contract with the Moscow Art Theatre—and to give Mabel his son Dionysus!—if she would work with him on it. For Craig, this idea became an immediate and all-consuming passion. For Mabel it was a passing fantasy, only one among other grandiose schemes. In her memoir, *Music at Midnight,* Muriel Draper recalls her own and Mabel's plan to buy a feudal estate that represented architectural styles from the eleventh through the eighteenth centuries. There they planned to create a historical commune that would be a living memorial to the past.[27] Like the plan Mabel suggested to Gordon Craig, this too came to nothing, although it foreshadowed her more serious schemes in Greenwich Village and later in Taos.

The Femme Fatale

Nothing Mabel did during her years in Florence seemed to fulfill her. She poured an extraordinary amount of creative energy into designing a world for herself at the Villa Curonia that fed her sensuous appetites and supplied her with a rich and varied store of human material to mix and match at her will. But she found that she could not subsist from feeding off of others' lives and loves, or from arranging and rearranging the dead forms of the past. So she convinced herself that she "was made for noble love, not for art, not for work, not for the life of the worldly world, but for the fire of love in the body. . . . Not lust, not merely appetite or hunger . . . but love the element like fire or wind or water." As in her schoolgirl days it was the idea of love that charmed her. She had built "a house for Love."[28] Now she must find someone beside the prosaic Edwin to validate her existence within it.

The Florentine ambience reinforced Mabel's desire to develop her powers as a femme fatale. Yet she had to be careful; she had seen examples enough of the price paid by women who left their conventional lives in order to live out their passionate dreams. Although Mabel was on the lookout for a man who matched her conception of Renaissance virility, she intended to keep her promise to Edwin that she would remain technically faithful. In her memoirs, she was extraordinarily frank about the absurd behavior to which this paradoxical attitude often led her.

Mabel's first victim was a British Colonel, Ernest Roupell, D.S.O. He had "a beak like a chicken hawk," but it was Mabel who was the bird of prey: "Something *morne* and indifferent in his aspect allured me to attack." She found herself more alive when she aroused his interest; yet when he tried to make love to her, she was offended and turned him away. It was one thing for him to press his bony knees into the skirts of her muslins in the back seat of her husband's Renault. For there was Edwin, in the driver's seat, providing her with the security of "the marriage net." But making love was outside the rules of "celibate athleticism" she set herself.[29]

Mabel's pursuit of men was related to her adoption of "art for life's sake." As was true for the figures on Keats's Grecian urn, bliss lay in the stimulus of the chase; consummation was always the promise of future fulfillment and one never had to know the disappointing aftertaste. The romantic sensibility that inspired her to become "La Belle Dame Sans Merci" was rooted in the supposition that she could maintain her superior position of power over men only if she withheld her sexual favors. In Buffalo, she had been the hunted. In Florence, she became the hunter, using her sexual allure to entrap the sex she had always felt entrapped her.

Mabel's second conquest could not have been better chosen for an adventure in romantic decadence. It offered a relationship with the most tragic figure in Florentine society, without the possibility of physical union to detract from it. Bindo Peruzzi de Medici, godson of King Victor, had been a handsome and distinguished cavalry officer in his youth. When a ruthless ex-lover exposed his homosexual inclinations after he broke off an affair with her, he was ruined. An outcast from Florentine society, Bindo lived at home with his mother, a friend of the Brook Farm group and the Brownings. His sole friend was Pen Browning, the apple-faced and somewhat epicene son of Elizabeth and Robert.

Mabel was attracted to Bindo for some of the same reasons she had been to her Uncle Carlos. There was something "satanic" in him, an "ancient weariness" and desperation that at once challenged and frightened her American innocence. Bindo visited her often, but their relationship was never more than intensely Platonic. Edwin, however, was certain that the Marchesa Peruzzi wished to marry Bindo off to Mabel in order to restore his financial losses and his reputation. Mabel did give Bindo some pearls to pay off a debt, and there is no doubt she led him on. At one point she told him impulsively she would like him to live with her in the Villa Curonia. Bindo's impassioned reply, "If they take you away from me now, they may as well put a knife in me," may have been a mark more of his financial than of his emotional desperation, but it certainly suited the role Mabel had chosen him to play. The rumors of their "affair" that spread through Florentine society thrilled her, as did Edwin's jealous anger.[30]

Edwin finally gave an ultimatum. He was going to Boston, and if Mabel did not come with him, she would never see him again. As usual when she reached a crisis point, Mabel's pragmatism cooled her romantic ardor. She went to America with Edwin and, upon their return, obeyed his order to stay away from the Peruzzis. When she did see Bindo by accident during a shopping expedition, she did not speak to him. That night, according to Mabel, he committed suicide.

Mabel's pursuit of romantic love finally drove her into the arms of death. Like Wagner's Isolde, she heightened passion within herself until it became an extreme form of self-torture. Gino, her chauffeur, became her Tristram. He was a "knight, a page, a courtier"; his presence raised the rate of her vibrations. She longed to have him near her "to have the stimulant keener": "He was nothing to me. Nothing. But to the furnace I had become, he was everything."[31] With Gino, Mabel's romantic fantasies crossed the border into psychosis. When she could bear her agony of passion no longer, she put shards of glass into a box of figs and ate them. She survived and went to the mountains with him. But when he tried to embrace her, he found himself paralyzed by her frigidity. Mabel responded to his impotence by drinking a bottle of laudanum. The romantic maze in which Mabel found herself led to suicide as the only possible escape. But the drug did not kill her; in fact, it revitalized her. Apparently she was so numbed emotionally, so lacking any sense of self, that it took a brush with death to bring her back to life.

Mabel's recovery from her attempted suicide did not lead, however, to any clearer awareness of her central problem. She still could not take hold of her life or see that she needed to. Instead, she retreated to a more calculated exertion of her female powers:

These different men who desired me and had never been able to overcome me, contributed to the feeling of life I enjoyed, sitting in the warm room, sunk in furs, breathing of drooping violets . . . noting the magnetism that I exhaled like a perfume, something tangible like the musk of an animal, and irresistably attractive to at least three of the men in my neighborhood. It seemed to me, as a substitute for love, the ascendency over the desires of others was a good one. And, I thought, probably lasted longer.

In a telling analogy, Mabel compared herself to a "crippled child" who looks out at children playing in the street and longs to call them in to play with her. Life within the Villa Curonia was not so dissimilar to life within her Buffalo nursery. It, too, was a "play-house" in which she was encouraged to indulge her whims and fancies, as long as she remained within "the ample security . . . the guarded boundary, the imprisoning rules."[32]

Within the boundaries set by her husband, her society, and herself, she began to discover the role for which she became most celebrated during the next two decades, that of Muse. If she could not find a satisfactory outlet for her creative energies in her own right, she might at least serve to inspire genius. Mabel turned to what Patricia Spacks has called an age-old tradition of the "corruption of the female imagination." Lured by the forces of social convention, the potential woman artist has often converted herself into a work of art, "perverting her imagination by limiting its scope, losing herself by intense concentration on how she presents herself." Paul Draper was the first likely candidate she set out to magnetize. At the time she met him and Muriel in Florence, he was the more famous of the two. Although he had "no mobility, no flexibility in his physique, and his profile had the straight, inanimate plumb line of a not-very-good Greek statue," he was a fine tenor. Under Mabel's tutelage, Paul broadened his repertoire from Schumann and Schubert to include the turbulent music of César Franck. He took Mabel on long drives and whispered fiercely in her ear, "God! Mabel! You are life. . . ." Paul informed his wife that he needed a great passion to increase his talent. Now that she was being used "by the demands of the musical life," Mabel felt she had an occupation.[33]

Mabel used Nietzsche's philosophy of the superman to justify her behavior: "I was . . . beyond good and evil, indomitable, unbreakable." There was no room for ethics in a "world of fire and force in which one was able to forget them and feel oneself alive." In order to live in that world, however, she needed the strong psychic stimulation provided by a vital person to whom she could attach herself. On her own she felt weak and partial; yet each new conquest increased her need to realize herself through someone else. The extreme mood swings that Mabel exhibited throughout her years in Florence—and later in New York and Taos—were closely related to this dilemma. When her "life-flow" was aligned with someone's genius, she lived in a state of ecstasy during which she felt she could accomplish anything she set her mind to. In her depressive phases, "the relapse back into the deficient, partial, insufficient life of my own organism separated from the . . . vitality and richness that I believed was residing in another and which I sought out and drank, intoxicating myself, was always terrible for me."[34]

The *fin de siècle* world of Florence in which she had immured herself seemed less and less satisfactory as Mabel approached her thirty-second birthday. Its sterility was epitomized by the games the Bernard Berensons played at their parties. They would spread out a number of art prints, cover up all but a small piece of cloak or apple, and ask the guests to determine who painted the picture from the "treatment" evidenced in the clues. Mabel realized this world had carried aestheticism to its furthest limit, and she saw the danger of her absorption in it. In his verses about the Villa Curonia, "The Upper Garden," Robert de la Condamine captured what her life had become: "For these are the blossoms that . . . are of no use to the world, no advantage shall come from them, but the Upper Garden is beyond the world, and its scented mazes enshrine but one hope—the desire of creation, creation for its own sake, beautiful and barren."[35] Mabel had reached a dead end with the forms of the past. The people and the objects she collected in Florence were the fabric out of which she had hoped to weave a life and identity satisfying to herself. And she had failed.

The year 1911 was crucial in Mabel's awakening to a new form of consciousness. That spring she met Leo and Gertrude Stein, who converted her to modernism and opened up to her the possibility of self-transformation through the language of art. Gertrude's admiring "Portrait of Mabel Dodge at the Villa Curonia" (1911) established both women's reputations in America as leading figures of the avant-garde. In the same year, Mabel commissioned the painter Jacques-Émile Blanche to immortalize the many roles she had taken in her "play" with the past. Blanche was both awed and horrified by the undirected American energy in which Gertrude Stein so much delighted. His novel *Aymeris* (1923) treats Mabel as a modernist symbol of the disintegration of Western culture.

Mabel was not alone in seeing her life as emblematic of important tensions and shifts in the social and intellectual life of her times. The literary portraits of the American character and cultural traits she seemed to embody began in Florence and proliferated over the next three decades.

A Postimpressionist Portrait:
Mabel Dodge and the Steins

> *Gertrude Stein was prodigious. Pounds and pounds and pounds piled up on her skeleton—not the billowing kind, but massive, heavy fat. . . . She intellectualized her fat, and her body seemed to be the large machine that her large nature required to carry it.*
>
> *Gertrude was hearty. . . . She had a laugh like a beefsteak. She loved beef, and I used to like to see her sit down in front of five pounds of rare meat three inches thick and, with strong wrists wielding knife and fork, finish it with gusto, while Alice ate a little slice daintily, like a cat.*
>
> *Yet with all this {fat} she was not at all repulsive. On the contrary, she was positively, richly attractive in her grand ampleur. She always seemed to like her own fat anyway and that usually helps other people accept it. . . . She gloried in hers.* [1]

Leo and Gertrude Stein were the first to help Mabel break out of her prison house of the past and into the twentieth century by introducing her to the revolutionary spirit of the postimpressionists. The break with traditional forms that the postimpressionists formulated opened to Mabel new modes of being that were particularly suited to her.

When Mabel visited Leo and Gertrude Stein at 27 Rue de Fleurus, in the spring of 1911, she was ready for what they had to offer her. The Stein salon was well established, and Leo was at the pinnacle of his reputation as the first prophet of the new art. Mabel adopted his underlying aesthetic axiom for her own approach to art: "Leo seemed to be an enemy of gravitation; he required more than just the natural laws when it was a question of art forms. The conventions of sound or painting were unutterably wearisome, always proceeding along the lines of least resistance. . . . 'Tension,' he used to say, 'is the requisite for a living work of art.'" [2]

Mabel justly credited Leo with the discovery of Picasso and the other postimpressionists he collected (unlike Gertrude, who, in her autobiography, totally ignored Leo's contribution to her aesthetic development). Leo remained a friend to Mabel and an influence on her long after she had been frozen out of Gertrude's life. But it was Gertrude to whom Mabel initially responded most warmly. Mabel immediately became one of her fervent admirers, displaying an understanding of Gertrude's artistic intentions that seems remarkable, considering how little known or understood Gertrude was at the time.[3]

Mabel's portrait of Gertrude in *European Experiences* reflects the rich sense of vitality and well-being Mabel felt she radiated. Her rendering of Gertrude also reveals one of Mabel's own literary fortés: her ability to capture vividly the essential characteristics of the vibrant personalities with whom she surrounded herself. Mabel "valued Gertrude for reasons that many other people were not alert enough to grasp. . . . She felt that Gertrude, as Leo's first disciple, had learned the necessity of being absolutely free to react to paintings as well as to people, to count upon one's own subjective taste as a first principle." In Mabel's words:

> Gertrude had direct first-hand reactions of her own about life just as Leo did about paintings. He had taught her this secret. I remember she was the first one of all those sophisticated, cultured people I had grown accustomed to, who made me realize how nothing is anything more than it is to oneself. For instance, Gertrude didn't care whether a thing was *bon gout* or not, whether it was quattrocento or not, unless it affected *her* pleasantly, and if it did please her she loved it for that reason.[4]

Gertrude Stein was at the cutting edge of a revolutionary period that could be called "the flowering of the age of ego." Diverse manifestos claimed for the artist's vision a truth as valid as any external reality, and, as Mabel put it in defining Leo's credo, a visionary power that saw beyond the obvious realm of appearances into the underlying structure of the dynamic tension between form and matter.

From the very first, Mabel understood Gertrude's linguistic contribution to this revolutionary breakthrough in modern consciousness. After leaving Paris, Mabel took back to Florence several chapters of Stein's manuscript *The Making of Americans*. Beyond the evident hyperbole, Mabel's response shows she understood the essence of Gertrude's linguistic revolution:

> To me it is one of the most remarkable things I have ever read. There are things hammered out of consciousness into black & white that have never been expressed before—so far as I know. States of being put into words, the "noumenon" captured—as few have done it. *To name a thing is practically to create it & this is what your work is*—real creation . . . your palette is such a simple one—the primary colors in word painting & you express every shade known & unknown with them. It is as new & strange & big as the post-impressionists in their way &, I am perfectly convinced, *it is the forerunner of a whole epoch of new form & expression.* . . . *I feel it will alter reality as we know it,* & help us to get at Truth instead of away from it as "literature" so sadly often does.[5] (Italics mine.)

Through Leo's theories and Gertrude's works Mabel first saw the possibility of achieving wholeness through language. Leo Stein's aesthetic, and Gertrude's adoption of it in her works, provided solutions to deeply disturbing psychological problems much like those that troubled Mabel. Both Steins had felt alienated from their world during childhood and both later suffered from identity confusion similar to that which marked Mabel's life.

The Steins were the children of a somewhat flaccid mother and an overbearing and autocratic father. Like Mabel, Gertrude attempted to disown her father psychically. In part because both she and Leo had been unplanned (they "replaced" two other children who had died), Gertrude presumed that she had never been wanted. For a great deal of her adolescent life, she felt unloved and unlovable, and she turned to Leo as a surrogate father (whom she later felt forced to disown). Leo was even more damaged by their upbringing. He suffered from a lifelong neurosis that he was never fortunate enough to resolve or transcend. From his studies of psychology at Harvard, and his pursuit of aesthetics in Florence during the early 1900s, he evolved a rather extraordinary psychoaesthetic theory which he termed "radical" or "practical solipsism." Through the application of this theory, he claimed, modern man's divided self could be integrated into the formal perfection of a living work of art. The application of this theory to himself became his life's vocation.

Leo evolved his theory by posing for himself the problem of learning how to see the way an artist does. He studied a china plate for several weeks in order to discover how it would look if it were "aesthetically significant." After several weeks of identifying himself with this object, he found that it was no longer an inert shape with various designs, but something "every part of which implicated every other part. . . . No longer a composite object, but an organism . . . a projection of my own organic sense, and that organism was experienced not as in myself, but as in the object." From china plates, Leo transposed his new vision to everything within his ken—paintings, scenery, and people. He trained himself to objectify himself into his various "parts"—psychic, emotional, and intellectual—and analyze them with the same severity "as a substance is treated by an engineer who wants to know that it is sound and capable of standing up to all conditions. If the substance retains any secrets, any undiscovered flaws, it has not been sufficiently examined and cannot be depended upon."[6]

This analysis would achieve the same results as his experience with the china plate. Leo's self would be realized, not as a series of dissociated parts, but as an organic synthesis. Although the integration was the result of his projecting his subjective "organic sense," it would be experienced *as if* it were objectively real. In one of the fragments of the book he planned to write on his self-analysis, Leo summarized the essence of his theory in a way that reveals its significance for Gertrude and Mabel: "The self turns into a reality of the fictitious kind, effective because it is believed in. . . . As in art, subject and form are part of a whole."[7]

Mabel shared with Gertrude a lesson they both seem to have learned first from Leo: that the act of creating the self through language could heal the psychic dislocations of their youth and nullify the hold of the past upon the present and future. Reading Gertrude's prose, Mabel realized the potential of rebirth through the word. As different as their upbringings were, both Mabel and Gertrude hoped to find salvation in the world of art. Throughout her life, Gertrude was puzzled over "the phenomenon of a multiple self." She felt sometimes that her identity was stable and at others that it was on the verge of falling to pieces. Richard Bridgeman attributes "a good portion of her stylistic experimentation" to the effort of reconciling "the sundered parts."[8]

Mabel made no mention of the American tradition of linguistic experimentation in which Stein worked and may have been unaware of it. She was, however, familiar with the works of Walt Whitman, as was Stein, who was well aware of her debt to him. In words remarkably similar to the ones Mabel used to explain Gertrude's "discovery" of the creative process, Charles Feidelson has noted that Whitman's contribution to poetics was the shift of the image of the ego as a "static observer" to that of a traveler or explorer: "the voyaging ego of Whitman's poetry records a large-scale theoretical shift from the categories of 'substance' to those of 'process'. . . . What seems at first a penetration of nature by the mind *is actually a process in which the known world comes into being.*" (Italics mine.) Gertrude's belief in the "continuous present" was an affirmation of the artist as self-progenerating, always able to start afresh by "beginning again and again." She believed that "the work of the creative imagination was not to reflect the world but to invent it."[9]

Gertrude and Leo Stein were the first to teach Mabel a lesson which later became part of the aesthetic philosophy that shaped her memoirs: the individual could overcome the bonds of heredity and environment and make herself anew. All three of them worked, each in his or her own way, at the center of this American paradigm. And all three shared the hubris of its imperial selfhood: the artist took the place of God and could create out of his own will new ways of seeing and being. Gertrude and Mabel had an equally detached view of human beings. As Gertrude put it in "Portraits and Repetition": "I had to find out inside everyone what was in them that was intrinsically exciting. . . ."[10]

James Mellow's description of Gertrude's relationships with people is equally revealing of the way in which Mabel used her friends and acquaintances as grist for her aesthetic mill:

She [Gertrude] had a passion for acquaintanceship . . . but a limited capacity for untroubled friendship. Except for several durable relationships, her friendships were like her collection of bric-a-brac: delicate objects, curiosities that took her fancy. . . . They were seldom priceless; they were not intended to display a cultivated taste; they were replaceable. . . .

The spectacle of human nature amazed and absorbed her. As the hostess of an international salon . . . she watched marriages, ruptures, divorces, reconciliations—enacted many times. As a writer she was fortunate in having the human comedy played out in her living room.[11]

Mabel Dodge was an ideal subject for Gertrude Stein's human comedy, and Mabel's life at the Villa Curonia was a perfect objective correlative for what Stein felt were the essential rhythms of twentieth-century American life. In "Portraits and Repetition" Stein wrote that "this generation has conceived an intensity of movement so great that it has not to be seen against something else to be known, and, therefore, this generation does not connect itself with anything, that is what makes this generation what it is and that is why it is American, and this is very important in connection with portraits of anything."[12] Her writing was, she says, like America in its fascination with motion and discontinuity.

By witnessing their coming into being, Gertrude was "creating" the individuals whose portraits she wrote. The portraits were a combination of the raw data of her subject's behavior and attributes and the transforming eye and ear of the artist. She rendered their permanence by paradoxically "fixing" them in a continuously fluid present where they could always be seen in the dynamic process of being "born."

Stein began writing portraits of people in 1908. Her early portraits were more or less representational. "The Portrait of Mabel Dodge at the Villa Curonia," written in October of 1912 while Stein was a guest at the villa, stands in a crucial place in the development of her prose style toward abstractionism. Leo Stein claimed that it was "directly inspired by Picasso's latest form," synthetic cubism. Arnold Rönnebeck, a friend of Gertrude's, remembered her saying about Mabel's portrait, "Well, Pablo is doing abstract portraits in painting. I am trying to do abstract portraits in *my* medium, *words*."[13]

Michael Hoffman has located four distinct varieties of portraits in Stein's work before 1913. He says that "The Portrait of Mabel Dodge" is the most famous portrait in what he calls Stein's "third type," which he defines as a series of non sequiturs "in which the sentences carry very little sense, and which gains its effects mainly by suggestion." The juxtapositions of images "have only the logic that their internal linguistic structures create for them." Hoffman compares this style to the work the cubists were doing at that period in their creation of portraits "that depended for whatever iconicity they had on suggestions that seemed to emanate from the associations connected with fragments scattered throughout the canvas. . . . "[14]

The attributes of Mabel's personality that Stein noted—in particular, her fluidity and discontinuity—may have inspired the direction of Stein's linguistic experimentation, for Gertrude always tried to match "her conception of a person with a style."[15] Synthetic cubism was far more appropriate to Mabel's "style" than analytic cubism, in which the intellectual and conceptual aspects of formal planes are emphasized. Synthetic cubism was expressive of imagination, surprise, and lyricism, which were the very qualities that caused Mabel to furnish each room in her villa in a different period in order to match the fancies of her mercurial moods.

What was it that Gertrude had seen and heard of her hostess at the Villa Curonia? The opening and closing lines of her portrait have the conventional quality of a thank-you note: "The days are wonderful and the nights are wonderful and life is pleasant. . . . There is not all of any visit." But between these lines lies a welter of objects, events, and passions connected in a disjunctive style that at first seems to mirror nothing but chaos. The non-sequitur style in which Hoffman says the portrait was written was certainly an appropriate one for expressing Mabel's mode of existence at this time.

In the villa, one walked from a room inspired by the nineteenth-century English arts-and-crafts movement to the grandeur of a cinquecento salon, rooms that were juxtaposed for no other reason than that they pleased Mabel's taste. The roles she played were, as we have seen, even more illogically juxtaposed than the villa's rooms. Depending on the day or mood, Mabel projected the mental habits of the *fin de siècle* femme fatale, the hauteur of a Renaissance princess, the lust after status of the *arriviste* (a quality in her that Alice Toklas could not abide), the innocent coquetry of a Daisy Miller, and a cautious sense of marital propriety. Her guests and friends ranged from those who were acceptable to the most proper Florentine society to those who were moral and social outcasts; from strait-laced Victorian expatriates to effeminate aesthetes.

Stein's portrait, however, does not evoke the baroque richness and lavish absurdities of Mabel's life at the villa. Rather, it renders the atmosphere of the life there in the most basic of "primary colors," focusing on simple textures. Elemental to the life of the villa, as Stein saw it, were all the necessities for a fully sensuous existence:

Blankets are warmer in the summer and the winter is not lonely.

A bottle that has all the time to stand open is not so clearly shown when there is a green color there.

Abandon the garden and the house is bigger. . . . This is comfortable. There is the comforting of predilection.

. . . although there was the best kind of sitting there could never be all
the edging that the largest chair was having. . . .
  There was not that velvet spread when there was a pleasant head. . . .

There is the use of the stone and there is the place of the stuff. . . .
There is the room that is the largest place when there is all that is where
there is space.[16]

The fragments of rooms and objects within them do not represent any
of the specific furnishings or the architecture of the villa. They are disembodied abstractions of particulars noted by Stein that have the kind of
timeless unity one finds in a still life by Picasso. The unity Picasso achieves
by balance of color and shape, Stein achieves through the equivalent value
of her verbal imagery. Each thing is noticed and cherished for itself. A
velvet spread is of as much inherent value as the space where a vase once
stood. The portrait also achieves balance through antithesis; for many of
the things and activities that "are," are also "not." This was equally true
of the villa's hostess, whose "personality" is rendered through the evocation
of objects and activities with which Stein quite astutely identified her.
  In order to understand the "logic" of the portrait, it is important to
know the context that helped to create Stein's perceptions. While Stein
was visiting, Mabel was engaged in a torrid love affair with her son's
twenty-two-year-old American tutor, which Mabel insisted was platonic.
Edwin was away on business, and Mabel had promised to be good while
he was gone. On the third night of Stein's visit, the young man came to
Mabel's room (which was next to the room in which Stein was writing
her hostess's portrait) importunate with passion. After a more-or-less silent
embrace on Mabel's bed, which apparently lasted for hours, the young
man left, unfulfilled in his desires. In his biography of Gertrude Stein,
James Mellow assesses the effect of this scenario on Gertrude's work-in-
progress:

  Mabel was relieved that Gertrude had remained in the study, unaware of
  the encounter. . . . But since an "adulteration" and a good deal of heavy
  "breathing" figure ambiguously in Gertrude's text, it seems possible
  that, subliminally at least, Gertrude may have been aware of the
  footsteps passing down the red-tiled corridor to Mabel Dodge's room.[17]

Gertrude's knowledge of Mabel's sexual habits was far from subliminal,
however. For Mabel made Gertrude her confidante in this matter and
attempted to have Gertrude function as a go-between for the triangle of
unhappiness that existed between her and Edwin because of the young
tutor (whom Mabel did not quite give up until after she returned to New
York).
  The triangle was complicated by the fact that Mabel believed Gertrude   49

to be erotically interested in her at the time she was writing the portrait. In *European Experiences,* she mentions a charged look that Gertrude sent her way one evening at dinner, much to the discomfort of Alice B. Toklas. Mabel says that she flirted with Gertrude as well. It is certainly true that her early letters to Gertrude are love letters, of a sort. She was continually writing after their first meeting in Paris how awfully she missed her. After her October visit, Mabel wrote, "Gertrude—If you love me you'll come back. I can't do without you—especially now. Won't you come & help me & E[dwin] out?"[18]

In her next letter, she told Gertrude that she wanted to spend the winter in Paris under her supervision, in order to escape her triangular complications at the villa. Edwin was not quite as dull as Mabel made him out to be. He suspected, with a good deal of justice, that Mabel was infatuated with Gertrude, and that it was Gertrude, not the tutor, who was Mabel's real interest. Mabel told Gertrude this and remarked that she almost believed Edwin was right; then she coyly asked Gertrude if she thought Edwin was right.

Gertrude's portrait is filled with sexual innuendos that mirror the conflicts and confusions of Mabel's emotional life. One gets the sense of desire fighting duty, with the result of a "yes-no" stalemate that must have been torture for the poor young tutor. Stein certainly captures the humor of the situation, while enjoying the contradictions:

> Bargaining is something and there is not that success. . . . That was not an adulteration.
> So much breathing has not the same place when there is so much beginning. . . .
> Any time is the half of all the noise and there is not that disappointment. There is no distraction. An argument is clear.
>
> . . . the forgotten swelling is certainly attracting . . . it is not sinking to be growing. . . . There cannot be sighing. This is this bliss.
>
> There is not wedding instruction. . . . There is the paling that is not reddening . . . there is that protection, there is that destruction . . . there is the argument of increasing. . . . There can be the climax.
>
> There is that desire and there is no pleasure. . . .
> Praying has intention and relieving that situation is not solemn. . . . There is not that perturbation. . . . There is no action meant.

The heavy breathing and the bargaining are interspersed with the green glass, the blankets, and chairs in such a way that one does get the impression of the non–point of view of a collage. Stein's continual use of gerunds and participles, which permeate almost every paragraph of the portrait, gives a sense of the on-going pleasure in motion created by the villa's mistress: breathing, beginning, regaining, feeling, undertaking, pressing, pleasing, drinking, directing, looking, laughing, smiling, beguiling, comforting, exchanging, acting in partaking. The energy, delight, and desire that Stein speaks of seem the basis of a life force that is directed as easily to love as it is to vases and visits.

It is obvious that Gertrude found in Mabel the kind of discontinuous motion and ever life-renewing energies that she associated with being an American, and, in particular, with being an American at the dawn of the twentieth century. Gertrude reveled in the new century, which she described as "a time when everything cracks, where everything is destroyed, everything isolates itself, it is a more splendid thing than a period where everything follows itself."[19]

It is also no wonder that Mabel was delighted with her portrait. She discovered in Gertrude's prose a realm of being where value did not lie in complex moral or psychological states, a realm in which self-contradictions were part of the necessary tension of a living work of art. Value lay in the aesthetic and sensuous pleasure to be garnered from the concentrated vibrancy of moments that had no logic or motivation outside themselves. The fluidity of her character was made to seem a cause for delight rather than dismay, while the incoherence of her "intensity of movement" was justified by the dynamic personality that generated it:

Villa Curonia [Nov. 1912]

. . . I consider the Portrait to be a master-piece of success from my (& your) point of view *as* a portrait of *me as* I am to others! . . . My English friend, Mrs. Napier . . . writes "it is bold effrontery to do this sort of thing" (*If* she only *knew me!!*) Others say (as they would of me! They know *so little* they *are* saying it of me!) "there is no beauty in it." . . . Muriel [Draper] who is here . . . says "Ducie Haweis and I wanted to wire from London "We understand *the cover*"(!) . . ."

Someone else says "it is all confusion, things do not seem to follow each other out of each other" . . . No one (but me!) can remember a line in it to quote without referring to it! In fact it is so faithful a portrait as, I think, to produce about the same effects as myself were the truth always said! . . . Some days I don't understand it, but some days I don't understand things in myself, past or about to come! When I tell people that my "precious coherence" is in it they roar, never having perceived any in me! When I say it seems to me "middleclass, confused, & rather sound," Edwin laughs with contempt at my daring to even mention the word "sound" in connection with myself not to *mention it!*[20]

Portrait of an American Expatriate:
Mabel Dodge and Jacques-Émile Blanche

He knew everybody worth knowing in France and England and a good many Americans. He was intensely curious about people, and tried to probe them with his paint brush. He was charming and a little wistful, with gray eyes over which the lids drooped, and that sagged at the lower lids like those of a mournful hound. He was a kind of hound. He hounded the souls of his sitters, trying to fathom them.[1]

Mabel Dodge hired Jacques Blanche shortly after her visit with the Steins. During her trip to Paris, she had seen Blanche's portrait of Nijinsky, "sumptuous in oriental silks, standing poised on one leg in the center of a strip of Turkish carpet." She apparently determined that Blanche might be her Diaghilev. The Russian ballet was "orientalizing Europe in those years, setting new fashions in turbans and languors, and every woman became an incipient Scherherazade. . . ." At the time Blanche came to the Villa Curonia, in the spring of 1911, Mabel was caught between the crosscurrents of the formalized past she had resurrected to structure her life and the heady liberation offered by Gertrude Stein's continuous present. The woman whose soul he was to probe with his paint brush did not have 1,001 tales to tell. But her extraordinary range of costumes and personalities, her appropriation of the European past and vehement defense of the new art shook his traditionalist's soul to its foundations. "We Americans, for whom the world is in its infancy," Mabel told him, "lay claim to the past of your continent—it is ours."[2]

Mabel informed Blanche that he could "do" her as anything "except an American for Mr. Sargent." Each morning, she sent her chauffeur to call for him. Blanche was never sure of the woman who would greet him: "Mabel in a cotton skirt, holding a blue parasol, and a basket of eggs" and Mabel "coming from behind a tapestry . . . with a turban like Thamar in Rimsky-Korsakoff's ballet" were only two of the many Mabels who greeted him. She could be placid like a Chinese divinity or a madonna, or move like "a fleshy odalisque, worn out by the heavy perfumes of the harem."[3]

Two paintings Blanche did of Mabel authenticate her image as a Renaissance lady. One depicts a highly idealized Mabel, draped in a flowing gown, her satin-shoed feet resting on a pillow and her arms elegantly crossed over her waist. The expression on her face is one of enigmatic serenity. She appears to be a woman at ease with herself and her position in life. The second, which Mabel referred to as "a very Raphaelesque mediocrity," projects ambiguity. Her face is once more given a classic grace and sensuality, but it expresses boredom and puzzlement. Her elaborate gown and turban are far more obviously a costume, juxtaposed to the contemporary togs of her son who kneels beside (but is ignored by) her.

The images of elegance and grace, ennui and restlessness that Blanche rendered in his paintings were charged with greater intensity and complexity in his fictional portrait of Mabel as Gisell Links in *Aymeris*. Unlike Gertrude Stein, Blanche felt that Mabel's "American" qualities of fluidity and dynamism were more a cause of destruction than delight. She served him as a prototype of his own version of the Jamesian paradigm (Blanche was a friend of James's): the clash between cultures, between innocence and experience; the confrontation between the sometimes dangerous naiveté of a new world on the make with the rich traditions of an old world that seemed almost eager to collaborate in its own annihilation.

Gisell is a wealthy American expatriate who lives in a sumptuous Florentine villa. Georges Aymeris, the novel's hero, is a conventional portrait painter who has become dissatisfied with the limitations of his traditional technique. He leaves his lover and child in Passy while he travels to Florence seeking a cure for his painter's block. There he meets Mrs. Links and through her discovers a whole new world. Entering his hotel room wearing a fur stole over a transparent skirt, with a large Renaissance beret on her head, Mrs. Links tells him that she has been commanded from the "world beyond" to have him do her portrait. Here, as in many fictional portraits of her, Mabel's idiosyncracies and behavior are exaggerated, while her person is mythologized to larger-than-life proportions. Georges writes to his lover that he sees only English and Americans in Florence, "like Henry James." In fact, Blanche creates out of Mabel a rather terrifying feminine version of James's Chrisopher Newman:

> Her admiration for our past and our traditions inspires her with vaguely defiant and ironic words; she has the suspicious look with which, in our country, the young look at the old. . . . She takes a cruel pleasure in

our decomposition, of which she seems to smell the carcass. . . . From her latticed window, she sees Florence at her feet, and thinks, while filing her nails: "I will buy the best, since everything is for sale; and may the rest sink with a civilization that has lasted too long! . . . Our libraries and our museums will suffice for the education of philosophers."[4]

Like Mabel's, the past that Gisell purchases is falsely colored by her *fin de siècle* lens. She views the art of the Renaissance from Aubrey Beardsley's perspective and worships the French symbolists while sitting among the bric-a-brac of fake Renaissance madonnas. She is, finally, committed to nothing in any permanent way. It is her openness to change and her intensity that attract Georges to her. Although he is disturbed by what she tells him of the new art, he says that she, more than anyone else, may cut the strings that tie him to academic art. Gisell has made him aware of marvels "at the four corners of the universe" so that the thought of continuing in his traditional mode torments him.

To Gisell, Georges seems an "invalid" who has returned from famous battles and can tell her historical "anecdotes." She collects names, dates, and stories like "a boa stuffed with food." Although Gisell had hired Georges to be her teacher, it seems that he is the one to play the role of student. Gisell gives Georges lessons in avant-garde literature and art, interprets the French symbolists for him, and recalls to mind verse, prose, and paintings that she makes him understand in new ways. She teaches him, as Max Eastman's surrogate Mabel would teach his hero in *Venture,* to stand before a work of art and experience it freshly, without preconception. It is even possible, Georges says, that Gisell is trying to make him into the man "I should have been." (As many other artists would be, Blanche was impressed by Mabel's ability to play the godlike artist who attempted to mold and shape the very lives she had chosen to give *her* form.) But while Georges notes Gisell's astuteness in perceiving the revolt and anarchy buried within him, he questions what his creator obviously doubted about Gisell's prototype—whether she knew the woman "she should have been." Georges calls her a jellyfish who allows the flow of whatever tide she happens to be on to take her along.[5]

Georges sees himself and Gisell as Blanche obviously saw himself and Mabel; they are symbolic representatives of the "war between two continents." Gisell's lust for European history and her eagerness to purchase its past to legitimize her wealth and self are matched by her willingness to fling it all away for modernity. Georges has faith in the ability of his realistic brush to penetrate the "ivory armor" of her masks. His brushes and colors will be his "ballistas" and his "catapults." He is confident in their ability to capture, define, and control the essence of his protean American "enemy." Sometimes she reminds him of "Chinese divinities

54

and Siennese Madonnas"; at other times, she shifts into an entirely different mode of being: "her eyes are frightening, in her dull and swollen face, framed with hair that frizzes like the wig of Ida Rubenstein in Scheherazade. Gisell's chest heaves with each breath, like the lever of a powerful machine. . . ." While she seems "steeped in the scents of the harem," she has the energy and resources to "organize a canning factory, a refrigerated meat store, a railroad trust or a musical movie."[6] Gisell is doubly fearsome because she combines the American hero's will-to-power with the sexual dynamism of the feminine archetype.

In his portrait of Gisell Links, Blanche embodies the antitheses of the Dynamo and the Virgin. He uses them much as Henry Adams did in his male allegorical fantasy of the decline and fall of Western civilization. Mabel Dodge serves as an important "link" in the transformation of Woman's role from the Virgin who presumably centered Man's spirit to the Dynamo that broke it. Blanche's Madonna-Mabel (whom he associates with both pagan and Christian traditions) is comparable to Adams's Venus-Virgin: "She was goddess because of her force; she was the animated dynamo; she was reproduction—the greatest and most mysterious of all energies. . . ." She was, Adams claims, responsible for four-fifths of the world's great art. Blanche's other Mabel is very much like Adams's other dynamo—the one he stands before in the Gallery of Machines at the Great Paris Exhibition of 1900. This modern dynamo, which men now worship, is a machine that harnesses the chance collision of atoms.[7] It represents an anarchical, centrifugal power with the potential for mass destruction. By embracing modernism, Gisell serves this dynamo. Against it, the "ballistas" of Georges's traditional art are impotent. One cannot fight the modern dynamo with medieval weapons.

In his introduction to the French translation of Mabel's biography of D. H. Lawrence, Blanche wrote that she "had passed over Italy like an aeroplane laden with explosives—I might add over all the earth."[8] The last view we get of Gisell in *Aymeris* establishes her apocalyptic role. Like Prince Prospero at the end of Poe's "The Masque of the Red Death," she presides over a landscape of the human damned at a ball that she gives in her villa. Her guests are all caricatures of humanity who mock traditional values and sacred rituals, and who symbolize modern civilization's dance of death. Gisell is at once their priestess and a member of the community of the damned.

At the ball, the men come dressed in stiff skirts and ecclesiastic habits, as pilgrims and singers. Women appear as Velásquez Infantas, as Carmens, and Neapolitans. The "Pope" enters to a march played by the orchestra. Gisell orders a Virginia Reel and as a "priestess forgets her sacred role; the monks' robes rise showing naked legs. . . . The Holy Father brandishes his tiara, the bishops' crosses fall to the ground: the women, hair dishevelled, take off their black velvet masks; always the same Negro rhythm, 55 the banjo, more strident. . . . At the paroxysm of the uproar, the candles drip wax, a lamp is smoking; you no longer see there, and the Virginia Reel ends when an Ophelia appears on a bed borne by four porters."[9]

After Georges returns to Paris, he finds that Gisell's effects on him are long-lasting. She has increased his emotional instability, for he now aligns himself with everything that is new. Georges destroys all the designs he made in Florence and speaks to his friends of the "dated method" of oil painting. He buys crates of postimpressionist works but never opens them. Depressed and moody, he feels that the world is stupid except for some "superior minds" to whom he had tied himself. He tells the narrator of the novel that he wishes to take him to see Leo Stein's collection. He plans to spend his winter in St. Petersburg, writing poems for Igor Stravinsky.

The novel ends with Georges being brought back to the reality of earthly responsibility by the death of his young son. The death of the child is a mute testament to the immaturity of the artistic soul that tries to nourish itself on aesthetic values. The ultimate decadence, embodied in the lives of Mrs. Links and Mabel Dodge, is the inhumanity of those who live entirely within the solipsistic realm of the imagination.

Blanche takes his stand with the conservatives who felt that the impulses which led to the attack against representational art and traditional aesthetic forms brought about the destruction of social and ethical norms which gave coherence and order to the lives of the individual and the community. Although his novel is hardly a paean to academic art or to Victorian morality, he finds the twentieth century's embrace of revolutionary art forms a source of fragmentation for the human spirit. In Mabel Dodge, Blanche found his objective correlative for the psychic and emotional dislocations of the modern temper. Muriel Draper remembers Blanche working on one of his paintings of Mabel at the same time that Gertrude Stein was writing her portrait "Mabel Dodge at the Villa Curonia."[10] It is fascinating to think of these two artists, the traditionalist and the modernist, simultaneously creating the woman who came to symbolize the death of the old order and the birth of the new.

Somewhere between the poles of Stein's and Blanche's imaginations the real Mabel Dodge roamed. She had found a milieu in Florence where she began to realize her talents as an artist of life, but none of the activities in which she engaged had secured her identity: not the pleasure dome she created, nor the romantic adventures she engaged in, not even the artists whose genius she had served with her "psychic" energy. She had come to Europe a depressed widow, and she was about to return to her native land an unhappy wife.

Edwin had become merely "the figurehead of my ship." Now that John was approaching adolescence, Mabel did not feel Edwin was as necessary to fill the role of father. Hoping to find a good private boarding school for John, she wrote to H. G. Wells, whose ideas she admired, asking his advice about a "socialist school" in England. Wells's response indicates that he must have read between the lines. He suggested that the place for a rich young American was America.

In *European Experiences,* Mabel says that she chose to leave Europe because she was tired of Florence. More likely, however, Edwin determined the move, in an attempt to salvage a marriage that by now he ought to have realized was hopeless. Mabel was not so very different from the indecisive woman he had taken charge of in July of 1904, when she disembarked in Paris. In spite of her divided yearnings for her son's tutor and for Gertrude Stein, she too could not admit the marriage was over.

Once she was faced with it, the idea of returning to America was abhorrent to Mabel because it meant beginning life all over again. In Florence, she had at least "made a lovely frame" for herself, even though it became more important over time than "the picture [which] never was painted." Leaving Florence meant going back to "a world of dull, grubby men and women, street cars, cigar stores, electric signs, and baseball games." In a rare maternal moment on shipboard, she admonished John to remember that America was "ugly, ugly, ugly!" made up, as it was, of money-making and machines. John responded with adolescent recalcitrance: "*I* don't think it's so ugly," he informed his mother, as he gazed with anticipation at the New York skyline.[11]

Mabel spent the five days of the November 1912 crossing in the stern of the ship: "I did not care to look back and I could not look forward." She felt suspended "between two worlds," as she quoted from her favorite Matthew Arnold poem, "one dead,/The other powerless to be born." She had no idea what kinds of lives she would find to "dip into" in New York. Because she believed that "the only way I was able to live was vicariously— imagining myself into other forms than my own," she had reason to be afraid. To exist, she still needed to know "what manner of being was cherished in the other's imagination" so she could "project just such a form before delighted eyes."[12] Yet it was just this protean quality that allowed Mabel to thrive better in the radically antiformal bohemian world of Greenwich Village than she had among the moribund traditions of Florence. Inspired by the Steinian revolution, Mabel would join the young prewar rebels of the lower and middle classes of New York in their efforts to *épater la bourgeoisie.*

Chapter 3

Movers and Shakers

The Mabel Dodge who was soon to take New York by storm moved quietly into her Washington Square apartment, in a brownstone at 23 Fifth Avenue, at the end of November 1912. Although she had no idea what she was going to do with herself, she had chosen exactly the right place to live. Her building was at the fashionable edge of Greenwich Village, the heartland of America's avant-garde.

Like the Villa Curonia, Mabel's new home became a testament to her current mode of consciousness. Its interior was a *tabula rasa,* a "slate" of white walls, muslins, velvets, silks, and damasks that dramatized her desire for a new cosmos: one that was dedicated to wiping out the past, her own as well as the oppressions of the collective human past. Here she and her radical friends would seek sustenance from the brave new world of social harmony, economic justice, and sexual and aesthetic freedom that they imagined in her living room.

At the time Mabel designed the apartment, however, it held none of this symbolic resonance. It was merely intended to protect her from the physical and social grime of New York City. "The front of it," she wrote, "had a blank look like a face that hides its thoughts and it gave one a feeling of immense security. It seemed a refuge from the street."[1] The European decor—pale grey canopied bed and Florentine chaise longues, porcelain Venetian globes ornately decorated with brightly painted birds and flowers to offset the blinding whites—further segregated her from the city in which she felt an alien.

The fact that Edwin and John adjusted smoothly and happily to the enticements of New York and the bourgeois delights of weekend football games drove Mabel further into herself. Once she had completed decorating her apartment, she felt paralyzed by having "nothing to do," and, just as she had after her marriage to Edwin, she fell "quite definitely ill." Mabel convinced herself and her doctor that Edwin was the primary cause of her nervous disorders, so within a few weeks of their arrival he was advised to move out of their apartment in order to help his wife recover. Mabel believed that Edwin stood between her and "real life." Though he may have doubted her intellectual capacities, there is no evidence that he ever prevented her from doing as she pleased, except in the area of sexual fidelity. More to the point was her inability to find a satisfactory identity as a wife. During their last years in Florence, he had been little more than a safe background against which she played out her unfulfilling romantic dramas. Faced with the "shock of uprooting," she found he was no longer a stabilizing force.

What Mabel called the "strain of making an entirely new adjustment" resulted in a brief but severe nervous breakdown. The disintegration of personality her symptoms reveal remind one of Poe's characters who are completely cut off from society and human affection. Like Roderick Usher, she experienced trance-like states during which she suffered from hyperesthesia. Lovely things became acutely beautiful, while daylight pained her eyes. When a friend brought a bouquet of flowers, Mabel says she smelled them long before they arrived. Her rarefied sensibilities brought her terrifying and tempting visions of self-annihilation, including a confrontation with her own "Satanism" which appeared as a devilish figure who grinned at her from sulphuric fires.[2]

Mabel was spared madness, however. In fact, the sulphuric flames seem to have purged the last remnants of her *fin de siècle* aestheticism. Edwin also helped. As Mabel quaintly put it, he was the captain of the ship in which she finally sailed away from him. To cheer her up, he brought their mutual friend, the sculptor Jo Davidson, to visit. Through Davidson, Mabel met Hutchins Hapgood, the man who became her closest confidant during her New York years. Through Hutch, Mabel met Lincoln Steffens, Walter Lippmann, Emma Goldman, Bill Haywood, Max Eastman, Margaret Sanger, Alfred Stieglitz, and many of the other "movers and shakers" of the day.

During the eight years that Mabel lived in Europe, the industrial system that her grandfathers had helped to finance reached its apotheosis. In 1912, 2 percent of all Americans controlled 60 percent of the personal wealth of the nation: stocks, bank income, property, and business goods.

One-third to one-half of the American people lived in poverty or so close to it that they were pushed over the line any time they suffered extended illnesses or industrial accidents—in which the United States led the world. During these same years, the ruthless exploitation of human and natural resources and the economic oppression of child and adult laborers created among some segments of the middle and upper classes what one historian has called "the Revolt of the American Conscience." Progressive reformers took as their mandate the extension of the political rights to life, liberty, and the pursuit of happiness into the economic spheres of life. Most, however, were interested in modifying and cleansing an economic and political system they believed was essentially sound in order to make it more responsive to a broader spectrum of American society.[3]

The radicals who formed the inner core of Mabel's circle were more sweeping in their condemnation of the basic ill health of bourgeois America and industrial capitalism, even though they participated in many Progressive efforts. Like other "clean government" reformers, Lincoln Steffens worked to expose urban corruption by pointing up the collusion between American businesses and party machines. But he also lectured and wrote about the debilitating social and psychological effects of the Horatio Alger success myth. Walter Lippmann shared with elitist Progressive intellectuals the belief that social scientists should regulate the nation's industrial economy because their commitment to rational principles would lead them to adjust the disparity among goods, services, and human needs. But in his more apocalyptic moments, he scorned the shibboleths of middle-class property and propriety. John Collier worked with "social justice" Progressives to improve the conditions of working-class people by supporting such causes as tenement and factory reform, unionization, and expanded educational opportunities for immigrants. But he also focused much of his energy on promoting ethnic hegemony for the millions of immigrants who were swarming to American cities in the first two decades of the twentieth century, because he was convinced that the preservation of their communal traditions was a necessary counterbalance to the anomie of urban life. Socialists and anarchists like William English Walling, Max Eastman, Emma Goldman, and Bill Haywood demanded even more fundamental changes in America's political and economic system: from the redistribution of the national wealth, through a graduated income tax and federal regulation of wages, to workers' wresting the national wealth and the means of production from the hands of their owners.

During the 1912 elections, even establishment politicians were using the rhetoric of revolution. The Democrats under Woodrow Wilson proclaimed a "New Freedom," and the Progressives under Theodore Roosevelt, a "New Nationalism," both of which were dedicated to rectifying the environmental and human costs of America's industrial empire. The Socialists garnered the highest percentage of votes they ever received in a national election—6 percent of the presidential vote—as well as scores of state and local government offices. Certainly liberals had some justification for believing that their programs would temper, and radicals some justification for believing their programs might transform, America's social and economic life.

Greenwich Village

Van Wyck Brooks opens his chapter on Greenwich Village in *The Confident Years* with the dramatic image of Mabel Dodge returning from Florence "to dynamite" New York. She had arrived, he notes, at precisely the right moment: "at one of those 'heats and genial periods' that Emerson described 'by which the high tides are caused in the human spirit.'"[4] In many other eyewitness accounts of the time, Mabel also appears as the harbinger of an *annus mirabilis*. Her "coming out" in January 1913 was a rite of passage that contrasts strikingly with the upper-class debut she celebrated in Buffalo and the art-for-art's-sake pageantry of her dedication of the Villa Curonia. Before the end of the month, she would be fully engaged in the preparation of the most important art exhibit held in this country, immersed in the anarchist politics of Hutchins Hapgood and Emma Goldman, and on the verge of launching the most successful salon in American history.

"Looking back on it now," she wrote in an oft-quoted passage, "it seems as though everywhere, in that year of 1913, barriers went down and people reached each other who had never been in touch before; there were all sorts of new ways to communicate, as well as new communications. The new spirit was abroad and swept us all together." The "new spirit" of which Mabel speaks found its leadership in Greenwich Village and its "spiritual home" at 23 Fifth Avenue. It permeated the theories of psychology, art, poetry, politics, and sexual relationships that made the men and women who lived there imagine themselves capable of changing "the mores, the artistic standards, and even the political course of the United States."[5] Free thinkers and lovers, disparate in their creeds, goals, and degrees of radicalism, they were united by their fight against those tendencies in American life that were driving their fellow citizens in the direction of increasing standardization, mechanization, and materialism: the Taylorites and their worship of efficiency and cost-effectiveness based on the principles of scientific management that were turning men and women into machines; the specialization of work that further segregated the class system and divided the educated from the uneducated; the manipulations of the mass media, which promoted the myth that the pursuit of happiness took place between the covers of a Sears Roebuck catalogue. They have been called a "Lyrical Left," whose cultural politics sought to undermine the property-oriented, regimented, guilt-ridden bourgeois civilization that had spawned most of them.

Walter Lippmann, one of the least radical among them, sounded the trumpet of their charge in his 1913 book *Drift and Mastery*. They opposed, he said, "the sanctity of property, the patriarchal family, hereditary caste, the dogma of sin, obedience to authority. . . . Those who are young today are born into a world in which the foundations of the older order survive only as habits or by default." Christopher Lasch attributes the rise of these self-conscious radical intellectuals to the development of a "new social type," products of the cultural fragmentation of an industrial society that led to the decline of parental authority, community cohesion, and traditional middle-class values.[6] This was not the first generation of middle-class American rebels to feel estranged from the dominant social and economic patterns of the Protestant work ethic. But they were the first to argue with equal fervor for aesthetic, sexual, and political revolution.

Unlike the more serious and orthodox Marxist intellectuals of the day, and most working-class labor leaders, theirs was a revolution as much devoted to "play" and self-expression as it was to unionization and the redistribution of wealth. No one incarnated their spirit of spontaneity better than John Reed. Their acknowledged poet laureate, he captured the essence of the new bohemian life-style. Mabel knew him first through the book of verses he published on life in Greenwich Village just after she returned to America:

The Day in Bohemia

Twixt Broadway and Sixth Avenue,
And West perhaps a block or two,—
From Third Street up, and Ninth Street down,
Between Fifth Avenue and the town,—
Policeman walk as free as air,
With nothing on their minds but hair,
And life is very, very fair,
In Washington Square.

Lives there a man with soul so dead, I ask,
Who in an attic would not rather bask
On the South Side, in lofty-thinking splendor,
Than on the North Side grow obese and tender?
The North Side, to the golden ladle born,
Philistine, suckled at a creed outworn!
Unnumbered Jasons in their motor-cars
Pass fleeceward, morning, puffing black cigars—
We smoke Fatimas, but we ride the stars!

> Yet we are free who live in Washington Square,
> We dare to think as Uptown wouldn't dare,
> Blazing our nights with arguments uproarious;
> What care we for a dull old world censorious
> When each is sure he'll fashion something glorious?
> Blessed art thou, Anarchic Liberty
> Who asketh nought but joy of such as we![7]

Small wonder that once she grasped the essence of the Greenwich Village revolution, Mabel gave herself over to it entirely; for she recognized within it the same kind of psychologically and aesthetically liberating forces she found in Gertrude Stein. Postimpressionism, anarchism, feminism, Bergsonism all proclaimed the power of the individual to shape the self and the environment in terms of an inner vision. Daniel Aaron has noted the defining terms that connected all the revolutions: "'Released personality,' 'expression of self,' 'emotion,' 'intuition,' 'liberation,' 'experiment,' 'freedom,' 'rebellion,'—these phrases and words connote the prevailing tone of the 'new' magazines, books, and plays as well as the manifestoes, art exhibitions, and political rallies between 1912 and 1917." They inspired the Pagan Routs, during which Villagers dressed up as nymphs and satyrs and thumbed their noses at uptown "Puritans." They informed the meetings of the Liberal Club held at Polly's Restaurant on Macdougal Street, where one was equally likely to find on any night an imagist poetry reading, a lecture by Alexander Berkman on the slaughter of coal miners in Colorado, or a discussion by Henrietta Rodman of working women's needs for cooperative housing and child care.[8]

Even Freudian psychology served the cause. The first American therapists were buoyed by a psychological theory that was optimistic about the possibility of curing nervous disorders. Freud rooted neuroses in environmental causes that could be cured through the "cathartic" method: "Over and over again the psychoanalysts insisted that Freud's method was radical in the literal sense: it eradicated the roots of symptoms." Freudians stressed the need for mental and physical activity—not drugs or physical immobility, but "the patient's own insight cured." Freudian psychology was also used to question the benefits of the "painful saving of energic capital," which had buttressed the nineteenth-century Protestant work ethic, and to argue for the healthy release of psychic energy that would occur when deadening routines and inhibitions were overcome. Its more radical proponents called for the release and enjoyment of sexual energies by both men and women as an antidote to the neurotic symptoms created by the genteel "civilized code" of middle-class life in America.[9]

If Freud provided the psychology, William James and Henri Bergson, whose lectures at Columbia in February 1913 drew enormous crowds, articulated the philosophy that shaped the world views of Mabel and her cohorts during the prewar years. James's open-ended, unfinished, pluralistic universe and Bergson's vitalism posited the centrality of the individual's mind and will as the creators of matter and meaning. Bergson's *élan vital,* which Mabel variously called "IT" or the "life-force," coursed through human and physical nature, attending the creative individual who could harness it in service to ever-evolving states of consciousness. His celebration of intuition as the primary vehicle of "truth" returned power to the poet and guaranteed it to women, who were, he believed, the guardians of nonrational and nonlinear modes of thinking.

It was an American poet, however, who was the inspirational godfather of this rebel generation. For Mabel Dodge, Isadora Duncan, John Reed, Alfred Stieglitz, and Emma Goldman, Walt Whitman's poetry was the gospel from which they drew the benediction for their various causes. His *Song of the Open Road,* according to Mabel, was their rallying cry:

> Allons! with power, liberty, the earth, the elements,
> Health, defiance, gayety, self-esteem, curiosity;
> Allons! from all formulas![10]

Like Bergson's *élan vital,* Whitman's "procreant urge" enjoined men and women to create and master themselves and the universe. In Florence Mabel had adopted Whitman's motto, which she had embossed in purple and silver as the "seal" on her stationery: "If I contradict myself, well, then, I contradict myself." The words were even more appropriate now.

Mabel's goal was to incorporate the chaos of the diverse social, artistic, and political movements proclaimed by the "republicans" of Washington Square and direct them through her liberated life-force. In an unpublished poem she wrote in 1912, whose title denotes the quality for which she became famous, she outlined her mission:

Magnetism

> The supreme task of the soul is to encompass all experience.
> In the circle of the compass lies the soul's activity.
> Drawn by every influence lies shivering the needle,
> Yet ever striving for an immobility more fixed.[11]

Her free-floating energies were ready for any cause that drew her soul's "shivering needle." How she would achieve an "immobility more fixed" for her elusive identity by encompassing "all experience," and how she would direct the influences she was "drawn by" were two of the Whitmanesque contradictions she was initially willing to embrace.

In retrospect, Mabel tells us that she was an involuntary "instrument of the times." While it is certainly true that she immersed herself in the vortex of radical activity swirling about her, she was not merely "Fate's chosen instrument." In fact, like Madame de Staël, she set out quite deliberately to make herself the mistress of the spirit of her age by meeting and learning from its most creative and committed men and women.[12]

Just a few blocks from her home on Fifth Avenue, she visited Alfred Stieglitz's "291," the center of avant-garde art in America. Stieglitz was one of the first who helped her "to See—both in art and in life. . . . He never gave into anything except what he believed to be the best; . . . he never did anything for money or prestige or power. . . ." He was one of the most outstanding photographers of his day and a patron and advisor to many of the artists who are now acknowledged as among the most important and innovative painters of the early twentieth century: John Marin, Arthur Dove, Marsden Hartley, Georgia O'Keeffe, many of whom became a part of Mabel's circle. His gallery and his magazine, *Camera Work,* were major forums for the newest aesthetic theories and practices of his day. The two cardinal principles of "291" reflected concurrent political and social ideals as well: "the work of art had to be a frank expression of the feelings of the individual who produced it, without regard for conventional rules or styles of any other artists; and the creator of the work was expected to add something new to what had gone before."[13]

The Armory Show

The combined influences of the Steins and Stieglitz had much to do with the first cause that consumed Mabel's interest and launched her legend as a leading "new light." For a month before its opening on February 17, 1913, Mabel worked on the promotion of the Armory Show. Though most of the plans were well under way by the time she became involved, she supplied and solicited much-needed funds and obtained for the show some paintings that were in private collections. Within ten years, she would be credited with hiring her own ocean liner and carting the exhibition over from Europe single-handedly.

Arthur Davies, president of the Association of American Sculptors and Painters, had initiated the idea for the exhibition of postimpressionist art. For the first time in America, the works of artists such as Cézanne, Picasso, Braque, Gauguin, Derain, and Kandinsky were displayed to a wide public audience that was, for the most part, totally unfamiliar with them. Public taste had been primarily formed by the conventional and sentimental "realism" of academicians, who stressed the importance of drawing and the use of classical models from the past. The academy was highly resistant to the new art. It had always controlled the exhibition— and thus the sale—of paintings and sculpture in America, enjoying a monopoly that the association hoped to break. This was one reason why Davies chose to hold the exhibit in the Sixty-ninth Regiment Armory instead of in a museum.

As soon as Mabel was made vice-president of the association, she began to feel that the exhibition was hers: "It became, overnight, my own little Revolution. *I* would upset America; I would, with fatal irrevocable disaster to the old order of things. . . . *I* was going to dynamite New York and nothing would stop me. Well, nothing did." While Mabel exaggerated her role in propelling the show, she did not exaggerate its importance as a major event in American cultural history. She expressed her understanding of its significance in a note to Arthur Davies, who had it printed up and distributed to everyone who came to the Armory. It was Mabel's "Common Sense," a call to her fellow citizens to participate in a second American Revolution:

> I'll be delighted to help in any way in the exhibition, because I think it
> is the most important thing that ever happened in America, of its kind.
> Anything that will extend the unawakened consciousness here (or
> elsewhere) will have my support. . . . The majority are content to
> browse upon past achievements. What is needed is more, more and
> always more consciousness, both in art and in life.[14]

The symbol of the sponsoring organization was, appropriately, an uprooted pine tree. Mabel, however, tried to allay the fears of the opposition in an article she wrote for the *Buffalo Courier Express* at the time of the show. She explained that the association was not concerned with pulling anything up by the roots except the prejudice of those who believed "there can be anything permanent or final in the art of a nation or of the world." But the conservatives were not pacified. The idea of an imageless art, whose primary reference was the internal world of the artist rather than the world of external things, revolted and frightened many critics and most of the public who attended the show. They viewed the exhibition as a desecration of traditional values and a violation of common-sense vision. Like Blanche in *Aymeris,* they recognized with various degrees of consciousness that "to accept the new art meant to further the outlook of modern culture as a whole. The rejection of the new art was for many an expression of an attitude to all modernism."[15]

One of the most talked about violations of "common sense" at the Armory Show was Gertrude Stein's "Portrait of Mabel Dodge at the Villa Curonia." Its publication and distribution at the show, accompanied by an article that Mabel wrote on Gertrude for *Arts and Decoration,* marked the beginning of Stein's recognition in her native land. It was also a "birthday" for Mabel Dodge:

> "Well, who is Mabel Dodge?!" they exclaimed. And thousands of
> copies of *Arts and Decoration* were sold, for Gertrude Stein's Portrait of
> her, serving as an example of her style, was in it, and she had signed

that article—and there was something new under the sun and everybody's blood ran quicker for it! A chance to laugh, to curse, to run cold from *words!* . . .

I suddenly found myself in a whirlpool of new, unfamiliar life and if Gertrude Stein was born at the Armory Show, so was "Mabel Dodge."

Soon after her return to America Mabel had 300 copies of the portrait printed and bound in various Florentine wallpapers. It was because of its circulation among her growing circle of artist friends that she was first contacted by the publicity agent for the Armory Show, James Gregg. In *Movers and Shakers,* Mabel tells us that her initial interest in the show was "desultory." Gregg found her "listless—Ariadne with the tide low." Reminding us that she was never a "self-starter," she claims that he had to press her to write an article on Stein.[16]

Mabel's correspondence reveals a very different state of affairs. On January 24, she wrote Gertrude that she was working for the show "like a dog." When Gregg told her that he was "all up in the air" about this postimpressionist prose of Gertrude Stein, she grabbed the opportunity to exclaim:

Well—You believe that there is too much smell of death in most of the painting you know. . . . You want fresh life. Why don't you see that you can apply that to words? Words originally in primitive man were pure sound expressing directly an emotion. . . . The life has gone out of them. . . .

Then she accepted the idea of an article without hesitation: "So there is my *confession. I* am your faithful and incomprehending Boswell."[17]

Mabel was not, however, a Boswell to take a back seat to genius. She was thrilled that Stein's portrait had helped to establish her identity so that her mail now read: "Mrs. Mabel Dodge" rather than "Mrs. Edwin Dodge": "That's what you've done for one thing!" For another, she informed Gertrude three days later, "people tell me that everywhere on account of my judicious scattering of the Portrait, *everyone* is saying '*Who* is Gertrude Stein? *Who* is Mabel Dodge at the Villa Curonia?'" The editor of *Arts and Decoration* gave them equal billing in a note that preceded Mabel's article: "This article is about the only woman in the world who has put the spirit of post-impressionism into prose, and written by the only woman in America who fully understands it." Impressed by her piece on Stein, her chastened and still-loving husband wrote her from the Brevoort Hotel, where he was living in exile:

I am still thrilled with the certainty of your fast approaching recognition. I am still humiliated by the knowledge that its arrival has been so long delayed by my blundering interference. You have been right these years—eternally right—I have not understood you. And nothing pleases me more in "Speculations" than its vibrant note of splendid optimism—for interest in vitality and distrust of the diseased are the highest and finest of human gifts. I marvel that you have been so good to me. Humility has entered the portals of Casa Edwin Dodge.[18]

The publicity and recognition that Mabel gained from the reception of Gertrude's portrait confirmed her belief that she could be made "real" through art. The belief was rendered more paradoxical by the multiple and contradictory portraits that followed, beginning with imitations and parodies inspired by Gertrude's piece. Leo Stein was the first to pen a literary reaction. Angered by what he felt was a conscious attempt at incomprehensibility, his was a delightfully testy reaction to the confusion he found in the portrait and, presumably, in the life of the woman who inspired it:

> Mabel Dodge
> Hodge podge
> What is up,
> What is down,
> What is smile,
> What is frown,
> What is passion,
> What is pose,
> What is guessing,
> What is nose . . .
>
> What is push
> What is drag
> What is hustle,
> What is lag,
> Somehow lean,
> Somehow stout,
> Half in
> Half out.[19]

One writer inspired by Gertrude's portrait belonged to the lunatic fringe of the literary Left. Donald Evans was the owner of a small, avant-garde press, Claire-Marie. He was a young man about whom it would be an understatement to say that he suffered from delusions of grandeur. Before he met Mabel he had hoped to achieve immortality by publishing a book of poetry in which he would describe in verse a dozen ways of committing suicide. (He never published the book, but he did commit suicide.) After they first met, Evans wrote Mabel that he was "intoxicated" by her freedom. A week later, he chose her as his vehicle for fame: "the golden voyage I have embarked on—a thousand and one sonnet portraits

of you. Of course, I only hope to do ninety-nine, but that will be enough. . . .
You yourself are quite ineffable; it is quite beyond belief that you exist. . . ."[20]

The portraits he created read like intentional parodies of the mental breakdowns Mabel suffered in Florence and New York. One sample will suffice:

The Last Dance at Dawn

And she was sad since she could not be sad,
  And every star flared amorous in the sky.
  Her pampered knees fell under her keen eye
And it came to her that she would not go mad.
The gaucheries were turning the last screw, . . .

She even dared be impudent again,
  And bit his ear; the deaths were far away.
The Bibles orgied in the treasure vaults—
  She tried to rouge her heart, yet quite in vain.
The crucifix danced in, beribboned, gay,
  And lisped to her a wish for the next waltz.

Among the nonsense, we can see glimpses of the original, whose knees were certainly pampered and who sometimes did feel sad because she could not feel. Might the lisping crucifix and Biblical orgies be emblematic of the decay of religion which her free spirit mocked? Mabel, in any case, says she found Evans's "*fin de siècle* attitude . . . rather boring and old-fashioned."[21]

Mabel's article on Gertrude Stein was a great deal more substantial than any such imitations would suggest. She displayed a fine sensitivity to Stein's technique and the theory underlying it, which she linked to Picasso "in a way that prefigured later critical approaches to her work." There is no doubt that she helped Gertrude, through its publication, to become known in America. Her analysis also reveals that Gertrude's linguistic revolution was the genesis of her own expanding passion for the idea of revolution in general:

. . . Gertrude Stein is doing with words what Picasso is doing with paint. She is impelling language to induce new states of consciousness, and in doing so language becomes with her a creative art rather than a mirror of history.
   In her impressionistic writing she uses familiar words to create perceptions, conditions, and states of being, never before quite consciously experienced. She does this by using words that appeal to her as having the meaning that they *seem* to have. . . .

Many roads are being broken—what a wonderful word—"broken"!
And out of the shattering and petrification of today—up from the
cleavage and the disintegration—we will see order emerging
tomorrow. . . .[22]

The Salon Dodge

One of the other roads that Mabel followed while she was working on
the Armory Show led her to the offices of *Mother Earth,* where she heard
Emma Goldman argue eloquently for the violent overthrow of capitalism.
Mabel had little awareness of what it meant to suffer economically, but
she understood what it meant to be a victim of the system that had starved
her of emotional nourishment and segregated her from knowledge of the
masses of people who worked for her leisure. It did not take Mabel long
to absorb the essence of the education that her hungry eyes and ears first
received from Hutchins Hapgood and Emma Goldman, nor to commit
herself to the full sweep of its idealism. Even before announcing her
presence at the Armory Show, she openly committed herself as a "radical."
She published her credo in January as a letter "To the Conservatives" in
a current periodical.

Mabel's words convey the impatience, excitement, and commitment
to a life of experimentation and self-conscious daring that make it a
representative document of its time and place:

The need of every growing thing is for room for expansion, for self-
expression. Have the limits of the academic in art proved wide enough
for this process? "The great master is he who expresses himself perfectly
within limits," you reply. Yes, but who shall fix the boundary? And in
the technique of life, which is convention, who shall decide the ultimate
horizon? In the institutions of today, is there room for unfolding? Does
marriage foster the inherent nobility of the human animal? Does our
prison system correct the mistakes of ignorance and give direction to
rudderless souls? If not, then our institutions are crystals thrown off by
civilization into the waste heap of the world, ready for the cosmic
melting pot. These are questions that have somehow to be answered . . .
we know that we will find them—out in the open space where we are
groping and where all the truth that we have already seized upon has
been found, and given to you others for your comfort and security. In
order that you may be conservative and skeptical (and cozy!) today, we
are out in the untried—feeling our way towards the truth of tomorrow.[23]

Of all the new friends that she was making, no one understood the
impulses that drove her to embrace the spirit of revolution better than
Hutchins Hapgood. Hapgood was a columnist for the *New York Globe*
who wrote about the sufferings of society's outcasts. A philosophical an-

archist, he supported revolutionary causes of every variety on principle. He was a "Victorian in the modern world" (as he appropriately titled his autobiography), who shared with Mabel the Arnoldean sense of living "between two worlds,/the one dead and the other powerless to be born." Like her, he suffered from the torment of feeling that he was a mere "spectator" of life, that he had known only the *forms* of religion, family, and community life. He identified with the ethnic working classes of the ghettoes he frequented because he longed to share what Jane Addams had called "the race life." Among the urban poor he found a vitality and sense of community that were lacking in the deracinated world of his middle-class midwestern boyhood.

Mabel and Hutch embraced the call of the younger generation of rebels in the hope that it would lead to a world in which they could feel at home. Their open-ended commitment to change was paradoxically motivated by a profound yearning for emotional and spiritual certainty. They shared what Willliam James had once described to Hutch as a "mad unbridled lust for the absolute," a nineteenth-century disease for which the twentieth century offered no cure. Hapgood acknowledged this when he looked back at the Mabel Dodge of the prewar years:

> Mabel Dodge, as she was then, is the only woman I know who might fairly be called "God-drunk." If at any time she became aware of something just out of reach, she was intensely restless until she had drawn it into her web. She was always talking about "It"; and this was really why Mabel and I understood one another. I have been conscious since my childhood of the unseen cause of all things, which gives to all seen things their superlative beauty; and have been engaged in the hopeless quest of the Cause. . . . I had been on the trail of the Infinite; and still the Infinite torments me.
>
> Mabel had no mental training; she never studied metaphysics or philosophy or logic. . . . She has never learned to express in abstract language the essential striving of her soul. The fact that I could at least appear to recognize some of her cosmic emotions appealed to her greatly. . . . And these desires of hers never sprang from mere curiosity, nor from physical or temperamental whims, though these were frequently obvious elements, but from that indescribable mystic search.[24]

In her quest for the "cause," Mabel did not commit herself to any of the political programs she was learning about. When Goldman's lover, Alexander Berkman, autographed a copy of his prison memoirs for her in the hopes of "a more perfect crystallization of a definite goal to make the world a better place to live in for men and women," Mabel admonished him that crystallization was the opportunity for "further disintegration," the springboard to new truths. As soon as an idea crystallized, it was ready for "spiritual dynamiting." The only real freedom lay in the Steinian approach to becoming: "I cannot imagine myself ever crystallizing into an anarchist or a socialist, any more than into a 'society woman.' . . . Because to become a member of a party signifies to me the exclusion of other parties."[25]

Mabel's aspirations were of a universal nature: she sought to maintain the ability to reshape continuously her own unique identity while striving to be Everywoman. Mabel outlined her mission in a poem that Stieglitz later published in *Camera Work*. It defined more broadly and boldly the intentions suggested in her unpublished "Magnetism." While the "I" of the poem obviously refers to the "life-force" that she felt must find expression wherever it would, it also reflects the public persona that Mabel was deliberately cultivating:

The Mirror

"Man is the measure of all things"—Protagoras

I am the mirror wherein man sees man,
Whenever he looks deep into my eyes
And looks for me alone, he there descries
The human plan.

I am the mirror of man's venturing mind,
And in my face alone he yet may read
The only reason for the every need
Of humankind.

I am the mirror of man's eager heart,
Within me lies the secret of his quest:
I hear the hidden part that is the rest
Of every part.

I am the mirror of the insatiate,
I am the good, the bad, the infinite all,
In me lie the answers to each human call
For I am Fate.

I am the many and the one, the odd
As well as even. Ever in my form
God is renewed each time a man is born—
For I am God.

I am the alternating peace and strife—
I am the mirror of all man ever is—
I am the sum of all that has been his—
For I am life.[26]

Lincoln Steffens was the first to recognize Mabel's potential ability to reflect the life of her times. When he saw that she had the ability to draw people out about the issues that were most important to them, he urged her to establish a salon: "You have a . . . centralizing, magnetic, social faculty. You attract, stimulate, and soothe people, and men like to sit with you and talk to themselves. You make them think more fluently, and they feel enhanced. If you had lived in Greece long ago, you would have been called an hetaira! Now, why don't you see what you can do with this gift of yours? Why not organize all this accidental, unplanned activity around you . . . Have Evenings!" When Mabel reminded him that "We don't believe in 'organization' because as soon 'as an idea is crystallized, it is dead,'" Steffens reassured her that he did not mean that she should actually *organize* the evenings.[27]

By Steffens's estimate, Mabel's was the only successful salon he had ever seen. He paid high tribute to her ability to choose the most important issues of the day as topics for her evenings, which generated intellectual excitement through the clash of opposing interests and theories within an atmosphere of artfully controlled spontaneity:

> Mabel Dodge managed her evenings, and no one felt that they were managed. She sat quietly in a great armchair and rarely said a word; her guests did the talking, and with such a variety of guests, her success was amazing. Practiced hostesses in society could not keep even a small table of guests together; Mabel Dodge did this better with a crowd of one hundred or more people of all classes. Her secret, I think, was to start the talk going with a living theme.[28]

Mabel began her salon (variously held on Wednesday and Thursday evenings, and sometimes on more than one night a week) in late January 1913. In *Movers and Shakers,* she spoke of it as a "wonderful new game" that sprang from her desire "to know the Heads of things, Heads of Movements, Heads of Newspapers, Heads of all kinds of groups of people. I became a Species of Head Hunter, in fact." Her desire for self-importance attracted her to some of the most stimulating and creative talents in America. But this was not her most important motive at the time. The "Socialists, Trade-Unionists, Anarchists, Suffragists, Poets, Lawyers, Murderers, 'Old Friends,' Psychoanalysts, I. W. W.'s, Single Taxers, Birth Controlists, Newspapermen, Artists, Modern-Artists, Clubwomen, Woman's-place-is-in-the-home Women, Clergymen, and just plain men" who came dressed in evening attire, jewels, sandals, and work clothes were intended to be participants in her laboratory for a new world order.[29]

Mabel understood that the new consciousness the radicals represented demanded new modes of communication, "as if men said to other men: Look, here is a new way to see things . . . and a new way of saying things." Her belief that the printed page would soon be superseded by the spoken word was announced in a lengthy interview by a New York reporter in June 1913. Mabel's prophetic remark, which headlined the article, foreshadowed Marshall McLuhan's theory that nonprint media would effect a worldwide synthesis, replacing linear modes of perception and logical analysis with the simultaneous gestalt of the spoken word and visual image. Mabel was trying "to loosen up thought by means of speech, to get at the truth at the bottom of people and let it out, so that there would be more understanding!" When asked if there would come a time when permanent records might be dispensed with, she replied, "No . . . but I imagine that somehow things will be recorded on the air with a kind of terrible permanence that we do not even dream of."[30]

Throughout the fall, winter, and spring of 1913 and 1914, Mabel's salon was a "medium" that broadcast the new consciousness simultaneously on all fronts. She expected that out of the clash of various ideologies and interests the best would survive and serve as the basis of the new world order.

Because of the combinations of people, their notoriety, and the importance of the issues that were presented and discussed, the evenings increasingly gained national fame. As one New York reporter acknowledged in a full-page spread on "The Salon Dodge" during its second winter of operation:

> You might find, for instance, one evening, a learned and eminent
> professor from Columbia University, holding forth on Freud's theory of
> psycho-analysis to a room full of absorbed "high-brows." Or it might be
> that Mr. Haywood and the I.W.W. would be expounding to the
> uninitiated what the I.W.W. really stood for. Or Lincoln Steffens, or
> Walter Lippmann, would be talking about "Good Government"; a
> correspondent just back from Mexico would be telling about the war, or
> a scientist from England would make eugenics the topic; or it might be
> feminism, or primitive life. . . .

Her role was that of an impartial overseer who made certain that a variety of styles and points of view were represented:

> Every lively topic, movement, and interest of the day has been
> discussed in her house, but Mrs. Dodge herself takes no part. Plainly she
> is not attached to any of these things, but her level brows and
> intelligent eyes make one know that she has an interest.[31]

Mary Foote captured Mabel's large, warm, and intelligent hazel eyes that attracted men and women throughout her life in a portrait she did during the salon period. Mabel is dressed all in white, except for an emerald green shawl that lightly covers her shoulders. Leaning slightly forward on her chair, she is obviously viewing with genial contentment the human menagerie gathered in her living room.

Not everyone who attended came for the intellectual sustenance alone. At midnight, Mabel offered a sumptuous buffet of cold meats and drink. As early as February 1913, Walter Lippmann was complaining about the crowds and encouraging Mabel to issue invitations, in order to keep her guests from being trampled underfoot. Mabel wrote a note to her "public" explaining her original motivation. She just "wanted to see if it would prove *constructive* or *creative;* just humans meeting together with no attempt at organizing, directing, or controlling the energies present."[32] Of course, she had directed them to the extent of choosing the theme for each evening and inviting the spokespeople who led it, but this was insufficient organization to suit the antagonist of "Drift" and the upholder of "Mastery." Mabel democratically allowed Lippmann to test out his theory and issued invitations.

The intellectual confusion and chaos that sometimes attended her salon have caused some historians to view it as representative of the incoherence of prewar radicalism:

> There was an atmosphere of pageantry in Mabel Dodge's "Evenings"—a parade of ideas and feelings, the display of which counted for more than clarity or precision of expression. . . . Though only a fragment of the intellectual life, [the Evenings] were symptomatic of a general, polite confusion in the matter of objectives. The guests were agreed upon the general need for reform in contemporary mores and institutions, but they were not anxious either for a revolution or for the sudden collapse of a society they found delightfully amusing.[33]

Frederick Hoffman's critique of the radical chic aspects of the salon is certainly valid, but his patronizing attitude fails in an important way to understand it within the context of its times. The naive faith in the force of ideas to effect radical political and social change that was shared by Mabel and her friends was not possible for the next generation of radicals. The word *innocent* that is so often attached to the prewar radicals speaks volumes about the world view that was an option before World War I. Men like Hapgood and Steffens believed that they could "deal Death" to social and political injustice through words. They and their more activist colleagues, who wished to deal death more directly, were not always clear or programmatic about their means and ends. Their belief in a free play of ideas and activities that would lead to the emergence of healthier individuals and a more equal social and economic order allowed them to tolerate and promote a logically incompatible variety of points of view. The salon revealed the full range of the strengths, weaknesses, and conflicts that marked the aesthetic and political avant-garde of the time.

Mabel Dodge, date unknown.

Portrait of Mabel Dodge, by Mary Foote, c. 1915.

John Reed, on the beach at Provincetown, 1914.

Interior, 23 Fifth Avenue, 1916.

John Evans at the Elizabeth Duncan School, Croton-on-Hudson, 1915.

Mabel Dodge at Finney Farm, Croton-on-Hudson, c. 1915.

Hutchins Hapgood, Big Bill Haywood, and Joe O'Brien in Provincetown, c. 1914. (Courtesy of Joel O'Brien.)

Elizabeth Duncan.

Maurice Sterne.

Mabel recalls an evening when she invited Bill Haywood, Emma Goldman, and William English Walling (a founder of the NAACP) to define the IWW, anarchism, and socialism. Although they spent several hours in the attempt, none of them could clearly articulate the differences. "There was a great deal of General Conversation but no definition." The bond that drew them together at the end of the evening is perhaps best summed up in the emotional outburst of the eccentric anarchist Hippolyte Havel: "My little sister! . . . My little goddam bourgeois capitalist sister!" he cried as he embraced Mabel with tears running over his spectacles.[34]

But there were also evenings that illuminated the differences among the various brands of radicalism as well as the conflicts between working and middle-class activists. Andrew Dasburg, one of the Stieglitz circle, wrote to his wife, Grace Johnson, on June 2, 1914 about an evening devoted to a "Protocol" that shirtwaist and undergarment workers were to present to the manufacturers. The agreement would bind workers and management to submit grievances to a board of arbitrators for settlement as a means of avoiding strikes. After a good deal of statistical analysis, suggestions, and name calling from groups representing different sides of the labor issue, Emma Goldman rose and told them they were all conservatives and "a curse on the cause of the workers." She condemned the social workers and "dilitant [*sic*] philosophers" who delayed everything with their "endless quibbles and hair-splitting of issues." She warned the working men and women present to act on their own and not leave their fates in the hands of "college professors and lawyers who with the philanthropically inclined ladies only succeed in sentimentalizing the cause and making compromises which in time become real evils again. . . ."[35]

During another evening Bill Haywood magnetized his audience of artistic modernists with his discussion of the need for realistic, proletarian art that would reach and mobilize the masses, while Janet Scudder furiously challenged his call for "mass art" with her eloquent description of the years of sacrifice and drudgery that earned her place as an independent sculptress. At another art and politics evening, the radical artists who drew for *The Masses* gained the attention of the editors of the establishment journal *Cosmopolitan* which up until then had refused their work because of their politics.

Most of the men and women who attended Mabel's salon were serious about their political and artistic ideals and commitments. Women like Henrietta Rodman risked their jobs (in her fight to have the City of New York allow married women to teach) and others, like Margaret Sanger, their freedom (in her fight to give birth-control information to working-class women). The social and political theories that Lincoln Steffens, Walter Lippmann, and Max Eastman espoused "represented the main trends in most of American intellectual life for the years to come." In his book *From Self to Society*, Robert Crunden begins his exploration of the relationship of twentieth-century intellectuals to their larger society with an essay on what he calls "the most famous salon in American history" because the "prize heads" Mabel collected there defined the issues that were central to social and political analysis in the following decades: "the impact of pragmatism and the related developments in social science; the impact of psychology, and what it meant for the unhappy and dissatisfied individual; and the impact of communitarian social ideas, and what they meant for a capitalist society that was in trouble."[36]

One of the salon's most important functions was the dissemination of new ideas, as Steffens recalled:

> It was there and thus that some of us first heard of psychoanalysis and the new psychology of Freud and Jung, which in several discussions, one led by Walter Lippmann, [and another by A. A. Brill, Freud's translator and one of the fathers of the American Psychoanalytic movement] introduced us to the idea that the minds of men were distorted by unconscious suppressions, often quite irresponsible and incapable of reasoning or learning. The young writers saw a new opening for their fiction, the practical men a new profession. I remember thinking how absurd had been my muckraker's descriptions of bad men and good men and the assumption that showing people facts and conditions would persuade them to alter them or their conduct.[37]

Ideas were more play than work for Mabel, in the sense that she was not committed to any one line of thought at the time. But the people she most respected were those who risked "shattering themselves for the sake of their ideas"—those most committed to discovering "the truth" about political, social, and interpersonal relationships. Her openness to the ideas and issues that played out before her in her living room allowed her to taste rich and variegated slices of the intellectual life of her times. Indeed, as Hoffman says of her, she "all but established the pattern of the 'free-lance intellectual' of the early twentieth century."[38]

Mabel was more than a spectator and catalyst, however; she also offered her purse and her person in support of the causes and people affiliated with them that she entertained. Steffens recounts her extraordinary generosity:

> . . . she backed everything with her person and her money, especially young geniuses, like Jack [Reed] and Robert Edmond Jones. She gave "Bobbie" Jones a back room in her flat to play in. . . . There he slept, worked, and played with the miniature stages and stage accessories he gathered to develop his childlike gift for stage-making and decorating.

Bobbie Jones was one of the most innovative and influential stage designers in modern American theater. He credited Mabel with saving his physical life during the period of poverty when he lived at 23 Fifth Avenue and later with salvaging his emotional life, when she took up a subscription to send him to be analyzed by Carl Jung in Zurich. At the same time, Steffens says, "she was backing . . . other trouble-lovers in a free speech demonstration or a sympathetic appearance for strikers. . . . There were arrests, releases on her bond."[39]

Upton Sinclair remembered Mabel's generous support for radical causes in his memoir *Money Writes!,* where he mentioned the day she sold her dining room chairs to raise the funds needed to post bond for a group of socialists. Among her unpublished correspondence during the years 1913–16 are numerous letters of appreciation written by anonymous workers and hungry artists to thank her for her monetary and personal intercession, as well as letters from those in power seeking help for the powerless, such as Frederick Howe's request when he was commissioner of immigration that she aid an Italian immigrant woman who was being held at Ellis Island because she had an illegitimate child and no job.[40]

The publicity that Mabel gained from her association with Gertrude Stein and from her salon was the starting point for the belief that she had only to be associated with a movement for it to be launched or successful. Because of her wealth, social standing, and reputation as a leading proponent of radicalism, she was asked to join, advise, call together, support, and sustain a staggering variety of causes and organizations. Her own writing and the letters and memoirs of her friends attest to her ability to organize and catalyze groups and to write with understanding on the important issues of her day.

Joe O'Brien was one who asked her to set up a meeting for the IWW Defense Fund because she had a "rare gift" for getting people together at committee meetings. In the fall of 1913, when John Collier became involved with the Industrial Relations Commission—the first congressional survey of the industrial system that included the point of view of radicalism—he invited Mabel to chair the executive committee that would plan programs and prepare evidence for the commission. In May 1914, Upton Sinclair wrote Mabel a fervent request to attend the meetings of the Socialist Party because even if she attended for only half an hour, the reporters would print anything she said. But he also respected her opinions and advice. He sought her help in putting together an anthology on revolutionary art, and asked for her suggestions about producing a play that his wife had written.

Mabel received letters from the Women's Municipal League of New York City, anxious to secure her aid in organizing a committee of 100 women to work for nonpartisan government, and from the General Federation of Women's Clubs, asking her to join their art committee. She joined the Heterodoxy Club, made up of prominent suffragist, feminist, and labor leaders like Charlotte Perkins Gilman, Crystal Eastman, and

Elizabeth Gurley Flynn, who met frequently for what a later generation would call consciousness-raising sessions.[41] Mabel supported the Women's Birth Control League and opened her home to meetings of the Sanger Defense Committee, after Margaret Sanger and her husband were arrested for distributing birth-control information. She was also a sponsor for the Twilight Sleep Association, which sought to educate women about medicated childbirth.

Mabel helped support William Walling's *New Review* and wrote for *Camera Work,* George Sylvester Viereck's *The International,* and *The Masses.* *The Masses* was the most popular journal of the Lyrical Left, and "perhaps the best example in American history of a nearly successful synthesis of poetry and propaganda, politics and art." John Reed defined its policy in January 1913: "a free magazine; frank, arrogant, impertinent, searching for the true causes; a magazine directed against rigidity and dogma wherever it is found; printing what is too naked or true for a moneymaking press; a magazine whose final policy is to do as it pleases and conciliate nobody, not even its readers. . . ."[42] *The Masses* published the illustrations of one of America's best realist painters, John Sloan, the brilliantly satiric cartoons of Art Young, the poetry of Floyd Dell, the fiction of Sherwood Anderson, the political analyses of Max Eastman, and the personal journalism of John Reed. Mabel became a member of the advisory board in the spring of 1913 and was asked by Eastman to take over the April or May issue in 1914.

Mabel achieved her greatest public notoriety through her presumed affiliation with the IWW, which began with one of her more extraordinary inspirations. In May 1913, she attended a meeting where Bill Haywood was discussing the plight of the silk workers, who were on strike in Paterson, New Jersey. He was searching for a way to tell his New York comrades about the hunger, oppression, and police brutality suffered by the strikers in order to get their aid. Mabel suggested that he bring the strike to New York City "and *show* it to the workers" by hiring a great hall, like Madison Square Garden, and reenacting the scenario.[43]

The idea of the Paterson Strike Pageant was born. The pageant, one of the most unusual cultural events in American history, united the labor of anarchists, socialists, philanthropists, painters, and poets. It was a symbolic culmination of prewar radicalism that combined the traditional qualities of a popular morality play with radical politics and avant-garde theater design. Mabel, Hapgood, Eastman, Bobby Jones, and John Reed devoted themselves tirelessly to the production: to set designs, fund raising, and publicity. But it was the workers themselves who were the actors. On June 7, twelve hundred crossed over from New Jersey and witnessed the startling surprise pulled off by the committee. Huge red electric lights lit up the New York City sky above Madison Square Garden, proudly proclaiming the initials *IWW.* Haywood remembers queues of workers twenty-eight blocks long waiting to get in. Everyone who attended was awed and moved by the scenes of workers, deadened by toil, finally organizing to strike; the shooting of the striker Modesto, his burial, and the march of hundreds who placed red carnations on his coffin; the parents sending their children off to stay with caretakers because they could not afford to feed them; Haywood speaking to reinspire the thousands of strikers and gain new sympathizers in the audience; the entire population of the garden standing at the end to sing "The International."[44]

A week after the pageant, with Mabel in the full flush of her triumph, Hapgood published an article about her in the *Globe.* It illustrates how she was transformed into a mythological figure in her own lifetime:

A Promoter of the Spirit

There is a woman in New York City who is a promoter of the spirit. . . . We are all familiar in America with promoters in business, in land speculation, in philanthropy, but not so familiar with promoters of the sport [*sic*].

This woman came to New York City about four months ago, a stranger to the town, and for many years to the country. . . .

I imagine her real purpose in coming here was to help advertise, exploit, and promote, what she thought was a new and important form of art, the kind of thing people now refer to as post-impressionism. She was associated with the big exhibition of modern art at the armory. . . . She made of her pleasant Fifth Avenue apartment a kind of "salon," in which . . . the spirit of post-impressionistic literature was continually promoted.

She believed she was called on by God to help a new spiritual impulse to take possession of the earth.

Then she felt herself called to the labor movement. She felt called upon to promote, advertise and exploit the spirit of the Paterson Strike. Surrounded by men and women in the thick of this great industrial conflict she felt something new in the spirit of the Paterson workers. She felt that this spirit ought to have the chance to take possession of the world. So she started out to promote and advertise it. At a gathering of radicals and strike leaders at which I was present, I heard her imagine and suggest the great strike pageant which took place last Saturday in Madison Square Garden. It was her idea, and it was the act of an imaginative press agent of a high order. Then, in the two weeks preparation, she threw herself into the game, sustaining, encouraging, and promoting the enterprise.

In one way . . . this woman has accomplished a great deal in these four months. She has got in behind what she thought is the beginning of a new impulse of the spirit in art and life and has pushed with all her might. She has been successful in helping to bring out into the light of day important impulses in the development of our time.

Ironically, however, Hapgood was praising the very traits that would lead to her private downfall:

> One of the immemorial functions of women is to stand behind, to encourage, to cheer, to stimulate—whether it is in the bringing up of children or, failing these, in the close personal enhancement of a man's activities, or of men's activities. To promote something, whether it is a child's growth and character, or the ideas and tendencies and work of men, has always been one of the passions of women.
>
> When a woman in whom this promoting impulse is strong feels any spiritual power in a man or a movement, she quickly and completely becomes a kind of active reflector. She reflects and at the same time intensifies his direction . . . in order to enhance, set free, to promote the spirit that he represents.
>
> The woman I refer to says she is nothing in herself. And this, in a way, is true. Before she becomes anything, she must be possessed—possessed by the spirit of something else. . . .
>
> So she does not create anything. She only promotes. But she promotes the best she can find. . . .
>
> This woman acts entirely on instinct. She knows and thinks of nothing except the thing that possesses her at the moment. . . . She believes she is controlled by God; that her every strong impulse is divine. . . .
>
> . . . I am sure that she has with uncritical, instinctive emotion promoted in these recent months very good things.[45]

The New Woman

Mabel's life-style seemed to affirm that the instinctive flowering of the individual would lead to a society blessed with personal, social, and economic well-being. But as an uncritical reflector of men's dreams, she fed this illusion at enormous cost to her psychological and intellectual integrity. She realized that for all her welter of activity, she was "leading an existence without any real direction," but she never recognized how much of this was due to her acceptance of the role of hetaira.

Instead of listening to her own Muse, as did the poet Whitman whom she aspired to emulate, she served as Muse for others. Because she devoted so much of her energy to being a mirror for men's imaginations, she could rarely focus her intelligence or gain the confidence necessary to take charge of the political and literary tasks she was offered or instigated. Thus she refused to take over the issue of *The Masses* that Max Eastman wanted her to edit. She declined John Collier's request that she head the executive committee for the Industrial Relations Commission because, she claimed, her "inexperience and ignorance of industrial problems was complete." At one point, she planned to move to Paris and begin a magazine like *Camera Work*, "but, alas, I had not the simple continuity and persistence. . . ."[46]

Mabel's public, and her friends, believed that she was radical, emancipated, and a leading female influence in her times. Mabel, however, felt the large gap between her image as a liberated woman who did exactly as she pleased and the very confused Mrs. Dodge, who "went alone, cut off from the ways of other people who all attributed to me far more participation in rich living than they themselves enjoyed."[47] This confusion between image and reality was not hers alone. It was fundamental to the identity of the "New Woman," whom Mabel was so often believed to exemplify.

Greenwich Village was the headquarters of radical feminism in prewar America, where most of the issues surrounding the New Woman were lived and debated. Here, Crystal Eastman, Henrietta Rodman, Ida Rauh, and other feminist leaders argued that a truly socialist society could only be achieved if it were premised on the intellectual, political, and economic equality of men and women. Communal nurseries, birth control, family planning, cooperative housing, professional child-rearing, and higher educational opportunities for women were some of the necessities of their "cooperative commonwealth." The New Woman was one who had the option to choose routes to happiness other than the traditional roles of wife and mother. Many feminists, however, felt a great deal of tension between their stated ideals and the tug of traditional loyalties and beliefs. The feminist fiction of the period is a particularly revealing indicator of the uncertainties that beset women like Mabel Dodge who were trying to figure out their "place."

The heroines of the most popular feminist writers, Neith Boyce and Susan Glaspell, belong to a "lost generation" of women. For the most part, they have no special training or talent that can serve them in a profession. Although "they want something more than motherhood and a home, . . . an ideology, a program, an experience," they are unsure of "what it is or how to get it." They share "a romantic view of life and love, a burning desire for experience, and a belief in nonconformity" that often leads them to engage in sexual experimentation. Like more traditional female heroines, however, they usually find that love is almost always the solution to their quest.[48]

The conflicts felt by women feminists (and reflected in the confusion of their fictional heroines) can be attributed partly to the male feminists of Greenwich Village, whose political rhetoric often contrasted with what they actually wanted in their women. Floyd Dell and Max Eastman argued in *The Masses* for equal job and educational opportunities for women and for "free love" as a necessary adjunct to artistic and political freedom. But what they sought in their own relationships and celebrated in their fiction were women who were joyful and exciting companions, willing to abandon or at least put home and family life second. They assumed that "all emancipated women wanted free love and would find it emotionally satisfying. . . ." Their focus on women's sexual freedom actually undermined the fight for women's economic, intellectual, and political equality.[49]

Mabel, of course, experimented with free love—and found it wanting. Choosing an acquaintance and going off to a hotel room with him was an unpalatable experience that she did not repeat. The doctrine of free love, in the sense of casual relationships formed solely for sexual pleasure, held no real attraction for her. Margaret Sanger, however, did transform Mabel's notions about sexuality, removing for once and all the furtiveness and shame she still associated with it from her Victorian heritage. Sanger taught her about the joys and the eugenic necessity of "sex expression." She spoke to her of the "heightening of pleasure and of prolonging it . . . the spreading out and sexualizing of the whole body until it should become sensitive and alive throughout, and complete."[50]

Mabel has been labeled by more than one historian as "a pioneer in the cult of the orgasm," but the new views of sexuality that she was absorbing led her to an acceptance of her own sensuality as the means to a far more important end. Sanger's final lesson, as Mabel interpreted it, was that fulfilling "sex expression" led "to that great end, the development of life, and the growth of the soul."[51] The theory of the New Woman that won her assent was propounded by writers like Havelock Ellis, whose sex psychology Will Durant had lectured on in the Village, and Edward Carpenter, who saw in the liberation of female sexuality the potential of redeeming Western civilization from the life-denying practices they associated with the law, order, discipline, and materialism of patriarchy.

Mabel identified herself with Woman as earth mother, with the "female" values of love, nurture, and intuition that she learned would regenerate society by inspiring its great male talents (a much more revolutionary notion of the Muse role that she had played in Florence with Paul Draper).[52] This "new" philosophy, however, placed Woman in a position where she was at once raised above and kept beneath Man—both literally and figuratively.

In *Love's Coming of Age* (1896), Carpenter claimed superiority for Woman by virtue of her closeness to the "unconscious processes of Nature" and called for her liberation from bondage as Man's private property: "it is to her that Man, after his excursions and wanderings, mental and physical, continually tends to return as to his primitive home and resting place, to restore his balance, to find his centre of life, and to draw stores of energy and inspiration for fresh conquests of the outer world." At its highest level, the love and restoration she offers sublimate erotic energy into spiritual force: "How intoxicating indeed, how penetrating—like a most precious wine—is that love which is the sexual transformed by the magic of will into the emotional and spiritual!"[53] (And how hard Mabel worked, once she discovered her potential, to effect that transformation with men of genius!)

Carpenter liberates Woman from her chattel status into another kind of oppression that is not fundamentally different from the "angel in the house" philosophy which compensated Victorian ladies for their domesticity by affirming their moral superiority. The angel in the house is replaced by the bedmate who partners Man's creative endeavors by serving his sexual and emotional needs.

Although the Village radicals worked to subvert the bourgeois morality and capitalist economics that kept Woman in her "place," the new theories of sexuality, both European and home grown, still defined her in terms of Man. Hapgood's highest praise for Mabel was that she followed the "immemorial" role of women who promoted important changes *through* men, and he was not the only Village radical who encouraged her in this role. Mabel's affair with John Reed provides a paradigm of what the modernization of that ancient role meant for the New Woman.

John Reed

On the same evening that Mabel suggested the idea of the Paterson Strike Pageant, she experienced the first taste of the kind of "intoxication" Carpenter wrote about. A young man with a "high shining forehead" and boyish curls enthusiastically responded to her suggestion with an "I'll do it!" In the ensuing days while she worked with him on the pageant, Mabel discovered that she inspired Reed's creativity through the magnetism of her "exalted spirituality": "I knew he couldn't have done it without me. I felt that I was behind him, pouring all the power of the universe through myself to him."[54] In Reed, Mabel found a distillation of all the revolutionary ferment she had supported and promoted during her first five months in New York. She soon gave herself to him with an utter abandon that brought her the greatest happiness and most intense misery she had ever known. Mabel played Aphrodite to Reed's youthful Adonis (she was thirty-four and Reed was twenty-six when they met), and their affair became a Village legend that epitomized the presumably revolutionary ideology of "love's coming of age."

John Reed was seeking the very kind of woman that Mabel thought she wanted to become. The spark that struck them both simultaneously came from the same torch. Both of them suffered from nympholepsy, the "yearning for the unattainable and 'sublime' induced by an arch-Romantic and mystical imagination." He wanted a female compounded of earth and heaven, "full of beauty, love and joy, and ready to follow her man anywhere—be a virtual slave—if only he spoke the magic words 'I love you.'" In 1920, Floyd Dell described him as a "hero out of a fairy tale background" who sought a heroic battle and a love to fight it for in a modern world that had "no sufficiently heroic tasks for such persons to perform. . . ." He was a transitional figure, one of those "epic characters who arise in times . . . when laws and traditions have begun to break down under the stress of economic change and when it is necessary for individuals to make new laws for themselves and to rely on their own powers."[55] Like Mabel, Reed was a modernist temperamentally rooted in nineteenth-century Romanticism.

Reed grew up in an upper-middle-class family in Portland, Oregon. Although he had a much healthier and happier childhood than Mabel, he was from an early age a dreamer who was given to imagining himself an orphan outcast from some other time and place. In 1905, he brought the humor, daring, and fertile imagination that got him through prep school to Harvard. He also brought a "large appetite for power and prestige" that he fed by writing poetry and fiction for various Harvard publications and throwing himself into sports. After a trip to Europe upon graduation, he settled in New York. His father asked their family friend Lincoln Steffens to look after him and make sure that he had plenty of opportunity to "play" with life before settling down.[56]

In the fall of 1912, just about the time of Mabel's return from Florence, Reed moved to Washington Square. "The Village, with its delicatessens, bookshops, art studios and saloons, its long-haired men and short-haired women . . . was the center of his life." Just as he had at Harvard, Reed "scattered himself in many directions," keeping late hours, trying his hand at poetry, satire, humorous essays, and exposés. He wanted to be a great writer, but he did not know exactly what kind nor whether he had the talent. At the same time, he was becoming increasingly interested in working-class people, whose poverty was evident in the ethnic ghettoes he frequented. He began to see them as oppressed by the same middle class that he felt was stifling the creative impulses of himself and his fellow bohemians. To oppose the bourgeoisie was "to live life as fully as possible, to love art, youth, heroism and all the glorious activities that made life rich."[57]

Reed joined *The Masses* in January and helped to formulate its irreverent philosophy. Under the influence of Max Eastman, John Sloan, and other already committed radicals, he began to read socialist literature and attend political meetings, although at this time he was more interested in the "types" of people who attended than in the causes they espoused.

At the time he met Mabel, in May 1913, Reed was suffering from sharp alternations of "euphoria and despair." He had advanced somewhat beyond his totally carefree bohemianism, but had not yet found a way to connect his two interests, art and politics. He was no less settled in his love life. In fact, he fell in love "with such startling regularity that among friends it was something of a joke." Reed was described somewhat harshly, but accurately, by Walter Lippmann at the time in terms that could have applied almost as well to Mabel:

> He is a person who enjoys himself. Revolution, literature, poetry, they are only things which hold him at times, incidents merely of his living. . . . He is many men at once, and those who have tried to bank on some phase of him, to regard him as a writer, a correspondent, a poet, a revolutionist, or a lover, lose him. There is no line between the play of his fancy and his responsibility to fact; he is for the time the person he imagines himself to be. . . .[58]

Through Reed, Mabel believed that she could develop her full powers as a Magna Mater. She could help this ebullient but amorphous revolutionary to become a personage who would shape the direction of his times. As long as they remained on a highly charged spiritual plane, Mabel was at the height of her efficiency and an equal partner in his social and political endeavors. The Paterson Strike Pageant brought art, politics, and love together in a supreme moment of ecstasy for them both. Mabel had suggested the pageant, and Reed brought it to life, taking charge of the nightly meetings at the Sangers', where the writing and production were planned. Although Paterson was an important turning point in the growth of Reed's serious commitment to radicalism, he still refused to tie himself down. The day after the pageant, his most urgent business was pursuing Mabel, whom he was planning to conquer as his lover after they set sail for her villa in Florence.

Mabel held off making love to Reed as long as possible because she sensed that her sexual submission would destroy their delicate balance of power. On board ship, she denied Reed entrance to her cabin in order "to preserve the intense life we had created together without (as I felt it would be) descending into the mortality of love. . . . Something in me adored the high clear excitement of continence, and the tension that came from our canalized vitality." Reed, however, was importunate. When she refused him entrance to her room, he wrote a seduction poem, in which he argued that their sexual union would precipitate "A New Age" and their love replace an indifferent godhead:

> I cried upon God, last night, And God was not where I cried—
> He was slipping and balancing on the thoughtless shifting miles of sea—
> Impersonal he will unchain the appalling sea-gray engines,
> But the speech of your body to my body will not be denied![59]

Bobby Jones, who was accompanying them to Florence, told Mabel that there was something "immortal" in the love she shared with Reed. Mabel fretted that she did not know how to keep it so. Yet once she gave

93

in to Reed's earthly demands at their hotel in Paris, she learned what a "honeymoon should be." She experienced the kind of love that Margaret Sanger had taught her was "the first duty of men and women . . . with the body so illumined and conscious that it would be able to interpret and express in all its parts the language of the spirit's pleasure."[60] Noble ideas, politics, art, meant nothing, now that she seemed to have found the answer to the emotional hunger and desire for completion she had craved since childhood.

But Mabel's ecstasy was intermittent and costly. In giving herself so completely to him, she lost the fragile independence she had won with her work for Gertrude Stein, the Armory Show, and the success of her salon. Once again, she was the adolescent schoolgirl in her "Book of Poetic Quotations," yearning for an ideal love that was all-encompassing. Each time Reed looked away from her, she suffered agonizing misery. After they arrived in Florence, she even found herself becoming jealous of the *objets d'art* that competed for his attention.

Reed's responses were less complicated. On board the Hamburg-American ship that took them away from days spent in service to deprived silk workers, he felt delight mixed with a slight lingering guilt. On June 27, he wrote to his friend Edward Hunt that they were traveling *"grande luxe,"* and that he found it a "queer sensation—that of money's being *absolutely* no object." Although he had been to Europe before, he was seeing it fresh, with the illumined eyes of love. From Florence he wrote that he felt like a fisherman who had been caught by a "genie's Daughter and carried to her palace on the mountaintop."[64] Like a fairy-tale lover, each night he descended the silk ladder, which Edwin had installed and never used, to enter the bedchamber of his beloved.

Reed's "magical" journey fulfilled many needs for him. He had an entrée into the realm of the social elect who had always snubbed him at Harvard. He had glorious adventures subsidized by an emancipated, radical, passionate woman, who was able to enjoy and conjure up the most exquisite sensual and sensuous delights. He reveled in the Tuscan hills that rolled under the starlight from his bedroom window and in the songs of the Italian peasants who serenaded them each dusk. He relished the elegant meals and wines, the damask and silver, the ghost that haunted the house with her undying love for the villa's mistress. Mabel gave him the best of all possible worlds.

When Mabel complained of his neglect, Reed humored her by writing a hilarious play about "Creation" in which she figured as God's formula for the archetypal femme fatale. It included some of the cast of characters she had invited to the villa that summer, whose talents and styles constantly clashed. Mabel was not so involved with Reed that she did not take the time to tempt such friends as Gertrude Stein to visit by proffering her a rich variety of people to serve her aesthetic needs: *"Please* come down here soon," Mabel wrote her from Florence, "the house is full of pianists, painters, pederasts, prostitutes, and peasants. . . . Great material."[62]

Arthur Rubinstein, who was brought to the Villa Curonia by his friends the Drapers, gives a vivid picture in his autobiography of the circus-like atmosphere that he felt pervaded Mabel's home that summer. He was, however, not in the best of moods when he came. Rubinstein was in love with Muriel, whose escort he had been the previous year in London whenever she visited her dressmaker, art dealers, or attended shows. (Paul was typically off on drinking or gambling sprees.) The young pianist was irritated by the fact that he and Muriel could never find any time to be alone at the Villa Curonia, unlike its mistress and her lover:

> Mabel Dodge was a young woman of around thirty with a pleasant face, a slightly too generous figure, and a fixed, absent smile of a Mona Lisa. She spoke in monosyllables, save when addressing her servants, and she answered any query with a short nod. Life at her Villa Curonia was a constant carousel. Our hostess showed a gift for gathering together the most incongruous combination of guests in the world. There was the art and music critic Carl Van Vechten, a genius at arguing; Robin de la Condamine, a charming, stuttering actor whom nobody had seen on a stage; . . . John Reed, a journalist and poet, and a militant Communist, was sullen and very aggressive. He was Mabel's choice companion. There were two shrieking Englishwomen. . . . We had Gertrude Stein, engaged in some interminable vocal battles with Van Vechten, Reed hating everything and everybody, Norman Douglas using with relish his most profane repertoire in swearing, and last, but not least, myself, persistently jealous and irritable. Whenever or whatever I played, whether Beethoven or Stravinsky, some of those present would leave the room, hating the one or the other.[63]

Reed, of course, was not a Communist then, and his typical mood during the summer was, in fact, euphoric. Mabel had no typical mood. What counted most to her was to empty herself "over and over again flesh against flesh," rejoicing that she had unending passion to lavish upon him. She was happiest when he fell sick with diphtheria, for then she had him totally to herself and totally dependent on her. Throughout their stay, her insistence on his undivided affection created minor frictions that became serious wounds when they returned to New York in the fall of 1913 and lived openly as lovers at 23 Fifth Avenue.

On her return to New York, Mabel cultivated the fields of art and politics even more intensively than she had the previous year. She did so, however, more to impress and "conquer" her lover with her increasing fame, than to express her own revolutionary consciousness:

I invited more and more people to the Evenings and I tried harder

than ever to interest and attract them, making the ancient mistake of
believing my victories would act upon Reed like an aphrodisiac and that
when my value appeared greater to others, it would appear so to him
and would make him want to be with me all the day.

On the contrary! My triumphs served to stimulate him to greater
achievement in that world where men *do* things in order to prove
themselves powerful to themselves. So a spirit of competition sprang up
between us! If I had power, he, then, must have more power.[64]

Mabel understood that the kind of power which counted most among her
radical male admirers was that which could be felt and measured through
art, language, and political action. She was attracted to men like Steffens,
Lippmann, Eastman, and Reed just because they accomplished what she
felt she could best achieve through them.

Mabel was much less in control of the sexual politics and much more
vulnerable than she remembered. Nor was she the sole victimizer in their
competitive tug-of-war. She had chosen for her Antony a man who was
incapable of giving up the world for love. Reed's constant need for adventure, his callous discussion of other women he met who attracted him,
and his relegation of Mabel to the role of nighttime paramour justifiably
fed her misery. Reed was as incapable of fidelity to any one person at this
time of his life as he was to any one mode of life or politics.

With rueful pathos, Mabel described their life together that fall. She
would claim him each night and lose him each day. Up and off before he
had swallowed his first cup of coffee, Reed went out on the streets to find
material for his *Masses* articles. Unnerved by her demands for constancy,
and by her increasing hysteria at his absences, he left Mabel for the first
of several times in November. Reduced to the terror of nonbeing that she
experienced during her worst depressions in Florence, Mabel took an
overdose of veronal.[65] Hapgood and Steffens brought a repentant Reed
back to her.

In a very moving letter that she wrote to Neith Boyce Hapgood at this
time, Mabel puzzled over her need for faithfulness and wondered where
the line should be drawn in love. When she asked Neith whether her
desire for monogamy was a "primitive, selfish, unworthy instinct that
must be *overcome*," or whether women "*have* to ask it until men learn to
love *one* person," she revealed one of the conflicts experienced by a number
of radical feminists of her day:

> Reed & I love each other as much as any people can—that's why we
> torment each other so—but one of us has to give in on this . . . Yet if I
> didn't *feel this* & feel this important it would be because I would have
> him as I would a whore—indifferent to what he did so long as he
> doesn't deprive me of himself. It *can't* be meant to be that way! . . . To
> him the sexual gesture has no importance, but infringing on his right to

act freely has the first importance. Are we both right & both wrong— and how do such things end? Either way it kills love—it seems to me. This is so fundamental—is it what feminism is all about? . . . I know all women go thro this—but *must* they go on going thro it? Are we supposed to "make" men do things? Are men to change? Is monogamy better than polygamy?[66]

Mabel asked Neith not to show Hutch her letter, out of fear that he would tell others and make it into a "thesis to discuss in Greenwich Village." But among their friends, private anguish was grist for the mill of public discussion. Both Mabel and Hapgood agreed to have an evening devoted to "Sex Antagonism." As Lasch suggests, "One does not need to travel very far in the contemporary world . . . to encounter the same intense involvement in group personal relations that was characteristic of Mrs. Luhan and her friends . . . the same need jointly and publicly to analyze them in all their details. . . ."[67] For these uprooted radicals, wives, lovers, and friends bore the emotional and psychological weight of needs once diffused among other social and religious institutions. (As Reed intimated in his seduction poem, their love would replace a God who was no longer available.) Sharing and publicizing their most intimate lives was one means of evaluating and validating them.

Hapgood asked Mabel for detailed observations of his relationship with Neith. He loved Neith desperately even though he was ideologically committed to having love affairs with other women, which caused a great deal of suffering both for him and for his wife. In *The Story of a Lover,* he described the private details of his married life and then circulated it among his friends. When Hapgood later began therapy with Ely Jelliffe, Mabel took it upon herself to send the document to his psychiatrist. Neith also took part in these revelations. She wrote to Mabel about the violence and desperation that Hutch sometimes revealed in his need for her love, but she could no more complete his "intense need for being needed," as Mabel put it, than Reed could Mabel's.

Mabel's intense concentration of her emotional life on Reed had much to do with her belief that he would "realize" her into being. She wrote John Collier that she felt like "an *entity* . . . *functional* & helpful & constructive to life" only when her force was being used to aid Reed in his work, as it had been when they first began to live together:

All these days Reed had been telling me that he'd felt a flood of energy passing out of me so strong that it was like being near some highly charged electrical battery, from which one could draw electricity & become enormously strengthened . . . & he told me that there was something about this generation of force that drew him all the time so that when he was away from the house it was all he could do not to come back every minute.[68]

Although Mabel's demands on Reed to provide her with the psychological security that she craved were excessive, he certainly benefited from the emotional largesse that she laid at his disposal. The fact that she was always "there" in New York for him to return to freed him to concentrate on his work. No sooner had they gotten back together after Mabel's attempted suicide than he left for Texas, in early December 1913, to do a series of articles on Pancho Villa. (Published as *Insurgent Mexico,* they were a milestone in his political reporting.) On an impulse, Mabel followed him to Chicago and took the train with him to Texas. Reed's description of the picture they made clearly shows how out of place he felt Mabel was in his working life, though some of his jibes were aimed at himself:

Mabel has already decided that the rebels are part of the great world-movement, whatever that may be. . . . I think she expects to find General Villa a sort of male Gertrude Stein, or at least a Mexican Stieglitz.

With me in my bright yellow corduroy suit and Mabel in her orange hat and satin-lined tiger-skin hunting jacket—with . . . an expense account, and a roll of blankets and 14 different kinds of pills and bandages . . . we shall descend upon El Paso.[69]

When Mabel found that there was nothing she could do for the man who had become her career, she returned to New York. She turned her attention to the Tannenbaum trial and intensified her notoriety. In early February, Frank Tannenbaum, a member of the IWW, had tried to gain entrance to several New York City churches in order to dramatize the plight of the unemployed. He was arrested for disturbing the peace. Mabel attended his trial every day and was reported on daily by the press, who found good copy in a wealthy lady's concern for a young radical immigrant. Mabel was open with the press about her lack of political commitment. On March 27, the *New York Evening World* headlined one of its stories, "Fair Society Woman Defends I. W. W.; Is Neither Anarchist Nor Socialist, But Thinks Unemployed Not To Blame." Mabel is quoted as saying that the unemployed were justified in doing "anything to call public attention to their condition." She explained to the reporter that she was not a joiner, but a student of human events.[70]

Mabel also wrote an article on the trial for *The International.* Her objectivity allowed for some judicious, if naive, remarks. Each person at the trial, she stated, was loyal to the system he upheld, and all who were on the side of labor "must have felt that a way must be found to get those honest men on their side." The media did not fail to exploit her entertainment of "wild-eyed" Wobblies during the trial with such headlines as "I. W. W. Throng Are Guests of Society Folk on Fifth Avenue. Women in

Evening Gowns Entertain Bill Haywood"; "I.W.W. Men Starve as Leaders Eat. Latter Make Merry in Dodge's Fifth Avenue Home." Mabel received several letters of condemnation from the general public, as well. One man wrote to tell her that women who smoked were like prostitutes and would ruin their health and give their children bad habits, "providing that they have children instead of dogs." Another queried, "Do you call the Bums who you took into your home your friends if you call yourself a Lady, the public don't. . . ."[71]

When she wasn't attending the Tannenbaum trial, Mabel was turning her attention to the men in her vicinity through whom she hoped to make an absent Reed jealous. The ethereally handsome painter Andrew Dasburg was her most successful target: "His eyes were blue as sapphires, and they had a mystical red spark in them. His skin was so fair with a tremulous rose that came and went in his cheeks, and his fine blond hair rushed electrically back from his round brow and seemed full of white sparks of light." Mabel's emanations were so powerful, apparently, that Dasburg had received them on his first visit to 23 Fifth Avenue, when Mabel was in Texas with Reed. Bobby Jones brought Dasburg to the apartment, and when he saw how disappointed Andrew was that Mabel was not there, he suggested that he retitle one of his latest abstractions the *Absence of Mabel Dodge* and hang it on her living room wall for her to see.[72]

When Mabel returned in January of 1914, she agreed to sit for a portrait that became the *Presence of Mabel Dodge*. Mabel later claimed to have inspired a new direction in Dasburg's art in much the same way that she had for Paul Draper. While there is little evidence of her influence on the development of his art, there is no doubt that Dasburg was, for a brief time, infatuated if not in love with her. When I interviewed him at age ninety-four, he had not forgotten how on their first drive together through New York in her chauffeur-driven limousine, she had made "advances" toward him. He wrote her on January 11, "I want to say it with red ink. *I love you.* It crowds my head and suspends me trembling, like an aspen in the wind. . . . I'm resigned to the role of fluttering leaf waiting for the strong wind that will blow me to earth to you as a lover and not this trembling angel with cold hands bobbing in the clouds for warmth."[73]

Mabel had no intention of consummating his passion and suggested that he sublimate his sexual desire for her in painting. The two portraits that resulted, along with the original *Absence,* gained him important public notice during his winter exhibition in New York. A critic for the *New York World* described the apparent effect the Muse had on her worshipper:

In her presence he seems to feel like a torso stripped of skin and
palpitating in roast beef flavors of deep red and shining white; away
from her his thrill collapses and the torso is jammed, twisted and

flattened as if a motor car had run over it. . . . In one of the sequences, witness the unfolding of the torso and the exposure of the artist's heart in blossom as a tulip, with an amethyst shining in place of the navel. . . . The third dedication is entitled "Absence of Mabel Dodge" and is the most perfect portrayal that can be imagined of mental, moral and physical smash.

Mabel asked Marsden Hartley to write a description of *Absence* for Reed, to rekindle Reed's ardor. But Hartley's hyperbolic effusiveness—he described Dasburg as "carried way beyond mediocre despair" into a "fiery lamentation of something lost in a moment—a moment of joy with the joy sucked out of it"—did not secure Reed's return. He did not need to be near Mabel to feel secure of her love, while for Mabel, "to be alone was to doubt my own being, so little did I live in the life about me."[74]

Almost as soon as he returned from Mexico, Reed lit out for the Colorado mines to cover one of the most brutal coal strikes in American labor history. His love for the woman he left behind continued to grow and to feed his increasing self-confidence: "You dearest old thing in the world," he wrote Mabel from his hotel, "You are so beautiful to me for just that soul of yours, and so alive. You are my life." The separations that increased his passions were beginning to have the opposite effect on Mabel, however.

They spent the first part of the summer together in Provincetown, among the colony of Greenwich Villagers who were driven by the heat and smells of New York to what was then a quaint fishing village of small, white clapboard cottages. Reed's contentment with his growing reputation as a writer and correspondent was completed by his love for Mabel. Mary Heaton Vorse recalled their sometimes spending the night in a silken tent on the beach at Race Point.[76] Because there were no stormy scenes or threats between them, he took her seeming tranquillity for acceptance of the status of their relationship. "Everywhere in the spring of 1914," Mabel reminds us, there had been "hope—everywhere expectancy." But during the early summer in Provincetown, she felt a "dreadful suspension of life." She sensed in the approaching end of her affair with Reed, during the weeks before the outbreak of World War I, more than a dramatic coincidence.

Love and Death

Mabel believed the obsession with power that drove her during her Village years had its counterpart in the lust for domination and national glory which drove the European powers into the most destructive war in human history up until that time. In July, she traveled to the Villa Curonia with Neith Hapgood and Carl Van Vechten. There her premonitions of the coming disaster were strengthened. Her own dissociated personality was a microcosm of a world about to explode: "I was like a child with a dynamo that required the most cautious and careful operation."[77]

Carl Van Vechten corroborated Mabel's mood in two stories he wrote about the time he spent with her that summer. He noted "the shadow of romantic disaster" that hung over the house. Within it, neither bird, beast, nor man could find happiness: "Certainly illness and desolation and a mighty despair spread their pall over the Villa Allegra," he wrote in mimicry of the last line of Poe's allegory of the death of civilization, "The Fall of the House of Usher." He also recalled Mabel's prophecy on the eve of World War I; only she, among the guests, "had any definite realization of the tremendous events about to take place. . . . She spoke a great deal about Wells's book, *The World Set Free,*" which predicted World War I fifty years before it occurred.[78]

Mabel's friends booked passage home after the outbreak of war in August, while she waited for Reed in Naples. They spent a few quiet days there and then moved on to Paris so that he could cover the war. Once again, his work kept him from her, except in the evenings, when she greeted him with depression and tears. Mabel made one "feeble attempt" to get involved with the Red Cross but did not have the energy or interest. She spent most of her days in bed, unable to share the excitement and enthusiasm for the war that was felt by soldiers, citizens, and journalists alike. Out of her experiences in Paris, however, came a very powerful antiwar piece that was published in *The Masses* in November 1914.

"The Secret of War" was subtitled, "The Look on the Face of Men Who Have Been Killing—And What Women Think About It." Mabel located the "secret" in the machismo of battle and captured the tragic absurdity of young men going to fight in World War I as though they were going to a picnic. Her description accurately calls up the spirit with which the Western powers sent their eager young off to die:

> With flags flying from every door and window, Paris never looked more gallant. The Germans, we heard, were only a few miles away. Yet Paris in the sunshine seemed smiling, like a great lady going to the guillotine *en grande toilette;* exquisitely French.

Her interviews with wounded soldiers brought home how this first "machine war" was transforming warfare. A wounded officer tells her: "I don't believe men could stand mowing each other down like that if they met in hand to hand conflict. But with the machine gun—you just go on turning the handle." Mabel also reported on the cranking of the propaganda machine which used the cinema to sell the war on the homefront:

> The cinematographs showed pictures of the "brave boys" at the front and of the unbelievably inhuman enemy.
> All these incentives were brought to a degree of art that was hard to

101

analyze, which seemed to be a mingling of the simple and sincere poetic feeling of the people and the self-conscious control of diplomacy. It was very real.

Behind it all, Mabel saw what only a few were willing to see at the time, the ruling classes of both sides fighting each other in their quest for power:

> To this Moloch they are sacrificing the first born—and all the others. To maintain the illusion of Empire, women are urging their men into the field, and fathers are sending their sons—up to the last.

The women, not the men, questioned the war, as Mabel discovered when she interviewed the wives of soldiers. One working-class English-woman, who had seven children and whose husband had been away with no word for six weeks, asked Mabel, "Wot I'm awskin' yeh is what it's all *for?* That's what I want to know. Wot's it all abaout?" Since the men were aroused by the bugles and fooled by their leaders, it was up to the women, Mabel concludes, to ask this question: "The only hope of permanent peace lies in a woman's war against war."[79]

This was the motivation for the founding of the Woman's Peace Party and of the Women's International League for Peace and Freedom that Jane Addams helped to organize in 1915 to unite the world's women against the war. After reading Mabel's article, Elizabeth Glendower Evans, one of the leaders of the Woman's Peace Party, wrote her that it was "about the best thing on the subject I have seen. . . ."[80] Mabel hoped to get it published by the party, and Evans suggested that even if she couldn't they could jointly issue 7,500 copies. (Mabel had apparently suggested 75,000, which Evans assumed was a mistake but may well not have been.)

Mabel also wrote an impassioned open letter to the Wilson government, entitled "We Women Want to Stop War":

> We don't want to go on knitting and nursing and binding. We want to live and to help others to live. We want peace, but we are afraid that the big businessman and corporations will think that they will suffer if the war comes to an end—too soon!
>
> Won't you make them realize that they need not lose by a speedy peace? Won't you tell them we will use the ships we have ordered for commerce . . . the munitions for reserve . . . our standing army to back us when we enter the League of Nations to insure peace.[81]

But Reed, not the war, was still uppermost in Mabel's mind. When she realized that she had once again lost him to his work, she returned to 23 Fifth Avenue "to be miserable at home where at least I could be comfortable." He vowed undying love and a few days later wrote her that he had spent the evening of her departure with a prostitute. Within a few weeks, he wrote that he had fallen in love with a mutual friend, Freddie Lee, whom he had convinced to leave her husband in order to marry him. When Reed and Freddie cabled Mabel about their love, she astonished them both by sending her blessings.

Reed's betrayal broke the hold on whatever remained of her passion for him, as she informed Walter Lippmann, when she called to tell him that she was "tired of being the mother of men!" Mabel was obviously feeling a profound sense of loss, however, for which she tried to compensate by finding a child to mother. After driving around to several orphanages in New York City, she located a chld who seemed suitable: a cherubic, blond-haired, blue-eyed eight-year-old girl, who had been "returned" the year before because she wasn't "good at her books." After dressing her up and showing her off to Walter Lippmann for his masculine approval, Mabel soon lost interest.[82] She never legally adopted little Elizabeth, as she was called, but she did take care of her physical needs and paid for her education.

Mabel was not easily rid of Reed, nor he of her. Their mutual friend Bobby Rogers wrote an estimate of what Mabel meant to Reed that Reed would accept as true, but too late to repair the damage he had done: "You gave him more than anyone else I knew possibly could—I began to think you might make him what it was in him to be, and I was very glad. I never doubted but what he would go on growing stronger and happier and more able with you. . . . He thinks he is freeing himself from weakness; he is only cutting himself off from strength!" Once the idea of marriage came closer to reality, Reed dropped Freddie Lee and recovered his love for Mabel. When he returned from Europe at the end of January 1915, he brought a much strengthened commitment to the woman he was sure would forgive him. Reed bought two gold rings and went off to visit Mabel, who was renting a cottage in Croton-on-Hudson at the time. He was full of dreams of marriage, although he had been warned by Steffens that Mabel only wanted him as a friend. "Only when she pushed him out the door to stumble down Mount Airy Road toward the tiny Croton depot did Jack realize this true-life romance would not conform to the convention of a happy ending.[83]

Two weeks before he set sail for Europe in March, Mabel came to Reed and consented to wear his ring. She says she did so because his friends convinced her that he was in danger of losing his sanity. Although Mabel exaggerated the state of his mental health, Reed was devastated by her rejection. It is just as likely that she wore his ring because she did not find it easy to give up her ties of dependence and her memories of what their love had meant to the world of radical innocence that was no more. As soon as he embarked for Europe in March, Reed wrote his first poetry in two years. "Pygmalion" reflects "his wonder over his renewed love for Mabel," and his acquiescence in the fact that "he was stronger, more

103

complete, more in touch with the reality of earth and life when connected to her being."[84]

In the poem, Mabel appears as the incarnation of their nympholeptic love: the love that drove Reed to deny the reality of her human needs and individual integrity; the love that unfortunately affirmed for Mabel that her noblest, if most irritating, calling was to be the mirror of men's imaginations:

> He wrenched the shining rock from the meadow's breast,
> And out of it shaped the lovely, almost-breathing
> Form of his dream of his life of the world's women.
> Slim and white was she, whimsical, full of caprice;
>
> Staring, he felt of a sudden the quick, fierce urge
> Of the will of the grass, and the rock, and the flowering tree;
> Knew himself weak and unfulfilled without her—
> Knew that he bore his own doom in his breast—
> Slave of a stone, unmoving, cold to his touch . . .
>
> Hot moist hands on the glittering flanks, and eager
> Hands following the chill hips, the icy breasts—
> Lithe, radiant belly swelling to stone—
> "Galatea!"—blast of whispering flame his throat—
> "Galatea!" "Galatea!"—his entrails molten fire—
>
> Rock is she still, and her heart is the hill's heart,
> Full of all things beside him—full of wind and bees.
>
> Despair and gnawing are on him, and he knows her
> Unattainable who is born of will and hill—
> Far-bright as a plunging full-sailed ship. . .[85]

When he went off to cover the war in the Balkans, Reed told his publisher, Carl Hovey of the *Metropolitan,* to treat Mabel as his wife and send all his correspondence to her. Wherever he traveled, he sent Mabel postcards, with brief messages of love and descriptions of the country.[86] When he was imprisoned in the Balkans, he drew plans for a magnificent home he planned to build for them at Ramapo on the Hudson River. In July, he received a letter from Hapgood informing him that Mabel had "changed her mind"; her love was dead. Reed threw the ring that Mabel returned into a canal in Bucharest and asked Hapgood to destroy her letters to him.

In the same month, in Provincetown, Neith Hapgood produced the first play of the soon-to-be-named Provincetown Players, who were laying the foundations for the beginnings of modern theater in America. Her play, titled *Constancy,* was based upon Mabel's and Reed's affair and was performed in the Hapgoods' living room (along with Susan Glaspell's parody of Freudian theory, *Suppressed Desires*). Neith dramatized the dilemma that Mabel had outlined to her in the letter she wrote about fidelity. She answered Mabel's questions and revealed her own position by giving the heroine of the piece the moral and psychological advantage over her slightly foolish and immature "free" lover.

From the opening of the piece, Moira, the heroine, shows a dignified self-possession that contrasts sharply with her ex-lover's puerile romanticism. She is seated, writing at her desk, when he whistles from below her balcony, waiting for her to throw down the "rope ladder" by which he usually ascended to visit her, that is, when he was not off on other romantic adventures. Moira has put the ladder in her desk drawer as a symbol of the fact that she will no longer allow him to fulfill his emotional life at her expense. Rex had just returned from a love affair with a woman (like Freddie) whom he had been sure he was going to marry, only to find that it didn't work out. He assumes, as Reed always assumed about Mabel, that Moira was a "constant" in his life. Her role was to fight for his love as a tigress would.

Moira wisely understands that the love he wants from her is "a disease, a madness," which drove her to give up "all her interests" in order to devote herself to keeping his love. Their definitions of love and constancy are, finally, as incompatible as the "sex antagonism" of the real life men and women they represent. Rex's idea of fidelity is that he "would always come back." When Rex insists that he wanted Moira to be free to have other interests than himself (though not other lovers), she teaches him the awful lesson their affair has taught her: "In love one can not be free. I was constant to you every moment. . . . I can't endure love without fidelity."[87] Moira decides that the only way she can keep her self-worth is not to love at all.

Mabel came to a similar decision when she returned Reed's rings. Like Rex, Reed vowed to return, and did. In October 1915, he visited her at Croton, where she was living with her new lover, Maurice Sterne. Mabel offered Reed friendship and a room to work in, but after a few days he found the situation impossible. Max Eastman witnessed their final scene when Jack stormed out of her bedroom and slammed the door, "plunging away into a heavy rainstorm, none of us knew where."[88] Just before his return from Europe, Reed had sent Mabel a new ending to his poem, "Pygmalion," in which Galatea finally awakens to passion in the arms of her supplicant lover.

The dream of love for both of them had always carried the greater weight of their passion. That December, Reed met the woman who he claimed was the first he ever truly loved. Louise Bryant shared with him the glory of covering the Russian Revolution and became his wife. Yet, when he was dying of typhus in Moscow, he talked much of Mabel to her. Mabel records that the last words Reed was heard to speak before he died were meant for *her* ears alone: "Listen . . . I am singing a little song for you. . . The whole world came between us. . . ."[89]

Whether or not these were Reed's last words, and whether or not they were meant for Mabel, is less important than their symbolic appropriateness. Reed's Marc Antony–like regret for the love they had lost to the world was a fitting emblem of the historic tragedy of their times.

Between the time of her New York debut in January 1913 and her retreat from the worlds of love and activism in the winter of 1915, Mabel was pulled by two conflicting desires. She had wished to serve and guide the spirit of revolution as a catalyst and promoter in order to bring about a world in which the expressive self would flourish. And she had wished to channel her energy and vitality into serving her lover's world-shaping visions.

What Mabel could not resolve in her life, two of her writer friends resolved for her in their fiction. In *Peter Whiffle* (1922), Carl Van Vechten celebrated a Mabel Dodge who was the godlike "eye" of the various radical hurricanes she unleashed. In *Venture* (1927), Max Eastman fulfilled the male Village radicals' romantic fantasies by creating a Mabel Dodge who sacrificed herself to the revolution's leading man. Both novels provide fascinating insights into Mabel Dodge and the possibilities she represented as a New Woman.

Through the Looking Glass with
Carl Van Vechten and Mabel Dodge

*With him "amusing" things were essential things; whimsicality was
the note they must sound to have significance. Life was perceived to be
a fastidious circus, and strange conjunctions were more prized than
ordinary relationships rooted in eternity.*[1]

Carl Van Vechten knew Mabel best during a period in her life when
she was most disposed to allow life to "happen." His re-creation of her
as Edith Dale was a tribute to the kind of womanhood he felt she represented: intelligent, amused and amusing, centered on a concept of self
that thrived on the vitality of contradictory human impulses. Like the
views of other writers who used her in their fiction, his was in part a
reflection of the woman he wanted to see, the one who reinforced his own
philosophy of life. Mabel became for Van Vechten, as she had become for
Stein and Blanche, a type of the age whose chronicler he became.

Mabel shone the exuberance and energy of her life-force on Van Vechten
without expecting him to give over to her the direction of his life. This
he yielded voluntarily: "Mabel was a great woman and she completed my
education. She had some bad qualities and the worst one was what made
her great. She adored to change people. I loved what she did for me and
accepted her guidance with pleasure. . . . I think Mabel had more effect
on my life than anybody I ever met, because she was so experienced in
the ways of the world, and what you could see, and what you could do,
and so forth."[2]

Van Vechten arrived in New York in 1906. Like so many other young
writers who came there at the time, he was eager for the excitement and

107

cultural stimulation that he felt had been lacking in his stultifying, boyhood midwestern town. Although Van Vechten did not meet Mabel for seven years, he later remembered having met her soon after he arrived in the city, so closely did he identify her with his education in the avant-garde. In February 1913, he was sent by the *New York Times* to find out about a strange new writer, Gertrude Stein.[3] Since Mabel was the American expert, he interviewed her. He came away with a profound interest in both women that led to lifelong friendships. Eventually he became Stein's literary executor, and it was he who was primarily responsible for Mabel's sending her 1,500 pounds of papers to Donald Gallup at Yale.

What Van Vechten liked most about Mabel was her voracious appetite to "know" and experience "everything," an appetite that he found informed by an extraordinary appreciation of the best in art, wine, and pleasurable living. Her rich knowledge of art and architecture, for example, gave him his first real view of Europe, when he traveled with her in the summer of 1913. Unlike many in her salon circle who thought her "sphinx-like," Van Vechten found her adept at argument and agile in conversation and at drawing people out. He enjoyed the fact that she forced her friends to test their hypotheses by confronting them with others who held alternate convictions and who perceived the same economic or political situation from different angles of vision. Mabel's proclivity for combining "dissimilar objects to their mutual benefits" became the structural basis of his fiction.[4]

In his life, as in his fiction, Mabel was the duenna who initiated young writers and artists into the cultural vortex of modern American life. Even before he met her, however, Van Vechten was an advocate of the avant-garde, a mocker of tradition and academic criticism. He was an aesthete who loved to expose pretentiousness and sham of every kind, without moralistic rancor. He dabbled in drugs and drink, gave orgiastic parties, and was somewhat of a voyeur who thrilled to the exotic and erotic night life of the Harlem cabaret.

Van Vechten also had a more serious side, which shows in the important contributions he made in fields other than fiction. He was one of the first music critics to champion Stravinsky and to proclaim the superiority of modern music and dance over their classical forms. He was also a gifted photographer, the first champion of Herman Melville's later works, the most important white benefactor of the black writers of the Harlem Renaissance, and an executor of half a dozen of the most important library collections of modern American literature.

It was Van Vechten's less serious side that appealed to Mabel. For a period of two years, she saw him almost daily. He was her "vacation from the real business of life," the first person to "animate" her lifeless rooms when she moved to New York:

Carl would come for me at eleven in the morning when the apartment was full of sunshine from the south windows and every light beauty showing cozy and warmed against the white walls, and he would be ruddy and washed-clean like a well-groomed young hog, his familiar clothes hanging nicely on his tall figure, bones embedded in small amounts of fine flesh. Then I, in long, flowing, soft things and a hat with drooping feathers, nicely veiled, would pin a flower into fur and move down the dim mahogany stairs past General Sickles's heavily bolted double doors out to the waiting Albert.[5]

It is easy to see why Van Vechten saw in Mabel a woman devoted to turning daily life into a work of art.

At the beginning of their relationship, Van Vechten was infatuated with her. He often wrote to her that he needed her as a stimulant and once compared her effect on him to that of cocaine. Although he spoke of his "love" for her in hyperbolic language, he was much given to self-parody, irony, and exaggeration. There is always a touch of the romantic grotesque in his phrases, which sound like parodies of the serious espousals of Andrew Dasburg and John Reed. In one letter he wrote, "I do love you so much that towns and cities seem only like fish-ponds until you appear to give them meaning." One of Mabel's teasing responses to his ardent pleas reveals much about the game-playing among her intimates: "I love you—that is I think I do—that is—Hutch says I do—that is I think Neith wants me to—as well I think she wants you to make love to her to make me love you more." This ploy will not work, she concludes, "because I am a super-female and free of myself and everyone else thank heaven. . . ."[6]

Mabel signed her letter "Aunt Mike," the name by which Van Vechten addressed her. Although he was only a year younger than she, she played the role of matriarchical super female to his somewhat effete youth. The fact that she never became his lover may have had much to do with her ability to maintain this position. Whatever dalliance they may have had in mind ended with his marriage to actress Fania Marinoff and Mabel's liaison with Reed. Fania shared Carl's admiration for Mabel, as did the wives of many of her male friends. Like Frieda Lawrence and Una Jeffers later, Fania was most enthusiastic about Mabel's imaginative daring. Addressing her as "Lady Mike," she wrote her regarding the Paterson Strike Pageant: "I know that I am terribly proud that a *woman* was inspired with the idea and God must be praised that the woman was *Mabel Dodge* . . . aside from being great, noble, and wonderful, you are also a *darling,* and I, yes, little *me,* loves you."[7]

In his memoirs and letters, and fiction, Van Vechten credited Mabel with feats that are often wild exaggerations of her real contributions.

Following Oscar Wilde's dictum that life imitates art, he affirmed the legend of Mabel that he himself helped to create through the nationally known figure of Edith Dale, the heroine of his best-selling novel, *Peter Whiffle.*[8]

During the 1920s, Van Vechten was one of the most fashionable and popular writers in America. Because his was a Jazz Age readership that wanted to be entertained and not instructed, he found that his best approach was to treat "extremely serious themes as frivolously as possible." The reviewers of *Peter Whiffle* took it as a light and delightfully "civilized" satire on the mores and manners of the prewar literati. His characters were appreciated for having been born "this side of Fitzgerald's paradise . . . without being self-consciously beautiful and damned."[9]

Unlike the critics, Mabel recognized the darker side in both Van Vechten's nature and his work. She found in *Peter Whiffle* "a terror lurking in your formulas though I don't know exactly wherein it lies. Maybe your smile is full of little daggers!" Mabel was right. Below the sparkling and witty exterior, there was a demonic grin. Van Vechten was trying to be for the Jazz Age what Herman Melville had been for the America of the 1850s, the chronicler of a nation betrayed by a lack of coherent moral, social, political, and aesthetic values. Aside from the obvious gap in talent, the major difference between the two writers was that Van Vechten enjoyed the life he satirized.[10]

Edith Dale is the wise and detached sophisticate who helps to initiate young Peter into the world of the avant-garde. She is the "perfect mask" through whom Van Vechten views prewar bohemian America. For her, people exist like bits of colored glass in a kaleidoscope that she turns at whim to form patterns whose value lies in their transient charm. Edith thrives in this world because she is so centered and secure. For her, the self is the ultimate point of reference. In this, she is very much Mabel's ego-ideal: the godlike artist who plays with ideas and people for the sheer pleasure of self-expression. Carl, the narrator of the novel, is her masculine counterpart.

Peter is a trifling shadow of Melville's hero, Pierre Glendinning. Devoted to the discovery of a formula that will allow him to create an ideal and lasting work of art, his search for truth leads to Marx Brothers' farce rather than tragedy. Peter wears as many disguises as Melville's confidence man: opera claque, park bum, piano player in a whorehouse, aesthete, revolutionary, necromancer. Yet even when he attempts to invoke Satan as a master, he botches the incantation and gets himself blown up.

Both Carl and Edith are attached to Peter, for reasons that are more easily found outside than within the novel. Peter is very much like Van Vechten's youthful self, the wide-eyed innocent from the Midwest who came east in search of the means by which to create great works of art. Peter is also very much like the Mabel Dodge whose search for truth drove her in so many directions. He, too, suffers from the psychological dissipation brought on by endless, random experimentation.

Peter throws himself into each new enterprise with total abandon, unable to complete any one he initiates because he is always beckoned by another. His trouble begins in the womb, where, as the child of a Freudian mother who held no brief for "suppressed desires," he had to "choose" whether or not to be born. Given no direction in his youth, he lacks the means to integrate the fragments of an almost pathological personality.

We first meet Peter in Europe, living a life much like Mabel's in Florence. He is the complete aesthete, who carries the doctrine of art for art's sake to its logical absurdity by working on a book that will be "about" 300 pages, that is, blank pages. On his return to New York (in the month and year that Van Vechten met Mabel), he drops his formalist credo and takes up the proletarian novel. Giving up his foppish ways, he joins the IWW, and decides to become a second Theodore Dreiser: form is now nothing; content is all.

In the most humorous scene in the novel Peter describes to Carl the climax of his magnum opus to be. Revolution has come to the streets of New York. The Rockefellers, laid siege to in their mansions, are forced to eat their canaries. The heroine, modeled on Peter's hump-backed, hare-lipped, Jewish garment-worker girlfriend, Rosie Levenstein, runs amok through the streets of the city. Dressed in a Bendel evening gown, she smashes store windows to cries of "Weh is mir." Carl responds to Peter's scenario:

> "It's wonderful." . . . Then, as it seemed, rather inconsequentially, "Do you know Edith Dale?" . . . "Well, she's a woman, but a new kind of woman, or else the oldest kind; I'm not sure which. I'm going to take you there. . . . Everybody goes there. Everything is all mixed up. . . . Edith, inscrutable Edith, sits back and listens."[11]

Although Edith does not escape Van Vechten's irony, his admiration for her is genuine. The New Woman that he envisions is not defined by her ability to be a conduit for men's imaginations. She employs her energies in shaping her material and human environment into imaginative forms and relationships without the neurotic "male" need to produce in order to achieve self-validation. Like Gertrude Stein, Van Vechten's celebration of Mabel as an artist of life was not a patronizing way of complimenting her womanhood but a genuine regard for what he saw as an intelligent mode of being. Edith, of course, had the good fortune to suffer from none of the self-doubts and conflicts of her original.

When Edith completes her Florentine villa, it seems to those present "like the inauguration of the reign of another Lorenzo the Magnificent. There was indeed, the prospect that Ease, and Grace, Beauty, Wit, and

Knowledge, would stroll through these stately and ornate chambers for indefinite months, while hungry artists were being fed in the dining room." On her return to New York, she arranges "the first great exhibition of the post-impressionist and cubist painters."[12] She then creates a salon as the focal point for the "storm centers" with which she surrounds herself.

Edith grasps "this faint idea or frail theory, tossing it back a complete or wrecked formula," or she sits "like a Madonna who had learned to listen." She "was the amalgam which held the incongruous group together; she was the alembic that turned the dross to gold." Like Mabel, she is no mere artist of the beautiful. Her guests are a democratic melting pot of the raw and vulgar, earthy and unpretentious, effete and highbrow. Actresses, celebrities, and tramps "were all mixed up with green glass vases . . . cigarette stubs, Lincoln Steffens . . . over the whole floated the dominant odor of Coty's cyphre and stale beer." When a young "school-marmish" woman asks for a definition of modern art and gets a line of jibberish, she explodes: "It's just like the last chapter of Alice. . . . Why you're only a pack of cards, you'd all fly up in the air, a lot of flat pasteboards. . . ."[13]

Carl relishes Edith's looking-glass world for its delightful incongruities. It can contain Carlo Tresca and a Yankee millionaire, a modernist painter like Max Weber and a tradionalist like the young lady, without any need for resting, finally, in any one political or aesthetic point of view. The reader who demands logic and consistency can always, like Alice, knock them all down and "awaken" from the dream world that is Van Vechten's vision of modern life.

Peter, however, will not give up his insistence that somewhere there is a systematic mode of truth and value that will give coherence to his life. When he visits Edith in Florence, he loses all sense of the meaning of art. The glories of the Renaissance are mocked by Marinettist futurists who hold that the past is "manure"; atonal music is played in rooms where Bach and Beethoven are on the bas-reliefs. Edith tries to provide him with her "cat" philosophy to help him cope:

> The cat understands pure being, which is *all* we need to know and which it takes a lifetime to learn. *It is both subject and object. Its own outlet and its own material.* All the rest of us are divided bits of self, some here, some there. The cat has a complete subjective unity. Being its own centre, it radiates electricity in all directions. . . . The cat is the fine specimen of the I am. *Who of us is so fully the I am that I am?* (Italics mine.)[14]

Peter applauds wildly at the end of this speech, but when he asks if the cat has the consciousness to appreciate its advantage, Edith does not answer. Not long after her soliloquy, he makes an anguished speech about the impossibility of finding truth in the modern world: "Truth implies permanence and nothing is permanent. Truth implies omniscience and no one is omniscient. Truth implies community of feeling and no two human beings feel alike about anything, except for a few shifting seconds."[15] Yet Peter continues his quest and wastes his life in the process.

On the day of Peter's death, Carl goes to visit him. Finally, he seems to have accepted Edith's dictum. He had set out to write a new "Comedie Humaine" in 1914 and thought he failed because he could not achieve it. But now he realizes that he was attempting something he had no right to. "Instead I have lived it. And now I have come to the conclusion that that was all there was for me to do. . . . The great secret is the cat's secret, to do what one *has* to do. Let IT do it, let IT, whatever IT is, flow through you." Just before he dies, Peter whispers, "But—if I had found a new *formula,* who knows what I might have done!" That whisper is the the only haunting moment in the novel, but it echoes back over the whole. Peter dies December 15, 1919, on the eve of the Jazz Age. Carl tells us that he felt deep personal grief at his death because he was tied to him by an "indestructible bond."[16]

Peter's death reflects Van Vechten's broken bond with his youthful self, which could not survive in a relativistic and hedonistic world. Mabel acknowledged this in a striking metaphor when she wrote him that the novel appeared to her "like a clot of blood on a white daisy." But in the same letter, she also reminded him of the philosophy she had taught him, the one her fictional surrogate tried to teach Peter: that they would never live spontaneously or happily until they outgrew *"magic formulas* in art & life."[17] The dramatic irony with which we are left is that she continued in her own life his hero's quest.

The Mother Postulate:
Mabel Dodge and Max Eastman

*My life was gathering and accumulating in me. . . . I contained a
deep pool of refreshment and delight. This I called upon often, always
naming it Nature. I felt the rich stream of life that rose out of the
earth and I loved to lie upon it. . . . Max, who was sensitive to
women, felt, I suppose, the mediumistic part I had come to play and
seemed to feel the earth life that was using me to pass through to
whomever could take it. (Mabel at Croton-on-Hudson)[1]*

Like Carl Van Vechten, Max Eastman projected into his fictionalization
of Mabel Dodge characteristics of the New Woman that were linked to
his own psychological needs. Unlike the independent and self-defined
Edith Dale, Mary Kittredge, the heroine of *Venture,* is the embodiment
of a male Oedipal fantasy. Heavily influenced by his readings of Freud
and his own Freudian analysis, Eastman created Mary as a "mother postulate," who nurtures young male radicals by providing them with the
emotional and financial security they need in order to "play out" their
revolutionary dreams.

If Reed was the poet of the Lyrical Left, Eastman was its philosopher,
whose wide range of cultural, political, and intellectual interests issued
in an extraordinary array of publications over his lifetime, from *The Sense
of Humor* (1921), *Marx, Lenin, and the Science of Revolution* (1926), *Art and
the Life of Action* (1936), to his autobiography, *Enjoyment of Living* (1947).
Eastman shared Reed's secular commitment of living "life flagrantly to
the full," and Mabel's "obsessive fear of being cut off from 'life.'" He
shared with both their "romantic insistence upon the natural" and their
rejection of the cultivation of the mind at the expense of the emotions,
which was fundamental to the belief system of most prewar radicals.[2]

Eastman's mother was the source of his devotion to revolution. A pioneer

114

preacher in upstate New York during the last years of the nineteenth century, she was his first exemplar of the New Woman (the one Mabel would remind him of). She transmitted to Max both a joy in living and a sense of inadequacy; for he sensed that his mother was equivocal about the occupation of motherhood, and he felt that he had not really been wanted as a child. When he later went to A. A. Brill for therapy, he was diagnosed as having a strong mother fixation. Brill told him, "You want to get away from your mother and yet be with her."[3]

Eastman's political awakening came about through his ardent support of the women's suffrage movement, into which he was initiated by his brilliant sister, Crystal. He was sincerely dedicated in his conviction that women needed to become "aware human beings and to satisfy their ambitions," as is attested to by his support and respect for Mabel's creative capacities and for what he called her "sagacity," which revealed itself in flashes of illumination rather than in any systematic thinking.

In April 1913, Eastman invited Mabel to become a member of *The Masses* advisory board, and over the next three years she contributed three short stories and two articles to the magazine. In 1914 he pleaded with her to take over the April or May issue, promising her "unconditional freedom of expression" along with all the proceeds from the sale of the issue. In 1916 he wrote to pay homage to the quality of a story she wrote about herself and Maurice Sterne, encouraging her to pursue what he saw as her life's work. Mabel took justifiable pride in his letter and published it in *Movers and Shakers:*

> You have a gift, an energy of creation that ought to be more sacred to you than any personal thing. You ought enlarge your knowledge, continually, so that you will have at the command of your talent every intellectual distinction, every subtle verbal power that analytic thinking has developed.
> This is an intense and compelling work of art, and I hope you know it.[4]

Eastman also harbored some very traditional convictions about women's roles. His own felt need for mothering combined with his belief in sexual expression as "a liberating and regenerating social force" to create his feminine ideal: the mother-mistress who provided maternal security and erotic freedom at the same time. Mabel became the vehicle through whom he expressed his ideal, even though he found her too aggressive, competitive, and demanding to suit his personal taste. In his autobiography, Eastman tells us that he once toyed with the idea of making Mabel his lover, and he implies that he was somewhat irritated that nothing came of it. He was her neighbor at Croton and a witness to the end of her affair with Reed. Mabel says he felt the "earth-life" that was emanating from her at the time. Eastman, however, wasn't quite sure what he was feeling. He says that he was in the midst of his lifelong pursuit of "beautiful and blithe-hearted" women and that it would have been "convenient" if he and Mabel had fallen in love. But he also says that Mabel "was on the hunt again," and "I was in a dangerously convenient position."[5]

Like Reed's, Eastman's ambivalence was rooted in the fact that he was a perennial adolescent who believed that to be married was to be "committed 'irrevocably . . . [to] the Folly of Growing Up.'"[6] Thus he engaged in casual affairs throughout his marriage to Ida Rauh and, when she got pregnant, resented that she was no longer as good a companion. Both men shared a perennial Huck Finn–ish hankering to light out for the territory and away from the presence of women who threatened to tie them down, but whose mothering they also wanted.

In *Venture,* this boyishness is an important key to understanding Eastman's hero, Jo Hancock, who combines many of the elements of his and Reed's personalities. *Venture* "took on generic significance as the story of an entire generation," partly because Eastman revealed the underlying psychology of the young men who shared the politics of joy in the golden age that preceded World War I. He re-creates the sense of the Village as "at once a post-graduate school, a playground and a clinic for those who had broken with the old culture and had not yet found a new one, or had not yet discovered and accepted the fact that they were irrevocably committed to the old."[7]

Mary Kittredge's most important function in the novel is as an emotional and cultural incubator who helps to prolong male adolescence by providing radical youth with the perfect postgraduate education. At the same time that she teaches them about the avant-garde in art, politics, and sex, she eases the transition from their traditional, middle-class backgrounds.

Jo Hancock has disowned his middle-class businessman father and cut himself adrift to make his own life from scratch. His motto is that "each hour should be lived as though it were an express creation in precious metal wrested from death and oblivion." His ideal is "to depart passionately from all patterns and be himself—something that had never been before and would never be again."[8] Mary Kittredge, a family friend, is close enough to his parents' age to be a source of emotional support and different enough from his parents to be exciting, since she is neither middle class nor respectable. She shelters, feeds, and makes love to Jo, while he is free to experiment with the variety of pursuits in which his creative fancies engage him.

Mary symbolizes the catholicity of experimentation that was celebrated in Eastman's and Reed's *The Masses:* "the impulse of her generation to cast loose from all bonds and assumptions, and 'try things out.'" But like

Blanche and Van Vechten, Eastman carries her real-life achievements to absurd and hyperbolic lengths:

> Mary Kittredge was an extravagant person. She was almost as
> extravagant as the God who made her, and he so loaded her with whims
> and vigor and talent and money and a thirst after the true meaning of
> life, that she acquired the renown and popularity of a circus. She was
> always just entering upon some new spiritual experiment that involved a
> complete break with everything that had gone before. Either she was
> getting married, or she was getting divorced, or she was testing out
> unmarried love, . . . or snake-dancing, or Hindu philosophy, or Hindu
> turbans, or female farming, or opium-eating, or flute-playing. There was
> nothing in the world that Mary could not want to do, and there was
> very little that she could not, in a surprisingly short space of time, do.
> She waged a perpetual war on habit, a war in which she had already
> routed and driven from the field three husbands, nine lovers, and a half
> a dozen religions, although she was only thirty-five years old. And as she
> possessed an enormous fortune, and by right of heredity a certain
> "position" in American society, her career and character were well-
> known. She was a public institution.[9]

When Jo first meets Mary, he is a young man possessed of little more than a poetic gift and a romantic temperament. His story (like Reed's) is that of his transformation from a playboy poet into a committed revolutionary. Eastman conveys better than anyone who wrote about Mabel how she created an environment in which young people were initiated into the world of radical art and politics. His is also the most human and affectionate portrait of her:

> Did you ever wander through a beautiful museum of art with a person
> who knew the pictures and statues, and knew how to love them, and yet
> did not have vanity about his own taste and sophistication? . . . If you
> have found a person who can show you how Cezanne is a greater painter
> than Gaugin [*sic*], and think meanwhile about Cezanne's superiority to
> Gaugin, and not about his own superiority to you, you have found quite
> a treasure. And Mary Kittredge was such a knower, and such a lover, of
> art. Mary was a selfish woman, I suppose, but she was not egotistical.
>
> "Jo, you have to see the pictures, feel them. You have to stand before a
> picture like a little child, without knowledge, without opinions, without
> judgment, without *habits*—with nothing in you but the pure thirst for
> experience—stand there like a neophyte at the altar, and *receive* what it
> gives you."[10]

Eastman makes Mabel the center of the Armory Show. The high point of the exhibit is *The Portrait of Mary Kittredge,* a postimpressionist painting (like Dasburg's) which inspires Jo to write his own word portrait. Published in a New York daily, it earns Jo his first job and his first public notice. The portrait obviously represents Max's mixed impressions of its prototype:

> She's American, plebian,
> Sexed all over in a way you laugh and like,
> Unintellectual, unsensitive,
> Unkind, if kindness is quick sympathy. . . .
>
> But once, or somewhere, deep, or long ago,
> There is, or was, in her a mighty wish, or attitude,
> To mate the universe with mystery in her own soul.
>
> Sit silent and secrete intensity;
> Go passionately nowhere and go fast;
> Have thoughts, but never, to their peril, think;
> Be meaningful and moonish and bizarre,
> A personage of art and ecstasy. . . .[11]

Mary captures Jo when he is down to his last few dollars and provides him with all that a young man with a large appetite for life could want. As a boy, Jo had sometimes confused her with his mother, whom he had relied on as "the rock of Gibraltar." He had worshipped her energy and magnetism and when she died in his twenty-first year, he was left emotionally destitute. Mary takes her place.

Eastman's description of Mary's and Jo's first lovemaking conveys the allure of Mabel's passively aggressive eroticism. First, Jo notices her scent, as she lies half-reclined on her couch, then her scarf, that lies "like a humming-bird . . . on her half-bare shoulders." As he listens to her breathe in the total silence of the room, he realizes

> she was not phlegmatic, she was intense. She was alive like fire. . . .
> She touched her lips with her tongue to moisten them. She did not
> move. The stillness of her body possessed him. . . . His lips parted as
> though he were thirsty, and he reached toward . . . her warm throat and
> then plunged under the blue scarf, as he seized her breast and her body
> in his arms, only half-conscious, almost carried out of this world by an
> emotion.[12]

Mary's love is everything that Max Eastman and John Reed wanted in a woman. She "came to him so simply and lovingly. . . . She seemed to pour her affection around him more lavishly than before, so that he felt not only happy but completely irresponsible." We can assume that Max's

118

concluding irony is unintended: "He decided that Byron, who lived in the days before women were free and independent of men, did not know what true love is." While the lover she supports establishes his calling, Mary's involvement with him eventually takes up all her energy. Eastman credits the latency period Jo spends with her for his growth:

> The reason why Jo was able to abandon himself so utterly to this love, may have been that he knew he was growing. . . . Mary could abandon herself to love because she was a woman. . . . But Jo had in him that overbearing impulse to attack the world with his own ego, which is the masculine principle—assuming for a moment that there is a masculine principle—and this might have made him restless in a period as long as five days, had he been merely loving Mary, and not also increasing himself. [13]

Unlike the real Mabel, Eastman's idealized vision does not ask any embarrassing questions, or demand the kind of faithfulness that Max believed so often "destroys the purity of love." Mary subsidizes Jo until he finds a commitment to which he is willing to sacrifice his hedonism. While he is trying to make his mark in the coffee distribution business, she submerges herself in Marxism, takes Jo to his first socialist dinner, and brings Bill Haywood to her salon. Jo becomes involved in the Paterson Strike Pageant, the major catalyst in his evolving political consciousness, as it had been for Reed. Having "lived his way into the depth of her," he now resents his dependence on Mary, in much the same way that Reed did after the first passion of his lovemaking with Mabel.

While Mary has become a "mere underlying mother-postulate" of Jo's existence, he is still everything to her, and she is devastated when he leaves after their first quarrel. In one of the more moving scenes in the novel, Eastman enters her consciousness and follows her desperate route to new modes of salvation, now that love has failed her. Finally, she finds peace, in much the same way as Neith Boyce's Moira. When Jo returns, she tells him she has changed: "I've simply come back to myself, that's all, and I find I like myself." [14]

Jo's first real sign of emotional maturity is his recognition that he failed to be firm and loyal enough in his love. Confusing Mary's rejection with his mother's death, he begins to blame his own weakness and shallowness for the fact that his mother left him. Feeling contemptible, lonely, and lost, he contemplates death for the first time in his life. Like a young child suffering from night terrors, he passes out on the street. A friend finds him raving about "Mary," unsure of whether or not he meant the Virgin, "or the other Mary." [15]

Chastened by the necessary sacrifice of her loved one, Mary, the madonna, comes and stays by Jo all night. She is wise, Eastman tells us, with a wisdom that "is the mother of science." She departs before Jo wakes in the morning and leaves behind her hummingbird scarf as a symbol of their bright but evanescent love. Jo's friend watches her but cannot see "the tears brimming in her eyes and the terrible sad courage on her lips." When Jo wakes, he is purged of sickness and sorrow: "perfectly free," he is reborn. Mary's visit "was as far away as the memories of his mother."[16]

Mabel could not have asked for a more romantic testament to her role as the Magna Mater of twentieth-century America's first rebel generation. In reality, of course, the psychological consequences of her adopting this male fantasy were less than ennobling. Maurice Sterne, the next creative genius who happened upon her life-force, would suffer the full consequences of her repressed hunger for self-realization.

Chapter 4

Art, Nature, and
Mind Cure

During the winter of 1915, Mabel retreated into herself. Although she was still receiving urgent requests and calls for help and action from her radical friends and associates, she had lost interest in "that fabricated puppet, Mabel Dodge, as a Creature of Importance in Her Time":

> I had said good-by forever to Reed in my heart. To the gay, bombastic, and lovable boy with his shining brow; to the Labor Movement, to Revolution, and to anarchy. To the hope of subtly undermining the community with Hutch; and to the illusions of being a power in the environment. My young lover was gone, and, it seemed, gone with him were the younger hopes of change. With a world at war, one somehow ceased to be at war with systems and circumstances. Instinctively I turned once more to Nature and Art and tried to live in them.[1]

The Duncans

Mabel's renewed connection to nature had much to do with the appearance of Isadora Duncan in New York in January 1915. Isadora expressed in her dance the archetypal Feminine: "Power rose in her from her Center and flowed vividly along her limbs before our eyes in living beauty and delight." Isadora had taken many lovers, but she had never dispensed her favors at the sacrifice of her self. She seemed to Mabel to have escaped the problem of female identity by basing her life "upon a principle, not upon a personality."[2]

When Duncan stood upon the stage of Carnegie Hall and pleaded for a school to teach the poor children of America the joys of dance, John Collier, Walter Lippmann, and Mabel decided to come to her aid. Collier arranged to have the mayor of New York visit Isadora in her "Ark"—a loft she had rented in a business building which she transformed into a floating Aegean Island bathed in blue curtains. She was going to demonstrate what she had taught the Russian children she brought with her in order to convince Mayor Mitchell that she could do the same for the immigrant children of the Lower East Side.

The visit was a fiasco. One could hardly imagine two more different types than the straitlaced Irish Catholic mayor and the high priestess of erotic dance, whose emotional instability had increased since the tragic drowning of her two children the year before. The mayor had barely entered her inner sanctum when she pressed a piece of paper into his hand, on which she had written a reminder that in Plato's ideal Republic kings would be philosophers. Disliking him instantly, Duncan harangued Mitchell about the recent imprisonment of a mother who had murdered her children. She then spoke about the kind of life that her schoolchildren led. One can imagine the expression on his face as Isadora scornfully violated every precept he held sacred: "*They* don't have to get up in the morning and go down to breakfast with their cross fathers and mothers! *They* don't have to go to school with horrid dirty school books in satchels! *They* don't have to go to church on Sunday and listen to stuffy old men in ugly buildings!" They lived on beauty, art, and poetry, she concluded, as her dress slipped from her shoulder to reveal her bare breast.[3]

The propriety-conscious Walter Lippmann was infuriated by Duncan's self-abandonment. He wrote Mabel shortly afterward, "If this is Greece and Joy and the Aegean Isles and the Influence of Music, I don't want anything to do with it. It's a nasty, absurd mess, and she is obviously the last person who ought to be running a school."[4] Mabel evidently agreed, for she worked no further on her behalf. Isadora made her uncomfortable for other reasons as well. Next to her, Mabel felt awkward and ungraceful, her own unexercised plumpness magnified by Isadora's agile and "intelligent" flesh. She found Isadora's sister, Elizabeth, much more congenial.

Elizabeth shared Isadora's educational ideals and her philosophy of life, but she was much more shrewd and down-to-earth than her high-strung sister. Mabel's description aptly focuses on the essential difference between the two: "I have a memory of Elizabeth sitting cross-legged with her soft, white handwoven dress of Greek draperies all heaped about her, sipping a minute glass of schnapps. . . . She had a long upper lip, sagacious like a nanny goat, and the bright, haughty eye of that creature. . . . Isadora drank thirstily to still a craving, but Elizabeth tasted."[5] Forced out of Germany by the war, Elizabeth had come to America with her partner, Max Merz, and some of her students, to found her school anew. She had protected and sheltered her girls by having them live at her school, where they were trained in diet and exercise and groomed to devote their lives to grace and beauty.

Elizabeth's philosophy of life as a daily work of art based on nature's rhythms was a compelling one for Mabel and for some of the other Village radicals, who were troubled by the human waste of a world at war. Mabel pointed out that the outbreak of the war had driven many people "frantically to find salvation outside themselves" when they saw civilization "going to pieces."[6] The war was a shattering blow to the generation of radical innocents who had invested their talents and most of their intellectual and emotional resources in the coming secular millenium. John Collier was one who had worn himself into a state of near nervous collapse after seven years of devoted efforts to cultural, social, and economic reform. He responded enthusiastically to the idea of promoting an Elizabeth Duncan School that would educate a generation of children to celebrate life rather than destroy it. He had no difficulty gaining Mabel's support and financial aid.

Mabel worked with Collier and with Hutchins Hapgood's brother, Norman, the editor of *Colliers,* to raise funds and attract students to a program that incorporated Dewey's progressive principles with the more ethereal Duncan curriculum. The prospectus promised not just an education, but "a way of living" that would provide students with the integrated learning necessary to the growth of both body and soul. The school was planned, in fact, as a microcosm of the world they dreamed before the war, one that would combine the "vocational" with "an education of the aesthetic, human and social nature of man."[7]

Mabel raised money wherever she could, even from the German-American owners of the New Jersey silk mills, whose exploitation of their workers she had helped to dramatize in the Paterson Strike Pageant two years before. By February, they had enough backing to look for an appropriate location. Elizabeth and Mabel found the perfect setting among the hills of Croton, rolling gently above the winding Hudson River. Mabel rented a small cottage near the school buildings, on what she called her "Mt. Olympus on Mt. Airy." Here she found the solid rural virtues of simple country living that her weary spirit demanded. At its best moments, life in Croton had the rich tones and earthy heartiness of a still-life: "To see the evening sun come in the door from the porch and fall on the supper table, shining through a tumbler of red wine, falling on the orange-colored cheese and the fresh brown loaf while we sat . . . idly at rest, after the purposeless day. How good it was!"[8]

Mabel's emotional detachment from lovers and causes helped her to feel "strong, serene, and self-possessed," although she experienced periodic undercurrents of anxiety, such as the one in early March, when she agreed to wear Reed's ring. In the spring, she purchased Finney Farm, a beautiful country estate surrounded by cultivated farmland. Her life, finally, seemed complete: "in that dignified and settled environment, supported by its deeply rooted walls, backed up by its respectability and permanence" she could ignore the realities of the larger world around her. She placed little Elizabeth and her son John in the Duncan School and spent her days watching Elizabeth Duncan train her charges to "touch the hills" with their fingertips.[9]

Mabel kept her apartment at 23 Fifth Avenue throughout the winter and spring but rarely visited it. She was convinced that she was done with the demanding hustle of city life and the tormenting questions of what she should be "doing" with her life. As she sat quietly in the living room of her new home, she compared her contentment with the frenetic lives of the feminists in the Village who "hurried to check the population, or to raise wages, or to 'swing' some urgent affair." *Vanity Fair* did a nostalgia piece on her in May 1915, headed with a stunning photograph by the noted portraitist Gertrude Kasebier. It shows Mabel in a cloak and plumed hat seated on a balcony overlooking the urban domain that had been hers. Describing her as "a post-impressionist in the art of living," Arnold Hughes recalled the great days of her salon.[10]

John Evans, now a perceptive fourteen-year-old, was skeptical of his mother's newfound salvation. For years Mabel had assigned him to write a theme a day, at school and at home, in order to improve his vocabulary and his power of analysis and expression. Because she allowed no criticism or correction of these exercises, he could say what he thought about her in a forthright manner. Based on her past behavior, he had little reason to believe his mother could be rooted anywhere:

> She changes so. Sometimes she's a Christian Scientist and at other times she's sick in bed.
> She hates to travel and yet she likes new places. She hates to have trouble with a cook and yet she likes different food. She hates parties and yet she likes to meet different kinds of people. She is impossible.
>
> She gets a nice house in Italy, fills it with everything, rebuilds a part of it, and then after six years of preparing she decides its [*sic*] too big to live in.
> We haven't got the Finney Farm yet but when we get it she might decide its too quiet to live in, but "you never can tell!"[11]

As John predicted, Mabel's country idyll did not last long. In April, John Collier was writing her from his retreat in North Carolina, where he had gone to recuperate from nervous collapse, about his dissatisfaction with the way Max Merz was carrying out his plans for the school. The increasing anti-German sentiment in America was also having an adverse effect on the school's reputation because of its German and German-American connections. Mabel wrote back to Collier with her own long list of sufferings over the past three years, asking his advice about seeking a psychiatrist. Her rejection of women who "did" things with their lives provided her with respite for a while but in no way mitigated her need to do something with hers.

Mother Nature restored her depleted powers, but without men of creative genius around, Mabel still felt she had no way to use them. Thus, not long after settling in at Finney Farm, Mabel began to gather about her a small "cooperative commonwealth" of artist friends who stayed in her guest cottages. Bayard Boyeson, a brooding Norwegian-American poet who came during a period of turmoil in his life, derived great solace from Mabel's emotional support, as did Bobby Jones, who needed periodic visits with his surrogate mother to renew their "psychic bond." For a brief period, Marsden Hartley found refuge there from destitution until Mabel could no longer stand his morbidity and asked him to leave.

Maurice Sterne

Not until she met Maurice Sterne in May 1915 did Mabel find a cause worthy of the powers that had been ripening in her all spring. They met in New York City, at a dance performance given by the students of the Duncan School. Sterne was immediately attracted to Mabel, particularly to her eyes which "reflected her complex emotions spontaneously," and to her voice, "like a viola, soft, caressing, mellow, with confidential overtones." Mabel was drawn by the look of suffering on Maurice's handsome, "noble" face, which reminded her of the "undisclosed soul of Russia." Within a few weeks they were embroiled in a mutually exploitative love affair that made Mabel's alliance with John Reed seem quaintly romantic by comparison. George Biddle, who wrote the introduction to Sterne's autobiography, summed it up with comedic flair:

> It was one of the most incongruous, incompatible and tempestuous
> adventures in the annals of love. From beginning to end it transcends
> reality. It transcends fiction. It is pure burlesque, Italian comic
> opera. . . . It is a five-year long ring fight. No Queensberry rules. And
> many more than fifteen rounds. Both back in their respective corners,
> breathing messages of renewed affection and desire, as they regain their
> wind. [12]

125

Mabel had chosen, and been chosen by, a man whose artistic philosophy suited her more conservative mood. In the early 1900s, Sterne had studied in Paris, where he was befriended and patronized by Leo and Gertrude Stein. He was impressed with Cézanne but repulsed by what he saw as the unnatural subjectivism of Picasso and Matisse. Sterne left Paris in 1907, disillusioned by what he saw as the perverse direction of modern art. The radicals, he said, "were deluded into thinking that by turning their vision inward and exploring personality, they would create new masterpieces. I am afraid that in this departure from nature in art, an ingrown soul is as perverse as an ingrown toenail." A student and admirer of Rodin's, Sterne was a conservative modernist who was seeking to develop an art that would convey the essential forms and rhythms of nature and the human body.[13]

In 1910, Sterne talked of finding a "Garden of Eden" where life would be simple and "where beauty might exist as a part of daily living, rather than as an escape from it." He moved from Paris, to Greece, to Russia, to Germany and to the Far East in search of his Shangri-la. He stayed in Bali from 1912 to 1914, where he at last found a people like the ancient Greeks—brave, silent, and proud. They had in "real life" the quality that Sterne had hitherto found only in great art, and that Mabel would later find in the Taos Indians: "completeness."[14]

Sterne's passion for symmetry and balance may well have grown out of the sense of rootlessness that pursued him from childhood, when his family was driven out of Russia and came to the United States as poor Jewish immigrants. He spent much of his maturity seeking an identity that would provide him with emotional stability. Sterne combined great strength and emotional weakness; a rugged, patriarchal demeanor and a vacillating character that begged reassurance and molding. Like Mabel, he both feared and desired possession by a lover. He longed to achieve an independent identity and to lose himself in love.

Sterne was exactly the kind of man to bring out the worst in Mabel, particularly at the time when she met him. The unacknowledged anger toward men that she had stored up found its target in Sterne. She was as calculating in her attachment to him as she had been uncontrolled in her love for Reed. Sterne, however, was not just an innocent victim. He had ruthlessly exploited women to serve his own sexual needs, and although he grew to love Mabel deeply over time, his initial interest was motivated by his need for financial security and a patron. At the time they met, Sterne was just beginning to make a name for himself and he recognized, rightly, that Mabel could help his career.

At the end of May, Mabel brought Maurice out to Finney Farm for a picnic. Here he made his first sexual advances. She informed him firmly that what interested her was his work, not his body: "I was immune, I thought, what need had I for men, I who so far outran them, and their limited understanding, and capacity for life? I was inflated and I felt very superior."[15] Mabel held out against Sterne for the same reasons she had held out against Reed. This time, however, she was not just fighting to preserve her own self-possession. She was engaged in an archetypal battle of the sexes: seeing herself as Mother Earth facing her "deadly enemy," the aggressive male who sought to dominate and subdue her.

Mabel would fight, not for equality, but for control. She would make a man and an artist of Maurice in accordance with *her* image of both. Finding his paintings too erotic, she determined that he must work in a medium that was less "excremental." In her memoirs, she described her plan in the ugliest possible light: "I would harry and taunt and enrage and injure him. I would light a real fire in him before I was through: when I had him malleable I would make him throw away his yellow green paint and take to clay. . . . I was grappling now with the essence of the man. . . . His essence was strong and pure . . . I turned to it and went forward."[16]

Mabel began work immediately. She invited Sterne to accompany her to Provincetown in June, where she gave him a life-saving station she had rented so that he could work on a series of portraits of her. She intended these portraits to establish his reputation and embellish hers. Mabel limited his palette to blue, hoping that his concentration on form would eventually bring him to sculpture. She continued to keep aloof from physical intimacy in order to remain spiritually remote and untouched. But Sterne outmaneuvered her. He insisted that he could not work without sex. Mabel agreed because she could not deny him anything that would further his work, which was, after all, her work. While there is no doubt that Mabel used sex as a means of power over him, she obviously derived a great deal of pleasure from the way that Sterne made love to her. His hands traveled over her flesh as though in preparation for studying her form. Once he achieved orgasm, he would expound upon his theories of curves, volumes, and masses. For a woman who was as eager to be shaped as to shape, Sterne's sexual aesthetics must have been sublime.

Once she became Sterne's lover, however, Mabel lost her independence, just as she had with Reed. When his roving eye began to focus on other women, she was overcome with jealousy. This time the jealousy did not result in helpless hysteria or attempted suicide, but in the decision to make him over: "He *wanted* his character shaped . . . it never occurred to him to do it himself. . . . As far as working on *himself,* regarding *himself* as material more worthy of an artist than paper or paint, oh, no!"[17] It was she, not Maurice, who was engaged in the most supreme artistic undertaking: that of "creating" a human being.

Mabel, however, was not in control. Depressed throughout much of the summer, she was angry with herself for betraying "nature" by succumbing to the demands of her mortal flesh. Her mental state is epitomized in her account of her reaction to Sterne's near-drowning off the Provincetown lighthouse. Finding his discolored face and swollen body unaesthetic, she was icily indifferent to his plight. At the end of the summer, Mabel sent Maurice back to New York. Over the next year they lived on and off together at Croton. They both found that their romance flourished best when they were apart.

During their separations, Sterne's letters to Mabel are filled with avowals of love and paeans of praise. She had awakened in him a "passionate love for truth" that went far beyond the visual. Like Reed, he credited her with being the source of his creativity and the very "undercurrent" of his being. In spite of her alternating moods of affection and disdain, Mabel did have a beneficial influence on his art. When he exhibited his drawings of her at the Montrose Gallery in December 1915, he received critical acclaim. An article on the exhibit in *Current Opinion* reveals both the quality of inspiration she provided him and the reason she was so eager to have him do her portrait. The author paraphrased the art critic of the *New York Evening Post* as saying that Sterne's "striking" portraits combined "the monumental qualities of Greek art with the primitive simplicity of his Balinese studies."[78] Mabel helped him to come closer to the natural forms he was seeking, while he affirmed her self-image as the earth mother who drew her power from nature.

During the winter and spring of 1916, Sterne's avowals of love deepened, though they were sometimes punctuated by anger at her coldness. In February, he wrote to her of their nine-month love as a wonderful child that she had borne him. In March, he praised her for the quality that he would later recognize as destructive of both him and his art: "other women begin a flirtatious 'spiritualized' relation with men, build it gradually and then as a finality end up with bodily self-surrender. You, Mabel, begin where other women *end. All* that other women have to give is only the starting point with you."[19]

Leo Stein, who was a friend to both, had a clearer insight than either into their affair. He wrote Mabel advice that she would have done well to heed:

> Now, my dear Mabel, I really like you far too much to have any patience
> with your making an ass of yourself. Sterne doesn't want a mother
> except temporarily and unless you succeeded in dominating him more or
> less completely—in which case he'd be of not much more use to you
> than a pussy cat—you'd find after a while that mother was out of a
> job. . . .

> Now I don't believe that you're seriously interested in what Sterne is
> doing and what's more I don't believe that in any vital sense you

understand the problems (artistic) that agitate him. Art is something vital to you, I believe, as an experience; I don't believe it's vital to you as a problem. . . .

. . . There seems to be no evidence that you love each other enough to make sacrifices cheerfully. . . . You can't effectively bury your past selves unless they're dead and I think that in both your cases you'd discover a little after the funeral that you had to do with lively corpses.

. . . Of course, as you know, I know very few women, especially of the kind that radiate, as one might say, both tentacles and influence. . . . I cherish you as my only specimen, and don't want to see you clipped either as to tentacles or wings.[20]

In her relationship with Maurice, Mabel was trying to fulfill Leo's definition of the process by which a great work of art is created. Through the tension of their opposing forces, they would "create a new form of life," a Mona Lisa she called it, one that would justify their liaison and provide them with the self-completion each needed. Mabel discovered that the vitality Maurice drew upon for his art left her depleted of will and energy. Whenever she was not with him, she found herself "sinking down to the old depressed nothingness, which was all I was without a man. Be he ever so unsuitable, a man was what gave me identity, I thought."[21]

Mind Cure

Mabel had dabbled in Christian Science healing, astrology, and theosophy at various times over the past few years when she was having trouble with men. But during the winter of 1916, she began to search in earnest for a therapy that would resolve her self-conflicts and bring her peace of mind. Mabel's approach to mental health was very similar to her approach to radicalism. Not knowing which therapy provided the best answers, she tried them all, with the expectation that the "best" would emerge. Her simultaneous involvement in treatments whose philosophy and methods were sometimes contradictory was not just a matter of personal idiosyncrasy, however. For cross-fertilization of ideas among the various schools of mental healing was common during the years when psychoanalysis was first being introduced into America.

"Mind cure" and mysticism actually prepared the way for psychoanalysis in the first two decades of the twentieth century in America. Freud's lectures at Clark University in 1909 came "during the high point of the greatest popular interest in mental healing, hypnosis, and suggestion in American history up to the Great War." Popular novelists like Robert Herrick wrote about a "crisis" of nerves that Americans seemed to be suffering as the result of the "great machine" civilization that came of age in the twentieth century.[22] Many prominent men and women among the Progressives and Village radicals suffered from various ailments labeled nervous disorders, among them, William James, Jane Addams, Woodrow Wilson, Frederick Winslow Taylor, Max Eastman, and Floyd Dell.

Psychotherapy and mind cure appealed to progressive and radical intellectuals for some of the same reasons. Chief among them was the claim that the mind was virtually independent of matter (and, by extension, of the "great machine" to which the nation sometimes seemed inexorably bound). Both taught that the crippling effects of heredity and early environment could be overcome, that men and women could break the chains binding them to their neuroses.

Mind cure's most important contribution was the insistence that nervous disorders be taken seriously: "no longer were neurotics 'vampires' or 'silly exaggerators,' chiefly upper-class females. Most psychotherapists argued that neurosis was intensely serious and painful and could attack the happiness of individuals and families more cruelly than many organic illnesses." Most practicing psychiatrists at the turn of the century were neurologists who treated their predominantly female patients with rest and water cures and a variety of drugs, which is how Mabel's neurasthenic prostrations were treated by the doctors who visited her in Florence. When she first returned to New York in 1912, she was treated by the prominent neurologist Dr. Bernard Sachs. To many of his profession, "mentalists," as the Freudians were sometimes called, were often associated with the quackery of mind cure practitioners.[23]

Many of the early psychotherapists and practitioners of mind cure were eclectic in their methods. Dr. James Putnam of Massachusetts General Hospital, for example, prescribed autosuggestive exercises and worked with a team of specialists that included clergy. The head of the Emmanuel movement, one of the largest theosophical groups, borrowed Freud's idea of the subconscious and filled it with "the Universal Spirit" that remembered everything and solved problems. Horatio Dresser, founder of the New Thought movement, argued that the new psychology shored up lay beliefs in the power of "mind." Popular journalists hailed both psychotherapy and mind cure as manifestations of a new spirituality that proved the human mind was not inevitably bound to the laws of nature.[24]

When Mabel thought about seeking psychiatric help in April 1915, she sent John Collier a long list of the bewildering variety of sensory and psychic ailments she had suffered over the past three years and asked his advice. Collier's diagnosis provides a dizzying array of available options. Drawing upon James, Freud, occultism, and neurology, he suggested that Mabel had suffered from hysteria, hysterical epilepsy, brain anemia, melancholia, and psychical invasion and extraversion. He thought that Adolph Myers or William James could judge her case as "corporeal" or "supernormal" or both.[25]

130

Mabel did not follow up on Collier's suggestions at that time, probably because her relationship with Sterne intervened. A year later, however, in desperation, she turned first to the Freudians, whose talking cure seemed to hold much promise. Freud's cathartic theory had been greeted by many American psychiatrists with the kind of messianic fervor that one usually associates with the birth of a new religious order. In recounting the pioneer days, Fritz Wittels remembered: "Some of us believed that psychoanalysis would change the surface of the earth, believed that the Victorian age in which we then lived would by way of psychoanalystic revolution be followed by a golden age in which there would be no room for neuroses any more."[26] Just by "talking out" one's life history and discovering the traumas and complexes that had injured and impeded one's development, one could be cured.

Mabel's first analyst was Smith Ely Jelliffe, a man of prodigious intellect, who was interested in fields as diverse as paleontology, mysticism, and drama. He wrote some 400 articles and books during his lifetime. Mabel corresponded with him for twenty years, and he sent her copies of his major works. She had, of course, first heard Freud's theories explained at one of her evenings by A. A. Brill. But not until she worked with Jelliffe did she begin to apply them to herself.

Jelliffe shared Mabel's enthusiasm for Bergson's ideas about the creative evolution of human consciousness, but he reacted with intense dislike to the evolutionary manifestation of the new morality and the New Woman, whom he considered "mannish and decadent." It is hardly surprising that he charged Mabel with intent to commit castration. She provided him with the evidence when she told him of her desire to cut off her hair. Jelliffe responded that her "real" desire was to shear Phoebus Apollo. While Mabel enjoyed being able to break down the symbolic codes of her neurotic symptoms, she found Jelliffe too dogmatic in his type casting of her complexes. She was uncomfortable with his diagnosis of penis envy, although she soon came to accept most of Freud's views on female psychology. Jelliffe's was the only diagnosis she published in her memoirs:

> If your unconscious says . . . "I am a man and I can procreate with my male organ," then I am dogmatic. You can not and you need not try. This is not forcing a philosophy on you. This is only telling you you are trying to do the impossible.[27]

Freud's theory of penis envy did not, of course, explain Mabel's situation. What she wanted was the creative power she believed was denied her because of her sex. Orthodox Freudian theory thus reinforced the less liberating aspects of the *lebensphilosophie,* which at least celebrated women's life-enhancing characteristics as preferable to a rationalized and materialistic patriarchal civilization. "Why," Mabel asked herself about her relationship with Maurice, "did I have to wrestle so with this man, compel him to an exact fidelity, determine him to be a sculptor. . . . Really, was it only myself I was working on?" Jelliffe gave her an answer, but he did not provide her with a means to act constructively on it. He did, however, advise her to give Maurice up, which Mabel refused to do, because she had invested too much of herself in making him over. He was "trying to overcome the handicaps of ignorance and stupidity with which life had conditioned him. Probably for the love of the struggles which were breaking him, I could not give him up. We were, Maurice and I, both so terribly earnest!"[28]

At the same time that she was seeing Jelliffe, Mabel was engaged in seeking help from practitioners of New Thought, which stressed the importance of "giving up" her mind rather than using it to probe the inner recesses of her unconscious. Mind cure had dramatically increased its adherents in the first two decades of the twentieth century, appealing to those who were alienated from mainstream Protestantism. For women, who predominated as its prophets and patients, mind cure offered a means to power and success that was not attainable through more traditional cultural routes. In weakness was their strength.

The essence of the various sects and schools that made up the broader movement was reliance on an all-loving God, who offered a continual supply of divine sustenance. One did not have to wrestle with the world, or with the self, because there was no real self to be concerned about: "Individuality did not mean a center of integration in the individual. It meant . . . identity with Divine Mind as the only integrating power. It did not mean life defined by the vicissitudes, perils and promises of a unique existence. It meant sharing a universal essence. . . . No individual was an individual by being unlike other individuals. No one was an individual because of experiences he alone had had."[29]

Mabel's attraction to mind cure was based on the same need that motivated her search for a powerful male to whom she could submit herself. The "super-self" it taught her to rely on "was the child's wish about his parents, perfect in their gratification of every need, perfect in constituting the sum of reality." Mabel's involvement in New Thought had much to do with the added comfort it offered of overcoming the social isolation that had always plagued her. Unlike the secular humanism she embraced during her Village years, mind cure did not demand that the individual actively work toward creating a new human community:

We have not to *perpetuate* the sorrows of our parents—it is our task to rub them out—to rub out *all* the sorrows in the world—old smudges—old mistakes—wipe them off the slate. . . . The one *thing* that the exchange of burden & energy—between people—always & indubitably proves, is the oneness of humanity—the at-one-ment of Us! And wasn't it this at-one-ment Christ tried to tell us about all the time? . . . All his teachings are in the two things. How we can be shriven by that Power he knew—if One is saved all are *safe*. Thus vicariousness *is* atonement.[30]

Hapgood, who was privy to Mabel's misery during her affair with Sterne as he had been to the affair with Reed, understood better than anyone else what drove Mabel in her search for "at-one-ment." He had been the victim of her unhappiness that winter when he was having an affair with Lucy Collier. When he refused to give Lucy up, Mabel wrote Neith in January 1916 about the affair. At the time, Hutch was furious with her and even warned Sterne against her. Not long after, he forgave her, and in his memoirs explained the source of her more bizarre and cruel behaviors:

> . . . she continually seeks the nourishment which some harsh fate has withheld from her, and which she can come in contact with only by the most violent effort.
> . . . Her eager, sometimes graceless searchings, her terrific but formless needs, her occasional sharp unkindness, her extraordinary and otherwise incomprehensible jealousy, her inability to let go of anything even for a moment casually within her domain; all this seems often ugly and reprehensible. But to me it is not so at all; for I know that even the harsher more unattractive elements of her activity are there because of her eager love of "It"—the infinite—with which she wants to be naturally, strongly, connected. She wants to repose quietly and physically on the bosom of God. . . . Feeling myself to also be one of the *disjecta membra* of life, I feel singularly akin to my sister Mabel, and all that she did was to me sympathetically comprehensible.[31]

Mabel first tried the Unity School of Christianity, one of the largest New Thought organizations. Located in Kansas City, Missouri, it was a national clearinghouse and one of the first of such groups to make use of modern methods of communication. Unity kept a large staff of correspondents who addressed in semi–form letters the problems of people around the nation and the world, sent via letter, telegram, and telephone. They did most of their work through "meditations" distributed to their clients. In particularly difficult cases, they had their workers concentrate on drawing upon the divine essence at various times throughout the day. In return for the prosperity and health promised to those who followed their "prescriptions," the faithful sent "love offerings," which were the financial mainstay of the institution.[32]

Mabel had received her first "meditation" on September 13, 1915, not long after her return from Europe. It read, "I am the illumined Child of God, filled with the spirit of love and wisdom, by which I am guided in all my ways." In February 1916, she asked for help with Maurice. On

March 2, she was reminded that they must both overcome their fleshly appetites, for these depleted the bodily fluids which supported their spiritual growth. Power and mastery would come only through "dominion over the appetites and desires of the flesh."[33]

At the time Mabel began treatment with Jelliffe, she was already seeing a Divine Science practitioner, Nina Bull, who had been a close childhood friend in Buffalo. Bull started a tug-of-war over Mabel's psyche that continued over the next few years between spiritualists and psychiatrists, who did not find their therapies compatible. The spiritualists argued that all of her problems were related to the overdevelopment of her mental powers and that to be cured she must give up her desire for consciousness and knowledge. Her psychoanalysts insisted on rational analysis as the only means to self-understanding and change. Mabel had hoped that Nina would help her to "give [Maurice] a soul," but Bull insisted that there was little she could do as long as Mabel continued to see Jelliffe.[34]

When Mabel stopped seeing Jelliffe in the spring of 1916, she turned to Emma Curtis Hopkins, who had trained the founder of Unity and also taught Nina Bull. Emma promised to get Mabel smoothed out "the effortless way." She had been a leading student of Mary Baker Eddy's and an editor of the *Christian Science Journal* in the 1880s. Hopkins established herself in Chicago after her expulsion from the Mother Church, where she devised a simplified version of Christian Science that could be taught in twelve lessons repeated until they took effect.

Hopkins's healing derived much more from her presence than from her philosophy and seems to have lasted as long. Her "patients" would lie down on the comfortable hotel bed she kept for them in a room with drawn shades, while she held their hands and spoke to them in a soothing, hypnotic voice. Mabel felt stimulated and renewed after each of these sessions which took place three times a week, but she was incapable of following the instruction she was supposed to take home with her: to rely on the powers of love and health within her "without interception of will." Although Hopkins's prescription that she relax into the "Intense Inane" did not offer her much to go on, Mabel brought many of her friends to Hopkins, including Andrew Dasburg, Elizabeth Duncan, Bobby Jones, and, finally, Maurice, and they found some comfort in her therapy.

Still unsure of where her future lay with Sterne, Mabel went off alone to Provincetown in June. On June 8, 1916, she received notification of her divorce from Edwin Dodge, who had gallantly allowed her to use the grounds that he had deserted her. The finality of her separation from him obviously increased her anxiety about Maurice, to whom she wrote: "We are able to mean so much more to each other than anyone else can mean to either of us. . . . My real self doesn't mean to hold you down, dearest. I love you." Stimulated by the psychic vibrations she sent out at a distance, Maurice wrote her that he had never felt so deep and rich inside; at last, he was convinced he was a sculptor. His bliss did not, however, prevent him from worrying about a trait in Mabel that had originally attracted him: "You have both a mental curiosity and a certain spiritual perception for the soul of him who loves you—at times it almost seems to me that you have a bodily craving to absorb his soul."[35]

Mabel asserted her "craving" again in July, when Sterne wrote her that he was going to Maine to paint rocks. Deciding that he must have "the rockiest rocks" to paint, she sent him to Monhegan Island, twenty miles off the coast of Port Clyde, Maine. Mabel found the island "austere" and "tragic," like the terrain of Charlotte Bronte: "A black rock in the Atlantic Ocean with cruel cliffs against which the water, always of nondescript color, angrily lurched and broke night and day." "It was," she decided, "a suitable background for the turbulent artist." Maurice's enthusiastic absorption in his rocks oppressed her almost as soon as she arrived in August, and she found that she could create nothing for herself there. She would have done well to heed Bayard Boyeson's advice, when he wrote her, "I think you need, above all else, a purpose outside yourself— a purpose that is *not* connected with a person. . . . To be specific: you should be, not merely a medium and instigator of work, but a worker yourself." When she and Maurice returned to Finney Farm in September, the atmosphere turned poisonous among Bobby Jones, Bayard, and Sterne because of the competition for her favor she stirred up among them. She recognized that she was the snake who had spoiled her own Arcadian paradise and reluctantly began to dismantle her "Croton Cosmos."[36]

Mabel had found the energy that summer, however, to write two very powerful short stories about the destructive and self-destructive nature of her relationship with Maurice. Published anonymously in *The Masses* in September and October 1916, these were the stories that Max Eastman referred to as compelling works of art. They convey better than anything else Mabel ever wrote the tragedy of her compulsive drive to realize herself through men. In both, a man and his wife are nameless symbols of the type of marriage in which the wife feels she has no identity outside her husband and punishes him for it. While the woman clearly bears the brunt of the responsibility in the story for their joint misery, she and her husband seem as much the helpless victims of an inexorable male-female dynamic.

The wife, in "A Quarrel," is a woman who exists in a death-in-life state whenever her husband leaves her: "He was the source of her life and she looked to him to animate her sense of living and to enliven her inert force, and she hated him in advance for being the only element in her experience that could work this magic for her." She "grappled" with him in order to achieve a sense of life that could only be gotten "at his cost." His escape from her into his work "signified her temporary extinction." She hated the immunity his work gave him and "coveted" it at the same

135

time. Her way of dealing with her envy and hatred was to use her emotional weakness as a weapon to make him feel guilty: "He sensed her strength as she sat there deadly to him—sapping the strength in him, deadly in her desire to mutilate and overcome him." He knew that he could not live with her if she chose interests outside his own life, because the only reason she would do so would be to destroy him.[37]

"The Parting" is a continuation of the previous story. The man and the woman decide to leave each other: "After the long, unsuccessful pursuit of his spirit she had a sudden complete sense of frustration." She had hoped to be "saved" by him and had attempted to penetrate the very roots of his nature in the belief that by "knowing" him she could absorb his strength and purposefulness. In her husband's absence, she finds that her environment has become as denatured as herself: "symbols that had lost their meaning." Without her husband to give her energies a sense of direction her "soul" becomes a whirlpool of "unrelated emotion." Lost in her dependency, she cannot penetrate the foundations of her behavior. At the end, she waits for the dawn to break, "uncertain—weary and unfilled."[38]

Mabel's fictionalization of her own plight revealed her understanding of the dynamics of passivity, punishment, and guilt that drove her to destroy the relationship she had come to depend on for her own survival. But she seemed no more capable than her surrogate of doing anything about it. The kind of impasse from which she suffered is illuminated by R. D. Laing's existential study *The Divided Self.* Laing posits "ontological insecurity" as the predominant malaise of Western civilization in the twentieth century, which affects men and women who have grown up without the nourishing social context they need in order to experience themselves as "real and alive": "If the individual cannot take the realness, aliveness, autonomy, and identity of himself and others for granted, then he has to become absorbed in contriving ways to be real. . . ." The anomic individual is incapable of the kind of "relatedness" that occurs when there is "genuine mutuality." For such a person, the only alternative to total isolation is a "vampire-like attachment in which the other person's life-blood is necessary for one's own survival, and yet is a threat to one's survival."[39]

Laing's analysis of a woman patient whose case is strikingly similar to Mabel's reveals how this lack of a sense of self has sometimes affected women who have experienced the breakdown of cohesive community and family life. "Mrs. R." has no existence outside her lover because he provides the only context she has to define her identity:

If she is not in the actual presence of another person who knows her, or if she cannot succeed in evoking this person's presence in his absence, her sense of her own identity drains away from her. Her panic is at the fading away of her being. She is like Tinker Bell. In order to exist she needs someone else to believe in her existence. How necessary that her lover should be a sculptor and that she should be his model! How inevitable, given the basic premise of her existence, that when her existence was not recognized she should be suffused with anxiety. For her, *esse* is *percipi*. . . .[40]

A. A. Brill

Before Mabel had left New York City for the summer in 1916, she had tried to see A. A. Brill. When he told her he was too busy, Mabel informed him that she would not be able to endure her melancholy until fall. In the brisk, no-nonsense manner that became the hallmark of his relationship with her, he told her that she could and would. During the fall of 1916, Mabel came into the city from Croton to begin therapy with him. For the next twenty years, he would serve as her analyst, confidant, and friend, offering her large doses of orthodox and simplified Freudian psychology, as well as practical advice.

Mabel was fond of pointing out that she always wanted to know the "heads" of things. In choosing to work with A. A. Brill, she selected the head of the psychoanalytic movement in America, the man who more than any other "helped to determine the shape of the American experience with psychoanalysis." Brill was the first practicing psychoanalyst in America; the first to translate Freud's major works into English; the author of the first major popularizations of Freud; and a teacher and trainer of other leading psychoanalysts, such as Ely Jelliffe. It was through Brill that Lincoln Steffens and other radicals in Mabel's salon circle first heard of Freud's ideas. And it was through Mabel that Brill met the avant-garde artists and intellectuals, some of whom he subsequently saw in private practice.[41]

Brill came to Freudian theory out of a background very different from Mabel's, although he was attracted to Freud for some of the same reasons. Born in Austria to orthodox Jewish parents who demanded a rigorous obedience to his religion, he fled his home at age fourteen and came to America. Repudiating his past, and the father who embodied it, he settled in the Lower East Side in 1889 and worked his way up against great odds to a position of national prominence in the medical profession, which at the time was not an easy task for a Jew. Before discovering Freud, Brill had considered both the priesthood and the Baptist ministry as part of his search for an "all-embracing spiritual system" to replace the religion of his fathers: "For him psychoanalysis and Sigmund Freud gave more than an explanation of life, they gave structure and meaning to life. To battle for psychoanalysis was to struggle to establish truth, to enlighten the world."[42]

137

Brill's own struggle with poverty and his subsequent rise gave him a rather Darwinian view of society and the individual's need to conform to "reality." Like most Freudians, he steered clear of attacking the political and economic system and analyzed radicals as malcontents whose rebellion against capitalism was a displacement of their personal problems. At the same time, he attacked prohibition, censorship, and the genteel code of sexuality, which he believed had too severely repressed the natural drives of men and women. Brill spoke of Freud as his "spiritual father," and of his adoption of Freudian principles as his "conversion" experience (as did many of the early pioneers). His conversion was so profound that he never followed Freud beyond his earliest formulations. He insisted that Freud's essence was contained in his earliest studies on hysteria, psychopathology, and the interpretation of dreams.[43]

Mabel absorbed most of her knowledge and understanding of Freudian theory through Brill. (When she wrote a lengthy summary of Freudian psychology in the 1930s, she credited him as the source of her ideas.) Brill's teachings reinforced what she had already heard from Jelliffe. In *The Basic Principles of Psychoanalysis* (1921), Brill wrote that "women . . . suffer from a marked need of love. If you find a woman depressed and out of sorts with herself and weeping, who cannot tell you what is ailing her, you may safely conclude that there is something wrong with her love life. She is not necessarily craving physical sex; give her the necessary love outlet through happy marriage and children, and she will have no more crying spells."[44] While his analysis of Mabel's problems was not that simplistic, one hears echoes of his reductionism throughout Mabel's memoirs, whenever she says or implies that all her worldly activities had merely been "substitutes" for inadequate love relationships.

Like his mentor, Brill believed that women were granted limited powers of sublimation because they were "the true guardians of the sexual interests of the race."[45] But he stressed more than Freud the importance of sublimation for cultural and social progress and achievement. From the beginning of his analysis, he encouraged Mabel to sublimate. He insisted that she not just bring him her dreams and free associate, but that she organize her life and find some meaningful work to do. When she tried to save time by telling him all her complexes and asking if he thought a manic-depressive could cure herself (so Jelliffe had diagnosed her), Brill told her that he was not interested in her speculations, her "Jehovah complex," or her mysticism. Mabel noted with some truth that had she spoken to him about the power that "impelled" her from within as the "unconscious," he would have assented more readily to her descriptions of her emotional life.

After reading Mabel's *Masses* stories about herself and Maurice, Brill suggested that she take up writing. She had tried two activities and felt some confidence in doing them: writing and interior decorating. Mabel gathered herself together and tried her hand at both. On January 13, 1917, the *New Republic* carried an advertisement that she was available by private appointment as an interior design consultant. In August 1917, the Hearst chain began carrying her biweekly advice column. Neither the consultations nor the columns were particularly demanding in time and energy, but they were a beginning. On one issue, however, Mabel did not yield to her psychiatrist. When he tried to impress upon her his theory of adaptation by insisting that she was not normal if she did not want to live in the city, Mabel refused to acknowledge that it was normal to adapt to filth, noise, and pollution. Their compromise was for her to live in Croton while finding herself a writing job.

Mabel later insisted that she began to write "to appease" Brill. She also claimed that this "was not *work* at all." Like her protestations that she wrote her article on Gertrude Stein only because impelled to do so by a man, her assertion that she wrote to please Brill was hardly the whole truth. She received much pleasure from seeing her name in print, even though writing for the Hearst publications was not the kind of work that she, or the men she most admired, held in high esteem.

Mabel Dodge Writes . . .

Mabel became a syndicated columnist through the help of Arthur Brisbane. He was the publisher of the *New York Journal* and the Ganson family friend who had laughed at the adolescent Mabel's dreams of making something of herself in the world. Mabel's advice columns, for which she received ten dollars each, were printed on the editorial pages of newspapers with the largest circulations in the country. She wrote on such diverse topics as making quilts, adopting babies, and setting up lending libraries for paintings. But she was most interesting in her role as mass psychologist, to which she brought her understanding of Freudian psychology, Bergson, and mind cure.

In fact, Mabel was one of Freud's earliest popularizers. While Floyd Dell, Max Eastman, and Walter Lippmann had written about Freudian theories in such magazines as *Everybody's* and *The Masses,* these journals did not reach as wide and diverse an audience as Mabel did with her columns.[46] She geared them to the lower-middle and middle classes, to the "shop girls and clerks" whom Brisbane was continually advising her to "write down to." Some of her columns were no more informative than the run-of-the-mill theosophist tract, but others were intelligent attempts to explain basic principles of psychology in language that demystified them and encouraged professional counseling.

Her first topic, which was assigned to her, was most appropriate. She was asked to review *I, Mary MacLane,* the second volume of memoirs written by a woman who reads like a caricature of Mabel. MacLane had been born and lived most of her life in Butte, Montana, in an atmosphere devoid of cultural resources. She had devoted her life to fantasizing about herself as queen of a universe in which she was all-important and powerful.[47]

Because Mabel was tempted by just this kind of solipsism at various intervals, she had no difficulty recognizing a case of "arrested development" that was so close to home. Her advice to MacLane sounds very much like the humanitarianism she had preached during her Village days: "Living is the outcome of being in relation to others of our kind"; exclusion from them is "death." Only now she recommended psychotherapy rather than involvement in radical causes.

Mabel's articles, however, were no more consistent than she was. On September 8, she turned to Nietzsche in an article headlined, "Supernormal, Normal, and Misfit: Which Are You?" in order to argue the "supernormal" person refused to accept the "thousand imperfections" of life and strove to make "his environment according to his own will." On the following day, Mabel outlined a theory of human development at the opposite pole from Nietzsche. Relying primarily on Bergson, she argued that the "Growth of Love" took place in three stages: self-love, object love, and love of humanity.

It is clear from an overview of her columns that Mabel was incorporating all the theories and philosophies she had tried out in the previous five years of her life. The three most important issues that she deals with are how men and women can cope with the problems of modern industrial life, the uses and abuses of power between individuals and in society at large, and women's "problems."

One can find strong echoes of Village radicalism, combined with Freud, in her critiques of industrial capitalism. On August 31, 1917, she had called on the master of "cosmic consciousness," Walt Whitman, to convince her readers that they should welcome the Russian Revolution as a symbol of a necessary "re-evaluation of all values"—particularly those of money, love, and class. But she warned, prophetically, that if those who had taken power from the tsar used it to oppress their own people, the goal of the revolution would be destroyed. "Power without vision," she concluded, would defeat the promise of "the New Age" that Whitman—and the Lyrical Left—had prophesied would liberate humanity from all oppressions.

Mabel's essay of October 31 on "The Crime of Stealing Energy" had as its thesis that the ultimate crime between humans is taking "the life out of another." She gives as one of her examples the male entrepreneur who piles up money by stealing it from factory hands and urges her readers to "Release your energy! Release your money! Release your love!" On November 29, she discussed the wheel as a metaphor for the destructive potential of a world in which men have created machines which master them. On December 19, she tried to arouse her readers' concern about what she believed was an excessive sublimation of human energy into machine technology (a subject that would become an *idée fixe* during the next two decades).

The advice that Mabel gave to her women readers came directly from her experience. She warned them against her own two worst problems when she wrote about women who try to become "the mothers of men" and about "women who seek masters." In the latter article, Mabel argued publicly, for the first and last time, an explicitly feminist point of view. Using a simplified combination of Freud's theories of the primal horde, the incest taboo, and the Oedipus complex, she explained that women who sought father figures in men were holding on to "an atavistic infantile idea." "For the mature woman," she concluded, "there is no father. There is no master. There is only herself, free and alone, in the brotherhood of man, bearing her own security within her own soul."

Mabel's "feminist" statement was published one week after she and Maurice were married. Sister Beatrix, a lay nun who ran a school near Finney Farm, prevailed upon Mabel to show responsibility for her growing public by legitimizing her relationship with Maurice. In spite of her analysis with Brill and her initiation of her own work, she was still unsure of who she was or what she wanted to do. All summer long, she had continued to receive treatment from Emma Curtis Hopkins, who had promised to help Mabel with Maurice. But they did not, as he put it, get "smoothened out." Perhaps hoping marriage would do it, Mabel got up on the morning of August 23, 1917, and suggested it. She and Maurice, with Ida Rauh and Andrew Dasburg as witnesses, were married by a justice of the peace in Peekskill. Mabel repeated her marriage vows in a cold, tight voice, obviously resentful that she was once again bound, even though this time she had initiated the binding. A few days later, an irate friend, the suffragist Marie Howe, called upon her and excoriated her for her betrayal of the cause of women. Mabel had been an example to all women who needed to know that it was all right to live and love without benefit of clergy. She had, Howe insisted, given strength and courage to thousands of women by her position. Genuinely bewildered by her own contradictory impulses and behavior, Mabel queried, "Which one?"

No sooner were they married, then Mabel sent Maurice off on a honeymoon by himself out West. On his first night back in New York, she saw him look at another woman. That was enough. In a few weeks, she packed him off for the Southwest. Sterne remembered their first two marital months together as having been harmonious. After the marriage, he says, his feelings for her moved beyond sexual attraction to love and affection, although his letters indicate that those feelings had developed earlier. When he told Mabel of his evolving feelings, she apparently burst out, "the moment sex is over between us, all will be finished."[48] Mabel's insistence that sex was her "due" was certainly not out of keeping with her belief that it was her one sure means of control over him.

Shortly after Sterne left for the Southwest, Mabel went to a medium, who predicted she would soon be surrounded by Indians. Lying in bed one evening in November, just after Maurice had reached Santa Fe, she had one of her "psychic" experiences. She saw Maurice's head floating above her bed. Within a few minutes it was replaced by a dark Indian face that affected her like "medicine." Sterne wrote to her on November 28, his letter, with which she ends the third volume of her memoirs, a prophetic revelation of all that was to come:

> Dearest Girl—
> Do you want an object in life? Save the Indians, their art—culture—reveal it to the world! . . .
> That which . . . others are doing for the Negroes, you could, if you wanted to, do for the Indians, for you have energy and are the most sensitive little girl in the world—and, above all, there is somehow a strange relationship between yourself and the Indians.[49]

Chapter 5

Edge of Taos Desert

Revelations of the hidden distortions, the cripple under the veils of civilization, the mind breaking under its strain, and the heart atrophying in its insulation—those were the intimate memories of my life until I came to Taos where I was offered and accepted a spiritual therapy that was cleansing, one that provided a difficult and painful method of curing me of my epoch and that finally rewarded me with a sense of reality.[1]

Even today, some sixty years after Mabel's journey, the drive to Taos leads us to the point where we stop and see "the dawn of the world." Rounding the corner of the highway that winds upward from Embudo through twenty miles of rugged hills, we look down at the 7,000-foot-high plateau of the Rio Grande. Its tawny flatness stretches out some 400 feet below until it reaches the edge of the Jemez Mountains, a blue haze in the distant west. To the north, the grey green Sangre de Cristo Mountains tower 7,000 feet more from the bottom of the plateau. Taos lies in the hollow of their encircling center, still far enough away to resemble the "straggling vista of smoking adobe houses growing up from the warm earth" that it was in 1917.[2]

At the beginning of the fourth volume of her memoirs, *Edge of Taos Desert: An Escape to Reality,* Mabel tells us that she went to the Southwest seeking "Change." The capital *C* denotes the seriousness of the undertaking which was to become the pivotal journey of her life. Reversing the import of Willa Cather's remark that "the world broke in two" after the war, Mabel says of her arrival in New Mexico: "My life broke in two right then, and I entered into the second half, a new world that replaced all the ways I had known with others, more strange and terrible and sweet than any I had ever been able to imagine."[3] Just as her previous journeys

143

had cultural significance beyond the personal, so too did this one. Mabel had arrived in New York in time to catalyze the political and aesthetic radicals of Greenwich Village at the peak of their prewar idealism. She reached New Mexico at exactly the right moment to serve as an apostle for the Anglo artists and activists who "expatriated" themselves in Santa Fe and Taos during and after World War I.

In discussing this movement, Van Wyck Brooks once again used Mabel as his cultural avatar:

> Mabel Dodge was a type of those who . . . felt that the white man was "spoiled" and "lost" and who wished to throw off a civilization that was buried under accretions of objects, invented or collected. . . . The high tableland of Taos was a region of magic where the air seemed full of an almost heard . . . music and there was always time, space and ease. . . . But perhaps it required a world war to provide the occasion for this coming-to-rest on the bosom of the Indian faith in destiny and nature.

Like their counterparts who fled to Europe after the war, the writers and artists who came to New Mexico found contemporary American civilization bankrupt. They shared "one of the most profound emotional experiences" of the 1920s decade, "the agony of a spiritual quest . . . for a structure of myth and an acceptable mode of belief" that would nourish art, society, and human personality. Many of them had belonged to the prewar avant-garde that could no longer find "an acceptable mode of belief" in revolutionary promises.[4]

The artists and writers who flowed into Santa Fe and Taos in the 1920s and 1930s as permanent residents or summer sojourners numbered in the hundreds. They were drawn to northern New Mexico by factors that set it apart for them as a region of unique inspiration: the strikingly diverse landscape of mesa, mountain, and desert; the high altitude and dry climate which "intensified light and clarified form" while seeming to reveal an "inherent order"; the native American and Hispanic peoples who had maintained their cultural integrity for centuries and who thus provided the newcomers with rich sources in their search for an aesthetic which would break the European cultural dominance over American art and literature.[5] In New Mexico's past, they discovered their vision of the future: a world of individuals rooted in communities whose traditions were life-enhancing and, therefore, worth protecting and learning from. Unlike their European counterparts, they created a literature and art of affirmation that stands in marked contrast to the art and literature of alienation with which we are much more familiar from the 1920s.

Mabel was one of the first to discover the healing qualities of the land and its peoples. She took the lead in promoting the utopian myth of the Southwest as a garden of Eden, whose climate, terrain, and indigenous

144

peoples offered cultural renewal for the dying Anglo civilization. Over the next decade, she earned the sobriquet "regent of New Mexico," as she built a cosmos far more ambitious than the one she had created in Florence or imagined in New York. Many of the architects whose help she enlisted— Mary Austin, John Collier, D. H. Lawrence, Willa Cather, Georgia O'Keeffe—felt as she did, that New Mexico was "the greatest experience from the outside world" that they ever had.[6]

Mabel traveled to the Southwest with the expectation that a totally "alien" world might satisfy her emotional and spiritual longing for a home. One month before joining Maurice, she wrote him about her premonition: "They [the Indians] *are* . . . totally unmixed with our known civilization. . . . In their unconscious lie things that neither they nor we can fathom. Perhaps I too would feel this curious affinity with them that you do. Certainly the live heart of me—the inner life—is a life that finds no counterpart in Western civilization and culture." But in spite of her hopefulness, Mabel undertook the journey with a greal deal of anxiety. She wanted Maurice to guarantee her that if she came to New Mexico they would live "as one" in a "rich and happy relation." He, of course, could give her no such guarantee.[7]

Brill had advised their initial separation for therapeutic reasons, and friends of Maurice had suggested that he might find among the Pueblo Indians of the Southwest the same sort of creative sustenance that inspired his Balinese paintings. Sterne established a studio in Santa Fe in October 1917. He was, as Lawrence would later be, both repelled by the Indians' "antagonism" and compelled by their "otherness." But he had no doubt that Mabel would find them instantly appealing: "It was the fascination that opposites have for each other," he later wrote, "and I suddenly realized that it was much the way I felt about Mabel. . . . I became convinced that she had some Indian blood, and that part of her interest in me was that I too was evolving from the somewhat exotic and complementary civilization of the Mediterranean."[8] When Maurice wrote her in November that he could not work without her and appealed to her to come and "save" the Indians, he convinced her that she was needed.

Mabel's mid-December journey to Santa Fe was not an auspicious beginning. For three tedious and uncomfortable days and nights, she rode the railways, impatient to arrive at her chosen destiny. By the time she reached northeastern New Mexico, she could no longer stand stopping at every small station and being subjected to the noise and smells of small children eating apples and bananas. She disembarked and hired a young man named Elisha to drive her to Santa Fe, in the hope that they could "beat" the train. The auto trip, however, turned into several hours of sustained physical torture. Not only did Elisha's car have no lights (it was after 5:00 P.M. when they started), but the road, if there was one, seemed to have been deliberately planted with ruts and upheavals, each of which registered individually thanks to the car's broken suspension system. While she was on the train, Mabel had imagined Maurice's and John's eager faces as she greeted them at the station. Instead, she was tossed and bruised all the way into Wagon Mound, where she left her chauffeur and reboarded the train. When Sterne met her at Lamy, her discomforts were not over. He brought her to "a dark street in front of a mud hovel" that was their lodgings in Santa Fe. "I could hardly believe it was true," Mabel recalled. "So *this* was the Southwest! *Well!*"[9]

Mabel had arrived in the capital city of a territory that had achieved statehood only five years earlier and was eager to attract both tourists and new residents. Local citizens, the Chamber of Commerce, the Women's Board of Trade, and the capital's leading newspaper, the *Santa Fe New Mexican,* had "mounted a vigorous campaign to attract visitors and future inhabitants. Proclaiming themselves residents of the oldest city in America, promoters emphasized a unique climate and a variety of cultural assets: Spanish-Pueblo architecture, the Museum and the School of American Archaeology, the art colony, and the surrounding Indian and Hispano villages."[10] Not long after her arrival, Mabel took tea with the small artists' circle that centered in the home of Alice Corbin Henderson, perhaps the city's most famous recent settler. Henderson had been an associate editor of *Poetry: A Magazine of Modern Verse,* which was one of the finest avant-garde journals of the prewar era. It had been among the first to publish Robert Frost, Carl Sandburg, Amy Lowell, Ezra Pound, and T. S. Eliot. She had come in the spring of 1916, with her husband—the artist William Penhallow Henderson—and their daughter to receive treatment for tuberculosis at the Sunmount Sanitorium. (Two years later she brought out Carl Sandburg, Vachel Lindsay, and Harriet Monroe, who became frequent visitors.)

Almost from the first, Mabel was restless in Santa Fe. Her claim that the city was too tame and conventional for her tastes was very likely related to the fact that it had already been "discovered" by another woman writer and patroness, and by Maurice, as well. Mabel wanted her own domain, and thus decided to visit Taos, a small village that a New York friend had told her about, located somewhere north of Santa Fe near an Indian pueblo.

Taos

In those days, the seventy-five-mile trip from Santa Fe to Taos took an entire day by train and by "coach" or private cars which had to travel over narrow and steep dirt roads often eroded during the winter months. The single-track railroad ended at Embudo junction, which consisted of a platform and a solitary adobe shelter presided over by Mr. Patchum, stationmaster. He was telephone and telegraph operator and guardian and purveyor of all the news coming into and going out of Taos valley. From the junction, "Long John" Dunn, or his rival, Oscar Davis, took over with their sedans that made the precarious trek up the east side of the canyon. Andrew Dasburg, who came a month after Mabel's arrival in New Mexico, has given the most vivid description of the harrowing journey:

> At Embudo where the river came thru the mountains . . . started the thrilling part of the journey, a thirty mile trip by auto over mountain trails that a goat must have planned. To say that at times we were wonder-eyed with fright is a mild description of our inner state. In precarious places the car did not take the grade, so our driver would back down several hundred feet and try again with a fresh start. . . . In one place . . . another car came down; they got by us. . . . How, is one of those things that sometimes happen contrary to the laws of gravitation. The drop on one side was at least four hundred feet to the river. At the very worst place where the car about stands on end and even the driver admits its risky, a large boulder had come down almost blocking the entire road. This he passed like a mountain sheep without quite upsetting the car. . . . The cook [Mabel had asked him to bring] looked green and [Bobby] Jones like an ivory Christ.[11]

The terrors of the journey were not, however, what most impressed Mabel, who made the whole trip by private car.

In Santa Fe she had been moved by the "fresh, beautiful world" that surrounded the city. The extraordinary clarity of the crystalline blue sky and the mingled odors of cedar, sage, and piñon that perfumed the air gave her a foretaste of the country to the north. As she traveled the almost uninhabited space between the two towns, she felt that she was witnessing the origins of life. She responded to a landscape uncomplicated by human invention with much the same shock of recognition that stimulated Lawrence's, Cather's, and O'Keeffe's creative impulses: "There was," Mabel noted, "no disturbance in the scene, nothing to complicate the forms, no trees or houses, or any detail to confuse one. It was like a simple phrase in music or a single line of poetry, essential and reduced to the barest meaning."[12] Here was a place where she might break the chains of heredity and environment and begin again.

Mabel and Maurice had arrived after dark, in bone-chilling cold. But it took Mabel only a few hours to decide that Taos was where they were going to live. After her first dinner, she had no doubt that she had discovered the New Mexican equivalent of Shangri-la. Sitting alone in the stillness of the evening, she heard the whole world singing in a new key: "Now the world and I were met together in the happiest conjunction. Never had I felt so befriended." Maurice, on the other hand, was traumatized by the same view: "I felt its void, a primeval space before concrete form began to take shape. It not only failed to stimulate my powerful sense of form, the absence was like an ache that made me feel empty myself."[13]

Mabel was undaunted by the fact that there were no accommodations to be had and insisted that she be taken, by flashlight, to the one man in town who might be persuaded to rent them space. On January 1, 1918, she signed a lease for the back rooms in the largest house in town. It was owned by an English remittance man, a Mr. Manby, who had settled in Taos with the idea of creating a country estate for himself, and whose paranoid nature was soon to create a great deal of trouble for Mabel and Maurice.

Mabel was not impressed with the town of Taos. It was a frontier community of about 2,000 people; its center, a dilapidated green enclosed by a crumbling adobe wall; its shops and stores bearing the marks of its status as a crossroads for traders. On a typical day, one could see there homesteaders in covered wagons on their way farther west; Spanish-American farmers bringing their crops to market; and Indians on ponies. The town did not yet have gas or oil heat, not to speak of electricity or street lamps, and fuel deliveries were made by burros loaded down with wood. Mabel was soon to find the townspeople quarrelsome and difficult and local society without much to recommend it: "There was no foundation to anything, no rights, no roots, and no security. . . . There was no law, no reverence, and very little beauty of living."[14]

Manby's behavior certainly contributed to Mabel's estimate. He was convinced that Mabel and Maurice were German spies, probably because of Sterne's name and his accent. His suspicions were further aroused when Andrew Dasburg arrived in mid-January, for he and Maurice often discussed the course of the war in Europe, and neither was unsympathetic to Germany. For a period of several weeks, Manby overheard their conversations by climbing on the roof and listening down the chimney. In the early spring, he reported their "traitorous" activities to a federal agent in Albuquerque, who subsequently came up to Taos to investigate them. He informed Mabel: "You are suspected of pro-German activities. It is said you are receiving arms and ammunition almost weekly in large boxes and storing them in your house [Mabel's possessions shipped from New York]; that one member of your family is going among the Mexican population and enrolling them [Dasburg was buying santos and Mexican and Indian blankets]; that you, lady, are inciting the Indians to rise" [Mabel was spending a great deal of time at the pueblo].[15]

If Mabel's reputation had preceded her, one could understand how the government agent might have been convinced that she was capable of arranging an invasion of the United States from Mexico. But given her relative anonymity in that part of the country at the time, the charges were but one more example of the repressive atmosphere created by an America at war to make the world safe for democracy. Not only were Mabel and Maurice harassed, but the cook that Andrew had brought for them, Mr. Seebach, was abducted by a self-appointed vigilante group who suspected him because of his German name. In April, Mabel decided it was time to use her connections. She wrote for help to George Creel, an old friend from her prewar salon days, who was now the head of the Committee on Public Information (the propaganda arm of the federal government that was helping to spread anti-German hysteria). Creel assured her that she could use his name to clear her, since he had every confidence in her loyalty.

On April 21, Mabel wrote Neith Hapgood a marvelous rendition of the absurd side of her new life: "We are in the maddest, most amusing country in the world—in the freakiest—most insane village you ever dreamed of & I would like to stay forever! . . . We live in a pink adobe house built like a hollow square owned by a mad Englishman. . . . We have been considered queer, then mysterious, then dangerous—& we were finally 'investigated.' . . . We were *so* queer that they thought we were German agents importing dynamite! . . . Life is like one long comic opera—with the most exaggerated costumes & colors, & impossible scenery and sunsets."[16]

This was actually the more mundane side of Mabel's existence in Taos during her first four months. Alongside the mad Englishman and the provincial villagers was another Taos that she discovered at the Indian pueblo just north of town. Here was a garden of Eden inhabited by an unfallen tribe of men and women who were the true possessors of the landscape she had loved at first sight. Mabel was immediately smitten. Where Maurice found the Taos Indians dirty, smelly, and lazy, she found them holy. Not long after they settled into the Manby house, Mabel began to visit the pueblo and to invite small groups of Taos Indians to drum, sing, and dance at her home.

Mabel chose the Pueblo Indians as her saviors for the very reasons Maurice had foreseen. They were the complete antithesis to herself and to both the materialistic world she grew up in and the chaotic world of new freedoms in which she had matured. For most of her life she had expressed a Dionysian drive to experience and devour all forms of life, in her frantic search to connect with something larger than her solitary ego. Over a thousand years old, Pueblo culture was one of timeless and stable values that maintained a highly integrated personal and tribal life-style. While there are important social and cultural differences among the twenty-two tribes, which range from eastern New Mexico to western Arizona, the ideal personality type has been described as Apollonian. Courteous, yielding, and generous, they are expected to avoid any semblance of personal authority or interest in personal possession. Anthropologists have noted the remarkable congruence between Pueblo behavioral norms and their everyday lives.[17]

Pueblo cosmology pictures a universe in which man, woman, and nature, body and spirit, cooperate in a "balanced, co-relative interdependence." Ritual, social, and political activities are "geared to harmonize man's relations with spirits and to insure the desired cyclical changes will continue to come about in nature." All their ceremonials are practiced to ensure this goal, including their fertility rituals, which are devoid of any specific sexual symbolism. Within this universe, there are no abstract concepts for time and space as Westerners understand them. The Pueblos measure time by the cyclical calendar that governs agriculture and space by reference to specific places, such as the sacred mountains that mark the boundaries of their physical world or the earth "navels" in the village centers that mark the place of their original emergence from the underworld.[18]

Mabel witnessed her first Pueblo dance at Santo Domingo, a pueblo south of Santa Fe, on Christmas day, 1917, about a month before she met Tony Luhan. In her memoirs, it is her first epiphany:

> For the first time in my life, I heard the voice of the One coming from the Many—I who until then had been taught to look for the wonders of infinite divisibility and variety, for the many in the one, the elaboration and detail of a broken infinity. . . .
>
> The more singleness, separateness, and individuality become the habit of our development (so that everywhere everybody was breaking away from old patterns of social and family life), the more ways there were of escaping mechanically . . . the by-product of scientific conquest was become the elaborate, unhappy, modern man, cut off from his source. . . . The living sacrifice of his scientific knowledge. . . .
>
> The singular raging lust for individuality and separateness had been impelling me all my years as it did everyone else on earth—when all of a sudden I was brought up against the Tribe, . . . where virtue lay in wholeness instead of in dismemberment.[19]

The Pueblos offered Mabel what no advanced twentieth-century society was able to: an integration of personality that was achieved through an organic connection between the individual and the community, work and living space, play and art. All were rooted in "a living religion that had its source in love." Mabel was also attracted by their celebration of a life-force which transcended the sexual passions that she felt had always trapped her in a limited and disordering sensuality. Earth Mother and Sun Father were cosmic dualities who represented the dichotomy of instinct and spirit she was already familiar with. But among the Pueblos they were both equally powerful, equally worshipped, and equally necessary to the continuance and health of human and natural life. The fact that Mabel rarely differentiated between male and female when she talked about the Pueblos was at least partly due to the essentially androgynous psychology she associated with them. "We are all," as the Tiwa said, "in one nest."[20]

The particular community that Mabel encountered was one of the most conservative among the Pueblos. The Tiwa had a long and proud history of staving off the onslaughts of other cultural groups during the 600-year tenure of their adobe village. Although they had borrowed elements of Plains Indian and Spanish cultures during that time, their religious and social practices had not changed markedly. The Taos Indians were first "discovered" by one of Coronado's men, Captain Alvarado, on his quest for the Seven Cities of Cibola, the mythical realm of gold which incited Spanish exploration and conquest throughout the Southwest. In 1680, the Pueblo leader Popé staged a revolt against Spanish rule, using Taos as his base of operations. He managed to kill or remove all the Spanish from northern New Mexico during his twelve-year reign, until the Spanish reconquered the region. By the eighteenth century, Taos had become a major trading center for Indians and Spanish, from the Great Plains to the Pacific. In 1847, the Taos were involved in another uprising. This time they assassinated the American governor, who had been put in charge during the U.S. war with Mexico. In 1922, Taos would rise again (with the help of Mabel and her activist friends), to unite the Pueblo tribes in an effort to save their lands from the depredations of Anglo and Hispanic settlers.

Taos's multistoried adobes, rising against the backdrop of the Sangre de Cristos, have earned it the reputation as the most beautiful of the pueblos. It has called forth a profound response from an array of writers, artists, and social scientists who have visited there, many at Mabel's behest. It has been particularly attractive to Jungians, including Jung himself, who have found in Tiwa dance and ritual the manifestations of "prehistoric" archetypes whose recovery they believed would benefit modern men and women. So Mabel had responded to the Christmas dance at Santo Domingo, an experience which she had the opportunity to reinforce in Taos on January 1. The date on which the Tiwa celebrate the emergence of their ancestors from the world below was also, appropriately, the date on which she officially began her new life in Taos.

As the first light of the frozen dawn tips the peak of the sacred mountains, the men come forth from their kivas (the underground ceremonial chambers) just as their ancestors emerged in the cold dawn of life on earth. Moving in silence between the snow banks toward the open plaza in the often near zero weather, they are naked, except for their breechcloths. The dancers are painted white on one side (for water) and brown on the other (for earth). Hunched over with large painted mouths, they represent the giant turtles who crawled out of the waters onto dry land.

When the men reach the plaza, the sacred center of the village, they begin their dance of life in the growing light of the day.[21]

As Mabel became more familiar with the tribe, and mixed more in tribal affairs, she learned that rivalry, jealousy, and dissension, as well as personal and family assertion, were also part of the Tiwa's social dynamic—a dynamic that she sometimes helped to aggravate. But in the beginning, in the first euphoric months that she spent among them, peace and harmony reigned. She was determined to become as much like a Pueblo as possible and began by having her son John cut off the long brown hair she had worn in rings about her ears. She sported a Dutch bob so that she would look more Indian, wrapped herself in shawls, and spent several hours a day among the Tiwa women, trying to absorb their warmth and ease by imitating their orderly and soft-spoken ways. "I knew I could arrive at this unconscious, full equilibrium, but that I could only do so by adapting myself. I longed simply to *be* so, as they were. . . ."[22]

Tony Luhan

Mabel was particularly taken with Antonio Luhan, a majestically handsome Tiwa who Maurice soon sensed was a rival. On one of her first trips out to the pueblo after the new year, Mabel met Candelaria, Tony's wife, who was standing outside their home smiling and beckoning her to enter. She was a beautiful woman, dressed in a full skirt, red belt, and white embroidered petticoat, and she radiated a warm content that immediately attracted Mabel. She, Maurice, and John entered a large, empty room with bare white walls and a sweet-smelling piñon fire. There they saw a tall man bent over his drum, singing in a low murmur. When the song was over and he looked up, Mabel recognized the noble face that had blotted out Maurice's in her New York dream.

Luhan was an imposing figure. Over six feet tall and somewhat portly, his broad shoulders and leonine head gave him the look of an ancient pharaoh, particularly when he was wrapped in his sheet or blanket. (Ansel Adams would capture this image in two stunning photographs.) Mabel soon discovered that Tony was as solid emotionally as he was physically, and of just the right temperament, as she put it, to cure her of her epoch. She invited him to come and play his drum at her home throughout the winter and spring.

In his own quiet, but persistent way, Luhan pursued Mabel, throughout the spring and summer. He took her on tours of the countryside, to other Indian villages and dances, and talked to her in his limited English about the Pueblo way of life. Mabel claims that their relationship was purely platonic through August, that Tony was her spiritual guide and friend. In May she learned one of her most important lessons. When Tony brought her two wild pink roses, the first of the season, Mabel unthinkingly tossed them aside. Although he was deeply hurt, he said nothing at the time. Two weeks later, he reminded Mabel what she had done with his flowers. She witnessed his hurt and "felt for the first time in my life another person's pain and perhaps this was the instant of my birth, certainly the awakening of a heart asleep since childhood."

Luhan's unceasing kindness and unspoken love did for her what no other man was able to. As mother-father and soon-to-be-lover, he "saw me into being." Mabel's acknowledgment of his feelings was the moment of her conversion experience: "As I stood there facing Tony when he spoke to me, perhaps it was only an instant in time, yet I was by grace born in that flash as I should have been years, years ago; inducted into the new world." No longer would Mabel be the psychic octopus who grabbed at anything she wanted and stuffed it into what Edwin Dodge had called her "insatiable maw."[23]

Mabel's euphoria was not shared by her son and husband, of course. Maurice and John both felt keenly her increasing physical and emotional withdrawal, not just during the hours she spent at the pueblo, but also when she returned, wrapped up in her shawls and secretive Mona Lisa smile, distant and apart even when she was in the same room. The more time that she spent with Tony, the more Mabel felt that Maurice was a "dry well" from whom she could derive little nourishment. Although she was pleased that she had accomplished her mission to turn him to sculpting—he was working on the heads of two Indians at the pueblo throughout the spring—she had lost interest in his career.

Mabel came to new life in May in a sudden burst like the onset of spring in Taos valley. During the summer months, she settled down to a "gentle organic growth," which reminded her of the fullness of being she had known when pregnant with John. Tony continued to make her realize how insensitive she had been, employing her so-called sensitivity in self rather than in fellow-feeling. It was not that they conversed a great deal; in fact, most of their time was spent in shared silence, a very new experience for Mabel. Mabel felt that she was ready to give up everything— nationality and income included—to become part of his world. The kind of companionship and love that Tony offered her would, she hoped, "finally overcome all the conditioning of the years gone by, and all the crystallizations of heredity and environment" that neither Freudian psychoanalysis nor all the prayers of Divine Science could heal: "It was the Indian life I was entering, very slowly, a step at a time. I was becoming acquainted with a kind of living I didn't know existed anywhere. I had heard, of course, of the Golden Age, and of the Elysian fields, but they had only been words to me. Now I found out what they meant."[24]

Under Luhan's influence, Mabel began to give away her possessions. He told her that Indians could not have "things," that only white people could. One day, he cautioned, the white people would be buried under all their possessions; the wheel of power would turn, and the Indians' turn come next. He taught her that the white man's religion was "machinery," while the Indians' was "Life." Mabel adopted his theory of the crush of mechanical civilization as the basis of her primitivist credo: "like cold flies at the end of the solar year, crawling separately up the frigid, unfriendly walls of our cooling spiritual universe. . . . We have reached the last outpost of the warm and loving world of our kind of relationships. . . . We will give out and fall to the floor of the world and be swept away."[25]

In a clearly autobiographical story that she wrote in 1920, Mabel described the deformed creature she had been before encountering Tony Luhan and Pueblo life: "It had given her a feeling of being more alive to wrestle with people like an artist does with his clay; she had assimilated a great deal in this way . . . the essential significances of art and of philosophy, of anarchy, of political concoctions, of psychology. . . . Sometimes, adding to herself, she deprived the other of his portion. He could only be reckoned the loser, and turned adrift, metaphorically marked 'empty'!"[26] Thus, Mabel believed, had a power-based, Anglo civilization produced individuals who lived by their wills: the men seeking to master the earth, the women seeking to master men.

Sterne had planned to go back East in August, but he was chagrined when Mabel encouraged his departure. He knew that something was developing between her and Tony; yet he was growing to care for her more just at a time when he had become totally dependent on her financially. Maurice claimed that Mabel and Tony became lovers in June, when he parked his teepee on their lawn and came each night to serenade her. Mabel sneaked out to join him in his tent, where they presumably made love. Infuriated by her behavior, Maurice decided to play cowboy to Tony's Indian. He borrowed a gun from the grimly gleeful Manby but was afraid to use it. One night, when Mabel returned early from her usual tryst, he accused her of going to bed "without your nightcap." Mabel ordered him to leave the next day. He went north to a mining camp in nearby Twining to complete his heads and returned to New York in August. Maurice had done the bust of a beautiful Indian girl, Albidia, in some haste, however. When he opened the crate in New York, he discovered that the wax mold was melting. He decided to finish the job—and finish Mabel symbolically at the same time—by hacking the head to pieces with a hatchet.

Mabel claimed that she and Tony did not become lovers until Maurice left to go back East. Only then, she says in her memoirs, were she and Tony free to confront each other openly for the first time about their love. When she told him that he would make her own kind of life impossible for her, he promised to give her "a new life, a new world—a true one, I think." That same day, he informed her that he would come to the teepee in the evening and wait for her. Their spiritual communion would, at last, be fittingly consummated by physical union. "'Yes, Tony,' Mabel said, 'that will be right.' And it was right."[27]

During the nine-month period of her gestation and rebirth, which is as far as Mabel carried her published memoirs, there is no doubt that her sense of well-being was as rich and full as she claimed. For a time, Mabel entered as far as she was able into the life cycle of the Pueblos. She did not rush or force this new growth of feeling but allowed it to unfold gently. But her break with the white world and her sanctification of the Indian were only a part of the truth she continued to live. Even though she had sent Maurice away, she was not yet ready to give him up. When he left in August, she wrote to him that they still meant "a lot to each other spiritually."[28] In future letters, she continued to assume that he would return to Taos. When he mentioned the possibility of divorce the following spring, Mabel was upset and implied that she would stop his monthly support check of $100 if he carried through with it. She kept him on a "retainer" until December 1922, when the divorce she granted him came through.

Luhan's relationship with Mabel was also complicated by factors that Mabel never publicly acknowledged. Their affair created friction at the pueblo, which Mabel tried to resolve by signing a contract that guaranteed Tony's wife Candelaria $35.00 per month for life in exchange for her not interfering with them. But the friction grew worse after their marriage in April 1923. Because intermarriage was forbidden by tribal law, Tony had to give up his participation in kiva ceremonies. He did, however, retain his position on the Tribal Council, the governing body made up of the heads of various societies that met to decide on issues of importance to tribal welfare. Tony continued to be influential in tribal matters, partly as a result of his connections through Mabel with men and women who had political clout.[29]

Some of the changes that Luhan underwent after he went to live with Mabel were not in keeping with the pristine image of him she always created for public consumption. When they became lovers, Tony began to wear very expensive riding boots and tailored pants, clothing that was not normally allowed in the pueblo. He also gained a tremendous affection for cars; one of his favorite activities was to act as guide and interpreter for the famous guests that Mabel brought to Taos, whom he carried about in her Cadillac. Just as Tony was not always enough intellectually for Mabel, she was not always enough sexually for him. During the 1920s, he sometimes returned to the pueblo to sleep with his first wife; in the 1930s he had an Anglo mistress for a time in Carmel; and in the 1940s and 1950s, he kept a Hispanic mistress at one of his ranches. Nevertheless, it is clear from all the accounts of Mabel's friends who came to know and respect him that he not only loved her unreservedly, but that he also maintained many of the most admirable qualities of Pueblo culture.

Los Gallos

Their relationship went through a number of serious crises, in the main precipitated by Mabel. But the deeper bond between them lasted for both their lifetimes. Tony began to cement that bond by building Mabel what she felt was her first real home. In May 1918 he encouraged her to buy twelve acres of beautiful meadow, orchard, and high land bounded on two sides by Indian fields. On June 22, Mabel signed the deed that transferred the land and the small three-room adobe from Manuel Trujillo to herself for $1,500.

Luhan supervised the Mexican and Indian work crew who built the additions. While he worked on the structure, Mabel designed the interior. It displayed the many worlds she had known within the rooted context of the adobe shelter that defined her new world view. Unlike the Villa Curonia, which was largely a stage setting for the various melodramas and shifting personae Mabel enacted, or 23 Fifth Avenue, much of whose decor denied the modern world it came to represent, Mabel's Taos estate integrated the elements of her past and present into a harmonious whole. The architectural historian Bainbridge Bunting has pointed out "the way in which these disparate elements and inspirations have been fused into a harmonious design by the builder."[30]

For Mabel, "building this house was more than constructing a dwelling, it was embodying a myth of creation," and self-creation as well. Her description of the making of the adobe was an analogue to her own transformation:

> Working with the earth was a noble occupation. To loosen it and make the adobe bricks, mixing the wheat straw from last year's harvest with it thoughtfully, laying them in rows to dry while the rock foundation is being built, and then fitting them carefully upon each other with the rich dark mud between that will turn hard as stone, all of it is a sacred matter, for the wonder of creation is in it, the wonder of transformation which always seems of greatest significance to Indians. To take the living earth from under their feet, undifferentiated and unformed, and shape it into a house. . . . Money has very little to do with all this.[31]

Throughout the summer, the adobe shapes emerged from and blended into the landscape of chamisa, sage, and low hills. The first room built was the "Big Room," two large rectangular areas with fireplaces. The ceiling was fitted with cedar saplings, layered with sweet clover and sage to spread the wet mud on, the inside and outside world continually intermingling. Mabel furnished the room with French, Italian, and Oriental sofas and chairs whose pale greys and yellows were accented with bright magenta and emerald green pillows. Indian blankets hung on the white washed walls and Mexican santos decorated the mantel pieces. Always in the room, there was the fragrant smell of flowers: sweet peas, roses, and bowls of gladioli.

The Big Room and the bedroom above it, where Mabel slept, formed a wing, and Tony and Mabel decided to build a portal that sheltered the other rooms that they connected. Mabel stained the cut edges of the seasoned lumber they used with a mixture of her own invention. The noted Pueblo artist Awa Tsireh painted a striking mural on one wall, and Mabel used tiles made by William Henderson to decorate another. The roof sported brightly colored ceramic chickens that she bought in Mexico which gave the estate its name, Los Gallos. Most impressive was the dining room, which they built a few years later. Reminiscent of the Villa Curonia, the room led down from the Big Room with five round, tiled steps in a larger room, whose floor was laid with burnt sienna and black tiles that were made by William Penhallow Henderson who worked at the house. The room was graced with long French windows and a ceiling painted in earth colors and striped to look like an Indian blanket. In the center of the room was a heavy oak table surrounded by handsomely carved studded leather chairs.

Mabel added a large kitchen onto the dining area whose windows took advantage of the sunlight, as did every room where she could capture light. Male guests took their breakfast there, seated at a large table covered with bright blue oilcloth that stood beside the huge wood-burning stove. Women guests often breakfasted in bed.

In 1921, Mabel built a sun porch as a third story above her bedroom. There she could lie on a serape on the bare, bright blue floor and view the sacred Pueblo mountain to the north and the mountains in Colorado to the east (later she enclosed the room with glazed windows). By the mid-1920s, Mabel could look out over five guesthouses that were spread about the common meadows, her corrals, stables, barns, and a 1,200-foot gatehouse where her staff of servants lived. The main house surrounded a magnificent courtyard, which was itself surrounded by massive adobe gates that incorporated the hand-carved balcony of a Taos church a friend had salvaged. She enjoyed electricity and indoor plumbing, thanks to her son John's installation of a private generator and pump. At the edge of the courtyard ran the stream from the pueblo, shaded by willows and straddled by a hammock for reading on hot summer days. By the time that Mabel's estate was completed, in the early 1930s, the main house had grown to seventeen rooms, was 450 feet in length, and had over 8,400 square feet of living space.

Mabel's expanding domain matched her expanding visions, which began to develop during the first year that she and Tony lived together. From the simple paradise in the humble adobe house that she left us with at the end of her memoirs, her dreams took on a cosmic dimension that made the new worlds she toyed with in her Fifth Avenue salon seem modest by comparison.

It started, as always, because Mabel could not sit still and continue to enjoy the contentment that the summer months had brought her. As Dorothy Brett (and many other friends) noted, Mabel was "born bored." If nothing was happening, she would feel compelled to stir something up. It was not enough that Tony loved her and that he had compromised his position at the pueblo to become her lover, helpmate, and spiritual advisor. She had to *know* what made him the way he was. She had to "penetrate" his serene demeanor and discover the "secret" of Indian life so it would be hers. As early as her first tribal epiphany, Mabel had sensed the possibility that she might always remain an outsider: "They [the Indians] did not exclude us. They did not have to: we were, in reality, not THERE where they were. We did not know what they knew, nor experience their mystical communion which was as natural and inevitable as the communion between the cells of the body. . . . No, lonely atoms like us could never participate in their rich, shared companioned being."[32]

Once she and Tony started living together, Mabel was convinced he could give her the key that would unlock the door to such communion permanently. There wasn't any key, of course, although there was much to be learned from Pueblo life, and Luhan taught her as much as he was able to. But he was absolutely forbidden by tribal law to reveal to her any of the specific elements of his religion and ritual obligations. In fact, the Tiwa were among the most secretive of the Pueblo tribes in terms of what they were allowed to reveal to outsiders. When the anthropologist Elsie Clews Parsons wrote a monograph on them, after spending two summers in Taos in 1923 and 1924, the furor of the tribe rose to such a height that the publisher could not release it west of the Mississippi.[33]

Mabel would not accept the fact that Tony could not give her what she wanted. When she refused to stop pressuring him over the following winter and spring with her prying and domineering will, violent scenes ensued that were often followed by Tony's going off in the middle of the night. Mabel was certain he was meeting a secret lover and became hysterically jealous. In her story, "An Intimation," she revealed how the nine-month rebirth her heroine (Martia) experienced gave way to the regressive behavior that almost destroyed her relationship with her Indian lover (José). Her attempts to probe the "mystical core" of his "secret" began to "poison her in her Garden" and diminish the first "ardor of living" she had learned from him. When José suggested she go back East for a while in the spring to visit with her old friends, Martia acquiesced.[34]

Big House, Los Gallos, Taos.

Dining room, Big House, Los Gallos.

Taos pueblo, 1920. (Photo by Burt Harwood, courtesy of the Harwood Foundation, Taos.)

Mabel Dodge (Sterne?) in Taos, c. 1917. Tony Luhan, c. 1920.

162

Tony Luhan, c. 1929. (Photo by Ansel Adams.)

Tony Luhan and John Evans, 1918.

Paradise Regained

Mabel returned to New York in April 1919 in the hope that the separation would help her find some perspective on her life with Tony. When a friend of hers took her to visit Mrs. Lotus Dudley, an occultist, she found what she was seeking. Mrs. Dudley informed Mabel that there has existed, since the earliest known civilization, a secret doctrine that has been kept alive throughout the ages by being transmitted through certain races. This doctrine, which was now in the possession of the Pueblo Indians, was the psychic key to Nirvana on earth. "Taos," she told Mabel, "is the beating heart of the world." Her next revelation was even more startling. When the time for transmission of this secret was ripe, "a bridge will be needed between the Indian and white people, and you have been chosen to be that bridge." Taos was to become the center of a new birth for Western civilization, and "the great souls will be drawn there."

Without her knowledge, Mabel had been specifically guided and prepared to be sent to Taos for the purpose of seeing in the millennium: "You are not to fail," Mrs. Dudley warned, "for there is a cosmic purpose you are to fulfill. . . ." But only if she gave up her destructive, "indefatigable human will." When Mabel returned to Taos, she told Tony about what had transpired with Mrs. Dudley. He told her that the Indians were indeed taking care of the sun, water, and earth, and that they prayed daily for white people. Mabel "now felt a new significance in her life. . . . Was she not specially prepared for some great cosmic purpose?"[35]

Mabel needed no further convincing. Taos was the place and postwar America the time to institute a revitalization of American life. Her alliance with Tony Luhan was a messianic "bridge between cultures" that would serve as the model. The Indian's blood consciousness, rooted in the verities of nature, would merge with the cerebral consciousness of the white woman, who would articulate the ancient traditions in terms that would effectively persuade modern men and women. Like other immigrants who have apotheosized their dreams of settlement in America, Mabel hoped to bring the "elect" of her Old World—Europe and the East—to her newfound land. In a major reversal of mainstream Anglo conventions, however, she did not celebrate the bringing of the Christian God's light to the heathen. In her eschatology, it was the white man who was the devil and the Indian who was godly and from whom the white man would receive his redemption.[36]

Mabel wasted no time in calling the "great souls" who Mrs. Dudley told her would come to Taos. She worked actively over the next two decades to make Taos "a city upon a hill" and her home the center of a new world plan. Here she would gather disciples in all fields to help her spread a gospel that would redefine and transvalue the society and culture of Anglo America.

Mabel began to advertise the merits of Taos even before she received Dudley's prophecy, in fact almost as soon as she settled there. Her last column for the Hearst papers, published on February 8, 1918, was the first essay to set out the terms for the mythic utopia she would spend the next twenty years promoting to regional and national audiences. At Taos pueblo, Mabel informed her readers, everyone had enough to eat and plenty of time to sing and dance. The Indians were good-humored and cheerful, the air vital and invigorating. The Anglos who settled there loved life for its own sake, unlike materialistic New Yorkers who lived in order to make money. She invited artists who could not make a living in the East to come to New Mexico and "start over."

Shortly after her arrival in Taos, Mabel had told Maurice that if other people actually knew what was there, they would come and destroy it. Taos was a fragile paradise that could easily be despoiled through too much publicity and economic exploitation. Yet Mabel was faced with a curious dilemma. If it was to become a center for reeducating white America, white America had to know about it, and if she was going to have success in preserving the Indian way of life, she would need a national constituency. At one point, Mabel succumbed to some of the same confusion of values that has been part of the myth-making about America since its European discovery. When she wrote Arthur Brisbane in April 1918, trying to lure him to Taos because of the power he wielded through the press, she used language that Cabeza de Vaca and John Smith would have no trouble recognizing. She promised him mountains filled with gold, copper mines, radium springs, and reminded him that the "old world" of the East was subject to "plagues, panics," and germ infestations. She addressed him "in the name of all pioneers and master builders" and told him that he "could put Taos on the *map*," while acquiring a large fortune for his family. Luckily for Mabel and the Pueblos, Brisbane declined her offer, for his attitude toward Indians did not differ much from General George Custer's.[37]

It was Mable who "put Taos on the map," as her friend the art critic Henry McBride insisted some years later. But she did not do it by promoting the exploitation of its human and natural resources. Her appeals were typically to the aesthetic, emotional, and spiritual needs of her modernist friends, who responded to the spirit of place for much the same reasons that she did. Although she never achieved her more utopian goals, it was in good part due to her that Taos served as "a fabulous honeycomb, irresistible and nourishing," to artists, writers, and social activists for over forty years.[38]

The first artists to discover Taos were Ernest Blumenschein and Bert Phillips, who formed the basis for the Taos Society of Artists, along with

Joseph Sharp, Oscar Berninghaus, Walter Ufer, and Victor Higgins. Phillips and Blumenschein had started out on a sketching trip in 1898 from Denver and lost one of their wagon wheels twenty miles north of Taos. The story has come down, and is celebrated each July during fiesta, that Blumenschein mounted his horse with the broken wheel and rode to Taos. Impressed with the people and surrounding beauty, he decided to settle there. Within a few years, he and Phillips were joined by others whose realistic and romanticized paintings of the Indians and Spanish-Americans, and of the landscape became widely known, especially after the Santa Fe railroad began to use them in its national advertising campaigns. Mabel may, in fact, have seen some of their work before she went out to Santa Fe, because the Taos Society had a show in New York in 1917.[39]

The Taos Society were primarily representational illustrators who were untouched by modernism. It was Mabel who "changed the direction of Taos painting" with her telegram to Andrew Dasburg. Dasburg got over the trauma of his car trip to Taos within twenty-four hours of his arrival. On January 14, his second day there, he sent his wife his awe-struck impressions: "The clearing day had all the crystalline clarity and brilliance of light that is like a vibrant tinkling icyness of sound. In the hard transparency of the sky were fractured stretches of clouds, their shapes vanishing into the blue, while over the distant ranges was a turbulence of clouds in storm tearing against the peaks."[40]

Dasburg's portraits of Mabel had helped to establish him as "one of the true leaders of the avant-garde" during the prewar period. Her summons to Taos once again influenced his career, this time resulting in a revitalization of his art: "Under the influence of the southwestern landscape," his biographer has pointed out, "his pictorial language ripened and his philosophy of life deepened. The elemental majesty and power of nature became the primary focus of his artistic expression. Pure form and color were subordinated to the task of measuring the land and people of New Mexico in pictorial terms quite different from, though related to, his abstract work."[41]

At about the same time that Hemingway was attempting to create a verbal analogue to Cézanne's landscapes in *The Sun Also Rises,* Dasburg was returning to that paradoxical father of modernism, who took liberties with "reality" in order to uncover permanence. Cézanne had probed for the timeless, geometric solidities that he believed underlay the shifting face of nature, seeking to fix forever the "appleness" of apples in his patient, disciplined work to achieve harmony of form and color. It was just this kind of permanence for which Hemingway strove in his generic landscapes of "the abiding earth" and which Eliot discovered in the ancient myths that offer the only solace in *The Wasteland.* In 1920, when he first began spending his winters in Taos, Dasburg wrote Mabel about the way in which Taos fulfilled his spiritual hunger. His sentiment expresses the   167 quest of other expatriates, in Europe and the Southwest, during the postwar decade:

> Taos is the setting that can still in us the confusion that so often gathers there. Taos has the quality of a place in which . . . to find God. In Taos one could create the condition, the form of discipline, that is like the tuning of an instrument of harmony; which we must be to receive and give ourselves the power of the mystic.[42]

Almost from the first, Dasburg brought students back with him to share his experience. Later in the decade Cather and O'Keeffe would also find in the land and peoples of northern New Mexico the objective correlatives for their aesthetic and spiritual visions.

At the end of May, the English portrait painter Jack Young-Hunter arrived in Taos, soon to take root and settle for life. The romance of the American West had stirred his imagination from boyhood, when he devoured stories of explorers and trappers on the Oregon and Santa Fe trails. Like Dorothy Brett, who accompanied D. H. Lawrence to Taos in 1924, he was indelibly marked by his childhood visit to Buffalo Bill's Wild West Show in London. Young-Hunter wanted to start life anew, in a place where artistic traditions and influences did not exist. He arrived with a letter of introduction to Bert Phillips, who took him to a dinner party at Mabel's. Tony Luhan sized him up, asked him if he wanted a house, and within a few days, Young-Hunter owned the land that bordered the property soon to be Mabel's. There he built himself a Renaissance banquet hall for a studio, with Spanish wrought-iron grilles, Venetian glass chandeliers, and a musicians' balcony, to which he brought his wealthy clientele. He continued to paint in the tradition of Sargeant and became one of the few derivative artists who were part of Mabel's circle.

In June 1918, Marsden Hartley arrived and stayed through the late fall. Mabel had not seen him since she had refused duty as his caretaker at Finney Farm in 1916. When Leo Stein arrived in November, he tried to convince Hartley to settle in Taos, but Hartley did not agree with Stein's assessment that here was "the only landscape . . . where Nature is as aesthetic as Art; the only landscape that can compete with the great painters." Hartley's response was closer to Maurice Sterne's; he was traumatized by what he felt was emptiness. When he returned to Germany after his visit to Mabel's, he painted his recollections of New Mexico as a way of exorcising the trauma he experienced there.[43] But Hartley was one of the few who received Mabel's call that did not succumb. That summer Leon Gaspard also came to Taos. A Russian artist who had lived among the avant-garde leaders in Paris during the prewar period, he was

a literal refugee from the war, during which he was shot down as a fighter pilot for the French. He sought and found his peace in Taos, where he settled permanently.

By 1925, the new art colony that Mabel helped to create in Taos was making news nationally, although the most famous artists were yet to come. Writing for the *New York Times Book Review* in December of that year, Elida Sims spoke of Taos as "the garden of Allah in the New World; an oasis of twentieth-century culture in a vast desert of primitive nature." The New York galleries, she noted, counted on the yearly showing of Taos and Santa Fe artists as among their most important exhibitions.[44]

Mary Austin

The most important literary personage to visit Mabel in her first two years in Taos later became her chief rival for the title of regent of New Mexico. Mary Austin had been among the circle of radicals who frequented Mabel's salon in Greenwich Village, although she had never really been one of them. She had spent much of her young womanhood in the deserts of central California and, at the turn of the century, was one of the founders of the bohemian colony of artists and writers at Carmel, which included Ambrose Bierce and Jack London. She was an established nature writer and partisan of Indian culture long before she arrived in New York. A willful, awkward, and imperious woman, she had to struggle to make her own way as a writer of essays and short fiction in order to support a sickly husband and their severely retarded daughter.

During her lifetime, Austin published thirty-two books and over two hundred and fifty articles. At the time Mabel first met her in 1913, she had already established her reputation in the East and in Europe, with her desert landscape classic, *The Land of Little Rain* (1903), and with her publication of Paiute Indian legends. In New York she enlisted herself in support of women's suffrage and birth control through writing and lecturing. It is possible that Austin provided Mabel with her first knowledge of Indians since she also lectured in Greenwich Village on the early stages of human society, focusing on Indian tribes of the West. In her memoirs, she mentions lecturing at Mabel's salon and says it was one of the few times when she was living in New York that she found an audience to whom she could express her interest in folk theater and folk arts.[45]

Like Mabel, Mary was a mystic. She too had had a painful and lonely childhood, which she had learned to deal with by splitting her personality. There was "I-Mary," as she called her, the young woman who walked apart from others and did as she pleased by creating her own private world of thought and deed. And there was "Mary-by-Herself," the good daughter and dutiful wife who did what she was expected to do. Early in her life, Mary came to believe in a "Voice" or "Presence," like Mabel's "IT," who

169

worked through her. She was fascinated by strong female folk figures, like the "chisera," or medicine woman of the Paiute Indians, the heroine of her play *The Arrow Maker* (1911). The chisera is required to be celibate in order to use her sexual powers to promote fertility for the tribe and comes to a tragic end when she breaks her vow to become the lover of a young warrior. The conflict her heroine suffers between her desire for human love and the power and status she holds when she keeps herself apart from men is one that Mary shared with Mabel. Unlike Mabel, however, whom she chastised for not doing her own work, Mary used this power for herself.[46]

Austin arrived in Taos in March 1919, just in time to see the Penitente procession on Good Friday, which reenacts Christ's route to Calvary with a literalness that includes flagellation. Shortly after, she returned to Santa Fe, where she was hired by the Carnegie Foundation to do a survey of conditions in the pueblos of northern New Mexico. Four years later she accompanied the Santa Fe artist Gerald Cassidy and his wife on a sketching trip through the Rio Grande Valley. The trip convinced her to set her life on a new path: "More than anything else [my life] lacked pattern, and I had a pattern-hungry mind. I liked the feel of roots, of ordered growth and progression, continuity, all of which I found in the Southwest."[47]

Like Mabel, Mary found New Mexico a place where she could finally be at home. Although she did not settle permanently until 1924, it took her very little time to decide that she, too, would devote much of her life's energy to the cause of preserving and celebrating the native cultures of the Southwest. She obviously realized that there was not room for two chiseras in Taos, and so settled in Santa Fe, where she could often be seen "crowned with queenly braids, wrapped in a Spanish shawl, enthroned on the bootblack's stand in the Chamber of Commerce." Her long, sometimes stormy relationship with Mabel was marked, as she later noted, by "little consenting approval" but much "genuine friendship." With Tony, she had no problems. She appreciated his kindness and marveled at his excellence as a guide and companion on trips throughout the region. She believed that Tony had so mastered the machine he drove that he had absorbed its mechanisms into the rhythms of Indian life: "Tony puts the car on, and when he begins, as he does usually, to sing the accentless melodies of his people which fit so perfectly to the unaccented rhythms of the machine, one has the sensation of sailing on the magic carpet along the floor of space."[48]

In spite of their personality clashes, Austin shared most of Mabel's ideals and activities. Both women played an important role, for example, in preserving Indian and Spanish crafts and establishing their value by gaining them national recognition. In the month she arrived in Taos, Mabel began to travel with Tony and Dasburg all over Taos County collecting native blankets and pottery from the Indians and furniture and santos from the Hispanic population. (Santos were carved figures of saints that were made on flat pieces of cottonwood and pine. They had been discarded from churches as inappropriate to contemporary taste and worship.) Austin, too, began to collect as soon as she came to the Southwest.

At the time they discovered them, Spanish colonial crafts were disappearing. Artisans who made chests, hammered tin, and decorative embroidery were losing out to the mass-produced, standardized products made in factories, while native Americans were being encouraged to work with commercial dyes and weaving machines. Austin joined forces with other artists to form the Spanish Colonial Arts Society, which preserved the best specimens of folk art, revived their practice, and raised funds for preserving colonial buildings that were in disrepair. She also worked with John Sloan, who moved out to Santa Fe for the summers after the war, to create the Indian Tribal Arts Association, which educated the public about native American art and encouraged Indian artists to keep to their ancient standards.

In the summer of 1919, Mabel sent her collection of santos to be exhibited in New York along with a series of Indian children's paintings. The children's artwork was done at the Santa Fe Indian School, whose teacher, Elizabeth De Huff, encouraged them to use designs and imagery based on their tribal heritage and experience, unlike the government school which forced them into conventional Anglo forms of representational art. Stephen Bourgeois, owner of a prestigious New York gallery, wrote her in the fall that he saw the exhibit in Tarrytown and wanted to arrange to show it in the city.[49]

In the spring of 1920, Mabel sent several Indian watercolors to be exhibited in New York City at the Independent Art Exhibition. Walter Pach wrote her that they were the success of the show, and they were reproduced in the *Dial* and the *Survey*. Mabel was also busily engaged in gaining recognition for archeological sites near Taos that had recently been excavated. She sent some shards to J. A. Jeançon at the Bureau of American Ethnology in Washington, who wrote her that if the material was typical, the ruin was one of the earliest in that part of the country.

Mabel and Mary both took up Emerson's task of calling for the establishment of a uniquely American literature and art. In *Land of Journey's Ending*, Austin argued that an organic art was needed to revitalize American culture. The inspiration should not come from Europe or the East Coast, but from its most ancient peoples, whose verse forms and imagery were expressions of the rhythmic forces and forms in nature. Her vision of the Southwest's role in this cultural renaissance equaled Mabel's in its scope and ebullience:

We can no more produce, in any section of the United States, a quick and characteristic culture with the worn currency of classicism and Christianity, than we can do business with the coinage of imperial Rome.

Here in the Southwest, and up along the western coast, where our blood-stream reaches its New-World journey's ending, it finds itself possessed with no effort, along with beauty and food- and power-producing natural resources, of a competent alphabet of cultural expression. Thus it gains so enormously over all other sections, where such notation is still to be produced, that one confidently predicts the rise there, within appreciable time, of the *next* great and fructifying world culture.[50]

In 1918, she had written an introduction for *The Path of the Rainbow,* a volume of seventy-eight songs by Indians from all over the country, some translated from their native languages, some reexpressed by Anglo poets. Austin had no more doubt than Mabel that this new world culture would arise from the fusion of Anglo-American and Indian traditions.

John Collier

In the winter of 1920, Mabel brought John Collier to Taos. Collier was her most important convert and a major contributor to the preservation of Pueblo livelihood and culture. Throughout the 1920s, he was in the forefront of the fight to protect Pueblo lands and promote the benefits of their social system. In the 1930s, as commissioner of Indian affairs, he created the Indian "New Deal." Although he was highly controversial and won both praise and damnation from his Indian constituency, he has justly been called "the greatest of all Indian Commissioners" in the history of the United States' relationship with the Indians.[51]

Mabel bombarded Collier with letters and telegrams trying to lure him to New Mexico for almost a year before he finally came. He had resisted "her stories of the magical habitation there of six hundred magical Indians" for months, convinced that her descriptions of the pueblo were "fairy tales," and that the anthropologists' beliefs that Indian cultures were dying and should die out were correct. En route to Mexico, the Colliers arrived in mid-December, in the midst of a snowstorm. Mabel took them to the Christmas Eve ceremony of the Virgin at Taos pueblo. Three days later, Collier attended the Red Deer Dance at Taos where he experienced an epiphany similar to Mabel's when she witnessed the Santo Domingo Christmas Dance: "Here, at Taos," he later wrote, "a whole race of men, before my eyes, passed into ecstasy through a willed discipline, splendid and fierce . . . as near to the day of first creation as it had been in the prime."[52]

Collier had been seeking all of his adult life to create a community in which art, ego, and spiritual values could be integrated. At Taos, he found "a religious creation as powerful and as subtle as ancient Greek orphic dramatic art could have been; a communal art, remotely impersonal while very passionate and very joyous. . . ." This trip changed his "life's plan," though not immediately. Although he knew little about Indians at the time he arrived, Collier had spent most of his adult life as a social worker promoting cultural pluralism. When Mabel first knew him, he headed the People's Institute at Cooper Union, which was devoted to educating immigrants in the utopian theories of the Russian anarchist Kropotkin; the English socialist, William Morris, who had called for a return to handicrafts; and Lester Ward's concept of "sociocracy"—"the scientific control of social forces by the collective mind of society." The institute also promoted ethnic pride through organized festivals and pageants. In *Movers and Shakers* Mabel captured John as he appeared during those years: "He was a small, blond Southerner, intense, preoccupied, and always looking wind-blown on the quietest day. Because he could not seem to love his own kind of people, and as he was full of a reformer's enthusiasm for humanity, he turned to other races and worked for them."[53]

Collier's activities on behalf of social reconstruction ended in 1917, primarily as a result of America's entry into World War I. Like many socialists and progressives, he had at first supported the war effort because he believed that nationwide planning for economic and social resources would continue after the war. Disillusioned by the antiworker, antiradical, and anti-immigrant hysteria that reached its apex in 1919, he moved to California in the fall to direct that state's adult education program. When he spoke openly and well of the Bolshevik Revolution during the Red Scare, his budget was decreased and he resigned. It was at this time that Mabel's letters made their impact. Among the Indians of New Mexico, he found alternatives to trends that had vexed him for years: "the uprooting of populations, the disintegration of neighborhoods, the end of home and handicrafts, the supremacy of the machine over man, the immense impoverishment of the age-old relationships between the generations, the increased mobility of the individual, the enormous expansion of commercialized recreation, the quest by mass-circulating newspapers, the movies, and radio for the lowest common denominator."[54]

Collier, however, did not commit himself to Taos at once, and when he decided in the spring to return to California to teach, Mabel was furious. His leave-taking without her permission created a very unpleasant exchange of letters and a brief rift in their friendship. Mabel accused Collier of using her facilities (and her) and leaving them in a state of disarray. Collier suggested to her that perhaps the poor should not live next to the rich. Still, he ended on a note of understanding for their

173

shared sympathies: "You are what you are—a seeker,—creative—a very large spirit—and you have fertilized our lives in a way we must know from within for all the time. Love to you!"[55]

Over the next year, Collier visited Taos a number of times. Mabel's new circle of friends, particularly Mary Austin, enlisted him in their effort to revive and preserve Indian life and culture. His hopes for what could be accomplished, not just for the Indians, but for the Anglos who needed to learn from them, were at least as grandiose as Mabel's, and would remain so for many years. Freed by the Pueblos from what he called "the imprisoning dichotomies of the Cartesian Century,"[56] he planned to devote much of the rest of his life to freeing others like himself. Collier was soon to find, however, that the fight just to protect Pueblo tribes from further depredations by the federal government would consume most of his time and energy during the first decade of his crusade.

While he was living in California during the fall of 1921, Collier had the good fortune to meet Mrs. Stella Atwood, chairman of the General Federation of Women's Clubs Indian Welfare Committee, which had been created to survey and investigate the Indian reservation system. Mrs. Atwood introduced him to a wealthy sympathizer who offered to pay him a salary to work for the Indian Welfare Committee. In May 1922 Collier started his official job as a research agent for them, and in September, left for New Mexico to survey and investigate economic and health problems among the Pueblos.

Collier and Mabel had their work cut out for them. Indians throughout the United States, including the Pueblos, had experienced increasing impoverishment and loss of territory since the late nineteenth century. At that time, the federal government committed itself to an intensive policy of assimilating them to the mainstream doctrines of Christianity, private property, and the Protestant work ethic. The Bureau of Indian Commissioners declared February 8, 1887, the day the Dawes Allotment Act was passed, "Indian Emancipation Day." The act was intended to help Indians conform to American economic practices by breaking up communal patterns of landholding and giving each Indian 160 acres to work on his own. (Indians who chose private allotment were granted U.S. citizenship.) This act left much of the 135 million acres controlled by Indian tribes as surplus available for the white settlers who were pushing westward. Although the act provided for the training of Indians in the kinds of land management they would need to convert to private ownership, little actual training was offered over the next twenty years, during which time many Indians sold their lands at much less than market value.

Between 1900 and 1920, Anglo missionaries, who supported the act, and officials of the BIA concentrated their efforts on eradicating "un-American" Indian customs and practices. Investigators sent to study Indian life reported immoral and anti-Christian practices, which led to the passage of a Religious Crimes Code. The code instructed BIA officials to prohibit ceremonial practices and punish tribal leaders who would not accept Christian doctrine and practices. Boarding schools were deliberately built far from tribal lands and children were forcibly placed in them, without parental consent, in order to uproot them from tribal ways. The federal government's attitude can best be summed up in the 1913 decision of the Supreme Court that declared Indians wards of the government: "Though they are sedentary and disposed to peace, they adhere to primitive modes of life, influenced by superstition and fetishism and governed by crude customs. They are essentially a simple, uninformed, and inferior people."[57]

The southwestern tribes had been granted title to some 700,000 acres of land by the 1848 Treaty of Guadalupe Hidalgo that the United States signed with Mexico. Over the next sixty years, they sold some of this land to Anglo and Hispanic settlers and lost some to non-Indian squatters who settled on it. When Mabel and Collier encountered them, most of the southwestern tribes suffered from hunger and disease even more than they did from cultural oppression. Drought, lack of crop rotation, and the appropriation of irrigable land by Hispanic and Anglo settlers had done much to denature their soil and deprive them of their best land.

Even by the standards of the 1920s, when 60 percent of the American people lived on less than $2,500 a year (defined as minimal subsistence by the Brookings Institution in 1929, before the crash), the Pueblos were greatly impoverished. The average per capita income at Taos was $30 a year; at some pueblos it was half that. Because doctors earned as little as $1,000 to $1,600 a year for their work on Indian reservations, many engaged in outside practice, which did little to mitigate such health problems as tuberculosis, dysentery, venereal diseases, and trachoma, a chronic contagious eyelid infection that was found in up to 30 percent of the Indians in many pueblos. Only two doctors treated all of the ten pueblos north of Santa Fe. Collier's investigation of the state boarding schools for Indians uncovered a series of horror stories: debased standards for faculty (teachers needed only an eighth-grade education); debased health standards due to severe overcrowding and lack of hygiene; brutal corporal punishment for minor infractions of the school rules. Children who weren't robbed of their health had to suffer the denigration of their family and cultural lives.[58]

Pueblo Crusade

As was true of her commitment to other causes she had taken up in the past, Mabel was more interested in the larger utopian promise than in the daily grind of politicking and compromise that were necessary to enact the promise. Yet she lent her efforts, time, money, and influence to the Pueblo cause with greater fervency and consistency than she had or ever would apply to any other. There were times when her help was more of a hindrance, but on the whole, her efforts were beneficial. Mabel began with an attack on the medical problems that beset the pueblos. When one of Tony's nieces died of double pneumonia in April 1918, she attributed her death to lack of medical attention.

Mabel carried her complaints about the BIA doctor's neglect, the lack of medication, and this particular case to Frederick Howe, commissioner of immigration and a friend from her salon days, who promised to take it up with the secretary of the interior. The BIA's investigation yielded completely opposite conclusions from Mabel's. She claimed that the Taos wanted their doctor removed, while the federal investigator claimed that the governor and tribal council gave evidence they were satisfied with his work. Whatever the truth of the matter, there was no doubt about the health problems Mabel uncovered. She had been receiving lists of needed medical supplies during the spring of 1918 from a W. H. Carter, who worked with the Pueblos. She paid for these items and had them delivered to him. Two years later she began a crusade against venereal disease when a Turkish physiologist, Dr. Eshref Shevky, who was visiting her at the time Collier arrived, discovered evidence of syphilis among the Taos Indians. A series of Wasserman tests he administered showed "that probably 12 percent of Taos pueblo had contracted the disease." Collier wrote to a Dr. Lucas, to get his help in obtaining a full-time physician, and explained to him that based on Shevky's findings, "a project for emergency health work for all the 20 pueblos had been laid before the Red Cross." The fact that Mabel herself contracted syphilis from Tony no doubt added to the zeal of her continuing campaign to eradicate it from the tribe.[59]

Although Mabel was frightened by this experience, it did not dampen the ardor with which she pursued her work. By the fall of 1922, she had every reason to believe that the cosmic purpose for which she was destined was well on its way to fulfillment. The crisis that precipitated her belief began when a BIA agent gave Collier a copy of a bill that had been filed by Senator Bursum of New Mexico, the passage of which would have been a serious threat to Pueblo land holdings. Bursum had filed the bill at the instigation of Interior Secretary Albert Fall.

The land tenure issue in New Mexico was extremely complicated. When the Supreme Court ruled in 1876 that the Pueblos were not wards of the government, their lands were left open for purchase and squatting. The ruling was reversed in 1913, when the court declared that the Pueblos were wards of the government. This reversal meant that the Pueblos did not have the right to sell or give up their lands, which threw 3,000 claims of non-Indians who held Pueblo lands in doubt. The resulting hostility and confusion climaxed in the threat of armed conflict among Indians, Anglos, and Spanish settlers in the early 1920s. Fall told Indian

Commissioner Burke that the legislation was necessary to settle the disrupted land titles.[60]

Bursum's bill, introduced into Congress on July 20, 1922, would have confirmed all non-Indian claims held by Spanish and Anglo settlers who could prove continuous possession. It allowed any "trespasser" to appeal for a special ruling and put Pueblo water rights and contested lands under the unfriendly jurisdiction of the state courts. Opponents of the bill estimated that it would deprive the Pueblos of at least 60,000 acres, most of it valuable irrigated land. Stella Atwood had known about the early stages of the bill since December 1921, but it was not until Collier learned of it in September, and informed Mabel, that the first national campaign in United States history to protect Indian rights got off the ground.

Although the campaign against the Bursum Bill started over a land crisis, it is impossible to understand its broad-ranging support without in part recognizing the appeal of the myth in which it was rooted. Collier articulated it in the article which launched the crusade. "The Red Atlantis" argued that the Pueblos' social life could become a model for all Americans; that their lack of envy and their communal spirit made them living exemplars of all that was lacking in modern society: "Today at Taos . . . life from infancy to the grave is a rhythm . . . of worship and of the quest through art expression for any ecstasy communally realized and associated with practical social aims." His essay set forth the reform ideals that he and Mabel would follow throughout the 1920s: "recognition of Indian civil rights, conservation of their lands through cooperative enterprise, preservation of their communal societies, and agricultural and industrial assistance programs sponsored by the federal government."[61]

The power of this myth to engage and activate creative and thoughtful people from all over the nation is striking for the time at which it occurred—a decade during which political and social intolerance of racial and ethnic minorities increased. The protection of Indian lands and cultures became a national cause célèbre, supported not just by the progressives and radicals who were already committed to policies of ethnic and racial tolerance, but also by artists and writers. Much of the impetus for this work came from activists in New Mexico, many of whom were part of the prewar alliance of artists and reformers that was mostly centered in New York.[62]

Mabel did much to reestablish that coalition in Taos, as did Alice Corbin Henderson in Santa Fe, by bringing together painters, writers, poets, and reformers, like Collier, to work together to change federal policy. Theirs was a cultural politics that drew upon Indian and Anglo music, painting, poetry, exhortation, and lobbying to effect their cause, and received support from club women and from Campfire Girls and Boy Scouts as well as from an elite of social scientists. Atwood, for example, used the power of the two million women who were members of the

General Federation of Women's Clubs to write letters and send telegrams to their congressmen against the bill. Artists and activists formed the New Mexico Association of Indian Affairs and the American Indian Defense Association as watchdog and lobbying groups. They joined forces with the conservative Catholic Bureau of Missions and the Eastern Association of Indian Affairs, made up of the wealthy and politically powerful.[63]

The contacts that Mabel maintained from her Village years proved especially helpful in their gaining serious recognition in the most prestigious national journals and in the halls of Congress as well. Mabel arranged for the illustrations of Taos pueblo that accompanied Collier's article and put Collier in touch with other artists, writers, and activists who took up the cause. She contacted Dolly Sloan, wife of John, and former business manager for *The Masses,* who contacted her New York friends. Alice Henderson was recruited to write an article for the *New Republic;* Elizabeth Shepley Sargeant, for *The Nation* and *The World;* Mary Austin, for *The Forum.*

As publicity agent for Collier, Mabel worked on getting support for the nationally publicized "Protest of Artists and Writers Against the Bursum Bill." The signers included Mary Austin, Witter Bynner, Zane Grey, D. H. Lawrence, Harriet Monroe, Carl Sandburg, Elsie Clews Parsons, William Allen White, Vachel Lindsay, and Edgar Lee Masters. Although Mabel was interviewed by James Rorty for the *New York World,* she was reluctant to write political pieces under her own name, even with "masculine support," as she wrote to Collier. Once again her refusal to do "man's work" kept her behind the scenes, as it had during the Paterson Strike Pageant. This time, Mabel had the added incentive of worrying about the potential controversy of her relationship with Tony. Yet she was a capable publicist. The materials she wrote for Collier provide a clear and succinct explanation of the genesis of the controversy and a powerful description of the boarding school system and medical problems endured by the Pueblos. She was politic in not casting blame on the teachers and doctors, but instead directed her attention to the "American people" who obviously would not stand for such policies once they were enlightened.[64]

Mabel helped to arrange speaking dates for a delegation of Indians who went East to testify before Congress. She got Mary Austin to arrange for a group of Indians to perform in New York, where they managed to reduce the New York Stock Exchange to silence as they played their drums and danced. In November, Mabel wrote to Elsie Parsons, who had first visited Taos in the summer of 1921, and who had important connections among anthropologists in New York and Washington. Parsons replied that she was outraged by the material Mabel sent her and promised to promote a resolution opposing the Bursum Bill before the American Ethnological Society, which she did. Impressed with a group of Indian folk tales that Mabel had compiled, she encouraged her to keep a journal of her notes on Indian life, which she believed would have scientific and literary value. She also asked Mabel to contribute her stories about Mexicans in Taos to a folklore journal and suggested that she get training in the East so that she could do more ethnological writing. At the same time, Mabel contacted Fola LaFollette, whom she had known in Greenwich Village, and urged her to have her father, Senator Robert LaFollette, intervene. He was perhaps the leading Progressive in Congress and, along with Senator Borah, became a powerful ally.

On the Indian front, Tony Luhan's role was equally important. He accompanied Collier to every pueblo in New Mexico in order to translate his explanation of the bill and its ramifications if it was passed into law. The pueblos sent delegates to their first All-Pueblo Council since 1680. When it met, on November 5, 1922, they decided to write an "Appeal by the Indians of New Mexico to the People of the United States." On November 3, Mabel had written the council and urged them to write such an appeal. She said she would have it printed and sent to all New York and Washington papers as well as every congressman. Collier had the appeal printed and distributed nationwide. This was the first time that any group of Indians had made such a nationwide appeal. Their prose was measured and moving as they explained their plight: how most of them had use of less than one acre per person of irrigated land; how they had never asked for the legislation nor been consulted regarding it. They concluded, "This bill will destroy our common life and will rob us of everything which we hold dear—our lands, our customs, our traditions."[65]

Mabel was ready, she wrote John Collier on November 21, to offer her whole self—"energy, time, and money"—to what looked like the beginning of an unstoppable movement. She admitted to him that she was initially worried that he and Atwood were committed merely to amelioration and reform. But now that she recognized the full sweep of their common vision, she was ready to offer her home as "a kind of headquarters for the future," as "a base of operations *really* for a new world plan." She was willing to marry Tony, if that "will make it more convenient from the worldly standpoint." Though Collier shared Mabel's vision, he was too shrewd a political activist not to realize that they were not about to take over the nation until they established a political beachhead in Washington. He wrote her on November 26, "We shall have to establish the right to dictate Indian policy, and build up a truly national movement, and get ourselves strongly 'on top' politically before we can demand for the pueblos the kind of thing you write of."[66]

Mabel wrote to Stella Atwood on the same day, outlining in greater detail her (and Collier's) scheme of saving "the whole *culture* and *agriculture* of the pueblos," for their own sake as well as to provide the basis of "a social experiment" that would reeducate Anglos. She was willing to devote her life to this vision because "It would be a wonderful & a *new* work on earth if it could be done."[67] There was absolutely no doubt in Mabel's mind that the audience had been readied and that Americans were on the verge of undergoing a national conversion experience which would bring them the spiritual peace and emotional plenty that were obtainable only through a return to their lost communal roots.

In December, Mabel wrote to Mary Austin in accents that echo the enthusiastic challenge she had announced to her fellow Americans in January 1913, when she published her radical credo. Referring to the publicity that followed the All-Pueblo Council meeting, she exclaimed:

> It shows that there was *a latent sympathy,* almost fierce, for the Indian, in "These States." The country has almost seemed to *go Indian.* There hasn't been a single denial or refusal. *Universal* response. Is it possible that the little drop of Indian *in* everyone awakened and answered the call?
>
> Anyway—what was *latent* is now awake and conscious and must be kept awake and nourished until vigorous and undeniable. We want *interest* and *appreciation* of the indian life and culture to become a part of our *conscious* racial mind. We want *as a nation* to value the indian as we value ourselves. We want to *consciously* love the wholeness and harmony of Indian life, and to *consciously* protect it. This publicity is invaluable. That it began as politics does not prevent its being channeled into aesthetics. Please get busy and write. . . .
>
> Keep the indian *in* the public eye and he will be an integral part of the public welfare.[68]

Just in case Mary should think of slacking off, Mabel reminded her that even D. H. Lawrence, who had been staying at Mabel's since early fall, was writing a piece on the bill. Lawrence's piece was published in the *New York Times* on December 24, and although he was equivocal in the attitudes he expressed towards the Indians, he did speak out against the bill.

The Bursum Bill was killed in January 1923. But in spite of all the political and social power that Mabel and her friends mustered, the fight was not yet over. No sooner was the bill dead than the Senate came up with a substitute in February, the Lenroot Bill. This piece of legislation was just enough of a compromise to tear the national and regional coalition of liberals and moderates apart. The New Mexican and Eastern Associations of Indian Affairs supported it, primarily because they sympathized with the claims of non-Indians who had tenure on the land, many of them for several generations. Collier, however, was infuriated by the bill and by what he considered the apostasy of his allies. Not only did it offer no compensation for land and water rights lost by the Indians, but, he believed, 75 percent of the claims against the lands were not based on legal title.

The split that took place had as much to do with personal and political rivalry as it did with political differences. There was a great deal of jealousy among the Anglos in Santa Fe over who spoke for and had control of the Pueblos. One camp supported the Lenroot Bill: the New Mexico Association, which included such writers as Witter Bynner. The other supported Collier's newly formed Indian Defense Association. It became clear, when the Pueblos publicly repudiated the Lenroot Bill, that it was Collier who had their full support and trust. In November 1923, he visited the new secretary of the interior, who responded to the national uproar of the previous year by appointing a committee to advise him how to handle the Pueblo lands situation. (Albert Fall had resigned the previous March, primarily because of the Teapot Dome scandal, but also because of his handling of the Bursum controversy.)

Meanwhile, attorneys for the Indian Defense Association met with the settlers to work out a compromise. The resulting bill, passed in June 1923, made significant concessions to the Pueblos. The Pueblo Lands Act created a lands board to investigate the status and boundaries of pueblo lands; non-Indian claimants had to show continuous possession from 1902, supported by tax records; compensation was given to both Indians and settlers for lost lands; and the BIA was required to use all money awarded to the Pueblos to purchase land and water rights for them.[69]

Collier won a great victory, for himself in terms of consolidating his power with the Pueblos and with the federal government, and for the Pueblos as well. But the rift that was created among the factions in New Mexico did not heal quickly. It certainly added to Mabel's increasingly controversial position. In the same month that she wrote to Mary Austin about the success of their campaign, Albert Fall launched a counterattack against what he called the Indian propagandists. He demanded an investigation of the charges leveled against his office. Mabel believed she was being watched by government agents who would expose her relationship with Tony. She was, for certain, being watched by the irrepressible Mr. Manby, who was forwarding reports about her undesirable influence on Taos pueblo to the BIA.[70]

As early as January 1923, Collier warned Mabel that the opposition campaign would probably go after her. He advised her not to come East with the Indian delegation that was going to testify for the Bursum hearings. A number of writers and artists in the New Mexico Association were concerned about the damage that would result if Fall decided to publicize Mabel's affair with Tony. In April, Mary Austin learned that the government lawyer in Santa Fe was attempting to intimidate Mabel's friends with threats of what the Justice Department would do to them all. Mary's alarm, and the divisiveness she saw Mabel's affair creating, led her to urge Mabel to marry Tony. When a frightened Alice Henderson came to Mabel's house with warnings about similar threats, Mabel was convinced that she must make their union legal. On April 23, 1923, Tony became her fourth—and final—husband.

The major reason for Mabel's hesitancy to marry him was her fear that her mother would cut off her financial support (a fear she also had when she married Maurice). Mabel's understanding of her money supply was primitive, to say the least. This time her son, John, who was working in a bank in Buffalo, finally straightened her out. Shortly after her marriage, he wrote to her explaining that her maternal grandmother had bequeathed her $100,000 that paid her $5,000 a year, and her father had left her a life interest in $175,000, that paid her $8,750 a year. The interest from the two bequests gave Mabel an annual income of about $14,000. Her mother, John informed her, had absolutely no control over these funds. Mabel had, however, come to depend on her mother for cash gifts that often more than doubled her annual income.[71]

Mabel's marriage to Tony Luhan was performed quietly, in the presence only of Andrew Dasburg and Ida Rauh, but it became almost instant news in the national press. The eastern press, in particular, did its best to report the marriage as soap opera on a grand scale. The *Pittsburgh Post* asked in bold headlines: "Why Bohemia's Queen Married an Indian Chief." According to the reporter, the answer was that Mabel "found the primitive simplicity in which the red man lived gratefully soothing" after "all the sophistications of New York and the European capitals." Tony had fallen madly in love, begged her to marry him, and she had fallen "into his muscular arms . . . to be smothered by his kisses." Mabel was not adverse to publicity, however, for she believed that their marriage was the wave of the future. Nine years later, the *Colorado Post* quoted her on the future of the Indian-white marriages that she still believed would follow hers: "the races may amalgamate and the Indians be the ones to save our race. A wealth of artistic sentiment will be blended in the new blood infusion with the white race."[72]

A Bridge Between Cultures

After her marriage to Tony, Mabel retreated from her total investment in political affairs. As she had told Collier in her November letter, she was not vitally interested in the practical aspects of reform. She continued to support and work with him, and keep him informed about issues that affected the well-being of the Pueblos, and she expected to be kept posted on every step taken in his work as head of the Indian Defense Association. But with a few important exceptions, she left to him and Atwood the day-to-day work of strategizing and lobbying. What most interested her— and what she was most effective at—was the creation of the "mythopoeic imagery" through which she defined the sacred space that drew Collier and other great souls to Taos.[73]

Throughout the 1920s, Mabel wrote a number of articles for regional and national journals that described Pueblo culture and set the terms for the personal and cultural regeneration she believed they offered to those who could understand and respond to them. Six of her articles appeared in *Laughing Horse,* a "little magazine," both whimsical and serious that was published by Spud Johnson in Santa Fe. While a few of her articles were primitivist doctrine at its most romantic, others reveal the kind of sensitivity to Indian life that Parsons encouraged Mabel to cultivate and formalize. "The Door of the Spirit" (1923), for one, is a convincing and artfully rendered description of decision making at Taos pueblo. Using the issue of whether or not one man's door should be moved in his house from the east to the north side, Mabel illustrates the unspoken communion among tribal members.

Mabel spent all day and most of the evening outside the house where members of the Tribal Council met, listening to the men chant a "cosmic music" that refreshed and restored them: "This is *their kind* of 'creative work,' which binds them in renewed solidarity, unlike our 'Leagues of Nations' which leave us spiritually fractured and at odds with one another." In "From the Source" (1924), she speaks more to the malaise she assumed in her Anglo readers, when she describes the Pueblos as vast reservoirs of ever-renewable life that continually "bubbles up" because they are close to the "source" of nature. They are "time-binders" who have the ability to transmit to whites the "power of life" itself, if they were able to receive it.[74]

In May 1925, Mabel published her most prophetic essay on Taos in the *Theatre Arts Monthly.* The essay was titled with Mrs. Dudley's prophecy about Mabel and Tony, "A Bridge Between Cultures." It was Mabel's call to the nation's creative geniuses to save themselves and Western civilization. Drawing on Spenglerian theory, she compared modern-day artists to the ancient Romans, claiming that they were foredoomed to perish because of their pandering to commercialism. No culture can flourish, Mabel warned them, that does not rely on the "absolute static virtues" of truth, beauty, and the eternal. During periods of barbarism, like the 1920s, people craved artificial stimulants: "jazz and the cruel laughter of the senile gods."

There was, however, the chance for a new birth of American culture and spirit: "The Southwest may be the land of new birth, of the synthetic American culture we have all desired." Quoting Vachel Lindsay's remark that Santa Fe was "the spiritual center of America," Mabel affirmed that the people drawn to New Mexico are interested not in Roman luxury, but in Spartan truth. She exhorted the best among them to come to the Southwest where the land is still a source of inspiration. Out of a reverence for the soil and the wonder of fertility have grown the great rituals of the American Indian. . . . And linked with these, the mysteries of propagation and of the fiery energies of the human soul and its transformable power have blended and fused into the pattern of existence that is at the same time both life and art. For with the Indians life is art—and religion is its testimony.

In the conclusion of her essay, Mabel envisioned a great outdoor theater arising from the foot of the Indians' Sacred Mountain, one that would restore the Greeks' original theater of worship. A band of artists willing to undertake her errand in the wilderness could build "this theatre of the new culture" that would be the bridge between the dying barbarians who reigned over America's cultural wasteland and the rebirth of a new civilization.[75]

Mabel's call ends with a sketch by Robert Edmond Jones of her intended theater. Bobby had first come to Taos with Dasburg in 1918 and was a frequent visitor. At the time Mabel wrote her article, he was associated with Eugene O'Neill in managing the Greenwich Village Theater. O'Neill had purchased the Peaked Hill Life Saving Station that Mabel and Maurice had lived in during the summer of 1917 in Provincetown. Mabel corresponded with him after he moved in and tried to get him to come to Taos. But the man whom she considered America's greatest living playwright was not interested. His cautious, cynical, and insular nature was hardly one that would have responded to Mabel's schemes very well, but one cannot help wondering what his tormented Irish Catholic imagination would have made of the Pueblo Indians.

Jones shared Mabel's mysticism and found in both the human and geographic landscapes inspiration for stage designs that he produced for two New York shows: *Till Eulenspiegel,* and Maxwell Anderson's *Night Over Taos* (1932), which was a dramatization of the 1680 Pueblo uprising. In 1923, he wrote her about his shared enthusiasm for the new world theater she envisioned: "It is the aim of all vital imaginative effort in the theatre to perceive everywhere . . . the outward tangible forms of these invisible energies. . . . Such a revelation in the theater of the spiritual energies of the world made manifest in us . . . would fuse and quicken the numberless aspirations of today in one common ideal and would illuminate all our activity with the blinding certainty of a new era of freedom, as with the light of a strange dawn."[76]

Mabel had been taking care of Jones sporadically since her Greenwich Village days, when he had a room in her apartment to work out his set designs for the theater. He was a devotee of Emma Curtis Hopkins and had received therapy from Mabel's first psychiatrist, Ely Jelliffe (whom he convinced O'Neill to see in 1923). Emotionally unstable and fearful that he was homosexual, he blamed his lack of security and sense of unreality on "too many generations of New England bastards" whose sins he believed he was paying for. In 1926, Mabel raised funds among mutual friends to have him analyzed by Carl Jung in Europe. Jones was euphoric about working with the analyst he considered the "greatest" in the world and wrote Mabel that just as she had once brought back life to his body, she was now responsible for bringing life back to his spirit.[77]

Jung in Taos

Jones hoped to get Mabel and Jung together, and for a short time, she considered the idea of going over to Europe to see him. Jung apparently discouraged the idea, skeptical of whether or not she "were really sick" as Jones put it. Although Mabel never met Jung, he did come to Taos during the winter 1925 (while she was in New York City). Jung was fascinated by primitive cultures. One of the reasons he had broken with Freud was his aversion to the contemporary urban-industrial world which cut men and women off from the sacred symbols and archetypes that he believed were essential for the nourishment of an integrated social and psychic life.

He was brought to Taos by a friend of Mabel's, Jaime de Angulo, a Frenchman who had come to America at the turn of the century, worked as a cowboy, studied medicine, and practiced anthropology and medicine among the Indian tribes of the Pacific Coast. Angulo met Mabel and Tony in California and came to visit with them while the Lawrences were in Taos. He shared her belief that the Indians needed "preserving" and wrote her, in the letter where he described how he got Jung to come to Taos, that "the white American *must* preserve the Indian, not as a matter of justice or even of brotherly charity, but in order to save his own neck." Jung agreed, although he extended his indictment to European as well as American civilization. Jaime had been contacted by Jung's American escort, who wrote him that Jung wanted to visit an American pueblo. "I made up my mind," he wrote Mabel, "that I would kidnap him if necessary and take him to Taos. It was quite a fight because his time was so limited, but I finally carried it. And he was not sorry that he went. It was a revelation to him, the whole thing. Of course I had prepared Mountain Lake [the Indian name of Antonio Mirabal]. He and Jung made contact immediately and had a long talk on religion. Jung said that I was perfectly right in all that I intuited about their psychological condition."[78]

Angulo did not exaggerate Jung's reactions. He had an urgent desire "to see the white man from outside" and to gain perspective on Anglo-European civilization by viewing it from an entirely different cultural perspective. His many talks with Mirabal at Taos pueblo were "the most

185

impressive moment of all Jung's time with the Indians," one that he recalled frequently in subsequent years, particularly after World War II, when Mirabal's condemnation of the white man seemed more-than-ever appropriate.[79] Jung was impressed by the secrecy with which the Pueblos guarded their sacraments, which he believed helped them to protect the power and cohesion of their community life.

When he wrote *Man and His Symbols,* he recalled movingly how the Indians preserved what the white man had irrevocably lost:

> It is the role of religious symbols to give a meaning to the life of man. The Pueblo Indians believe that they are the sons of Father Sun, and this belief endows their life with a perspective (and a goal) that goes far beyond their limited existence. It gives them ample space for the unfolding of personality and permits them a full life as complete persons. Their plight is infinitely more satisfactory than that of a man in our own civilization who knows that he is (and will remain) nothing more than an underdog with no inner meaning to his life.[80]

The second major controversy in which Mabel involved herself was Collier's fight to see that the Pueblos did not lose the religious practices that gave them that inner meaning. The BIA was committed to a policy that had been lobbied for by Christian missionaries who insisted that Indian religious ceremonies were lewd and corrupting. In 1921, Commissioner Burke had issued regulations that children in government boarding school attend Sunday school and church. He threatened to punish by fine and imprisonment anyone involved in religious ceremonies that involved self-torture, drugs, or idleness. In 1923, he limited religious dances to one a month in the belief that such a moderate policy would hasten assimilation. When the BIA began a campaign to educate the public against the dances, Collier battled such allegations as the one that Pueblos withdrew their children from government schools at puberty to give them a two-year course in sodomy.

The BIA first attempted to enforce their bans on April 17, 1924, in Taos, where Commissioner Burke appeared to insist that two boys who had been withdrawn from school be returned. The governor and Tribal Council refused, informing Burke that their religion was more important to them than time or money. Although the debate divided Indians throughout the nation into two hostile camps (a group of Christianized Indians sided with the BIA), the secretary of the interior was forced by public pressure to back off on Taos. In the fall, he conceded religious toleration and liberty for all Indians, for the time being. Religious conflict broke out again at Taos the following spring, however, when officers of the pueblo disciplined two Indians who were members of the peyote cult for entering a religious ceremony in nontraditional dress. The BIA rather cynically sided with the two Indians and gave the superintendent of the New Mexico pueblos the power to arrest the entire Taos governing body just before their most sacred ceremony in August. The Pueblos called another All-Pueblo Council on August 31, 1925, and issued an appeal denouncing the BIA's efforts to destroy their self-government. When a group of Pueblos went to Berkeley to raise money to fight for their cause, the BIA chief spread the rumor that they were being financed by Moscow.[81]

Once again, Mabel used her publicity skills to gain attention for the Pueblos' plight. In May 1925, she wrote a long and impassioned letter to H. L. Mencken urging him to make public the religious persecution of the Indians by the Catholic church. She included a letter written by the bishop of Albuquerque who had himself condemned the missionaries' treatment of the Indians. Mencken replied that he would not publish the letter, but that he would consider an article if she would write it.[82] But Mabel once again avoided public political polemic and did not write the article. Instead, she worked on enlisting the help of the latest literary lion whom she captured that June.

Willa Cather

Willa Cather had visited Taos in 1912, long before Mabel ever thought of going there. She became increasingly interested in returning to that area of the country as she searched in the postwar era for a time and place in American history where one could find a stable community and enduring human values. In *The Professor's House,* she included the story of Tom Outland, an uneducated herd rider who discovers Indian cliff dwellings in Arizona. They so compel him with their simple, timeless beauty that he spends two years collecting artifacts to take to Washington, hoping to gain recognition for what he believes is a great national treasure. Put off by the officials of an obviously uninterested bureaucracy that cares only for European finds, Tom travels to the Midwest, where he becomes a student of the professor. Tom's story absorbs the professor, who sees it as a symbol of a bygone America, a country that is now cursed by grasping materialism and the need to get ahead.

When Cather remarked that the world "broke in two" some time after 1918, it was the sense of the radical gap between the pre- and postwar worlds that she had in mind (she has Tom die in World War I). Her desire to use the Southwest material she had stored over time is evident in the fact that Tom's story all but takes over the novel. Her 1925 trip was very likely motivated by her desire to rediscover those materials in order to solidify the subject for her next novel. Her close friend and traveling companion, Edith Lewis, believed that Cather got the idea for *Death Comes for the Archbishop* (1927) almost as soon as they arrived in

Santa Fe. She drew eagerly from everyone she could the information she felt she needed, talking to priests, old settlers, Indian traders, and poring through history texts and church records. Cather was staying with Mary Austin when Mabel wrote her a note asking her to come and stay in one of her guesthouses. Although Cather rarely visited people, Lewis tells us that Mabel "was very persistent in a quiet, persuasive way." (Mabel was excellent at adapting her style of invitation to the temperament of the guest she was courting.)

Mabel offered Cather and Lewis the Pink House, where the Lawrences had first stayed. She left them alone except for meals, which they took in the Big House, and she provided them with a willing and always available Tony to be their guide and driver. Cather had intended to stay for only two days and remained for two weeks, returning the following summer for another stay. According to Lewis, she was very impressed by Tony and felt an instant liking and admiration for him: "with a noble head and dignified carriage; there was a great simplicity and kindness in his voice and manner." Tony took them on long drives about the country surrounding Taos during which Cather learned many stories about the land and its peoples. "He talked very little," Lewis recalled, "but what he said was always illuminating and curiously poetic." She was convinced that Cather modeled the Indian Eusabio in *Death Comes for the Archbishop* after him.[83]

Eusabio is a gentle guide who helps to initiate Bishop Latour into the ways of Indian living and consciousness. As Cather describes him, he has many of the characteristics that Mabel and others associated with Tony:

Travelling with Eusabio was like travelling with landscape made human. He accepted chance and weather as the country did, with a sort of grave enjoyment. He talked little, ate little, slept anywhere, preserved a countenance open and warm, and like Jacinto he had unfailing good manners.

When Cather was later asked how Mabel could have married an Indian she replied, "How could she help it?"[84]

Cather was also impressed with Mabel, who respected her powerful response to the creative stimulus of a "country . . . still waiting to be made into a landscape" and had been a supremely understanding and unobtrusive hostess. As Lewis astutely noted, Mabel was "essentially an artist herself—knew the conditions that contribute to an artist's work, and was able to create them. She had, too, a large ungrudging generosity toward people she admired; one felt that she enjoyed helping them toward their aim and seeing them realize their desires."[85] Of course, it helped when her guests' goals suited her own, for she was also known to interfere with them and to remove them on short notice, if someone she was more interested in accepted an invitation.

Mabel had not been able, however, to enlist Cather in her fight to protect the Pueblos' religious freedom. She was not interested in the "tribal side" of Indian affairs and found Collier's style fanatical. Her contribution, which Mabel obviously appreciated, was her sensitive and appreciative portrait of the Indians in *Death Comes for the Archbishop*. Mabel could justifiably claim that Cather received some of the inspiration and forming ideas for her novel during her visit. In August, Cather wrote to express her gratitude for the "fine reality" of her weeks in Taos. Both women needed the society of cultivated men and women, and the sophistication offered by more "advanced" civilizations. But like Bishop Latour, they agreed the Southwest was the place of renewal:

> In New Mexico he always awoke a young man. . . .
> Beautiful surroundings, the society of learned men, the charm of
> noble women, the graces of art, could not make up to him for the loss
> of those light-hearted mornings of the desert, for that wind that made
> one a boy again.[86]

Unlike Cather, Mabel felt that she needed a man to help her express that sense of renewal. Thus she had spent much of her time during the early 1920s pursuing the man she believed to be the greatest living twentieth-century writer. Mabel "summoned" D. H. Lawrence "across continents" so that he would help her to usher in the brave new world that Tony promised her. Lawrence did not accomplish her mission, but he was profoundly influenced by his stay in Taos and by his relationship with Mabel who, in turn, was profoundly influenced by his views.

Chapter 6

Sybil, the Phoenix, and the Queen Bee: The Luhans and the Lawrences

Constantly remembrance came back to me of his expressed intention to destroy me—repeated so often—so often defied. It occurred to me that had Frieda let him write that book with me, he would have attempted by the means to annihilate the strong creature whose will was so evil in his eyes, for he held me to be the prototype of that greatest living abomination, the dominating American woman.[1]

In April 1935 Angelo Ravagli returned to Taos with the urn containing D. H. Lawrence's ashes. Frieda intended to inter them at sunset, to the beat of Indian ceremonial drums, in the chapel she had built to Lawrence's memory. According to Frieda, Mabel not only drove the Indians away by telling them there was a curse on the ashes, but also plotted to steal and scatter them over the Lawrence ranch. When the plot was discovered, Mabel apparently threatened to wait until Frieda's death to take her revenge. On Frieda's orders, Angelino mixed the ashes with mortar and concrete, forming an immovable block as Lawrence's permanent memorial. This was the last time that Mabel and Frieda would struggle over possession of Lawrence's soul.[2]

Frieda triumphed over Mabel in Lawrence's death as she had done during his life, for no woman was ever a serious rival to Frieda for his deepest affection. Yet Mabel had her triumph as well, though a very mixed one it was. Mabel profoundly influenced Lawrence's life and art. She captivated him and also evoked in him a hatred so passionately intense that it startled his friends and frightened his wife. Mabel has the distinction of being the only person reported to have caused Lawrence to declare himself capable of murder and to have inspired him to describe in intimate detail the exact method he would use to commit it.[3]

To Lawrence, Mabel was the murderer of male potency. According to Mabel, it was Frieda who "answered to" Lawrence's sexuality. She was the physical, the generative life-seeker, rooted in the natural spontaneity of unself-conscious flesh. Mabel believed that she "answered to" Lawrence's other side—the mental prober and sublimator who attempted to universalize an intensely personal religioaesthetic vision. She and Frieda objectified the polarities of Lawrence's nature:

> When he was in a temporary harmony with Frieda, he would, in brilliant vituperative talk, sling mud at the whole inner cosmos, and at Taos, the Indians, the mystic life. . . . Then, sometimes, . . . forgetting Frieda's presence or defying it, [he] would talk . . . of the power of consciousness, the growth of the soul, its dominion and its triumph.[4]

Mabel was right. Lawrence would have wished to have his ashes scattered to the winds as a final gesture to the anomic spirits that drove him ceaselessly throughout the world in search of his Rananim. Frieda was also right to mortar those ashes and affix them to the mother earth whose imago she was as the primary inspiration of his art. Lawrence, of course, would have been equally angry at both of them. For if Mabel threatened to destroy the source of his inspiration through her mental probings that struck at the "quick" of life, Frieda threatened to annihilate the ideological value of that inspiration in the hearty mockery with which she often greeted his passion to achieve success in the world of men. His nickname for her—the Queen Bee—was an apt one.

For all their differences, there was a bond among these three that makes their meeting seem almost a matter of predestination. Mabel and the Lawrences had separately embarked upon life journeys that led them simultaneously back into the historic and psychic past of humankind. Like Mabel's trip from New York to Taos, the Lawrences' journey from Germany through the Far East to "Red" America was part of the postwar modernist disillusionment with and flight from Western civilization. Their fascination with lost harmonies that could presumably be recovered by tracing mental life backward into earliest race memory had all begun before the war.

Born in the same year, Mabel and Frieda became mothers at the same time and took lovers who were revolutionaries. The ideals of the *liebensphilosophie* that Mabel absorbed in Greenwich Village and practiced with John Reed were the same ones Frieda was learning from her lover and Freud's radical disciple, Otto Gross, in Schwabing. Frieda taught Lawrence the necessity of a sexual revolution whose values were love, growth, and spontaneity, as opposed to the patriarchical values of law, order, and material wealth. Like Mabel, Frieda was a "love goddess" who hoped to regenerate society by inspiring its great male talents. The key difference between them was that Frieda accepted this role and Mabel, who resented its restrictions, continually subverted it.[5]

The war that killed the social and political aspirations of these revolutionaries reaffirmed Lawrence's belief in the "Great Mother" as the source of life-wisdom and psychological well-being. She represented, as Jung's disciple Erich Neumann explained, "the original situation of the unconscious, which consciousness has not yet dissected into its antithesis . . . [of] good and evil, friendly and terrible." She was the center of a mode of perception and symbology through which the world appeared to primitive men and women "as an original and natural unity" and thus was "the creative source of the human spirit." Lawrence, as Mabel understood, believed that "a man gets his power from *a* woman. There is something to be learned from her; for, being 'centered' as he called it by his woman, sheer power emanated from him. This, perhaps, is the lost meaning of continents, lost in these days of outlets, canalizations and self-expression."[6]

After reading *Sons and Lovers* and *Psychoanalysis and the Unconscious,* Mabel was convinced that Lawrence held the key to unlock "the lost Atlantis" of her being as well as the power to divine the "secret" of Pueblo life and reveal it to the world. At the time that she called him to New Mexico, in September 1921, she was a woman of forty-one years, who had found love and a mission she believed would transform the world. But she had not become the "clear channel" Mrs. Dudley told her she was destined to become. Lawrence was to serve as midwife to the birth of her millenial vision. Once again, Mabel felt that she must rely on male genius to see her and her dreams into being.

Lawrence seemed to offer more than any other man she had known except Tony; in some ways, more than Tony. As a psychologist who incarnated the "eternal feminine" in his fiction, he might help her to center herself. As a prophet who shared her apocalyptic insights about the race suicide of Anglo civilization, he had proved his ability to reach the kind of audience she sought to convert. As a writer, he shared with her a belief in the regenerative power of the "Word." He was, she felt, the one twentieth-century writer who could best "speak" Taos for her and thereby locate it as the center for the redemption of the Western world. He would "take *my* experience, *my* material, *my* Taos, and . . . formulate it all into a magnificent creation."[7]

Lawrence was trying to achieve through language what Mabel believed the Pueblos had achieved through their ceremonial practices: to arouse modern men and women from their worship of the false icons of money and mechanism and restore them to a nonexploitive relationship with nature and their own bodies. To Mabel, he was a John the Baptist "crying in the wilderness," who would translate her vision into a new gospel.

When Mabel wrote to Lawrence, in the fall of 1921, that Taos was "like the dawn of the world," she whetted an appetite already stimulated by a vision of America as the potential locus of his long-dreamed-of Rananim—a community of like-minded men and women who would practice a simplified economy and live by the organic consciousness that he preached. His coming to America was, in fact, the beginning of an experience in which Lawrence sought the means to personal and artistic regeneration for himself, and to religious, political, and cultural regeneration for society. He came with no illusions, however, about postwar American society—its commercialism, mammon worship, and obsession with mechanical contrivances were what he expected to find and what he found confirmed by his visit. These social and commercial aspects of American life were the result of what Lawrence saw as an American personality type that suppressed feeling and sensuality in favor of mental life. Yet Lawrence saw America as being at the beginning of a rising cycle of historical importance that he believed he could influence by redirecting American consciousness toward organic expression.[8]

In his essay, "America Listen to Your Own," published in the *New Republic* before his trip to America, Lawrence stressed the importance of America's lack of a past and traditions. He expressed his belief in the possibilities of a new aesthetic arising from a continent that had the opportunity to regenerate its art and society. He warned, however, that America would have to turn to "the spirit of its own dark, aboriginal continent" to do so. That which the Puritans abhorred and called Devil, they must now recognize and embrace: "Americans must take up life where the Red Indian, the Aztec, the Maya, the Incas left off. . . . There lies the real continuity: not between Europe and the new States, but between the murdered Red America and the seething White America." Although Lawrence was never of one mind about the Indians, he shared Mabel's belief that the Indians cherished some esoteric life secret. While he was aware of the materialism of the East, he was optimistic about the Indian West.[9]

Lawrence's correspondence with Mabel over the winter and spring of 1921–22, when he was slowly making his way to America via India, Ceylon, and Australia, anticipated the mixed response he would have to Taos and the Indians. His first letters were hopeful. In November, he wrote: "our own thin end, and the last dark strand from the previous, pre-white era" must be brought together. But he warned, "I also believe in Indians. But they must do *half* the believing: in me as well as in the sun." Lawrence's experiences with dark peoples in the Far East brought out his latent racist paranoia: "all dark people have a fixed desire to jeer at us," he warned her. Frieda shared none of Lawrence's reservations, either about the Indians or the "arty" people they heard populated Taos. She wrote enthusiastically about coming and shortly after arriving told Mabel, "I only wish with all my heart we had known you long ago!"[10]

Mabel had resorted to everything, including witchcraft, to ensure that the Lawrences would end their journey in Taos. She had Leo Stein write Lawrence that Taos was the most beautiful landscape he had ever seen and that Mabel was the "all but perfect hostess." She sent Frieda an Indian necklace that she had steeped in potent Indian magic. She drew her power down into her "solar plexus" and willed Lawrence and Frieda to her home. She also enlisted Tony's concentrated efforts after convincing him that Lawrence could be of immeasurable help to the Pueblos. Mabel left no possible access to Lawrence's mind and spirit unexplored. She even sent *Sons and Lovers* to Ely Jelliffe for analysis. He wrote her that Lawrence had a severe homosexual fixation which he was trying to compensate for. (Two years later, he elaborated on his diagnosis to include "an inferiority and Jehovah complex.")[11]

When Mabel and Tony finally met Frieda and Lawrence after a year's correspondence and waiting, it was Frieda who most impressed Mabel. Lawrence appeared "agitated, fussy, distraught." Slight of stature with his dark, piercing eyes and bright red beard, he seemed unsubstantial next to Frieda's imposing bulk, "tall and full-fleshed in a suit of pale pongee, an eager look on her pink face. . . ." Characteristically saving the worst for last, the mark of her acid word portraits, Mabel did not fail to note Frieda's "green, unfocused eyes, and her half-open mouth with the lower jaw pulled a little sideways. Frieda always had a mouth rather like a gunman." Mabel was convinced that Lawrence's initial discomfort in the presence of Tony and Mabel resulted from his ambivalent feelings about miscegenation. The next day on their way to Taos the car broke down. Lawrence sat "helplessly" by, much to Frieda's annoyance, as Tony fixed the car. [12]

In spite of their awkward start, Lawrence and Mabel formed a bond during his first two weeks in Taos that was never completely severed. Mabel was certain that she could accomplish her goals through him by providing him with a higher form of inspiration than Frieda was capable of. Her belief was related to the fact that she was undergoing menopause at the time of the Lawrences' arrival in Taos. With the loss of her fertility, Mabel was convinced that she gained the ability to inspire artists to go beyond primary sexuality in their search for a Muse. She articulated her new role in a poem she wrote for Lawrence in 1923, entitled "Change."

Mabel begins by lamenting the seeming death-in-life existence of the woman whose blood flow has stopped:

> Scarlet days fading out to white,
> What shall I do with white days, God?
> All my years have been
> Crimson, scarlet and orange. . . .

But the loss turns out to be a disguised blessing when she discovers that she is no longer bound by her "ego-insistent flesh":

> Here in this place, my own,
> You receive at last
> The power of the virgin.
> This is the happy time.

Turning a biological disadvantage into a psychological coup d'état, she implies her powers are Promethean.[13]

Mabel sensed the curious asceticism that underlay Lawrence's theory of "blood consciousness" and knew that he celebrated a sensuality he sometimes longed to escape—a desire that increased during the 1920s along with the decline of his health. This is evident in his adaptation of Mabel's poem, which he entitled "Changes of Life." While he used her opening stanzas almost verbatim, he had a very different view of how postmenopausal women were supposed to behave. His new "Eve" has gone through the "auto-da-fé" of life to emerge a "softened springtime," whom he celebrates as an example to men and women of the tranquility of non-combative, passionless love.[14]

Mabel was convinced that she could help Lawrence into this new Eden by giving him "the womb behind the womb—the significant, extended, and transformed power that succeeds primary sex, that he was ready, long since, to receive from woman." There is little doubt that Lawrence encouraged her belief in postmenopausal power when he condescendingly informed her that "the burden of consciousness is too great for a woman to carry. She has enough to bear with her ever-recurring menstruation." But Mabel had an even more important incentive. She admitted many years later to Una Jeffers that she had always been frigid, in the sense that she was incapable of enjoying sexuality with anyone for more than a brief period of time. Mabel attributed this to her early relationship with her father, but it was also a response to her ambivalent conceptions of womanhood. She told Una that frigid women were "capable of strong psychic relationships" and that they "set an enormous value upon a spiritual or psychic or subtle form of love such as there is between Tony & me." Menopause released her from the need to play earth mother, or so she thought.[15]

If there was one thing for which Mabel especially disliked Frieda, other than her possession of Lawrence, it was that she was a "creature" of sex—lustful and joyful, at home in her body, proud of her contribution to the "religion of love" that Lawrence celebrated in his works. Mabel wrote Leo that Frieda could not possibly understand Lawrence's desire to collaborate with Mabel on a book about her life because Frieda was "obtuse—retrograde—stupid spiritually and definitely *hostile* to anything spiritual—

Lawrence has summed her up this way himself. Of the sublimation of the sexual impulse in human relations she is absolutely *unaware*—& consequently most distrustful of any friendships or interests outside of her."[16]

Mabel was astute enough to recognize that Lawrence both needed and resented Frieda's healthy animality and her ability to react freshly to every new experience. In spite of her own predatory objectives, she never lost sight of Lawrence's intensely symbiotic relationship with Frieda. Frieda was the "medium" through whom Lawrence "received" life. She had achieved the role Mabel had dreamed of fulfilling with Reed and Sterne. Mabel, of course, exaggerated Lawrence's repugnance to the sexual. She had to, since this is what gave Frieda her power as "the mother of orgasm and the vast, lively mystery of the flesh."[17] She claimed to find Lawrence physically repellent, although it is difficult to know whether this was because he felt the same way about her. (Each of them intimated that the other attempted seduction.) Lawrence certainly demonstrated a strong puritanical streak while he was visiting. When Mabel greeted him one morning on her sun roof, dressed only in a blue burnoose, he was shocked. He was more shocked by her uncovered bathroom windows, on which he painted brightly colored designs to keep out the prying eyes of anyone who wanted to take the trouble of climbing upon her roof in order to peer in.

Whatever the truth about their physical response to one another, Lawrence was a willing partner in Mabel's plan to have her life story told. Almost as soon as he arrived in Taos, he decided to write his "American book" around her. His letters to her during his first few weeks in Taos reveal that he was as eager about the project as she. He asked her for detailed notes and written remembrances of her coming to Taos and her meeting with Tony, including the short story she had begun ("An Intimation"). It was for this, Mabel told him, that she had "called him from across the world—to give him the truth about America." He would "polish" the "indigestible jewel" she had harbored for four years and display it in its appropriate lustre.

Lawrence had a long history of collaborating with women on his fiction: Jessie Chambers had read and edited his first version of *Sons and Lovers;* Frieda had helped to write parts of the final version; an Australian nurse worked with him on *Boy in the Bush.* He was perfectly willing to have his collaborators' voices heard in his fiction—as he told Mabel when he said he would use her writing in his novel—though he was not willing to share authorship in any public way. The *gloire,* as Gertrude Stein called it, was to be his alone. In fact, Mabel recognized that Frieda's lifelong grievance against Lawrence was based on her need to be recognized as a person in her own right and not just as an appendage to Lawrence's creative needs. Joseph Foster, a struggling young writer who lived on the fringes of the Taos art colony and was an observer and minor participant in their

197

affairs, remembers Frieda shouting with well-justified anger during one of her famous battles with Lawrence, "You lovely Phoenix! You are the bird and the ashes and the flames all by yourself. . . . I don't exist."[18] She felt the same narcissism at work in Mabel: she once accused them both of being golden cows, prancing about in self-worship.

Frieda did everything she could to make their work together unpleasant. When Mabel came over to the Pink House in the mornings, Frieda was ready with her broom, singing and sweeping as loudly as she could about their feet. She was intensely possessive of the man in whom she had invested her life's purpose and for whom she had given up her children. She found it intolerable when Lawrence looked to other women for inspiration. As she admitted, she "always regarded Lawrence's genius as given to me."[19] Her jealousy was especially aroused when the women who attracted Lawrence were articulate and intelligent, since she had to fight his ridicule whenever she expressed herself intellectually. He needed wealthy and well-spoken patronesses from time to time. Frieda felt that all he ought to need was her.

Lawrence fostered their rivalry and seemed to get a perverse pleasure out of pitting them against one another. As soon as she recognized what Mabel was after, Frieda wrote her, "You never cared a rap about me, you don't want a *relationship* with either Lawrence or me, you only want people in your *power*—the game that you play with him *bores* me in both of you. . . . I despise it—it's the same man-hunt, the female on the hunt—lo taliho! The hunt is up!" In a fictional fragment she later published, Frieda wrote of Mabel as "R": "a very energetic and powerful American woman who had learned all the tricks of the mind and the will, had decided that she was the person to 'run' Andrew's [Lawrence's] genius and he was the man to reveal to the world her great self. But there was no self to reveal. . . . The very fact that she had no genuine self gave her the frantic desire for dominion over others."[20]

At the same time she bitterly resented Mabel's sinister intentions, Frieda admired her enormously for her energy, style, and lust for living. Her admiration, like that of Una Jeffers at a later date, had much to do with Mabel's drive to achieve an identity on her own terms that was always stronger and more persistent than her desire to give over her life and person to any male. In spite of Lawrence's attempts to keep them at a distance, they enjoyed each other's company when he was not around. Mabel recalls one richly comic scene when the two of them were seated like plump goddesses surrounded by the apples in her orchard, sharing a pleasant camaraderie. Unknown to them, Lawrence was in the upper branches of a nearby tree. From there he espied the twin furies who possessed his imagination. Dropping to the ground in despair he moaned, "O implacable Aphrodite!"[21]

Mabel, however, was clearly the more frightening fury. How could

Lawrence help shuddering once he recognized her intentions: "I wanted to seduce his spirit so that I could make him carry out certain things. . . . It was his soul I needed for my purpose, his soul, his will, his creative imagination, and his lighted vision." Lawrence was not the only victim of Mabel's spiritual vampirism that summer. In a letter she wrote to Leo Stein at the time, she expatiated on her household full of male psycho-neurotics:

> Andrew Dasburg stayed for four months but his mother complex grew worse and worse until he was a blight and he couldn't hardly swallow his food at the table. . . . Bobby [Jones] has a family complex and two mother complexes. One is the pathetic, starving at-the-foot-of-the-cross mother, and the other is the warm-cheerful-bountiful mother. These two aspects he claps on to Mary (Foote) and me. John Evans also has a mother complex and is very jealous of all my friends except Tony . . . and really when all these mother complexes sat down with me at my table this summer *I* couldn't eat a thing—it was so tense! . . . I finally decided that meals were evidently appallingly sexual in character and had much better be conducted à deux like other matters.[22]

At the same time Lawrence recoiled from Mabel's conception of her Muse role, he was attracted to those very qualities in her that made her a kindred seeker. In fact, Mabel's quest for spiritual and emotional redemption became the central theme of his American fiction. It was not the journey of the hero of classical myth that provides the archetypal structure of Lawrence's works, but that of the twentieth-century heroine: "when Lawrence came to America . . . he became absorbed in the theme of the woman in search and made it the dominant one in every important piece of fiction that he wrote from the inspiration of this continent. Most of [these heroines] possess traits of character drawn from Mabel Luhan and have experiences suggested by the events of her life."[23]

Lawrence's six-page penciled draft, all that he completed of his first American novel, contains some of the best prose that he wrote in America, as well as the major motifs that he developed over the next five years. He interweaves the specific and concrete with the mythic so ingeniously that the three dominant images in the story—the heroine (Sybil), the landscape, and the train—take on the primitive powers of a medieval morality play, without ever losing their roots in natural fact.

As a symbol of industrial America, the train is supposed to be the vehicle which transports her to the promised land; instead it holds her back:

> They ought to arrive, soon. There is already the desert of grey-white sage and blue mountains. She ought to be there; soon, she ought to be there. This journey alone should be over. But the train comfortably

stretched its length in the stations, and would never arrive. There was no end. It could not arrive. She could not bear it.[24]

When she hires a car to get to her destination more quickly, Sybil finds herself carried helplessly through a "god-forsaken" landscape, "like wilderness, the wilderness of the temptation, for example." Lawrence implies that Sybil has the choice of being the Jesus or the Judas of the spirit of the place. She can accept its stark fierceness and beauty, or betray it for the kingdom and glory of mechanical and mental power. The destiny of this female prophet, as she looks down upon her "terra nova," is a highly ambiguous one.[25]

The ambiguity is increased by Lawrence's use of folk humor. Sybil is carried to her promised land in a broken-down Dodge (as Mabel was) with no headlights; she is bumped and bruised as she careens across the rocky landscape. Her Charon is an incompetent boy she hired on sight in a scruffy western town. The woman who stands at the center of this grandiose mythic scheme is the victim of a comically rendered symbolism which exaggerates her importance while cutting her down to size. The irony is Lawrence at his best because it is self-directed, aimed as well at the pretentiousness of this typological patterning.

Lawrence gives Mabel a name to match her presumed powers—Sybil Monde. The disjunction between the masculine, industrial metaphors he uses to describe her physical being, and the prophetic powers evoked by her name, are emblematic of the split he saw between the potential and achievement of the American Dream. Sybil's glance had "the bright candour of youth resolving into something dangerous as the headlights of a great machine coming full at you in the night. Mr. Hercules better think twice before he rushed to pick up the seductive serpent of loneliness that lay on the western trail. He had picked up a snake long ago without hurting himself. But that was before Columbus discovered America."[26]

The evil that the modern male hero must tangle with is incarnated in the American female dynamo: "Mark is her husband, her third. One dead, one divorced, and Mark alternatively torn to atoms and thrown to the four corners of the universe, then rather sketchily gathered up and put together again by a desirous if still desperate ["dangerous" crossed out] Isis." Lawrence's ideal woman was a magnetic center who focused man's creative powers. When the center no longer held, the modern Osiris was reduced to a "humpty dumpty" who could never be put back together again. This machine Isis is the "new" Woman who symbolizes for Lawrence the perversions created by the twentieth-century industrial wasteland.[27]

As a frontier "hero," with the "energy of a small bison," Sybil is both ludicrous and dangerous. To protect herself from man's abdication of his masculinity, she borrows his masculine pride of will, which she uses under the guise of femininity. She thus trains her mind to match the mechanisms man has created to supplant her original fertility: "Perhaps she felt that some power of her will could at last neutralise altogether the power of the engines. . . . So there they would sit forever, the train and she at a deadlock on the Santa Fe line." Lawrence's evocation of Mabel's physical duality mirrors the moral duality he found at work in the American psyche: the seemingly fair benevolent spirit that masked the evil, bullying will beneath: "Her thick, dark brows like carved horns over the naive-looking face, and her bright hazel-green eyes, clear at the first glance as candour and unquenchable youth, at the second glance, made up all of devilish grey and yellow bits as opals are." She is the culmination of the worst and best of "the old colonial vigor" that had collected "as in some final dam" waiting to burst.[28]

During the first two months of his visit, Lawrence's feelings for America and Mabel—always closely intertwined—underwent a significant shift. His earliest notes to her were warm and friendly, filled with appreciation for her generosity and interest in serving her and her cause. Mabel achieved the coup of getting Lawrence to contribute his talents to the Bursum Bill controversy, although he concluded his article with some irritation: "what business is it of mine, foreigner and newcomer?" The irritation displayed in this article can also be found in his correspondence during this period, as he felt more and more smothered under the wing of his "padrona." In a letter to Harriet Monroe, he expressed a reaction to Taos that shows how easily he made the leap from the particular to the universal in translating Mabel and Taos into archetypal images. Taos, he told her, was "soft and unwilling" like a "free woman" who never gives of herself. "America," he concluded, "affects me like that."[29]

Lawrence found this inability to "give" not only in Mabel, but also in the soil and in the very harsh extremes of the Taos climate. Beneath his love for the beauty and thrill of Taos lay the horror of a landscape where, he wrote, the heart "is never touched at all." In October, however, he was still thinking of Mabel as a potential member of his Rananim. He wrote to an old school friend of Mabel's that he wished to go up to Lobo Ranch and "make a *real* life there" with Mabel and no servants.[30] He was also working hard to make Mabel over into his image of what a "true" woman should be.

Lawrence began with her outward appearance. Mabel's mode of dress at the time was full and flowing, really the only style a woman of her short stature and bulk could wear gracefully. Lawrence made her replace these clothes with tight-waisted mother hubbards, white stockings, and aprons with hair ribbons to match, a get-up which made Mabel look like an overgrown Alice-in-Wonderland. Next, he attempted to get Mabel to relate to her body by having her attempt housekeeping chores at which she was completely inept. Lawrence has the distinction of being the only man for whom Mabel was willing to cook and to get down on her knees to scrub floors. Both attempts ended in disaster, which Mabel took rather good-humoredly, considering how foolish they made her look.

Lawrence worked simultaneously on her will, which he insisted she must give up or be destroyed. But her need for intensity and excitement, which he felt would "break" her one day, were the very attributes he most stimulated. When he talked of things of the spirit, he was "god-like." Mabel felt as though he were saying that "nothing else matters save this excitement, this flow, this ecstasy."[31] For all his vicious temper and macho bossiness, Lawrence was extraordinarily charismatic and also very witty and charming when he wanted to be. Mabel spent some of her most memorable times with the Lawrences playing charades and enjoying his parodies of their behavior. Without the daily exchange of "power and life" that he seemed to provide her, she felt empty. Each time he left her, she felt physically ill and highly antagonistic toward him.

In November, Lawrence borrowed Mabel's Lobo Ranch some six miles north of Taos up in the mountains. Much to Mabel's annoyance, he not only moved away from her control, but also brought two male painters to live with him. She and Lawrence had their first open fight just before Christmas.[32] Lawrence had intended to spend the holidays with her, but Mabel refused to have him out of jealousy and spite: the war was on.

In December, Lawrence wrote his mixed impressions of Mabel to Frieda's mother, the Baroness von Richthofen:

> [She] wants to be "good" and is very wicked, has a terrible will-to-
> power, you know—she wants to be a witch and at the same time Mary
> of Bethany at Jesus' feet—a big, white crow, a cooing raven of ill-omen,
> a little buffalo.

To Knud Merrild, one of the Danish painters staying with him and Frieda at the ranch, Lawrence expressed his darkest desires about murdering Mabel and his most racist views. At one point, he remarked that he wished Mabel would stop "dragging that fat Indian around. . . . Why don't people know their place? I hate having servants around me."[33]

For Lawrence, Mabel's betrayal of their common vision was that she was not really engaged in reintegrating her fallen white consciousness with its aboriginal roots, but in using what she learned about Indian life to strengthen and market her own ego. In trying to "sell" the Indian cause to the guilty conscience of a nation, he felt that she was politicizing what had to be worked out on a personal level of redemption:

> Don't trouble about the Indians. You can't "save" them: and politics, no
> matter *what* politics, will only destroy them. I have said many times
> that you would destroy the Indians. . . . The same with Collier. He will

Ralph Myers, Witter Bynner (seated left and right), Alice Corbin Henderson, Mabel (Sterne?), William Henderson (standing left to right).

Dorothy Brett, standing in front of a mural by Awa Tsireh at Big House, Los Gallos, c. 1925.

Awa Tsireh, noted Pueblo artist.

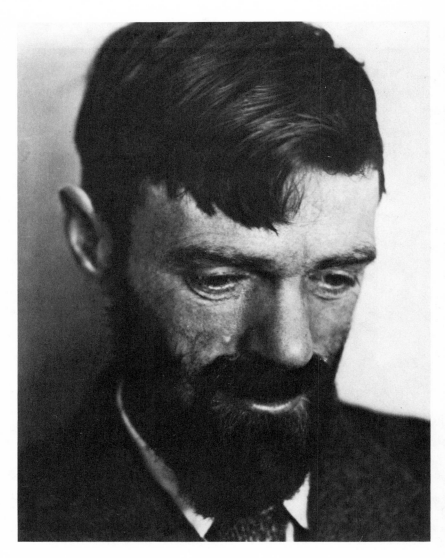

D. H. Lawrence.

D. H. Lawrence in Taos.

Lorenzo's first drawing for "Ballad of a Bad Girl"—

Illustration by D. H. Lawrence for "Ballad of a Bad Girl."

Mabel Dodge Luhan. (Photo by Edward Weston.)

destroy them. It is his saviour's will to set the claws of his own White egoistic *benevolent* volition into them. Somewhere, the Indians know that you and Collier would, with your salvationist but poisonous white consciousness, destroy them.[34]

This is one reason why Mabel became for Lawrence the incarnation of evil that was masked by America's benevolent will. American benevolence, as he well understood, had a way of making dependents of the less fortunate others it felt morally bound to liberate as a means of affirming its sacred "mission."

Lawrence's increasing dislike of America and Americans followed a well-established pattern. He would react enthusiastically to a new environment only to reject it and wish he were elsewhere within a short time. But he had invested enormous hope in America and Taos as the destination of his long-dreamed-of utopian colony, which he expected to serve as spiritual leader. Lawrence's dashed hopes for a shared communion with Mabel and the Indians had an effect on his life equal to what he believed was John Middleton Murry's Judas-like betrayal. His disillusion with Mabel deeply affected his feelings "to the point of his repudiating *all* of America. This could be a sign of the depths of his feelings for her—and his disappointment."[35]

Lawrence's disappointment with Mabel, and his depth of shared feeling, permeate the third version of his *Studies in Classic American Literature,* which he worked on during the winter of 1922–23. Where the male Puritan had received the brunt of Lawrence's invective in the versions of his essays that were written in England, the woman "redeemer" is now the force to be reckoned with in American life. She doubly betrays her sex, by sublimating her sexual power in search of the life of the spirit and by trying to appropriate the task of the male as world-builder. The hysterical misogyny that permeates these essays was also fed by Mabel's sexual relationship with Tony Luhan. It came to symbolize for Lawrence the loss of his hoped-for communion with the Indians and fed his racist fantasies of annihilation by them.[36]

Implicit in his diatribes against modern woman is Lawrence's belief that the Protestant ethic and the white man's homoeroticism have given her no choice: either she denies her sexuality by appropriating the worst elements of white male consciousness or she betrays the white male by taking his red brother.

Revenge! REVENGE! It is that that fills the unconscious spirit of women to-day. Revenge against man, and against the spirit of man, which has betrayed her into unbelief. . . .

These leprous-white, seducing, spiritual women who "understand" so much. One has been too often seduced, and "understood."

What drove Lawrence to such a pitch of fury against the "noble savage" fad was his belief that Mabel had not taken up the Indian in order to reintegrate her white consciousness with its aboriginal roots, but in order to emasculate the white man intellectually and sexually: "White Americans do try hard to intellectualize themselves. Especially white women Americans. And the latest stunt is this 'savage' stunt again. White savages, with motor-cars, telephones, incomes and ideals! Savages fast inside the machine; yet savage enough, ye gods!"[37]

In Lawrence's essays on Poe and Hawthorne, Mabel functions as the prototype of the avenging fury. Where Ligeia had been a victim in the earlier version of his Poe essay, she is now victimizer. Although doomed by 200 years of white American males' rebellion against the flesh, "her own lustful will" is primarily responsible for the diseased relationship between the sexes. Mabel had both corroborated and altered Lawrence's earlier views on the nature of the American psyche:

Beware, oh, woman, of the man who wants *to find out what you are.* And, oh men, beware a thousand times more of the woman who wants to *know* you, or *get* you, what you are.

These terribly conscious birds like Poe and his Ligeia deny the very life that is in them; they want to turn it all into talk, into *knowing.*[38]

In his essay on *The Scarlet Letter,* Lawrence reincarnates Hester Prynne as Mabel Luhan: "The deliberate consciousness . . . so fair and smooth-spoken; and the underconsciousness so devilish." On a more peevish note, it seems that Lawrence could not forgive Mabel for not accomplishing the household tasks in which he had tried to train her. Hester is blamed for loathing physical labor like washing dishes and sweeping floors. She is too busy victimizing men: "The greatest triumph any woman can have, especially an American woman, is the triumph of seducing a man. . . . 'Seduce me, Mrs. Hercules.'"[39] Mr. Hercules was warned about seeking out a mate on the western trail in Lawrence's manuscript on Mabel's life.

Lawrence's opening essay in *Studies in Classic American Literature,* "The Spirit of Place," reveals those aspects of Mabel's philosophy and character that he believed might make the New World the site of Western man and woman's regeneration. He proclaims his interest in the messianic role Mabel had encouraged—"Look at me trying to be midwife to the unborn homunculus"—and defines freedom in the very terms she had used to describe the essence of Indian life: obedience to an inward voice of belief and participation in a "living, organic, *believing* community." Lawrence adopts Mabel's favorite terminology for describing her relationship with the powers that be (terminology found nowhere previously in his writing): "If one wants to be free, one has to give up the illusion of doing what one likes, and seek what IT wishes to be done. . . . The true liberty will only begin when Americans discover IT, and proceed possibly to fulfill IT. IT being the deepest *whole* self of man. . . ." His use of Mabel's "IT" to define the whole soul of America as the "dusky body" underneath the "democratic and idealistic clothes of American utterance" reveals the primitivist bond that drew them together.[40]

Writing about Whitman, Lawrence eulogized other qualities in American life that he had discovered in Mabel. The "dauntlessness" and "fierce recklessness" that he attributes to Whitman he admired in Mabel. They were attributes of the "Yankee kick" that had driven America to break its bonds to kingship and fatherhood in its rebellion against "the old parenthood of Europe." Her life reaffirmed the courage and energy that had driven Americans continually to confront new frontiers: "You happen to have been born an individual. . . . Yours, anyhow, was a fierce direct negation: as there are gods of pure destruction, pure in its way, and necessary as creation." This assessment of Mabel provides an interesting clue to Lawrence's paradoxical statement in *Studies* that Americans were the closest to potential regeneration because they were the furthest gone toward the extreme of consciousness and mechanical will. Only after the furthest verge of soul destruction could the apocalyptic breakdown come that must precede the birth of new organic life. Not long after Lawrence's death, Frieda wrote Mabel, "You know Lawrence had a great respect for something incorruptible in you—some kind of truth & facing things." At the end of the letter, she inscribed the symbol of the phoenix, with Mabel's name beneath it.[41]

Lawrence was away in Mexico with Bynner and Spud during the spring, summer, and fall of 1923. During this time, Mabel wrote and asked for forgiveness, and he graciously agreed to forget the "bad things" because of his beautiful memories of Taos. On October 19, he advised Mabel to stop trying "to *compel* life," to become passive and allow the "vast invisible god that lives in ether" to interpenetrate her, the very resolution that he gives his heroine, Lou Witt, in *St. Mawr*. He wrote to Spud Johnson that she had put out the "flag of peace." "Let it be peace. . . . It may be that she is another woman."[42] Despite the quarrels and curses, Lawrence was genuine in his desire to establish their friendship on fresh and less destructive grounds.

While he was in England, during the winter of 1923–24, he wrote her about what he hoped would be her role in their future. Discouraged and unhappy in London, he encouraged her to believe that he had great need of her love and understanding. In December, he wrote her he was depending on her spirit "at the back of me, over there no matter what is over here." He was happy to hear that she had given up "taking thought": "Perhaps it is because you are learning to *give* your life into the creative future. For a woman, the greatest joy, I think, is to give her spirit and know it is not in vain, that the gift is needed. Which it is." By January, he was admiring her "dauntlessness" and looking forward to the good times they would have the next summer. She, he averred, was one of the few people capable of having the seriousness of the Great God Pan: "this fierce recklessness, based on trust . . . trusting deep down to the springs of nature, the sources: and then the laughter."[43] Lawrence wrote his essay "Pan in America" on his return to Taos.

While Lawrence was feeding her ego and psyche, Mabel was in the midst of a creative outburst of poetry writing that addressed her longing to be able to play the part he wanted her to. In "False Start" and "The Land of Flowers," she used wasteland imagery to express the barren state of her body and soul. The first dealt with Lawrence's perception that Mabel contained within her a seed that could be nurtured to regenerate her being. Tired of trying to "reach the fruit in the seed," she asks to be left to "recover in darkness" and for Lawrence to "bear with my weakness, my failure, my pain. . . . I sicken from sunlight, but give the rain, for I am but seed." As in most of the poems she wrote for and to him, Mabel bestows on Lawrence the power of a fertility god who can quicken the roots that have withered from her overexposed ego. In "Land of Flowers" she awaits his "interpenetrating ray" that will bring the desert wilderness of her body to life, while in "Tell Me Master," he is the prophet who alone can interpret the secret that will soften the "frozen" soil of her being.[44]

In "Best to Tell All," Mabel revealed to Lawrence the opposite impulse that drove her to imitate rather than submit to him. She writes of the need to make the transition from the primary demands of the flesh to more controlled forms of creativity. Wishing to purge her body of its craving for physical love, which she feels has drowned her in a limiting sensuality, she hopes that the revelation of her past through language will be the catharsis of the body lust that has consumed too much of her life.

The poem is significant not only because it was the first that Mabel wrote to Lawrence as a mentor, but also because it was the first to express one of the major impulses that led to the writing of her autobiography:

> Best to tell all.
> Maybe earth-cast words will carry away
> Desire from this clay.
>
> Wring the tear dry.
> Maybe this salt will burn
> Lust from this eye.

> For over me, forlorn,
> Love, old love, hovers still,
> Seeking new form.

In "Grey Gulls" she recognized Lawrence's similar impulse when she compared him to one among a greedy flock of birds who hungered for food. Because he was "eager and unappeased with our morsels," he veered "true and straight towards the sun," the center of spiritual light.[45]

These poems, however, were the exception. After Lawrence accepted her apology, in the summer of 1923, Mabel celebrated her feeling that she was "a new planet" by once more revering him as the prophet of female submissiveness. In "Sapphic," she recalled how she spent her life "dancing with God," and, as the aggressor, did the leading. Wearied of this, He "threw her down hard." But she was unwilling to dance with anyone but the best, so she waited for the man who would take up her hand. Mabel understood Lawrence's hatred of her Sapphic qualities. When she was on the outs with him, she wrote to Van Vechten about his belief that he had the godlike power to destroy men and women through his fiction. Calling him an absolutely "mal hombre" who would do the worst, she confessed that "he has tried to destroy every friend he ever had—in his books." He had told a friend in a rage that he had destroyed Lady Ottoline in *Women in Love* and followed this up by saying, "And I shall destroy Mabel."[46]

Lawrence wrote Mabel on January 22, 1924, that he refused to think of her as a "knower." While he was amused by her poetry (and obviously flattered), it is clear from his response that he exacerbated those very qualities he disliked in her and in his American heroines: "the essential you, for me, doesn't know and could never write: the Eve who is Voiceless like the serpent, yet communicates." Mabel acceded to his views in her most self-revealing poem, which was published in the May 1924 issue of *Laughing Horse* and was illustrated by Lawrence. While the poem sounds parodic, Mabel intended it as a serious antifeminist tract. She wrote Van Vechten that it was "an indictment against all Feminism" and an "earnest appeal to women to leave off trying to steal the world away from men." Women should return to motherhood—symbolic, that is: "There's enough power in that for any woman—Let them leave off stealing the masculine secrets of the will-to-power." In trying to achieve "the godhead" by emulating men, women will be destroyed: "a woman genius is scarce."[47]

Mabel is, of course, the "bad girl" of the poem. Her lust to violate a male godhead is rooted in her early childhood, in the failure of her parents to fulfill their traditional roles. The "Ballad," in fact, reads like a comic version of a classic American literary theme—the "orphan" betrayed by his parents who seeks out an enigmatic God in his quest for identity. Here, however, the hero is female, and the quest profaned by that fact:

> When I was a baby Mother pushed me from my cradle,
> But I didn't fall! Oh no, sir! Tho' it's odd, odd, odd.
> I snatched up in the hall Father's silver-headed walking-stick
> And, a straddle it I hastened after God, God, God.

Passing into the airy regions, she learned the secrets which kept the world going as she feasted on honey cake and ether. She dabbled in mystical realms where she learned things she was never allowed to in school. Her father died raving and her mother remarried, but she does not allow herself to feel the pain of human life on earth. Her life's quest is to push past all barriers in the Promethean search to find out God: "And I knew he had the secret that it wasn't His to keep!"

Just as she is about to plunge her hand into his burning breast, out jumps a very angry D. H. Lawrence, "with blue, blue eyes and a red, red crest." He informs her that she has taken a wrong turn because there is no place for women in heaven. Stamping his foot, he orders her down below. With the help of his kick, the bad girl returns to earth, having learned the only secret she needs to know: "That a *Woman* can be saved by a fall, fall, fall!" She puts her father's cane back in its place and gives up her search for phallic consciousness. Lying down in the pansy bed, she calls for her mother to "mother me,/And teach me how to mother and that's all, all, all!"[48]

Beneath the poem's surface silliness is the genuine tragedy of Mabel's lack of mothering. Her humiliating herself so publicly before Lawrence is a measure of the depth of an inadequacy that was often masked by her seemingly gargantuan ego. She could have done no more for Lawrence, short of prostrating herself before him. When he returned to Taos in the spring of 1924, she was determined to win him by proving how "good" she had become, how sweet and feminine. She put on a show of weakness, riding decorously beside him instead of tearing ahead on horseback as she had previously done. Lawrence was evidently pleased with this new Mabel, as indicated by his warm and friendly notes during his first few weeks back. His renewed appreciation had much to do with his own situation as with her seeming change, however. Lawrence had expected to recruit converts back in England for his New World colony. He had managed to bring only one, the Honorable Dorothy Brett. Brett had nothing but contempt for the "stuffy" friends back home who could not free themselves to come to America. Of all those who were part of the Lawrence ménage during his life, no one adulated and idolized Lawrence more than she. Four months before her death at age ninety-four, her eyes still bright with the memory, she told me that there was no man ever like him. "One would go anywhere in the world with him." And, after all, Frieda *bored* him. She "had as much brains as that bird over there in the cage," Brett informed me as she pointed to her parrot.[49]

Brett was a painter who had been on the fringes of the Lawrence-Murry circle. Although she admitted that "Lawrence's ego never permitted a woman any creative ability," she came with him to America to serve him as a combination secretary and idolator. Like John Young-Hunter's, her appetite for America had first been whetted when she was treated to Buffalo Bill's Wild West Show. It was a very different Indian she came to know and respect after her move to Taos. She captured him in some of the most beautifully rendered paintings of Indian ceremonial life done by Anglo artists in the Southwest.

Brett was a witty, perceptive, and delightfully eccentric woman who came to Taos predisposed to be enthralled. She was awed by Mabel's poise and self-assurance and admired her "warm glow" and "rich personality." Although Mabel was not conventionally attractive, Brett found her, as many of her friends did, "compelling"—"a small, powerful woman with a beautiful voice and beautiful eyes." Brett remembered those first days as wonderful, with Lawrence profligate with his "gift of enhancing life, of making the chores . . . gay, exciting, and fun," and Mabel full of "keen perceptions" and "vigor." She was continually arranging joyous occasions for their benefit: charades, hot baths in mountain springs, picnics, and horseback rides into the high mountain forests, and the Indian dances that Mabel and Tony delighted their friends with and often gave at home. The large dining room would be cleared, "the drum suddenly throb, the singers softly sing," and through the kitchen door the feathered Indians dancing to the ever-strengthening beat of the drum, "fantastic, gorgeous figures" in the low light. On midsummer evenings, they were spellbound outdoors by "the wild beauty of the songs, the unbearable rhythm of the drum, the bells and light swish of the feet of the dancers." The festivities would end with a Circle Dance the Anglos joined, coming as close as they ever would to experiencing the fusion they hungered for with a peace whose "haunting beauty" followed "one through sleep all night."[50]

Brett also experienced Mabel's "desire to control" and her "insatiable appetite for tasting life in all its aspects" which drew people into intimacies that she sometimes used to break up relationships. She felt the full fury of Mabel's mood swings, jealousy, and pettiness, which could turn favor into disfavor like lightning. Brett was to suffer banishment at various times throughout the rest of her life at Mabel's hands, but she also benefited tremendously from the loyalty and generosity that Mabel bestowed on her.

Although Mabel later became a fervent supporter and promoter of Brett's paintings, she was anything but enthralled by her entree into an already complicated ménage. Brett intruded herself and her ear trumpet, "Toby," everywhere she could, in order to miss as little as her defective hearing would allow. Her presence served, ironically, as a release for Frieda's and Mabel's tensions with one another. They both joined in despising her, ostensibly for her sexlessness but just as much for her hero worship of the man toward whom each felt proprietary.

After a few weeks, the up-and-down cycle of Mabel's and Lawrence's relationship began again. In the morning, following a lively evening during which Lawrence did one of his amusing imitations (he was particularly good at caricaturing Mabel's mother), Mabel would rush over to his house to let him know how wonderful she felt. Lawrence was cross, unsympathetic, and distant from the woman to whom he had seemed so close the night before. The more marvelous Mabel said she felt, the more sullen Lawrence became: "You think it's good health, but it isn't. . . . It's just sheer unrestrained ego, that's what it is. It's the destroyer." Mabel strolled over to Brett's. Hoping for a more sympathetic ear, she screamed into her trumpet, "Isn't it a wonderful day?" only to get back in reply, "Hay? Is José cutting hay?" When Brett finally understood, she replied, "Well, what of it? What about the day?" "Oh, *shut up!* Mabel snapped, all her ebullience gone. When Lawrence's "daemon took possession of him," however, just to be near him "was to be destroyed, and possibly, re-created. . . ."—that is, until the next dip in the cycle with his and Mabel's rhythms out of synchronization and the two jockeying for power and attention. Camping one night on the appropriately symbolic Continental Divide, Lawrence wanted his coffee weak, Mabel, strong. They made it twice as they sat "in a venomous silence, each conducting furiously an inner dialogue with the other."[51]

Lawrence's distaste and revulsion for human flesh and physical contact were more in evidence than during the previous summer. One can see them in the dehumanizing impersonality that pervades his work and particularly in the assaults that brutalizing men make on women. Mabel claimed that Lawrence sometimes beat Frieda after making love to her because of his disgust at "sinking" into the flesh. Mabel was not the new Eve he evoked in his letters and she envisioned in her poetry; in fact, the effort she put into reforming the bad girl she had been the year before only exacerbated her willfulness, especially once she recognized that she would have to share Lawrence with Brett as well as with Frieda.

The distorting effects that Mabel and Lawrence had on one another's personalities can be most strongly felt in a bizarre dance that took place in Mabel's Big House that summer. Mabel had under her wing at the time an effete young man named Clarence who she believed was in love with her (later she claimed he had sexual relations with Lawrence). Frieda and Clarence were dancing quietly, when Lawrence in a frenzy of jealousy grabbed Mabel and, using her strength for a "battering ram," flew about the room bumping and kicking Frieda at every opportunity. Mabel believed that she and Lorenzo were, "united at last, one will, one effort, to break, to crush, to shatter if we could, the ease and beauty of those two others." Brett recalled that it was Mabel who was dancing decorously with

Clarence when Lawrence seized *her* and went bumping and crashing into Mabel. Brett was, however, drunk during much of the affair.[52]

Both Brett's and Mabel's memories highlight the sexual tensions that were destroying the hoped-for reconciliation in Taos that summer. If Brett's memory is correct, Lawrence was using a woman he believed was frigid as a weapon to nullify one sexual state which he dreaded—the castrating, masculine woman locked in the embrace of a homosexual. And if Mabel is right, he was using a woman who intellectualized sexuality to attack the other state which he dreaded—the fecund earth mother locked in an embrace with her eternal son. In either case, Lawrence was using a woman as a weapon-like surrogate for his own sexuality, a situation reflected in his two most misogynistic American stories, "The Woman Who Rode Away" (whose heroine is based on Mabel) and "The Princess" (whose heroine is based on Brett).

In retrospect, Mabel blamed a great deal of Lawrence's aberrant behavior on the women who she felt dragged at, wrestled with, and "ground against each other and against him" like rocks at the foot of a sea-sprayed cliff. The image is an apt one. Lawrence and Mabel needed people with and against whom they could "grind" in order to form their attitudes and behavior. Both of them violated social expectation by turning their personal battles into public spectacles, as though their lives were performances that needed an audience to ensure their value and significance. Lawrence needed an entourage to bear witness to his life and legitimize his role as prophet—Murry, the Danish artists, Mabel and Brett, the Huxleys. Mabel, of course, sought out the elect of the world to come to Taos and legitimize her role as prophet by immortalizing herself and Taos.

Mabel's transformation of her private life into a public act with "aesthetic significance" is most revealing in her relationship with Lawrence, who was her peer in this as well. After one of their many quarrels, Mabel commanded Lawrence to come to her. When he refused, she went to his house and begged him, breaking down and sobbing about the way he had treated her, while he quietly sat regaling her with his distaste for the way she had walked that morning. Mabel sobbed on, keeping up her tears long past the point where they would have naturally subsided. Various people came by to look in—Frieda, Brett, Clarence, some Indians—for no one had ever (apparently) heard of Mabel crying and they wished to see this phenomenon.

Mabel had staged a wonderful event for the community, given a great "gift" to Lawrence, and achieved catharsis by sharing the luxury of her weeping with a sympathetic audience. She had always tried to give her life symbolic import, but to do this she reversed the normal symbol-making procedure; she hoped to make her scenes stand for more than just themselves and in this way to prove to herself that the concrete situations out of which they arose had meaningful content. This constant, conscious

217

shaping of life was one of the things that most irritated Lawrence about Mabel, for he felt that living should be natural, spontaneous, and unself-conscious. Yet his vocation demanded a conscious process of observing, shaping, and ordering human behavior in order to derive its symbolic import. He too was not above staging his own real-life scenarios to serve his art.

Mabel and Lawrence believed that imaginative literature, as the integrator of human, natural, and spiritual forces, was the primary vehicle for their message. But the "mankind" to whom they proferred this salvation largely saw the artist as an effete entertainer of the educated and wealthy; many of them saw Lawrence, specifically, as obscene. One way to respond to the discrepancy between how he viewed his role and how society at large did was to surround himself with an appreciative audience. Third parties were necessary for both Lawrence and Mabel to assure them that what they did and said mattered.

When the third parties did not measure up to their standards of an ideal audience, they often found themselves punished in prose as well as insulted in real life. But when appreciative, such an audience could often give back only a reflected glory that distorted their personal lives and their ability to measure their own influence. Lawrence often failed to see his friends as individual people and tended to view them as "types" of his own or society's inner demons. Thus Murry became a Judas and Mabel a Medusa, or, when he was feeling affectionate toward her, a "voiceless Eve."

Fiction, as Hawthorne noted, depends on this public-private inversion. Lawrence borrowed Hawthorne's definition of the unpardonable sin as the violation of the sacred "otherness" of a human being and then committed the sin over and over again in his fiction. At one point in her autobiography, Frieda acknowledges this practice, when she says that Lawrence sometimes treated her as a scientist treats his "dissecting rabbit." As even his most sympathetic biographer noted, Lawrence used his friends in his fiction in such a way as to reveal elemental flaws and idiosyncratic characteristics that made them instantly recognizable to themselves and to those who knew them.

Tony absented himself a good deal during the Lawrences' visits. He seems to have taken his wife's behavior with stoicism, at least up until the night of the dance. When he saw Mabel creep after Frieda and Clarence in order to spy on them, he called after her to come back. When Mabel refused to return, Tony left. During the dreary hours of the night she waited for his return and wrote the poem which expressed the loneliness she sometimes felt as an "eternal alien." In her conclusion, she summed up all the roles Tony played for her: the spiritual father, who offered her a mystery she could not fathom; the earthly father, less remote, who guided her by example; and the lover who was "no stranger to my heart!"[54]

As much as Tony had to offer, however, it was still not enough. In the fall of 1924, Mabel fled from Lawrence's rejection to A. A. Brill. He once again insisted that she learn to do her own work. Although Mabel went to him in a very doctrinaire Laurentian mood, she recognized that he was right. Lawrence rejoiced in her submission to Brill, apparently pleased with the fact that she had submitted to a male authority, and he recommended housework as an exercise in self-discipline. Lawrence's chauvinistic views corroborated Mabel's belief that as a woman she was capable only of minor sublimations. She was prevented from writing both by her own inertia and by his remarks that he would never consider her a writer or a knower. "And these words paralyze me. . . ." Yet, she would not give up and asked him if he thought she should start a "life-history or something."[55] In this endeavor, Lawrence encouraged her.

While Mabel was living at Finney Farm during the late fall and winter of 1924–25, she heard rumors of Lawrence's vituperations against her that finally made her realize "there is nothing except what one creates oneself." It was at this point she began to think about writing her memoirs, about shaping her life through the formal control of *her* own language, although she did not, for a while, intend to publish them. Mabel wrote Leo Stein about her break with Lawrence and the inception of her autobiography: "I finally couldn't stand his meanness & untrustworthiness any more & wrote him when he went to Mexico in October that he was *too* treacherous and unreliable [to] keep a friend. . . . I am writing on a kind of honest autobiography. . . ."[56]

Lawrence, meanwhile, had continued to develop his reactions to Mabel's life and character in the fiction he published about his experiences in America, most of which deals with women who are solitary wayfarers from civilized society. It is as though he were compelled to tell her story over and over, each time casting a different shade, and sometimes a contrary light. Through his retelling, Lawrence was able to project his own ambivalence toward giving up his manhood and individuality in order to recover a primal sexual and tribal experience. When his generic heroine risks penetration by an upwelling of unconscious forces, she is rewarded with fulfillment. When she seeks new life out of willful curiosity, the thrill of adventure, or a conscious, prying ego, she is punished with insanity or death.

In *St. Mawr*, Mrs. Witt is easily recognizable as Mabel. Once again, Lawrence measures the decline of Western civilization by the decline of woman's traditional role. Mrs. Witt runs about Europe looking for "real" men and confronting them as the perennial castrator: *"Your virility or your life."* Paraphrasing Mabel's poem "Sapphic," Lawrence says that Mrs. Witt wanted to cry out for God to conquer her. But she had contempt for Him and felt she could make *"Him* kiss her hand."[57]

In spite of Mrs. Witt's forbidding nature, Lawrence admires in her what he admired in Mabel—her courage to face new experiences in her unending search to be made "real." Having lived much of her life as a public figure, she felt, as Mabel often did during her New York years, that her identity was no more than "a daily sequence of newspaper remarks." Mrs. Witt is much like the Mabel Luhan that Lawrence first encountered in Taos: "Here she was, a woman of fifty-one, past the change of life. And her great dread was to die an empty, barren death." Unlike his biographers, who consistently viewed Mabel as a lustful seductress, Lawrence understood Mabel's views on sexuality: "Sex was a mere adjunct. She cared about the mysterious, intense, dynamic sympathy that could flow between her and some 'live' man. . . . But she had never rested until she had made the man she had admired: admiration was the root of her attraction to any man."[58]

Like Sybil Monde, Mrs. Witt is described as a goddess who has been dispossesed of her birthright by her times. Her attempt to find a mate worthy of her leads to one of the great comic moments in the novel, especially if one is aware of the in-joke involved. Looking at his relationship with Mabel from the luxury of distance (he was in England when he worked on the novel), Lawrence relishes the humorous dimension of her pursuit. Mrs. Witt chooses her groom, Lewis, an uneducated Laurentian, who is childlike in his language and perceptions and distrustful of strong women. She gives him the nickname that Mabel gave Lawrence in a poem she wrote for him that satirized his pretensions as a sexual prophet. Referring to him, with what I assume is a deliberate pun, as "Jack Horner of the Midlands," she wrote:

> Oh, bitter, sacred fruit of women!
> Bitter, flaccid, perpetual harvest!
> Lorenzo!
> Thyself plucked only by thyself from women's hearts.
> Thyself.
> Eternal fruit uneaten of men—
> And uneaten of all creatures.
> . . . self-harvested only!
> The mystic Plum.[59]

Lawrence's rather attractive portrait of Mrs. Witt can in part be attributed to the renewed feelings of affection that came with his first winter away from Mabel. His conflicts are felt more markedly in his portrayal of Lou Witt. She is a rootless American who has wandered Europe like a gypsy, with a marriage to a minor landscape painter that reveals a "tension of will" very similar to Mabel's and Maurice Sterne's. In the mountains of New Mexico, she discovers a place she can call sacred, where she is able to cleanse herself of centuries of civilized refuse and be reborn. Expressing the same repulsion to the flesh that Mabel's and Lawrence's poems of this period do, she decides to consecrate her life to the "unseen gods" and the "sacred fire" of the mountains.

Just as it is unclear whether Mabel was asking Lawrence to nourish her sexuality or help her to transcend it, it is unclear what Lou wants from "the spirit of the mountain." It arouses in her a "sex passion" that is violent and terrifying. Although Lawrence tries to affirm her actions as redemptive, what she really worships is "the sexual annihilation that is pictured in the loveless, savage energy of the landscape." Through Lou Witt, Lawrence identified himself with the earth mother, who, like the persona of Mabel's fertility poems, waits expectantly to be violated and possessed by the male spirit of the mountain. By this identification, Lawrence could appropriate the fecundating principle responsible for the generation of his art. But the attractiveness of this identification was matched by a revulsion that was aroused by his desire to retain his manhood and his individual identity. The only way that Lawrence could deal with his conflicting desires to escape and accept his phallic maleness was "at the bitter cost of sending his female persona to destruction."[60]

Lawrence's fictional sacrifice of Mabel Luhan may well have been his means of avoiding literary and psychological suicide. By reducing her to her "essential femaleness" he could at once experience and expiate his own desire to be violated by the savage gods and men that haunted the American landscape, while punishing her for her attempted usurpation of male prerogative.

In "The Woman Who Rode Away," Lawrence carried out both his own and Mabel's desire to serve a messianic role by making his heroine the sacrificial fulfillment of an Indian myth. Reduced to "Woman," stripped of ego and personality, she becomes the archetypal savior (she is thirty-three and her journey takes three days) who gives up her life so that the Indians may regain the power and supremacy wrested from them by the white man. In one sense the story is, as Frieda wrote to Mabel, an extraordinary tribute: "did I ever tell you, or he, that he said: 'The Woman Who Rode Away' is Mabel's story to me." In Lawrence's terrifying allegory of the rise and fall of American civilization, the woman redeemer symbolizes the victimization of women. Her husband is a withered heir of the Protestant ethic who exploits his land and rapes its wealth. His relationship with his wife is purely economic—she is a prized possession like the silver from his mines. Like Sybil and Mrs. Witt, the Woman has been unsexed by a civilization that has committed the sin of abstracting women from their inherent sensuality.[61]

If one pays less attention to the story's mythic structure, however, and more to its details, it reads like a revenge fantasy. Mabel was closer to its import than Frieda when she described it as the one where "Lorenzo thought he finished me up." Although we are not told very much about the Woman, she is hardly presented as a heroic figure. She undertakes 221 her journey with what Lawrence calls a "foolish romanticism" and a willful curiosity to find the strange gods of a savage Indian tribe. She is described as being dead almost from the beginning of the journey, and very soon after arriving at the Chilchui village, she is kept in an almost continual state of hallucination by the drugs the Indians give her. The Woman does not go to her sacrifice willingly or even consciously. Lawrence blames her "half-childish, half-arrogant confidence in her own female power" for getting her into this position.[62]

In her one moment of apocalyptic insight, the Woman reveals Lawrence's terror of the modern woman whose death is necessary for the resurrection of male prerogative: "Her kind of womanhood, intensely personal and individual, was to be obliterated again, and the great primeval symbols were to tower once more over the fallen individual independence of woman . . . womanhood was to be cast once more into the great stream of impersonal sex and impersonal passion." As in *St. Mawr,* one perversion is met by another, more loathsome: the extreme of the modern woman's self-consciousness can only be overcome by the extreme of a dehumanized phallic consciousness. That the death of the Woman is eroticized as the ultimate religiosexual experience is most horrible of all.[63]

"The Woman Who Rode Away" bore a close resemblance to Lawrence's fantasized death wish for Mabel. It appeared in *The Dial* during the summer of 1925 while he was living in Taos. He and Mabel did not see one another that summer; in fact, they never saw one another again. After spending some time in Mexico, Lawrence returned to Europe in the fall. In January 1926, he and Frieda moved to Italy, where they lived until his death.

On January 26, 1926, Lawrence wrote her about the publication of *The Plumed Serpent,* which he sent her a copy of and hoped she would like. Mabel resented the fact that the novel was set in Mexico rather than in New Mexico, but she recognized that it was as close as Lawrence would ever get to portraying their shared messianism.

In this novel, Mabel's quest for new life, and her supposed regeneration through her marriage to Tony, provided Lawrence with the key to his lost Atlantis. As Witter Bynner wrote him, Mabel "got" (i.e., took over) his novel; for Lawrence reveals the same naive belief that the ancient mythos of Indian tribal religion might provide the key to modern man's and woman's salvation. The rebirth of Western civilization is exemplified in the marriage of Indian and white cultures that Mabel dramatized in "An Intimation." Indian-white miscegenation becomes the only way for white men and women to recover their original harmony with their bodies and with nature, as well as the only way for the Indian to advance out of his "degenerate" state of mindless despair. The brotherhood that the European conqueror (Ramón) achieves with the "best" of the native Indians (Cipriano) fulfills Lawrence's old Cooperian fantasy. In this novel he has it all:

the blood brother he had always yearned for, and the submission of the white woman over whom they both exercise their machismo.

Unlike his other American heroines, however, Kate is a fully realized character. This may well be because she is an amalgam of Mabel, Frieda, and Lawrence at the points where they were most congenial. In her enthusiasm for finding a purpose in life and in her relationship with Cipriano, Kate is Mabel. In her skepticism of Ramón's pretentions to godhood and her acceptance of her sensuality, Kate is Frieda. In her aristocratic distaste for Mexicans and Indians and her equally strong attraction to their warmth and phallic power, Kate is Lawrence. What holds her together is the bond Frieda wrote Mabel they all had in common: "The bond between us is really that we weren't satisfied with the old way of consciousness & wanted a new one, each in our own individual way & that mattered more to us than anything."[66]

Kate's life history and transformation, however, are closely modeled on Mabel's. Her gradual initiation into the revivified tribal ways of ancient Mexico parallels Mabel's own autobiographical descriptions of her road to salvation in the final volume of her memoirs. Like Mabel, Kate had lived in restless pursuit of lovers who were involved in reshaping the world through art and politics. She is middle-aged when she discovers that she can center herself and "be born again." When she attends her first Indian dance, Kate is pierced by a rhythm that speaks of the human family in communion. All she had known before were the broken strains of individual consciousness. Here Lawrence idealizes the experience he depicts with horror in his other American works: the consummation of Kate in "the greater womanhood . . . beyond the individualism of the body." Reiterating his words to Mabel after her marriage to Tony, Kate tells herself that this is not a "panic reversal: 'We must go back to pick up old threads. We must take up the old, broken impulse that will connect us with the mystery of the cosmos again.'"[67]

Kate comes to see her mating with Cipriano as the "rounding of the great circle" Lawrence wrote Mabel about. Like Mabel, she sees in the fusion of the old blood consciousness with the verbal and rational powers of the white race the germ of a new world order. Lawrence elevates Kate and Cipriano to the level of joint godheads who reenact in their marriage ceremony the original sexual act of heaven and earth. The integration of body and soul, individual and communal life, that Mabel and Lawrence longed for with equal intensity is here achieved through a sexual dialectic firmly rooted in a religious and ritualistic context. The symbols through which the poet-prophet calls this new world into being are the outgrowth of and analog to the act of coitus—the momentary meeting of opposites in which spirit and flesh are joined.

In November 1923, Lawrence had written Mabel, "One day I will come to you and take your submission. . . . I was your enemy. But even saying things against you—and I only said, with emphasis and in many ways, that your will was evil masquerading as good, . . . even as an enemy I never really forsook you."[68] In *The Plumed Serpent,* he took what he had always told Mabel it was in her power to give him. Through Kate, he rewarded Mabel with what he saw as the true fulfillment of her womanhood. The optimistic side of Lawrence's racist fantasy is seen in his portrait of Cipriano as the dark other. He alone is able to teach modern woman to lie prone under the all-powerful and revered phallus. Yet he is, ultimately, uninteresting to her without Ramón, just as Mabel needed the white prophet Lawrence to articulate what Tony stood for in silence.

The Plumed Serpent is a wish fulfillment of what Lawrence's and Mabel's relationship might have been. Neither could give up cerebral consciousness and the need to dominate the other by force of will. What Lawrence and Mabel sought was power; what they wanted was love. When Kate at last turns to Cipriano, pleading with him to need her, it is not as Malintzi, the earth mother, she speaks, but as a lonely woman who wants to be loved for herself. In his recoil from the "cold egg" of militarism that pervades *The Plumed Serpent,* Lawrence wrote *Lady Chatterley's Lover* to restore tenderness between man and woman.

Lawrence's departure from America did not, needless to say, restore Mabel to tenderness. In fact, it seems to have stimulated her attentions to a man who she believed might assuage the spiritual hunger that Lawrence left unsatisfied. Mabel's ardor for Jean Toomer was one more sign that her "intimation" about her marriage serving as "a bridge between cultures" was in trouble.

Chapter 7

The Other Side
of Paradise

What aloneness it is to awaken in the night
Away from native air and earth!
The heart is appalled by the eternal alien and everlasting
Unknown land.

What incomprehensible aloneness for the white woman
Who crosses over into the Indian heart![1]

Rarely in her public life and letters did Mabel indicate that she was anything less than content and fulfilled by the new world she discovered in Taos, whose "good news" she was spreading throughout the nation. Even the sentiments she expressed in the poem quoted above, which she included in her biography of Lawrence, were resolved a few verses later in the arms of her dark lover. But Mabel did not always resolve so easily the doubts she had about her final cosmos and her fourth husband.

Her restlessness is evident in the amount of time she spent away from Taos. Almost every year from 1923 on, she took at least one extended trip to New York, California, Arizona, and Mexico. These trips were undertaken for a combination and variety of reasons: for a change of scene and climate, to raise money for Collier's Indian work, to reestablish contacts with the cultural life of the city. In March 1925, Mabel published an article that described her need to breathe the "native air" of New York, the city she spent the rest of her time convincing others to leave. The "reviving embrace" of the latest in art, theater, and intellectual life was something she missed in Taos, no matter how many great souls she brought out there.

Mabel was also brought back to New York by the emotional upheavals and manic-depressive cycles that continued after her marriage with Tony, and that often resulted from her dissatisfactions with herself and with him. Much as she wished to she could not become an Indian, could not transform herself into the placid, intuitive, egoless ideal she admired. Nor did she always find Tony's incarnation of these qualities life enhancing. At various times throughout their marriage, Mabel was bored and repelled by Tony, when his long silences and lack of intellectual interests frustrated her. In a few of her most private papers, she admitted that their "utterly opposite characteristics" sometimes drove them to hurt one another cruelly and that there were times when she felt chained to him irrevocably by a fate that was more painful duty than love.[2]

Mabel turned to men like Lawrence because they could articulate what Tony, more often that not, stood for in silence. They could stimulate that part of her which never ceased wanting to know, control, and shape other lives. There was, however, only one time when her marriage was seriously threatened by such a man. In November 1925, she met Jean Toomer, the strikingly handsome charismatic disciple of the Russian mystic Gurdjieff. Toomer offered her a spiritual medicine that promised to cure her continuing psychic ailments and take her beyond the limits of Tony's expertise.

In 1923, with the publication of *Cane,* Toomer had been widely acclaimed as the most gifted and talented Afro-American writer of his generation. That same year, he began his dissociation from the black race. Wishing to be identified as neither black nor white, he claimed to be American, a new race he believed was evolving from the melding of the many racial and ethnic strains in the Unites States. In the fall of 1923, he met Gurdjieff, whose philosophical system he spent the next three years mastering and teaching. Like other exiles who attracted Mabel, Toomer was a "Flying Dutchman" in search of an identity and a haven. Deserted by his father as a child, uncomfortable with the personal and social limitations of his black identity, he searched for a father-substitute and a role that could both secure and liberate him.[3]

Mabel first learned of Gurdjieff's teachings and his Institute for the Harmonious Development of Man (established just outside Paris at Fontainebleau, in 1922) two years before she met Toomer. In the winter of 1924, when she had returned to New York to work with Brill, Gurdjieff gave a series of lectures about his work. When he left in February, his English disciple, Orage, who was by all accounts the better speaker, took over promotion and fund-raising. Mabel and Tony heard Orage speak at Janice Heap's studio, along with Muriel Draper and Margaret Anderson.

Gurdjieff's system appealed to Mabel because it combined a critique of Western civilization with a course of self-study that presumably led to total psychic harmony through mastery of the universal laws of "cosmic consciousness." Gurdjieff spoke of modern man in terms Mabel was quite familiar with: he was an automaton who allowed things to happen to him; he was made up of many conflicting selves and maintained only the "illusion of unity"; his three "centers"—mental, emotional, and instinctive—were perpetually out of balance. Drawing upon Freudian dream analysis, Nietzsche's theory of the transcendant Will, Buddhist practices of mysticism, theosophy, and the occult, plus his own idiosyncratic regimen, Gurdjieff designed a program that promised to lead his students beyond the shifting mask of "personality" to the permanent "I" that was the center of their "essence." Once they had full knowledge of "I," they could break the habits of social conditioning that had damaged them and create themselves anew.[4]

Gurdjieff created an exacting daily routine for his students at Fontainebleau. They awoke at five each morning, worked for two hours building, repairing, and farming; ate a light breakfast, did more domestic labors; ate a light lunch and after a brief rest devoted one or two hours to exercises; after dinner, there were four or five more hours devoted to ritual dances and rhythms, as well as talks by the master. Gurdjieff often declared fasts, sometimes lasting for up to a week.[5] One can hardly imagine Mabel adhering to such requirements. It was fortunate for her and for Gurdjieff, who profited greatly from her interest in his work, that she never went to France to study with him and that she never convinced him to open up an institute in Taos.

When Mabel heard Jean Toomer speak about Gurdjieff in public, and then talked with him in private, she was convinced she had found the system and the man who could help her reach the pinnacle of evolutionary consciousness. Mabel was not alone in her admiration. Toomer was extraordinarily attractive to women in general, and there were several Gurdjieffan disciples whose conversion was primarily a matter of personal adoration of Toomer. Part of his attraction was his power as a speaker, which seems to have been mesmerizing. One can feel some of what drew Mabel to him in the words he later wrote about his own conversion experience:

> Our economic system had run away with itself and was doing damage not only to the proletarians and the petty bourgeoisie, but to the capitalists as well. All classes and all groups were involved in the mutilation.
>
> Our psyches were split and chaotic. Our spirits were shrunken. Our souls were empty. To compensate for this emptiness, to avenge our tortured slow deaths, we had grown fangs and sacks of poison; and we used these fangs—race fangs, sex fangs, class fangs, national and religious fangs, all manner of personal fangs—with typical man-insanity against each other.[6]

Toomer's discovery of Gurdjieff had given him the personal direction and way "out of the chaos of modern civilization" that Mabel once believed

Tony had given her. Meeting Jean made her realize how far she had to go and how limited Tony was in his ability to help her get there. While her passion for Toomer did not last more than a few months, it was one of the most intense of her life. In December and January, she wrote him several lengthy letters that were filled with her wonder that the joy of his presence brought her, with expectations of the heights of consciousness to which she felt he could bring her, with her need and love for him, and, finally, with her recognition of how the pain she was causing Tony was lacerating him with jealousy and despair.

After Toomer's first talks with her in New York, she wrote to tell him that he called forth in her a desire to communicate more deeply, intensively, and significantly than she ever had. Tony "awakened my heart & my altruism, & kept it alive so that it is alive for good—& he made me maturer and stronger," but Jean was able to "transmute" her fire "to another centre where it is no less fire but is burning somewhere else,—& in this more lofty region—every cell is filled with light & no more weight remains in matter. . . ."[7]

Mabel well understood that the way to Toomer was through Gurdjieff. She told him that she was now convinced that everything she had done up until the time she met him had been "preparation" to receive the wisdom he had to teach. To prove her loyalty, she offered Gurdjieff, through him, her home in Taos and as much of her income as she could afford. Mabel convinced Jean to come to Taos, which he did in late December. There, both her passion and Tony's misery increased. When he spoke to a group of her friends in Santa Fe in early January, Mabel wrote him from the hotel where she was staying that she felt for him what she had felt for no other man. She had lost interest in Tony, who felt Mabel's total absorption in Toomer and was bewildered and angry. Her need for a new teacher was incomprehensible to him, for he believed he had taught her how to live. Tony threatened to expose Mabel to her mother and son; he warned her that the stone coldness of white people would cause them to crumble and become the "foundations" for the Indians who took over; he threatened to smash her with a hammer. Refusing to "be a shield" for her, he went home to Taos.

Mabel was not insensitive to Tony's plight, nor was she so infatuated with Toomer that she failed to recognize that he could survive without her. She wrote him that if Tony lost her, he might lose his life, but then, in the next breath, said she had to live near him: "I need you—*Need* to love you the way I do." Mabel cemented her love with a loan of $14,000, which she hoped would tempt Gurdjieff to open an institute in Taos. She reminded Toomer how much the Anglos in New Mexico needed what he had to give and recalled Alice Henderson's husband's remark after hearing Toomer that New Mexico was a "magnetic, an attracting centre" that would draw many more.[8] After he left, Mabel wrote her most impassioned letter. It revealed the depth of her feeling as well as a new maturity in terms of her sense of responsibility to Tony.

Mabel was certain that she had ruined Tony, that he was "weak and crippled." While she exaggerated the extent to which she had cut him off from the pueblo and made him a "spoiled" and "captive indian," she apparently did not exaggerate his wretchedness. According to Mabel, Tony told her that he wished to die: that his car would turn over or a bullet would find him. Mabel wrote she had outgrown him but could not break the "net" that bound them: "To break it & jump free is to repeat—at one hundred per cent more ruthless a level the heartless & selfish escapes of the past. That is not the solution. . . ."[9]

And how did Toomer respond? He did not meet her passionate outbursts with anything like her intensity, but there is no doubt that he encouraged her interest and to some extent exploited her feelings. The day after he left Taos, he wrote her from the train that leaving Taos "was like leaving home. This was the first time in years that I've experienced an emotional attachment to place and people. . . . I *feel* as though I could leave New Mexico forever; I *know* I never will." The weeks ahead would bring to light how much they had already accomplished together. Six days later, he insisted that she come to New York, which she did, in order that he could continue the "genuine stimulus" that was already moving her "up the scale." After he returned to Fontainebleau, Toomer told Gurdjieff about Mabel's offer and provided him with an unflattering portrait of the woman who had just provided them with $14,000.[10]

By the end of 1926, Toomer began to feel differently about having a center in Taos, and for the next six years he worked to convince Gurdjieff to move to America. He wrote Mabel in 1926 that Taos was one of the three places in the world Gurdjieff was seriously considering, and he reminded her of his own continuing interest in her: "I've never for a moment lost the sense of basic relationship and joy in being with you, and somehow I've also felt that you too sustained this sense and joy. It is a *damned* good thing in this life to know someone whom one can *live* with, difficulties included."[11]

The following year, Mabel's ardor seems to have cooled as she began to recognize that Tony was the someone she would "live with, difficulties included." She wrote Toomer in 1927, in a friendly but dispassionate vein. She was glad to hear that he was writing after a fallow period and offered him space in Taos if he wanted to work there. She was removed enough at the time to ask him about the arrogance and narcissism she had failed to note during her love-blind stage: "Do you still love yourself as much as ever with that half-pitying–half-patronizing but quite considerate love you felt two years ago? I wonder." In 1929, she asked him for the money back that she had loaned him. She asked him again in 1932, although she was still very cordial about her request and interested in seeing him. By that time Toomer had begun to recognize the dishonesty of his mentor, who had not only misappropriated Mabel's money, but was drinking and philandering with women. In 1934, Toomer sent Mabel a full account of the confused misuse of her funds and apologized for having no means to pay her back. Mabel never corresponded with nor heard from him again.[12]

Restoration

In the summer of 1926, Mabel's life returned to patterns that were more familiar to the rhythms of her life before Toomer had broken upon the scene. She entertained Willa Cather for a second time and also had a new conquest to add to her pantheon of those who enriched the Taos art colony. Nicolai Fechin was a Russian emigré from Kazan who was a well-known portrait and landscape artist when he first visited Taos at the Young-Hunter's invitation. Fechin had been living in New York City since he came to America. He found in Taos a vivid reminder of Georgia and the Caucasus Mountains, which he had visited and loved while living in Russia.

When Fechin became ill the following winter, he decided to leave New York forever and move to Taos. Mabel built him a studio out of a garage in the summer of 1927, but he soon began his own home. He spent the next six years designing and building a monument to his artistic genius. Fechin was a skilled woodworker who carved the entire interior and most of the furnishings of his new home: the posts, windows, fireplaces, desks, bowls, sculptures. The rugged beauty he created with his own hands is a testament to what his daughter believed he found in Taos: "Fechin had found his 'place'; he was in love with the land and the natives. His work sang."[13]

In 1927, Fechin painted the most striking portrait of Mabel during her New Mexico years. It makes a fascinating contrast with the dreamy-eyed romantic of the Villa Curonia created by Blanche, and the captivating brown-eyed innocent of Greenwich Village, created by Mary Foote. Fechin's Mabel is Indianized; bold, dark, and regal, she rules from her Florentine chair in a black dress and turquoise jewelry. She dominates her environment with a compelling gaze that invites your curiosity, at your own risk.

It was this Mabel who greeted Carl Van Vechten when he visited in January 1927. After several years of invitations and entreaties from Mabel, he finally came out to Taos. Here he met a very different woman from the detached and amused hostess he celebrated in Edith Dale. As early as January 1920, Mabel had tried to lure him by piquing his interest as a music collector: "You never saw such people!" she wrote him. "*Such* music

& movement. You should come out here & study this music & write it up. . . . Come with a phonograph or a dictograph & you could make the finest collection of records in the world."[14]

Van Vechten's visit was an interesting measure of the distance Mabel had come from the world he still inhabited. Mabel dramatized it in a short story she wrote after his departure, entitled "Twelfth Night." Her surrogate heroine is about as different a creature from Edith Dale as one could imagine. Edith was supremely tolerant of the moral laxity and self-indulgence of her ménage. The Mary of "Twelfth Night" is a Mabel who has been redeemed from the sins of the flesh by her stay in a southwestern garden of Eden. Carl's intrusion on this idyllic scene, in the guise of a Mr. Van der Comp, is the snake's entrance into paradise. He brings with him a jaded sensibility that prevents him from appreciating the simplicity and ethical profundity of Indian dance and music. He looks like someone "who had sucked his fingers overlong" and never outgrew the oral stage of infantile sexuality.[15]

Mabel's description of Van der Comp's life in New York City reads like a scene from one of Van Vechten's novels. Only here there are no amusing ironies. As Mabel portrays it, his life is empty and vicious. People drink and dance at endless parties and come and go with no ostensible purpose other than coarse amusement. Mary's life is a stark contrast to this Jazz Age debauch. When he begins a round of dirty jokes that goes on for three days, she feels "live charges of poison drenching the place." The dirt brought into the house is clearly that of white male sexuality, crude and unrelated to any connection with the living power of the earth. Respite is provided by the coming of the Indians, whose eroticism has nothing to do with Western decadence. It is not until Van der Comp leaves that paradise is fully regained.

Mabel wrote Carl after he left and pleaded with him not to use Taos or the Indians in any of his works because he had not received the kind of impression Mabel had hoped for. Van Vechten got his licks in at Mabel's world, although not at Mabel, in *Spider Boy* (1928), the last in his cycle of cynical Hollywood novels. His hero leaves Hollywood, after the fiasco of working with a director who knows nothing about art, and flees to Santa Fe. When a friend offers to take him to see Edith Dale, living in her refuge up in Taos, he declines. Instead he is taken up by Marna Frost, an "indian lover" in the ambiguous sense of the word, who wants to use his talents to help her with her cause to save the Indians. Marna is a brutal portrait of Mary Austin, whom Carl used as the butt of his satire on noble savagery.

There is little doubt that Van Vechten's visit reinforced Mabel's rededication to Tony and to Pueblo life. Shortly after he left, she wrote a fine essay on the value of Indian art and its importance as a national resource. Mabel explained that the stylized patterns on pottery and blankets were produced because of the "order and symmetry" that the Indians were able to intuit in the landscape. Where whites had ceased to experience life directly because of their faculty of analysis, the nonrational Indian was able to discover a pattern of meaning which unified human sensibility because it was based on the same "laws" that directed the seasons, balanced the forces of nature, and gave rise to religious and aesthetic expression.[16]

Eight years later, Mabel came as close as she ever would to conveying that pattern of meaning when she wrote her finest prose work, *Winter in Taos*. In the meantime, she took pleasure in Alice Henderson's 1928 anthology of poetry, *The Turquoise Trail*, which showed the marked influence of Indian culture and the New Mexican landscape on a large variety of Anglo writers: Vachel Lindsay, Mary Austin, Alice Henderson, Witter Bynner, Arthur Ficke, D. H. Lawrence, and Mabel Luhan. Henderson's *Preface* proclaimed the benefits of a "distinct regional personality" that had been created through the Indians' enrichment of Anglo culture: "On the common ground of poetry, indeed, the living Indian poets and the Anglo-American poets of New Mexico now meet in friendly contact; and the influence of this primitive verse and thought on the later poets is obvious."[17]

The regional myth that Mabel had so strong a role in shaping continued to nourish the artists and writers who lived, moved to, and visited Santa Fe and Taos throughout the decade. Their support for the protection of Indian life also continued. In 1926, Commissioner Burke devised a bill that would make all federal civil and criminal laws effective for Indians, who had previously settled all but eight federal statutes by tribal adjudication.

Collier worked with progressive congressmen over the next year to get the bill withdrawn. It was clear that the BIA had singled out the Pueblos as a test case for their increasingly repressive Americanization policies, when they created a rival Pueblo Indian Council to air Indian views and grievances. Collier successfully urged the Pueblos to boycott it. He was also successful in persuading congressmen to defeat the Leavitt Bill. With its demise went the last major threat to Indian religious freedom.[18] The fight, however, once again left scars. Mabel had kept Collier posted on the divisions that the BIA was fomenting with its attempt to preempt the All-Pueblo Councils, but she was fearful that if the Pueblos angered the federal superintendent they would lose their chance to recover several thousand acres surrounding their sacred Blue Lake, which they had petitioned to get back. When Tony refused to have anything to do with the government's representatives, some members of the Tribal Council accused him of betraying his people.

Mabel was obviously in a difficult position, but she played a mediator's role. She urged Tony to cooperate and to tell the governor and council to treat the federal agent with courtesy, at the least. The agent who came to hear grievances was apparently satisfied with his talks. While he did not think the Tiwa would get Blue Lake back (they didn't until 1971), he admitted that legal measures could be taken to stop prospectors from mining up in the mountains and thus from polluting the pueblo's water supply.

The federal government's abuse of Indian water, oil, and mineral rights was the third crucial issue that Indian reformers had to confront during the 1920s. Under Albert Fall, who believed in unrestricted use of America's natural "wealth," many Indian reservations were opened up for private exploitation. After two years of fighting, Collier, Atwood, and their allies in Congress finally got the Senate to submit a bill giving the Indians 100 percent of the royalties for oil found on their lands. It passed in March 1927. At the same time, Collier convinced the Senate to authorize its Committee on Indian Affairs to make a general survey of Indian conditions and report their findings, with recommendations for the correction of abuses and changes in the law. The two most effective progressive leaders in Congress, La Follette and Burton Wheeler, were put in charge.

Commissioner Burke also approved a private investigation of federal Indian policy by the Institute for Government Research. In 1928 it issued the Mirriam Report. It was a scathing indictment that, as one representative predicted, told a story worse than anything Harriet Beecher Stowe portrayed in *Uncle Tom's Cabin*. The report primarily blamed Congress for its refusal to appropriate adequate funds for medical care and education and for its destructive policies on land and natural resources. It concluded with a series of recommendations for major changes. The report certainly justified Collier's own work and gave him and his supporters, Mabel among them, reason to feel that they had brought about "a provisional revolution" in Indian affairs over the past six years. During the next decade, he would be given opportunity to bring that revolution to fruition.[19]

Although 1928 was a year of political and artistic promise, it was also a time of financial insecurity for Mabel. She had continued to build her guest houses throughout the 1920s, and the money she had so generously lavished in making life comfortable for herself and her guests, as well as the funds she expended on Toomer and on her Indian work, brought her to a point where she felt forced to earn some income. For a brief period of time, Mabel considered turning her homestead into a ranch resort. She opened the main house briefly in the spring of 1929 to serve meals, but closed it to the public after a short time. The lack of privacy her business would have entailed and her lack of business sense were very likely the main reasons for her decision. Tony fared much better in his new venture. In the spring of 1929, he began to hire out both himself and his Cadillac to take tourists through the Indian pueblos and Spanish settlements.

O'Keeffe, Adams, and Marin

Mabel's financial concerns did not prevent her from playing hostess, in the summer of 1929, to the most stellar array of guests she had attracted since the fall of 1922: two of America's greatest painters—Georgia O'Keeffe and John Marin—and the man who was to become one of America's most noted twentieth-century photographers, Ansel Adams. Marin was stirred to tremendous creativity by his visit; for O'Keeffe and Adams, it changed the course of their careers.

Mabel had kept up her correspondence with Stieglitz from the time she came to New Mexico, hoping to convince him to visit. Stieglitz, however, believed that he had all that he needed in the way of natural inspiration at his family's summer home on Lake George. Mabel and Georgia had never been more than acquaintances at the time Mabel lived in New York, although O'Keeffe evidently admired her. In 1925, she wrote Mabel that she wished she would come to see her new show at the opening of Stieglitz's "Intimate Gallery." O'Keeffe had recently seen a piece Mabel wrote about the actress Katherine Cornell and believed that she "could write something about me that the men can't." She was infuriated with the incessant Freudian readings given her work by many male critics, who reduced it to an "outlet" for sexual expression and frustration. O'Keeffe told Mabel that "there is something unexplored about woman that only a woman can explain." She had apparently forgotten that Mabel brought psychoanalysts to her first show in 1916, when her openly erotic designs were causing a stir in the press.[20]

If O'Keeffe ever read the essay which Mabel wrote but never published about her 1925 show, she must have been shocked. The revulsion Mabel expressed toward her art, and toward Stieglitz as the presumed guardian of it, was hysterical, to say the least. Her disgust had much to do with jealousy as well as with the change her sexual philosophy had undergone since her Greenwich Village days. O'Keeffe and Stieglitz had the kind of mutually nurturing and productive personal and professional relationship that she had dreamed of for herself from the time she met Gertrude Stein. Stieglitz was O'Keeffe's friend, lover, supporter, mentor, patron, and business manager. He had absolute faith in his wife's original genius and felt that she expressed the best of what he had always loved in the American spirit—"a direct, clear, strong—even fierce—force" that was untainted by European training or influence. His discovery of her renewed his own art, as well.[21]

Although O'Keeffe was a shy and diffident person in public who very much needed the push that Stieglitz gave her work, she was also a very tough, independent, and strong-willed woman. She was completely devoted to her craft and to her role as a pioneer fighter for women's right to equality in the arts, during a period when women's aptitude for artistic genius was still seriously in doubt among establishment critics. It was not, however, the boldness of Georgia O'Keeffe's paintings that offended Mabel, but rather the openness of her sensuality. At a time in her life when she was working to evolve beyond her "primary" sexual instincts, she found O'Keeffe's seemingly exaggerated adoration of genitalia disgusting. Her attack went beyond that of any of the male critics of the time. One "feels indelicate looking upon these canvases," Mabel wrote, because they are unconscious outpourings of the "sexual juices" which "permit her to walk this earth with the cleansed, purgated look of fulfilled life!" But such art is the "negation of being," not a genuine cathartic. It is one "among the other 'comfort stations' of our civilized communities." Stieglitz is the "showman" who uses "this filthy spectacle of frustration" to market his wife's work.[22] Mabel's venom was a strong indicator of her still painful confusion about her own sexuality and the role it had played in her identity as a woman.

By the late 1920s, Mabel seemed to have overcome her objections to O'Keeffe. In the winter of 1929, she was in New York with Dorothy Brett, whose Indian paintings she wanted Stieglitz to show at his gallery. When she invited him and O'Keeffe out to Taos, she whetted Georgia's appetite. During the past year, relations between O'Keeffe and Stieglitz had been strained. He was happy with his routine, but Georgia was growing increasingly restive and eager to find new subjects and inspiration. She found the wet weather, constant intrusions, and lack of privacy of their summers with his family at Lake George increasingly difficult to take. In September 1928, Stieglitz suffered a heart attack that required total bed rest and quiet. Georgia now had the added responsibilities of being his nurse and secretary. Her concern for his health, the constant visits, and the work she had to do for him took a great deal of time and energy away from her own work.

In the winter of 1929, O'Keeffe was invited to show at a Museum of Modern Art exhibit. She had by now established a notable national reputation and critics looked with expectation to each of her winter shows. This year her new paintings were her weakest in years and the exhibit was not, by her standards, a success. Mabel invited her to Taos at the lowest ebb in her personal and professional life. She recalled the happy years she had spent in Texas as a young teacher and a visit she had made to Santa Fe in 1917, which she had loved. Although Stieglitz was not at all happy about her decision to spend the summer of 1929 in New Mexico, Georgia left on May 1, with her close friend Rebecca Strand, a painter who was married to the noted photographer Paul Strand.[23]

No sooner had they arrived in New Mexico than Mabel met them at an Indian dance and insisted they come to Taos. O'Keeffe may not have been eager to go, for Rebecca and Paul had found Mabel a difficult hostess when they visited in the summer of 1926. But neither woman resisted when Mabel apparently told them she had already sent their trunks to Taos so that they had no choice.[24] Whatever her initial feelings about going there, O'Keeffe's response to Taos was immediately positive. Mabel put her and Beck, as Rebecca was called, in the Pink House and also loaned Georgia an adobe studio. O'Keeffe felt completely at home in a landscape whose "bare essentials" called forth her deepest creative instincts. The semiarid terrain, the dryness, the spectacular vistas and clarity of light, the vast scale of mountain, mesa, and sky offered her a vision of enduring beauty that she, more than any artist who lived there, has defined for the nation as the symbolic Southwest.

Mabel captured O'Keeffe's sense of discovery in an article totally different from her earlier essay:

Things appeared to her visually enhanced, people were revealed more fully to her and seemed brought further into being than those she had known. "Wonderful" was a word that was always on her lips.

"Well! Well! Well!" she exclaimed. "This is wonderful. No one told me it was like *this*." No one could have understood how "this" appeared to her who had not experienced that almost miraculous acceleration of awareness that climates and altitudes can accomplish in mortals. . . .

When Georgia came to the high table-land of Taos it made her heart beat high. She was exultant and enchanted.[25]

O'Keeffe was not the ony one whose vision was "freshened" that summer. Ansel Adams was visiting at the time of her arrival. Adams was twenty-seven years old and had spent most of his life preparing for a career as a concert pianist, while practicing photography as an avocation. He had visited the Southwest three times before and was now engaged in photographing it for the Sierra Club. That summer, he decided to collaborate with Mary Austin on a verbal-pictorial celebration of Taos pueblo. When he returned to Mabel's the following summer to work with Austin, he met Paul Strand, whose work conveyed a "luminousness and clarity he had not believed could be captured by a camera." Taos was his "Paris and Rome" and Strand the mentor whose work "hit him like Saul's vision on the road to Damascus." Adams put aside all thoughts of a concert career as well as "the use of soft focus, atmospheric effects, and the simulation of painting that marked many of his early photographs." He adopted the style that brought him fame.[26]

Like O'Keeffe, Adams was tremendously taken with the solidity and timelessness of the Indian's architectural integration with the landscape and with the paradox created by the combination of weight and light that evoked a spiritual purity firmly rooted in the earth. The series of photographs in *Taos Pueblo* was "an important step in Adams's artistic evolution" because of his commitment to "light and form as the essential building blocks of a picture. Every exposure was made in the most brilliant sunshine which in turn created deep shadows." Shortly after its publication, Adams helped to found Group f/64 and define "the visual manifesto of straight photography." Light and shadow were the "essential ingredients of the new purist sensibility," which created "the illusion of touching the untouchable that is such an important theme in Taos Pueblo."[27] This was, without doubt, one of the finest products of all the artistic collaborations Mabel had fostered.

Not long after O'Keeffe's and Beck's arrival in May 1929, Mabel greeted the third remarkable member of the artistic trio who were guests that summer. They suggested she invite John Marin, and when she asked him out for the month of June, he wasted no time in getting there. Marin was the most ebullient among the artists that Stieglitz had helped on their way to national prominence. He was a slight, puckish-looking man whose brown bangs and weather-beaten gaze greet one with great candor, in the portrait that Paul Strand did of him the following summer. Marin had been one of the first members of 291, and Stieglitz had worked hard to establish him. By the mid-1920s, he was considered by many art critics the greatest watercolorist in America.[28]

Like O'Keeffe, Marin was ripe for a change. Just a year before he came, he wrote Stieglitz that he was tired of "living in herds." He was looking for a new landscape as a means of clarifying and renewing his aesthetic vision: "Seems to me," he wrote Stieglitz, "the true artist must perforce go from time to time to the elemental big forms—Sky, Sea, Mountain, Plain— . . . to sort of re-true himself up, to recharge the battery." Although Marin had spent several summers on the Maine seacoast, he was immediately impressed by the strikingly different terrain: "He liked the jagged forms of the mountains; was struck most of all by the vastness of space in that lofty region and by the washed clarity of the atmosphere after the showers which occurred almost daily during the rainy season in the summer. He set out to paint space, unbounded space, and produced pictures sharply different from the crowded houses and boats" of his Maine watercolors.[29]

Ella Young, an Irish poet and folklorist, remembered him as a "slave" of the Sacred Mountain. "Every day he set forth with paper, paint, and pencils, vowing that this time he will escape, he will not be captured by Taos Mountain. He comes back and somewhat shame-facedly exhibits another study of Taos. 'I just looked at it in passing,' he declares, 'and the Mountain held me!'" During the two summers he spent in Taos, from June to October 1929 and mid-June to mid-September 1930, Marin made nearly one hundred watercolors. When he returned to New Jersey in the fall of his second visit, he wrote Strand that "the East looks *screened in*. The West is a memory that we are constantly talking about."[30] Unlike

Adams and O'Keeffe, whose works stress stillness, balance, and formalism, Marin's watercolors of Taos capture the ever-changing dynamism of the always changing light and shadow that the clouds create across the land-scape. His mountains tower above plains that seethe with a motion matched by the drama of the storm clouds that usually hover overhead.

Another arrival that summer meant a great deal to Mabel in a more personal way. She had kept up her friendship and correspondence with the Hapgoods over the years, but it wasn't until this summer that she had convinced them to make a visit. Neith arrived with her daughter, Miriam, who "fell madly in love with the place as soon as I got off the train." The altitude was too much for Neith, but Miriam, who had been in a very depressed state before her arrival, stayed through until November and benefited greatly from the climate and Mabel's attention. Hutch bought her a small home, with Mabel's encouragement, and Miriam lived there for the next fourteen years. Miriam feels that she "became a new person" after moving to Taos, in good part because of Mabel's care and interest in her over the next few years.[31]

Stormclouds

Thus the summer of 1929 saw the beginnings of another triumph in Mabel's conversion crusade. Mabel did not, however, have much time to enjoy it, for she was soon plunged into the middle of a personal storm that once again threatened her marriage. This time Georgia O'Keeffe and Tony were the villains of the piece, at least as Mabel saw it. Mabel's internist discovered fibrous tumors in her uterus in June and insisted she have a radical hysterectomy at once. Mabel decided to return to Buffalo General Hospital, where she had been treated after John's birth. While she was waiting in the hospital for the operation, which took place on July 10, she received messages from home that informed her Tony had returned to the pueblo and was sleeping with his first wife. This was apparently not the first time.

The fact that Mabel was 2,500 miles away, waiting for an operation that was psychologically traumatic, increased her anxiety. She had under-gone menopause in 1922 and had spent much of the decade trying to transcend her "earth motherhood." But the removal of her womb was an event of such finality that she could not help fearing it would unsex her and that she might lose Tony as a result. To make matters worse, all of her correspondence with him during July went through the hands of Georgia O'Keeffe, whose admiration and interest in Tony added to Mabel's apprehensions. Because Tony could not write English, Georgia wrote his letters to Mabel and read Mabel's letters, full of suspicions and accusations, to him. Georgia did everything she could to allay Mabel's fears and reaffirm the profound love she believed that Tony felt for her. When Mabel wrote threatening divorce, Georgia replied, "I just feel like breaking your head if you don't stop even thinking about leaving Tony." After she and Beck had just come back from a camping trip with him in early July, she wrote:

> Right now as I come fresh from six days spent mostly with your Tony—
> I want to tell you that next to my Stieglitz I have found nothing finer
> than your Tony and—I feel about the same between you and him as I
> have told you before—if Tony doesn't love you—according to my
> notion—then nobody ever will. . . . I have rarely seen something in two
> people . . . as I feel it between you and your Tony and I feel you have
> got to let him live and *be* his way—however much it might hurt
> you. . . . Even if he goes out and sleeps with someone else it is a little
> thing—oh dear this sounds like twaddle but I love something that I feel
> together in you—and when I see such things being destroyed—it just
> makes me not want to live.[32]

Mabel did not fail to note the passion with which Georgia wrote about Tony and her remark that "if Tony happens to go out to women with his body it is the same thing when one goes out for a spiritual debauch." She knew that Georgia could not have sexual relations with her own husband and had certainly not forgotten her past concerns about Georgia's highly charged erotic nature. Mabel's threat of divorce may well have had more to do with her conviction that Georgia was making love to Tony than her upset about his visits to his first wife.

While O'Keeffe was playing marriage counselor (or betrayer, as Mabel saw it), Mabel was writing some of her most moving letters to Stieglitz. Like her, he was suffering physically and emotionally that summer and was equally concerned about the mate who had sustained him throughout the last decade. Mabel acknowledged her own failings: that she was selfish, hysterical, difficult, and demanding (Georgia once said she had the ability to "paralyze" an entire room of people if she so chose). She poured out her struggles to come to terms with her damaged and damaging ego:

> I now perceive my self—this Mabel Dodge or Mabel Luhan—mythical—
> invented—some true, some merely fantastic—quite powerful but
> evidently destructive—as a thing in space—& I completely refuse to go
> on being her. Then I must die—or be reborn—or converted. . . . I long
> to *live* in that free, dis-embodied,—*carefree*—functioning way that you
> know about . . . Georgia has a great faculty for living this way. How
> she enjoys herself!

Affirming her love for Tony, she told Stieglitz that he was "the live cell that the new ones will congregate around!"[33]

Ten days after her operation, she wrote him her most anguished letter.

She was fearful that all her talk about suffering—his and her own—had added to Stieglitz's misery that summer (she may well have shared with him her suspicions about Georgia, at least indirectly). "How shall we get free of this suffering?" she asked. "I go mad when I think of humanity in its anguish. What other cure save to somehow turn a cold eye upon one's ordeals, watching their alchemical effects, saying somehow—aside— 'Yes I see it but *I* am not *that.*' . . . Let us say to our suffering flesh & hearts & minds, 'Go to hell,' *I* am not that!"[34] Mabel's heart went out to Stieglitz, but she continued to nurture a great deal of suspicion about Georgia's role in her unhappiness. When she returned home in August, O'Keeffe left abruptly, without saying good-bye. Mabel evidently had made it clear that she was no longer welcome.

O'Keeffe returned home "radiant from her trip to Taos" and soon found renewed happiness with Stieglitz. Her 1930 exhibit was acclaimed by critics; two-thirds of it had been inspired by her stay in New Mexico. She went back the next summer and stayed in one of Mabel's studios, but the two women gave each other wide berths. Mabel wrote to Brett of Georgia's propensity to "grab" people, which she noted the very first day of her return: "But when she came and started in on Tony the first day & asked him to go & ride etc—etc—I had it out with her, *as you suggest,* & told her she was to lay off Tony this summer as I am well now & able to do things with him myself." O'Keeffe's decision to move to Abiquiu (where she still lives) has usually been attributed to her wanting to avoid the strains and stresses of Mabeltown.[35] The separation, however, was clearly mutual. Mabel may have regretted Georgia's autonomy at times, but she was at least as eager as O'Keeffe to keep her distance.

Twenty-five years later, Mabel still hadn't quite forgiven her. Walking with her granddaughter, Bonnie Evans, on the plaza in Taos, she pointed to Georgia O'Keeffe in a car across the way: "Look how 'that woman' has her hands dangling out the window so that everyone can see them. Ever since Stieglitz made all those photographs of them, she makes sure that they are visible at all times." Mabel then told Bonnie how Georgia used to "hang around" Tony and was "always trying to give him her father's gold watches." One night she had actually caught her "standing outside Tony's bedroom window in the middle of the night yearning after him. 'Well! I couldn't have that.'" Bonnie recalled "how pleased and wicked she looked when she said that, as if the whole thing had been great fun."[36]

Some forty-four years after the original incident, O'Keeffe still recalled Tony's love for Mabel: "Mabel and Tony Luhan really met their match in each other, I always thought. Tony stayed on top of the heap, and he did it through silence. Sometimes he'd get mad at Mabel and fling his blanket around him and say he was going back to the pueblo. Mabel always worried that he'd decide not to come back. But the time Mabel went East to have an operation, Tony lay like a log across her bed for days, missing her. They needed each other—no doubt about it." Georgia also recalled a time when Mabel refused to allow her to visit, and Tony went to stay with Georgia out of loyalty to his friendship with her.[37]

The summer of 1929 was not only a time of private anguish and self-reassessment for Mabel. It was also a time of public shaming. In 1926, Witter Bynner had written a scathing satire of contemporary American society and mores, whose heroine's life and character were modeled primarily on Mabel's. In July 1929, it received its first performance by the Santa Fe players.

The American Bitch Goddess
in the Theater of the Absurd:
Mabel Dodge Luhan and Witter Bynner

Witter (Hal) Bynner was a Santa Fe poet and a patron of the arts. Like Mary Austin and Alice Henderson, he hoped to make Santa Fe the capital of southwestern culture, and southwestern culture an important contributor to a revitalized national culture. A New Englander educated at Harvard, Bynner began his career as an assistant and poetry editor at *McClure's,* one of the best of the Progressive muckracking journals. Bynner arranged for Ezra Pound's first U.S. publication and introduced A. E. Housman to American audiences.

Bynner delighted in humor as the "great democratic leveller and equalizer" as was evident in his attempt to "reform" what he believed were the excesses of modernist poetry. Along with his friend Arthur Davidson Ficke, he dreamed up one of the great literary hoaxes of the early twentieth century as a spoof on the "isms" and manifestos that proliferated during the prewar era. Using the pseudonyms Anne Knish and Emmanuel Morgan respectively, they published two books of "spectrist" poetry, which were reviewed seriously and generated an interested audience. The hoax lasted for two years, until Bynner gave it away during a lecture in Chicago in 1916.[1]

Bynner was, at this time, on the faculty of the University of California, where he had met the man who became his lover for the next several years and his co-editor of the "little magazine" *Laughing Horse,* Willard (Spud) Johnson. Over the next few years Bynner became what he called a "commercialized troubadour," traveling around the country giving readings until, in 1922, Alice Corbin Henderson invited him out to Santa Fe on one of his tours.

While teaching at Berkeley, Bynner had learned about the T'ang poets and the philosophy of Laotzu, founder of Taoism, whose precepts they incorporated in their work. One of the earliest translators of Chinese poetry in America, he also adopted the brief, precise lyric form of T'ang poetry for his own work and the philosophy of Taoism as the means by which to live a sane and simple existence in a confusing and overly complex modern world. He discovered striking parallels between the world views and codes of behavior of the Taoists and the Pueblo Indians, views that he undoubtedly shared with Mabel and that he measured her by in *Cake,* his savage satire on her life.

Taoism was an intuitive philosophy based on a belief that men and women are microcosms whose bodies reproduce the plan of the cosmos. Subject to the ebb and flow of the complementary yin/yang energies, they are capable of perpetual transformation, at the same time that they are tied to an underlying primordial essence which connects them to all other life forms. As in the *liebensphilosophie,* the female is preferred to the male as the source of life energy, and men are encouraged to "feed on the mother" in them.[2] The Taoist view of civilization as "a degradation of the natural order" is very similar to the variety of primitivism celebrated by the Anglo expatriates of New Mexico.

It may well have been through Bynner's influence that Mabel first made the connection between Taoism and Pueblo religion, a subject she speculated on in her final book, *Taos and Its Artists.* She asked her readers to consider whether the name Taos could have derived "from the small band of devotees who followed Lao-tze [*sic*] westward out of China, imbued with the teaching of the Tao," whose "non-aggressive, moderate politesse of the heart" she found so consistent with Pueblo ideals of conduct.[3] Taoists insisted that personal passion, individual urges, and material wealth must be given up for the mystical union that brought renewal.

It was just such a promise of inner peace and emotional plenitude that attracted Bynner to Santa Fe and made him decide to adopt it as his permanent home. Writing about his move in 1924, he expressed the same kind of discontent that drove other Anglos to settle in New Mexico. The city "had held its own against man and his mechanisms. . . . I was washed clean of the war, I was given communion each night when the sunset would elevate the host on the Sangre de Cristo mountains. I was writing to friends who lived on another planet." In this environment, he felt that he could restore poetry to its early function of providing a vehicle for telling us how to live, just as Mabel believed she could do with her dream for reviving ancient drama.[4]

Bynner was an early supporter of the New Mexico Association for Indian Affairs and wrote pieces about the Bursum Bill, as well as essays on Indian art and music. Like Mabel, he contrasted the jazz that appealed to easterners with the very different dance expression of the Pueblos. In "Pueblo Dances," he mocked an unnamed New York friend who could not appreciate Indian dance because he was seeking "the personal, the immediate, the physical; something to excite his nerves with outward sensation." Among the Pueblos, he found the kind of intense spiritual experience that his Puritan ancestors would have appreciated, although they certainly would not have approved the source.[5]

Bynner spent part of his first summer in New Mexico as a guest of Mabel's. In July 1922, he wrote to his mother about his high regard for his hostess's generosity and kindness. Mabel provided him with a house, food, and the peace and quiet he needed to write poetry. The spirit of her house, he averred, was "ease and calm: may it never be crossed out!" Bynner's early admiration for Mabel is evident in a poem he wrote about her in 1923, entitled "New Mexican Portrait of Mabel Sterne." Here he presents her as a dignified goddess, the kind of earth mother Laotzu urged men to find within themselves as a source of emotional sustenance. Although she is rooted in the verities of nature, she also retains some of the refined attributes of a Renaissance lady who is accustomed to arranging the universe to suit her pleasure. Mabel is pictured against a background of rainbow waterfalls that join the earth, uniting the physical and spiritual manifestations of the life-force. Her regal countenance crowns a body whose fecund symbol is a shawl of undulating flowers:

> Those eagle eyebrows under peaceful sky:
> That contemplative look, proportioning
> Italian lounges to the universe.[6]

Within the year, Bynner's admiration for Mabel had turned to full-fledged dislike, as the two of them embarked upon a round of complicated rivalries which kept them at odds for much of the next thirty years. First, Mabel hired Bynner's lover and business partner, Spud Johnson, to become her secretary. This infuriated Bynner, who felt she had no right to interfere with their contractual arrangements. The fact that Spud became Mabel's secretary and remained in that position for most of his life, while promoting her fame and glory at every opportunity in the variety of papers he wrote for, certainly did not help matters any between Mabel and Hal.[7]

Mabel also had jealousies that fed their feud, for D. H. Lawrence had gone off to Mexico with Bynner and Spud his first summer in the United States. While Bynner had mixed feelings about Lawrence, he was a great admirer of Frieda, whom he felt was in danger from "she-wolves" like Mabel who pursued her husband.

Mabel was convinced that Bynner wrote *Cake* in "revenge" for the fact that she tried to "help" Spud. She refused to read the play (although it's hard to imagine that she did not finally succumb). Bynner admitted to Lawrence that "some aspects [of the play] were said to be a satire of Mabel Lujan. The slant was sportive, but not, I thought, malicious and, since I had visited her several times at her home in Taos, I inscribed the copy I sent her: 'Cast your bread upon Witter and it shall return to you as Cake.' I have heard that she was not amused." From the internal evidence, it is clear that Mabel's life history and salient personality traits were major sources for the play's inspiration.[8]

The contrast between the Lady, who is the unnamed heroine of *Cake*, and the earth mother of Bynner's "New Mexican Portrait" is striking, to say the least. Instead of the nurturing mother lauded by the Taoists, she represents the very worst kind of "New Woman": one who uses her "liberated" energies to deprive men of their power. She is both the cause and the effect of an Anglo civilization whose disintegration of culture and personality we have come to associate with the Theater of the Absurd.[9]

As a self-proclaimed modernist, the Lady lives in a social, moral, and political vacuum in which the only danger she faces is boring herself to death. She has gone through seven husbands, free love, mysticism, drugs, and drink, always seeking in some more *outré* pleasure a surfeit for her jaded appetites. She is a solipsist who has no context within or against which she can define herself because her wealth and power free her from any resistance to her fantasies.

In *Cake*, Mabel's lifelong dream of being ruler of her own cosmos is given ironic fulfillment. Sitting upon a golden throne, wearing a coronet of eagles, the Lady rules only the desires which she spins from a febrile imagination. These are carried out by her Chamberlain, an asexual Unicorn who is the spokesperson for the playwright (and seems to be based on Spud, as well as on Bynner himself). The symbol of his emasculation is the horn he carries in his hand as his staff of office. That a unicorn, according to legend, could be seen only by the chastest of virgins, and that the word's sound is also meant as a pun (eunuch horn) are two of the wittier absurdities of the play.

The Unicorn alerts us in the Prologue to the absurd world of the play when he tells us that there is no plot (implying conscious action that has some coherent purpose and progress) and no dramatic tension (in a world where one communes only with oneself there is no room for genuine conflict). The Lady reveals her modernity at once: "The world has moved, since women kept their hearts/As sticky as a dish of apple tarts./It's different now: I know what I'm about;/I am a modernist." The Lady's chief accomplice in modernism is the Psychoanalyst whom the Unicorn

245

brings forth to loosen up her "frontier libido."[10] While men are implicated in her evil because they affirm her powers, her unrestrained libido is the chief object of Bynner's attack on contemporary moral corruption. The cake of the title is a continually transmuted sexual and economic symbol of a female-dominated civilization that is transfixed at the oral stage of self-gratification. The Lady calls for it each time she embarks upon or is frustrated by her search for new experience.

Landing first in Paris, the Lady is spellbound with *fin de siècle* enthusiasm over a postimpressionist artist who is "Corruptly pale, romantically thin/ Who will narrow his eye to a demi-tasse of after-dinner sin!" Bynner magnifies Mabel's sometimes blatant inability to distinguish the real from the fake into a perennial inability to judge the quality or worth of any experiences. Her democratic lust equalizes all experience. Thus she tells Judas, whom she meets in Paris, that she would "like to meet Freud,/ People with minds, people with dash/A notorious artist, or an Apache." She even tries to seduce Judas, but he is interested only in the financial reward she offers for a tour of Heaven.[11] In fact, his conduct is that of a rather mild-mannered and conventional confidence man in comparison with her outrageous behavior.

On her next journey, to China, Bynner moves us from the personal to the political level. Here Mabel represents an updated version of Blanche's Gisell Links, one who inhabits a postwar America that is swollen with newfound military and economic might, and that uses its power to exploit other races and cultures for its own self-gratification. The Lady represents the ultimate perversion of America's international mission in the twentieth century. She does not wish to establish the Kingdom of God on earth, but to sweep the earth's kingdoms of their riches in order to provide for her own personal pleasure. When she travels to China she asks the Mandarin whom she meets to take an interest in her. He cynically replies, "At what percent?" The Lady coyly lifts a bottle from her hamper and says, "I am the dividends—after a cocktail." A follower of Laotzu, the Mandarin to whom she proffers her basket of goodies tells her that Americans are "asses with blinders made of perfect plumbing." He defines America as a land that loads its guns with missionaries, breeds babies in motor cars, and teaches other nations "that the sign of the cross is a dollar sign."[12]

Mabel, of course, would have been the first to agree with the Mandarin's perceptions of contemporary America. But Bynner felt that Mabel's use of her wealth and social prestige smacked of some of the same imperialistic methods she abhorred. He was also an eyewitness to the fact that she lived in comparative luxury while preaching the virtues of Pueblo simplicity. Indeed, Bynner twists the knife no more cruelly than in his section on the Lady's conversion to primitivism. Rejected by the Mandarin, she now believes herself disillusioned with civilization:

> Make me drunk with the smell of moony blood!
> I am sick of civilization. Put gigantic drums
>   into my ears!
> Cake me with mud![13]

When the Lady lands in Africa, she rhapsodizes lovingly over what she presumes is a genuine cannibal until she discovers that he is really a Harlem hipster on location for a Hollywood jungle film. Before she discovers her mistake, the actor tatooes on her back a symbol of her Americanhood—a collage of red, white, and blue poker chips.

The Lady then embarks on one of Mabel's lifelong pursuits, Eastern mysticism. Dressed as a beggar, she decides to leave the world altogether in search of the disembodied wisdom of the Swamis, but the Swami she meets in India is a true fakir. After she prostrates herself before him, he returns the compliment by noting the expense of the gifts she has brought him. She tries meditating for a while but finds herself sexually aroused by the Swami's disciple, who turns out to be a hair fetishist. In the last act of the play, the Lady is lying in bed, bereft of her hair and her vitality. Only the pituitary glands of a mastodon, stolen from the Smithsonian, can bring her back to life.

Revitalized by a cake of yeast, the Lady is ready to write her memoirs. She has learned the importance of sublimation now that her years of sexual allure are over: "Only a woman like me could have known from the first/ That to yield to the senses is to be accursed."[14] But the Lady is unable to carry out any of her own desires. Like Mabel's, her visions must be carried out for her by a man; in this case, by an unsexed Unicorn who despises her but whom she cannot do without as the best "cake maker" in her kingdom.

Mabel's need for a male amanuensis, and the temptation to serve that was felt by struggling artists, enraged Bynner. During one scene in the play, the Unicorn breaks through the thin veneer of farce. In a "released frenzy" he speaks what may have been Bynner's own voyeuristic visions of phallic revenge as he imagines increasingly horrible ways for the Lady to die: she will be crushed to death in a jungle haunted by obscene birds and reptiles: "Oh, to see you feel your soft flesh torn with a rush/Of horny finger-nails and your throat purple from the push/Of great thumbs!" Or she will be trampled to death by the hooves of a horse while a vulture plucks out her eyes.[15]

The Unicorn, however, does not quit her service. He has been bought willingly and is implicated in his own emasculation. He can only dream about murdering her; he no longer has the power to do so. Beyond what she represents socially and politically, Mabel finally symbolizes the prototypical Female Destroyer: Bynner's incarnation of the myth of feminine

247

evil that has haunted the imaginations of men for centuries. At this level, the most conservative and repulsive elements of his and Lawrence's sensibilities were in perfect accord. Lawrence wrote him in 1928 that while the play was "not particularly 'Mabel'—rather a type than a specific person," he had to admit that Bynner had noticed "the chief mischief in Mabel in your letter—her effect on the ————s [*sic*]."[16]

Yet if Bynner contributed to the worst of Mabel's legend, he also appreciated the power, drive, and intelligence that made her a worthy match. As his biographer has noted:

> Mabel and Hal were royal wags. . . . They played for the court's entertainment. Mabel might have hated the play, but she loved the attention. Bynner might resent Spud's departure, but he knew the love affair was over—he just minded losing *anything* to his great rival. Each was possessive and arrogant, but each loved a good fight and a good rival. . . . They could never be friends or admit to affection—that would let down the court watching the battle of the sexes—but underneath the game was a respect for a *peer.* In that area, neither had many who could be considered an equal in their royal sphere.[17]

After the Sturm und Drang of the summer of 1929, Mabel was not feeling very regal, however, and the year closed for her on a subdued note. She finished her story "An Intimation" with a sense of resignation for the lapsed sense of promise with which she had begun the decade of the 1920s:

> Little by little the years went by, and little by little Martia drew the white world about her again, almost unconsciously. Where her walls had been bare, she hung Chinese paintings that had been stored in New York. Instead of water drawn from the well she had it piped—hot and cold, now. More pipes for the furnace—more colds in the head! Books—books—books again! And People. More and more people, less and less Indian.
>
> After a while, she ceased thinking about the cosmic purpose of her life. Perhaps she let it ride. Life was not so ecstatic any more, it was more difficult to maintain, but it seemed right. There grew into their house, then, a strange balance between the white and the Indian modes of life. . . . And in herself, when it grew strong enough, there was a sense of waiting. An unachieved waiting. And sometimes, after sleep, she had a flash of knowing about life.[18]

Mabel's sense of resignation was also fed by the impending death of D. H. Lawrence, with whom she had made her peace. Lawrence had never quite given up on her after leaving America, nor did he go back on his belief that New Mexico was "the greatest outside experience" to affect his life. He had dedicated *Mornings in Mexico* (1927) to her, with the inscription, "To Mabel Luhan, who called me to Taos." From his home in Italy he wrote of his and Frieda's desire to come back to Taos, although he knew he could never live there permanently. In May 1927, he expressed to Mabel his hatred of the English who did not appreciate Americans, "not even the *real* menace: and none of the grim Yankee dauntlessness," both of which traits he associated with her. In the same letter he spoke of undergoing his "change of life" and agreed with her assessment of it.[19]

Lawrence used the occasion of Mabel's hysterectomy to urge her, for the last time, to put her spiritual cravings to rest, as he had recently done:

> You must do the same—try to give up yourself, try to yield yourself
> entirely to your body, and let it take its own life at last. You have
> bullied it so much. . . . Lie still and gradually let your body come back
> to its own life, free at last of your will.

Even on his deathbed, he spoke of the possibility that they could start a fresh life together:

> If we can manage it, and I can come to New Mexico, then we can begin
> a new life, with real tenderness in it. Every form of bullying is bad. But
> you must help me about coming over, when the time comes.
>   Love from us both.[20]

Not long after Lawrence's death, Frieda wrote a generous estimate of what Mabel and her cosmos had meant to Lawrence. The conflicts that generated pain and disillusionment had also prepared the way for healing:

> You wanted a more personal & direct relationship—but what you gave
> him was so infinitely greater than you know to his greater self. . . . He
> could even never have written Lady C—nor the "Apocalypse" nor died so
> unflinchingly in *utter belief,* if he hadn't known Taos and *lived* in it.[21]

And without Lawrence as nemesis and stimulus, Mabel's most important contribution to American letters, *Intimate Memories,* might never have taken shape.

Chapter 8

Intimate Memories

I started out to try & show the inward picture of a person of my own period; what heredity & environment had made of her. I did not believe, & do not believe, that she was inwardly so different from a lot of others. She was a 20th century type. But others & she herself always conceal the inner thoughts, egotisms, & separations from the outside world, under the "persona" they push around in front of the mask; so I tried to take off the mask & show the actuality.[1]

Mabel had worked throughout the 1920s to turn the nation's attention to the aboriginal Southwest as a source for its social and psychic renewal. In 1930, when Anglo-America faced the wreckage of its individualist and materialist ethic, she should have faced the decade of her triumph.

In some important ways, she did. During the 1930s, Mabel achieved her greatest public notoriety in the press, much of it related to the publication of her memoirs. Her dream of seeing a turnabout in federal Indian policies came closer to reality when Harold Ickes appointed John Collier commissioner of Indian Affairs in 1933, and Collier began to implement his Indian New Deal. In 1935, the cacique of Taos pueblo publicly announced his benediction on the marriage of Mabel and Tony, which had stirred up animosities a decade before: "God has done this," he asserted. "He sent you the white woman so we would send you away, because on the outside you could do so much more for us, but now since you have labored so well, God has sent you back to us and we receive you with great joy."[2] Throughout the decade, Mabel continued to attract "great souls" to Taos; among her new visitors were Leopold Stokowski, Edna Ferber, Thornton Wilder, Thomas Wolfe, Robinson Jeffers, and Myron Brinig.

Since the early 1920s, Mabel had been written up in the media as the rich, mysterious lady who had promoted radical causes, collected geniuses, and had thrown over civilization to marry an Indian. During the 1930s, she was not only credited with foresight and daring but also spoken of frequently as prophetic. The *Saturday Evening Post* reporter who wrote "Back From Utopia" after a visit in 1929 observed that Mabel's aesthetic judgments were "ten times ahead" of those of the average art critic's in the prewar era. In other newspapers and journals, she was named "first lady of Taos"; acknowledged as "the pioneer, one of those who foresaw in Taos an American Florence of American art"; congratulated for "putting Taos on the map" of the art world; described as a "hostess and angel to numerous writers, and the modern incarnation of the French dames who ran their salons for the struggling and successful writers of all national-ities." A Midwest reporter claimed her as one of the few women in the country who could be called "national institutions," and a New York reporter as "the big priestess of the earnest literary and artistic colony for which Taos is now famous."[3]

The popular image that established Mabel as a cross between Madame de Staël and George Sand had much to do with the public relations work of Spud Johnson, and of such newspaper friends as Elizabeth Shepley Sargeant and Henry McBride. In a typical article, Spud wrote of her as "a woman who has left her mark on her century. . . . One of the first salonniers of her time, an international figure, she has known most of the world's creative artists of the twentieth century, fostered and influenced not a few." The *Taos Star* frequently focused on its most famous citizen. One impressive photo of Mabel standing regally on her garden steps was captioned: "America's first woman columnist, a militant champion of individual liberties and human rights, a perennial drum major of the band leading various new movements in the world of arts and letters."[4]

Aside from the exaggeration of Mabel's genuine abilities and accomplishments, and the idealization of her personal characteristics, what is most notable about these articles is that they mainly look back to achievements of the 1910s and 1920s. Mabel herself faced the 1930s in a mood of nostalgia, even as she continued to track down artists, musicians, and writers who she felt could appreciate and translate Taos to the world. In 1931 she published a retrospective essay in *Creative Arts* under the title, "Taos—A Eulogy." She recalled the many artists who had gathered there, spoke of Collier's campaign to stem "the tide of mechanistic civilization," and quoted John Dewey's remark that Taos "was a survival among the most precious places of the world." Referring to Jung's assessment of Taos as a national treasure, she concluded that psychologists, educators, states-men, as well as artists, have determined that here indeed is "sacred ground."[5]

Mabel's essay has many of the qualities of those she had written in the previous decade, but it is marked by a subtle shift in tone that creates the impression of Taos as an oasis cut off from the harsher realities of contemporary America, rather than of the "city upon a hill" that was to serve as a beacon light to the Western world. The shift presages a truth she would not really come to terms with until the post–World War II era: that the days of glory she dreamed about lay more in the past than in the future. In the 1930s, America was too beset by economic disaster and social blight and by competing ideologies of reform and revolution to give serious attention to her primitivist philosophy.

During the 1920s, Mabel's lack of a specific program to reshape Anglo-American values was less noticeable. Her call for spiritual renewal, her work on behalf of the Pueblos, and the productivity she nurtured among artists and activists were notable accomplishments when measured against the Babbittry that ruled the nation and the alienation of many writers and intellectuals. Mabel had, however, always preached in aesthetic, religious, and psychological terms, not in political or economic ones. In the 1930s, when more than one-third of the population was "ill-housed, ill-clad, and ill-nourished," Mabel's call to Americans to take up the Indian way seemed overwhelmingly simplistic, particularly since the nation's Indians were still among the poorest of the poor. Measured against her own life-style, her call seemed hypocritical.

Just as Hollywood provided an escapist dream world for a hungry nation during the depression, so the mass media focused on the high-society aspects of Mabel's life-style. Although her daily pattern had not changed significantly, and her ordinary style of dress was still quite simple, Mabel had begun to experiment with new clothes and new friends that had little in common with her tastes a decade before. Jack Young-Hunter's 1936 portrait of her in an elegant black dress was one such indicator of change. When Nicholai Fechin returned to Taos in 1936, he was shocked by the woman he had painted in 1927 as an Indian princess—strong, powerful, and unconventional. This "new" Mabel had been coiffeured by Evangeline Stokowski, and outfitted by Adrian, the designer for Greta Garbo, Jean Harlow, and other Hollywood stars who bedazzled America in the 1930s, some of whom were new accretions to Mabel's social circle. Mabel also began writing for the kinds of publications usually seen in the homes of the women she grew up with in Buffalo: *Cosmopolitan* and *Town and Country.*[6]

Remembrance of Things Past

Given her media image, it is understandable that Mabel was not held in high regard by most of the serious intellectuals and leftist activists of the 1930s. It is one of the many ironies of Mabel's life that the publication of her memoirs in 1933, 1935, 1936, and 1937—the most radical public act of her life—reinforced their worst impressions.

When she began work on her memoirs in 1924, Mabel's purpose was primarily personal. After her second break with Lawrence, Brill insisted she start writing for herself. Dorothy Brett witnessed the extraordinary discipline that Mabel brought to a labor that continued over the next ten years: "When she started to write her memoirs, she wrote incessantly, without stopping, day after day, lying on her sofa with a copy book and pencil. She poured herself untiringly into those books. The energy concentration was boundless, until all of a sudden the book was finished and Mabel resumed normal life—which was energetic enough, Heaven knows." After Henrietta Harris typed her pages, she had them read (to whoever was available to listen) by the daughter of Alice Corbin Henderson, "little" Alice, who had married her son in 1923.[7]

Mabel's decision to write her memoirs was inspired by Freud's theory of abreaction, which Brill explained as a "Cathartic Method" based on the belief that "words are almost the equivalent to the action." Reliving the past through language, the "painful emotions associated with the experience" are presumably exorcised and cease to cause disturbances.[8] The memoirs were thus another form of therapy: through verbal expiation she might free herself from her still-existent neuroses and find the psychic equilibrium denied her by her past. Unlike her other therapies, however, this one demanded an active and creative use of her intelligence.

In this endeavor, Lawrence was as important an influence as Brill. Although he did not believe that Mabel had the discipline to write fiction, he not only encouraged her to write her life history, but provided her with enthusiastic feedback and incentives to continue during times when she needed him. He recognized how much her work corroborated and was influenced by his own views of American life. On April 12, 1926, he wrote from Italy in response to her first volume:

> I should say it's the most serious "confession" that ever came out of America, and perhaps the most heart-destroying revelation of the American life-process that ever has or will be produced. It's worse than Oedipus and Medea, and Hamlet and Lear and MacBeth are spinach and eggs in comparison. . . . It's not the absolute truth—but nothing ever is. It's not art because art always gilds the pill, and this is hemlock in a cup. It seems to me so horribly near the truth, it makes me sick in my solar plexus. My dear Mabel, I do think it was pretty hard lines on all of you. . . . Life gave America gold and a ghoulish destiny.

When Mabel was having a difficult time with her New York years because she felt very much out of touch with the woman she was then, Lawrence reminded her that her passion for revolution had been genuine and urged her to read Upton Sinclair's tribute to her in his autobiography, *Money Writes!*[9] Some of his most interesting, and amusing, advice dealt with the disposition of her memoirs. Concerned that she avoid both immorality and censorship by not publishing them, at least openly, he suggested a number of options: disguising all the names of her friends and swearing them to secrecy; getting the books out privately by subscription in Paris; having them published in German; leaving them buried in the vaults of the Académie Française for future publication.

In the meantime, Mabel was circulating the memoirs among other friends and acquaintances: Havelock Ellis, Willa Cather, Brill, and many others read all or part of them. Although it is unclear exactly when Mabel decided to publish them, there is little doubt that the high praise with which her writing was greeted by men and women she respected encouraged her to do so. Lawrence's analysis, in particular, reinforced her own belief that her symptoms and behavior were not unique but representative of the destructiveness and contradictions within Anglo-American culture.

At some point in the late 1920s, Mabel recognized that her life's story could serve a public as well as a private purpose. By "showing the crude and unflattering aspects of the past," as she stated in the foreword to her first published volume, she could practice therapy on a national scale. Mabel hoped to redeem the future by exorcising the sins of the past. She wrote compellingly to Leo Stein about the broader intentions of her work:

> How any of us have ever survived at all the system we inherited & were conditioned by, is more than I can understand. Of course we are crippled & malformed & always will be but I do *not* see why those who come after us go on in this same pattern, if some of us try & expose the way . . . we thought & felt & how we were motivated: the lack of suitable outlets, ambition, activity, stimulation; the sensory and psychic insufficiency. . . . The whole ghastly social structure under which we were *buried,* & that must be torn down, exposed, so those who follow us will have peace & freedom to make a different one. . . .[10]

Mabel offered her life on the public altar because she wished to facilitate the destruction of the system that produced her. In an important sense, this act was motivated by a radical impulse. Here, as she says particularly well in her first volume, is a social system that taught her that the only way to succeed in life is by having power over other human beings. She grew up in a family that trained her how to speak and dress, but had no time for the growth of her ethical or emotional life. She understood the crippling effects of a society that rewarded "power, prestige, and possession" while preaching love and brotherhood. That Mabel had to create more pain by opening old wounds in order to achieve her goal was a sacrifice of herself and others she was quite willing to make, since her suffering and their pain would thereby be redeemed: "if Background can

255

make a few grownups, with guilty, intimate childhood memories, realize theirs was a common and almost universal experience, then I have done the right thing in publishing it."[11] With this apologia, Mabel justified the exposure of her family life that some of her Buffalo friends and relatives believed hastened or even precipitated her mother's death.

Mabel's therapeutic purposes provided an impetus for the writing of the memoirs. But she turned elsewhere for the aesthetic theories and literary models that helped her to structure them. From the Steins, Mabel had learned about the uses of the aesthetic imagination in the creation of the self, while Lawrence had deepened her understanding of the power of language as a source of social renewal. Her primary literary model was Proust's *Remembrance of Things Past,* in which sin, selfishness, pride, and envy abound in the hero's allegorical search for truth and redemption.

Most interestingly, Mabel developed her life story within a major American literary tradition of autobiography, one rooted in conversion narratives that imagine history as a journey from imperfection to perfection, where new beginnings are often associated with new frontiers. Within this tradition, she shared many characteristics with writers like Cotton Mather and Margaret Fuller, who also wrote in the prophetic mode: "restless types, searching for truth, undergoing personal metamorphosis, interpreting the holy mysteries of their tribe, forecasting the collective destiny." She writes, too, in the heroic mode, for she has "taken the journey prescribed by the myth," although she reverses the import of the traditional American myth by portraying the Anglo as the barbarian who must be brought the light of true faith by the Indians.[12]

In *Background,* her first volume, Mabel sets the stage for the willful woman who appears in the second and third volumes as a symbol of the fragmentation generated by Anglo-American civilization. In *Edge of Taos Desert,* her fourth volume, she presents an integrated self. Restored by her Indian lover, she is at last able to see the world in its "original" state of unity and harmony.

Unfortunately for Mabel, most of the serious critics of the 1930s were not interested in her intentions. Nor were they taken by her subject matter, her hyperbolic style, or her romantic sensibility. As Frederick Lewis Allen has pointed out in his popular history of the 1930s, the decade "was the golden age of literary sociology." It was not the upper or middle classes who were subjects for serious writers and artists, but the rural and urban poor. The proletarian realism of James Farrell, Clifford Odets, Erskine Caldwell, and others had little in common with the self-absorption of Mabel's work. In the Southwest, some writers, like Edna Ferber and Oliver La Farge, wrote romantic and historical fiction, but most were working in a realistic or folk mode. Conrad Richter wrote tales of nineteenth-century Texas and New Mexico that focused on hard toil, childbearing, and death; Paul Horgan described the effects of economic insecurity and government relief in New Mexico; Mary Austin collected folk tales and wrote stories that detailed native customs.[13]

Mabel's worst treatment came at the hands of the radical Left, who looked back upon the rebels of the prewar generation as tender-minded and foolish bohemians. Hers was one of a host of confessionals published during the 1930s, along with those of Hutchins Hapgood, Max Eastman, and Lincoln Steffens. *Intimate Memories* was the longest, perhaps the most ambitious, and certainly one of the most widely condemned by Marxist critics.[14]

Background was the exception. It received high praise from friends and critics alike. The *New York Times* reviewer described Mabel's career as one "that is important to the cultural growth of this country" and called hers a "frank art that is admirable from beginning to end . . . a social history as well as a personal book." The *New Republic*'s reviewer was even more enthusiastic: "Here is the beginning of a life work as significant in its own right as any one of a chosen number of French eighteenth century memoirs written before the revolution." Its authenticity is hardly surprising, when one considers that Mabel spent much of her adult life in therapy, but the praise for her vivid accounting of child-rearing practices that were widespread among the upper classes of the Victorian era was justified.[15]

The second volume, *European Experiences,* was her weakest in terms of unity of form and content. (She had felt forced to delete the most important crisis of her young adulthood, the affair with Dr. Parmenter that led to her banishment from Buffalo after the death of Karl Evans.) Her reviewers were often more than dissatisfied, though sometimes for the wrong reasons. Louis Kronenberger of the *New York Times* was typical: "As for Mabel Dodge herself," he concluded, "the woman who refused to be bored and who liked power, who if it added to her development or enjoyment would engage in any kind of hazardous relationship, who loved a life of pure sensation . . . as for this woman hugging the ego from which her life derived, one respects the honesty . . . without quite seeing that it has any great importance." In October 1935, Mabel wrote to Leo Stein complaining that the critics attacked her unfairly when they accused her of being unconscious of the sometimes nauseating narcissism she displayed: "I try not to be any other than the one I was at the time I write about, not to know or feel more than I did at that time. And at that period I was very stupid, and unhappy, indeed quite desperate, with no heart at all nor any brains."[16]

Volume 3, *Movers and Shakers,* is Mabel's most absorbing and illuminating portrait of herself and her cultural milieu; in fact, it is one of the best eyewitness accounts of Greenwich Village before the war. Most critics on the left, however, dismissed it as one more piece of evidence that the prewar radicals were little more than hedonists. It is ironic to see the

Mabel Dodge who was touted during her salon days as a harbinger of revolution viewed as the very personification of bourgeois degeneracy that had brought on the depression. Malcolm Cowley summed up her life as "the case history of an art patroness under capitalism—a fable told round the fireside to edify and frighten little Russian children," while Granville Hicks recommended the book to social historians as an incomparable account "of the destruction that can be wrought by money when it is in the hands of intelligence and determination." Floyd Dell was one of the few radical reviewers who assessed the book within the context of its times, but then he was rejected by most of the others as a bohemian leftover. Although he agreed with the 1930s credo that "we" were silly, naive, and eager in those days, he recognized that Mabel's book was "quite a marvelous recapturing of the scent and flavor of that lost young world; it is because it is so true that it seems so fantastic."[17]

Just before the publication of *Movers and Shakers,* Mabel wrote to Neith Hapgood:

> I think there was a period in New York before the war when we were all keyed up to pretty high vibrations & we *knew* a good deal & then lost it. That was before I stepped out of that queer exalted sort of state & got very diminished over Reed. . . . I don't see what's coming to the world unless something really jars it into a change of heart. The war actually stopped or was stopped before it was finished—it seems to me. It was like closing up a running sore from the outside. What is ever going to clean the inside festering in sickness of this world?[18]

In *Edge of Taos Desert,* Mabel tried to answer that question. Stylistically and thematically, it represents a sharp break with the previous three volumes. Mabel explained this in an interview. In each of her four books, she attempted to imitate through language and syntax the particular phase of her life she was recalling. Thus her European and New York volumes were written with complex sentences, highly charged, allusive phrases, and uneven, sometimes frenetic, prose rhythms. This style was intended to indicate the complex world of ideas and the intensity of emotional entanglements in which she was engaged. Her final volume focuses our attention on the stripping away of her civilized veneer.

Here Mabel simplifies her words and syntax so that we may view her new world through eyes that are unencumbered by the weight of "dead" philosophies and books. Her initial responses to the Indians and the landscape are described in terms of analogies. The Indians are compared to Maxfield Parrish illustrations; the mountains, to da Vinci backgrounds. The analogies grow progressively fewer, until two-thirds of the way through the book she informs us that she must have an original confrontation: "I was impatient because I did not want to connect this new world with the old—I wanted it to be itself alone and not a part of any past that I had ever known."[19] Mabel keeps enough of the old in the form of biblical and mythological analogies, however, so that her readers will make the appropriate connections between Taos and the various paradises that preceded it.

The reviewers of *Edge of Taos Desert* took cognizance of the "new" Mabel and her unencumbered, leisurely prose rhythms, even when they distrusted her self-portrayal or winced at her Rousseauisms. Some responded positively to the book's spirituality. As with her other volumes, the eastern establishment tended to mock, while the western press was appreciative. Reviewing for the *New Yorker,* for example, Clifton Fadiman reduced it to a dime novel: "a passion-fraught story of two lovers who found each other in the wide open spaces of the great southwest. Real Indians for the kiddies. Bingo every Friday night." In contrast, the *Dallas Morning News* spoke of the author as "a brave and courageous spirit, deadly serious in purpose. . . . There is good reason for believing now that her outrage against established conventions arises not from a lack of reverence for life, but from a driving search for the realities of living in which she would accept no compromise."[20]

Most of Mabel's friends thought very highly of the work and its message. A few even revised their estimation of her after reading it, recognizing the sensitivity and idealism that were sometimes buried beneath moodiness and petty cruelties. One such reader was Ansel Adams, who had been invited to stay with the Strands in one of Mabel's guesthouses in the summer of 1930, much to Mabel's annoyance. Adams wrote her about *Edge of Taos Desert* on December 6, 1937:

I finished it in a state of amazed revelation. . . . It is so beautifully compact and consistent; it seems to draw to a fine point all the complex threads of your life and gives your decision a clarity and brilliance matched only by the sunlight and air of Taos.

Not unlike you, when you first came to Taos, I am confronted with finding a real way of life and real vital simplicity. You found it, even though it required ruthless action and decision. Your book has made me confident in the necessity of such action in myself. . . . Your transition was effected in a mood of strength and inevitability, and it is going to help many another woman and man to "take life with the talons" and carry it high.[21]

Among the congratulatory and condemnatory responses to *Intimate Memories,* perhaps the funniest was a delightful parody written by the actress Cornelia Otis Skinner and published under the title, "A Brief Digest of the Intimate Memoirs of Mabel Fudge Hulan." Mabel's role as chief headhuntress of her century is dealt with first, her tendency to write about the great and not-so-great with the same breathless enthusiasm, equalizing the value of her trophies with the polish of her lustrous prose:

'Tis my gift to gather together the most brilliant personalities of my century. My soirées have become famous. At the time I am writing about they were just beginning to be the talk of the intelligentsia. My dynamic temperament attracted to the little house on Mott Street the titans of the day. Henry James, Picasso, Stravinsky, Oscar Wilde, and Ty Cobb, not to mention Ibsen and Loie Fuller. . . . We sat about on bath mats (all of us except Yeats, who lay quietly on the stove) and discussed psychoanalysis, child labor, the Dreyfus case and the race problem.

Skinner captures what is often Mabel's real focus of attention, amidst the multitudinous issues and personalities she discusses: her view of herself as the continuing incarnation of the Female Principle: "Freud would remark, 'Mabel, you are extraordinary! The eternal hetaira.' I can't help it. I was born that way. (Aspasia . . . Astarte . . . Amnesia.)" In Florence, Mabel's villa is "vibrant with the iridescent quality of my aura. In some curious way I became the reincarnation of Lucrezia Borgia." Her dress, of course, suits the atmosphere, setting, and personality she is wearing at any particular moment: "I was majestic and picturesque . . . glamorous in asphodels and conch shells and an exquisite Etruscan toga, my spaniel had dug up near the Farnese cesspool." Mrs. Hulan's *fin de siècle* world-weariness exhales through a prose punctuated with smatterings of foreign idioms (a favorite device of Mabel's): "I would wander about the *boiseries* of my *pied-à-terre, ad libidum,* suffering from a combination of *Weltschmerz* and *dolce far niente.*"

Mabel Fudge, like Mabel Dodge, is most impressed by the number of men who, crossing all international and class boundaries, are unable to resist the call of her "magnetic intellect." First, there is her husband, whose name she cannot remember. Then "X," who was "caught in the golden net of his love for me. . . . His wife resented me. She came from Maine and was incapable of the finer emotions." Lolo, the butler, also wanted her and suffered accordingly: "One evening he flung down the soup tureen and caught me in his arms. He, too, had fallen hopelessly in love with me. . . . Although I hated him, I deliberately roused his lust by sending my essence out over the salad course." Devastated by her rejection, Lolo clawed himself to death with a jeweled backscratcher he had brought her from Afghanistan.

The climax of the piece is an evening spent with Frieda and D. H. Lawrence, which capitalizes on most of the parodic elements in the rest of the essay, with the additional shock value of the *outré:*

Little happened except when Brett threw an *omelette fines herbes* at Mrs. Sanger. I said nothing, but sat remotely on the mantelpiece in shimmering satin. I wore also a wreath of sagebrush and little crickets.

> Suddenly the door opened and in walked Pinto, his face suffused with
> heroic anger. He was completely naked.

Skinner concludes with Mrs. Hulan's promise to produce twenty-four
more volumes of memoirs.[22]

The Indian New Deal

One of the things that most disturbed Mabel about the reception of
her memoirs was how misunderstood her intentions were. She had, after
all, displayed her ego to reveal its flaws and contrast them with the
healthier mode of being induced by the Indian's communal way of life.
More distressing, however, were the kinds of criticisms leveled at her by
Mike Gold, who visited New Mexico in 1936 and dubbed it "Mabel
Luhan's Slums." Gold was a proletarian novelist and the editor of the *New
Masses,* a Marxist journal. His Southwest was as different as possible from
Mabel's. The landscape was inhabited by coyotes, burnt up by the sun,
and "stretched tight, league after hopeless league, like the dry red skin
of a feverish animal. . . . At the end of the vast, infernal plains rise the
mountains. Rattlesnakes, cactus, and the evening sun, and the lips cracked
with heat; one must learn silence and stoicism."[23]
    While Gold was impressed by Indian dances and understood their
attraction for neurotic intellectuals like Mabel and Lawrence (who, he
says, were "sickened" by the capitalist civilization they helped to build),
he had no tolerance for the way they romanticized poverty. The Indians
lived in dirt, filth, and disease worse than anything he knew in the worst
New York slums. Even Taos, the wealthiest pueblo, was no more than
"Mabel Luhan's favorite slum." He recounted with horror the stories he
heard of medicine men who maimed and killed their patients, of Indians
who sickened from drinking water from polluted sacred water holes rather
than from hygienic wells. Quoting federal health survey statistics that
revealed a standard of living among Indians far below any in the nation,
he concluded that the only way they would survive was by entering the
"mainstream of modern life, of science, of democratic struggle."
    While Gold's anger at the human misery he observed is well justified,
his knowledge of what was happening in the Southwest, and why, was
limited. Mabel did not write publicly about the suffering of the Pueblos
in the 1930s any more than she had in the 1920s, but neither did she
and her fellow regionalists ignore it. The backward glance demanded by
the completion of her memoirs was accompanied by efforts to alleviate
the continuing health and economic problems of her Indian neighbors.
Witter Bynner, Ina Cassidy, Allan Clark, and Mabel Luhan formed the
New Mexico Roosevelt League in 1932, which raised funds and endorsed

261

state party nominations of politicians who supported these interests. In the same month that Gold's article was published, Luhan donated one of her properties, La Posta, to Taos County for a much-needed county hospital, and she worked hard over the next few years to raise money for beds and equipment. Along with her fellow artists and writers in Santa Fe and Taos, she continued to demonstrate a commitment to community activism during the depression in helping to raise money, provide work, and protect the cultural integrity of the Anglo, Hispanic, and native American communities.[27]

When Harold Ickes, Secretary of the Interior, appointed John Collier Commissioner of Indian Affairs in April 1933, Mabel had reason to hope for much more than amelioration.[24] Collier's Indian New Deal had a twofold purpose. He planned to integrate the best of the Indians' old-world economy with the latest scientific methods of land preservation, irrigation, and health care in order to help them establish permanent means of economic viability. He also intended to protect their religious and cultural practices, which he believed were vitally necessary to the spiritual health of the nation as a whole.

Collier's desire to use the Indians as "laboratories" for progressive social, economic, and cultural change took on greater urgency because of the depression, as millions of Americans suffered displacement from their homes and the loss of self-sufficiency and community. The fact that native Americans were under federal jurisdiction gave him reason to believe that he had an extraordinary opportunity to make them "pioneers" in Roosevelt's efforts to establish "conscious planning" as the basis of a revitalized economy and society.[25]

In 1933, Collier began with the most pressing problems. He immediately enlisted the support of all relevant federal agencies to make their benefits available to Indians: the Civilian Conservation Corps began an Indian program that included leadership training; the Agricultural Adjustment Administration provided money for the purchase of cattle; the Public Works Administration provided money and jobs to repair and build roads, schools, and hospitals. Other agencies provided funds for crop loans, drought relief, self-help projects. Collier replaced many boarding schools with day schools and decreed full religious freedom by executive order. The Pueblo Relief Act provided the Pueblos with veto power over federal funds spent on land and water purchases. Taos benefited from a fifty-year renewable permit to use the government land surrounding Blue Lake for economic and religious purposes.[26]

As useful as much of this effort was, Collier recognized it as piecemeal reform. In 1934, he drew up legislation that incorporated much broader-ranging changes. Known as the Wheeler-Howard Act, after the two senators who co-sponsored it, the legislation was intended to restore tribal self-government and communal land ownership.

The bill was very controversial among a number of factions. Many congressmen opposed the economic aspects as segregationist or communistic, while most Christianized and assimilated Indians opposed the idea of reestablishing tribal life. In order to explain his proposals and generate support, Collier called a series of Indian congresses during the spring of 1934. Tony Luhan worked tirelessly on his behalf among the Pueblos, just as he had with the Bursum Bill. He traveled from pueblo to pueblo patiently explaining to often skeptical listeners the benefits that would accrue to them if the Wheeler-Howard Bill were enacted into law.

In a letter that he dictated for Collier, Tony made clear the great faith he placed in his integrity: "I said," he reported of one visit,

We have got a real friend in John Collier. He really likes Indians. In past time, we had Commissoners against us who tried to stop our ceremony dances and our dances-religious. They nearly destroy us; call our ways bad or moral [*sic*] or something, and put in the paper they are going to stop us. But John Collier fight for us with the Indian Defense Association and he save us. Now, he look far ahead and it is like he is putting a wall around us to protect us—and this Wheeler-Howard Bill is this wall. And no white man or grafter can come inside and take away our land or our religion which are connected together.[27]

Passed in June 1934 as the Indian Reorganization Act, the law bore little resemblance to the more radical bill Collier had initiated. But it did mark a major shift in Indian affairs. It ended further land allotments and allowed for the consolidation and purchase of new lands; set up a revolving fund for economic development; gave preferential hiring to Indians within the BIA; offered tribes the opportunity to charter themselves as municipal corporations so they could be competitive in a modern economy; and encouraged them to write constitutions that would give them greater political self-control.

Over the next ten years, Collier used the IRA, and implemented other policies, to restore millions of acres of land to Indian tribes. He helped them to gain increasing economic and political control over their lives, while protecting their cultural and religious freedom. But there were many factors that strongly qualified his achievement. First and foremost was the fact that the other New Deal agencies he relied on were set up to deal with short-term relief, rather than to eradicate the effects of long-term poverty. By 1935, an increasingly conservative Congress began funding cutbacks that ultimately vitiated the IRA's relief and self-help programs. Just as important to the defeat of Collier's more utopian hopes, however, was a tragic irony of his own making.

Collier had chosen the New Mexican Pueblos as his models for all other Indians and majoritarian democracy as the means of self-rule. In doing so, he ended up imposing "rigid political and economic ideas" on tribes that varied greatly in their economic practices and social and political attitudes. While most Indians supported Wheeler-Howard, the majority at the Indian congresses had insisted that their individual property and heirship rights be protected, which they were in the amended bill. After the passage of the IRA, few tribes engaged in cooperative economic ventures or used the option to create constitutional governments. Even among the Pueblos, who had most fully supported Collier, there was little enthusiasm for the implementation of the democratic ideals of majority rule because they did not agree with their hierarchical structure of authority.[28]

The most painful personal blow Collier had to sustain in his early tenure as head of the BIA came when the man and woman who had given him his initial vision of the "Red Atlantis," and who had been two of his staunchest supporters throughout his career, became his public enemies. The good feeling and cooperation that existed between Collier and the Luhans did not last long after the passage of the IRA. Mabel's first quarrel was over Tony's meager payment of $75 for the two-week, 1,200-mile trip that he took to promote the Wheeler-Howard Bill. In December 1934, she wrote to Collier complaining about that injustice. In the same month, she wrote to Ickes, demanding that Taos be given a government-owned and -operated water and light plant to get control away from a small group of private owners.[29] When Collier used his power to stop a government irrigation project that was taking place on land that she controlled, however, she was very upset. The breach widened greatly when Collier reorganized the administration of the southwestern pueblos into one United Pueblo Agency in 1935 and placed at its head a female superintendent, Sophie Aberle.

Mabel insisted that Aberle mismanaged the twenty-two tribes under her jurisdiction and wrote increasingly hostile letters about her to Collier over the next year. Neither she and Tony, nor the leaders of Taos pueblo, would deal with Aberle. Collier was furious, not just over this issue but over another confrontation he had with the Taos Indians early in 1936. This second controversy had to do with the use of peyote by a native American church group. Tribal leaders insisted that their new rights to self-government allowed them to prohibit this practice, which was allowable under Collier's religious toleration policies. They arrested a group of "peyote boys" and when they could not pay the alloted fine, confiscated 300 acres of their land. Mabel and Tony supported this action, Collier was sure, as revenge for his stopping the irrigation project on their land. Collier mediated a solution that allowed the peyote users to practice their rites in an out-of-the-way place and granted them their land back.[30]

Antonio Mirabal, the law enforcement officer who had arrested the peyote boys, did not carry out the mediation orders. When he (and Tony) spoke out against Dr. Aberle at an All-Pueblo Council meeting in April

1936, Collier fired him. Furious with what she saw as Collier's high-handed methods, Mabel turned their quarrel into a national scandal. She accused Collier of coercing the Pueblos into silence about Aberle's mistakes and wrote Ickes that Collier was covering up for Aberle. She openly attacked Collier in the local and national press for blackmail in his firing of Mirabal. At the same time, she wrote to Roosevelt complaining about the poor performance of the superintendent of the local Indian school. The *New York Times* carried her charges that the Indian administration was ruining the morale of the Pueblo tribes.

At the root of these controversies were Mabel's presumptions that her friendship with Collier meant that he would devote immediate attention to every issue she thought important and that she would have influential sway on local matters. One can sympathize with her frustration, voiced in 1936, over the problems that still persisted: "You used to feel that health and education were the major problems, after the land was secure," she wrote him, "but these have not been *touched* yet." But Mabel ignored the fact that he was commissioner of all the Indians, and that he had a large bureaucracy and an increasingly recalcitrant Congress to deal with. Collier only slightly overstated the case when he wrote his son that she wanted to "run the show, and not from behind the curtains."[31]

Aberle was apparently well qualified for her position, having lived among the Pueblos for seven years conducting important medical and anthropological studies. There is little doubt that Mabel (along with some of the leaders from Taos and Zuni) disliked the fact she was a woman. Although she might have been critical of anyone appointed to her domain, the last thing she could deal with was a woman in such a position, particularly one who had a great deal of control over Collier. As far as the peyote controversy is concerned, Mabel's insistence that the drug was dangerous and disruptive to tribal life is not borne out by research that shows peyotists were among those who most fully participated in cere-monials and that they often held leadership positions.[32] In any case, her open attack on Collier and Aberle was highly counterproductive to her own most important goals.

Mabel handled her legitimate differences of opinion, as well as her disappointments and jealousy, very badly. But Collier used poor judgment as well. When he appointed Aberle without consultation, refused to listen to any complaints about her from others besides Tony and Mabel, and fired Mirabal, he displayed the kind of arbitrary behavior he had deplored in the Indian administrations of the 1920s.[33]

The Stream of Great Souls

Mabel's open break with Collier was a severe personal and political blow, for she had counted on him to realize her dreams for Taos. He was not, however, the only person she had relied on. Throughout the 1930s, she continued to call to Taos the creative artists she felt could best represent its blessings to the nation. Streams of visitors arrived continually, beginning with the Jefferses and the return of Adams, the Strands, and O'Keeffe in the summer of 1930. After Mabel made her peace with Carl Van Vechten in the early 1930s, he came in the winter of 1935 to do a series of photographic portraits of her. That spring, the sculptress Malvina Hoffman arrived. Financed by the Federal Arts Project, she was en route around the world to create a group of heads and figures representing all the basic "types" within the human race.

Malvina had last seen Mabel in Florence in 1910, and so was not quite sure what to expect of her. But she was captivated immediately, both by her hostess's warm reception and by her estate: "The fields outside were lavender and gold; a sea of iris seemed to surround the house, lapping up against the frames of the windows, . . . I was entranced. Here was a pristine beauty on such a scale that it made one inarticulate." Mabel took immediate possession of her and insisted that she stay and work. Hoffman recounted the summer guest list, which included the Jefferses, the writer Myron Brinig, and Cady Wells, a modernist painter who lived in Santa Fe. Mabel took Hoffman to visit the "much-heralded" Frieda, but her most impressive memories were of the Indian dances Mabel held at her house and the dedication to Mother Earth that was celebrated by the Taos Indians on May 1.[34]

A. A. Brill spent part of the summer of 1937 with Mabel, as did Margaret Sanger and Carl Hovey (editor of the *Metropolitan* magazine) who was married to Sonya Levien, a scriptwriter for Fox studios. Sonya, who became a close friend, wrote Mabel soon after her visit that "every minute of our stay was blessed with something better than mere excitement or charm—I can only put it by saying that we fell into a way of living that we loved." The fact that Mabel's estate was a center of cosmopolitanism in the Southwest was a matter of great local pride. The New Mexico papers were fond of keeping track of and marveling at her guests. Harvey DeLong noted in the November 14, 1940, *Taoseño* that Mabel's home was a model of interethnic harmony. At the time, her visitors were the Catholic archbishop of New Mexico and Bertha Gusdorf, an orthodox Jew. When paired with Mabel, Protestant and divorced, they represented "the liberality of spirit that prevails in the Taos region."[35]

There was a significant change, however, in the influence of the region on the artists and writers who stayed with Mabel. Although most were personally nourished by their stay, as Edna Ferber, Malvina Hoffman, and Sonya Levien attested, few settled there or drew on Taos (or Mabel) as inspiration for their work. Mabel indicated as much to Sonya when she complained to her that people came to Taos and felt the magic, but then went away and forgot it. The four most impressive conquests she made during the decade—Robinson Jeffers, Leopold Stokowski, Thornton Wilder, and Thomas Wolfe—did little to help her continued efforts to build a "bridge between cultures."

Thomas Wolfe was undoubtedly Mabel's most magnificent failure. With the publication of *Of Time and the River* in 1935, Wolfe entered the ranks of major American writers, while his legend expanded to meet the scope of his intended project: to write the great American novel and get the entire American continent into his works. Wolfe's faith in his potential to fulfill a remarkable destiny, his epic vision, and lyrical power made him an ideal candidate to appreciate and celebrate Mabel's garden of the New World. He also shared her belief that the American artist could not find suitable traditions and structures for his work in the cultures of Europe. In *Of Time and the River,* he promised "I will go up and down the country, and back and forth across America. I will go out West where States are square; *Oh, I will go to Boise, and Helena and Albuquerque . . . and the unknown places.*"[36] Mabel wasted no time in tempting him to fulfill his promise about coming to the Southwest.

Mabel's first letter to Wolfe, in May 1935, expressed her admiration for his ability to render a generic spirit of place in language that was at once specific and timeless. She had come close to this in her just-completed *Winter in Taos* and had struggled for it on a broader scale in her memoirs. Beside his achievement, she felt, her own paled. Her letter reveals both her genuine humility about her own talents as a writer, and the seductiveness of her appeals to talented men. She informed Wolfe that she was overwhelmed by his novel, "where the tempo, color, feeling, taste, smell & sound of this continent is right *there* so that to read it is to be right in it. . . ." She spoke of her own failure to make a picture of life in America in her memoirs, although she felt her struggle was "the only thing worth trying, & the deepest kind of living is in the trying & doing of it." He had accomplished what she had only approximated: the unification of time and place with himself, an aesthetic unity that was at the same time the highest achievement of self-integration.[37]

Mabel concluded with an invitation that he come to visit if he were ever in the Southwest. On July 8, Wolfe wrote back that he was "happy and proud to get your wonderful and generous letter." He told her that he knew he was capable of better work and generously stated that "one reason I am going to try is because of the letter you wrote me."[38] Wolfe planned and postponed his trip to the Southwest a number of times. When he finally did arrive, he stopped first in Santa Fe, where a lunch was held in his honor. There he met two society women who offered to drop him off at Mabel's. Toasting the scenery with alcohol all the way, he arrived in Taos drunk, hours after he was expected to dinner. He phoned Mabel and "roared in his throaty, resonant voice, 'Sorry I'm late!' Pause. 'Well, can I bring along two whores who're with me? You'll like 'em!'" Mabel abruptly hung up.

His two women companions tried to sober him up, but he appeared at Mabel's at 9:30, still inebriated. He yelled imprecations at his hostess when he learned she had retired for the evening, and later compared her to "a big fat spider ready to pounce on any celebrity." But his biographer points out that "he had been flattered by the invitation to her web, and this ambivalence had no doubt brought on the dramatics."[39] That night was the first and last time Mabel almost encountered the man she believed had written "the most American great piece of something in the language I have ever read."

In Leopold Stokowski, Mabel had, initially at least, a much more willing enthusiast. He came for the first of several visits during the summer of 1931, when Carlos Chávez, his friend and Mexico's greatest modern classical composer, was also visiting Mabel. Chávez was noted for his incorporation of Indian and folk themes and instruments into his music. He and Diego Rivera had recently collaborated on an avant-garde ballet which Stokowski would premier in March 1932 with the Philadelphia Orchestra. *H.P.* (Horsepower) symbolized the economic relations between the United States and Latin America, contrasting the easy-going life rhythms of the South with those of the hectic, industrialized North. In the last act, the workers take over their machines in a triumph of the sensuous and lyrical over the mechanical. Stokowski, who was interested in Chávez's message as well as his music, was captivated by what he saw and heard at Taos pueblo.

At the time he first visited Mabel, Stokowski was probably the best known, best loved, and most controversial musician of his time in America. He was another who challenged the European dominance over American art that was even more prevalent in his field than in others. He made the Philadelphia Orchestra a first-rank world symphony during his twenty-six-year tenure, and was both praised and condemned for his progressivism and his popularization of classical music.[40] Stokowski's openness to new musical forms—he had traveled to Asia to study Oriental music—and his interest in experimenting with the latest technology in sound reproduction aroused Mabel's hopes that he could accomplish what Van Vechten had tried and failed in 1927: to record Indian ceremonial chants and bring them to the attention of the nation. In Stokowski, Mabel discovered someone who responded fully to the culture and communalism of the Pueblos.

In the winter of 1931–32, Stokowski wrote Mabel of his eagerness to see her and Tony again in order "to learn all I can about Indian culture and perhaps be able to pass some of it on to others." He agreed with her that "Taos feels like the *center* of this America" and "was enthusiastic about the idea of a great center in Taos," which he planned to talk over with her when he visited in July. After his arrival, he showed great interest in Mabel's and Collier's work with and for the Indians and promised to help in any ways that he could. He had brought along with him a specially designed recording machine, but the recordings he got were very poor. In August, he wrote Mabel of his difficulty in finding an adequate notation system for transcribing Indian music.[41]

Tony, who was very fond of Stokowski, tried to help. But he had difficulty trying to explain how he made the music for which he was famous in Taos and Carmel: "I don't read & I never speak to any man about music," he told his friend, "but, I listen to the world & the mountain & I learn from them & that comes. You know music is not just sound, it is what you make from own life & heart. Afterwards you make the brain work. I have to think a lot about it. Everyone can't make it—they try but it don't come out."[42] After his recording failure, Stokowski planned to write an essay on Indian music for a book he was publishing on American music.

In 1934, he resigned from the Philadelphia Orchestra and set his sights on Hollywood, in order to find new directions and greater audiences for his music (he was soon to collaborate with Walt Disney on *Fantasia*). En route, he stopped at Mabel's. Brett remembered vividly the famous conductor's appearance at Mabel's for dinner: "Through the glass doors walked this amazing, fantastic creature. Tall and slim, with ash-blond hair and one of the most finely chiseled, sensual faces I ever saw, he walked straight out of a fairy tale. I just gaped. With all the charm in the world and with perfect understanding of the effect he produced, he bowed, and we were swept into the dining room." Mabel and Brett were the only Anglos in attendance for a lavish feast given in his honor at Taos pueblo. Three or four steers were killed, mounds of squash, corn, chili, vegetables, and beans were served between dances and songs, while posted guards kept out tourists.[43]

When he was asked in 1935 to make a movie about music from all over the world, Stokowski informed Mabel he wished to include the Indian dances and music of New Mexico and Arizona. At the time, Mabel was working on her own movie scenario. Her fifty-eight-page typescript, "Conquest," was her rendition of Spanish-American history. While the scenes, weapons, dress, and cookware that she annotated were authentic, the historical conclusion of the drama was her own fabrication. After the Spaniards finish conquering the Pueblos, they are conquered "spiritually" in turn. Mabel gave the script to Stokowski during his summer 1936 visit. He took it quite seriously and brought it to Hollywood, where D. W. Griffith read and rejected it.

That summer, Mabel also wrote an essay about Stokowski. "Bach in a Baggage Car" is a wonderful description of the drama and showmanship   269 he brought to classical music as well as an insightful analysis of his appeal to women as a "dream-man." Stokowski was, she asserted, "living proof that men may exist on this earth who understand Everything: everything about Beauty, Spirituality, Art and Consciousness. . . ." Mabel focused on his playful side when she recounted how he handled a problem with broadcasting equipment in Denver. He moved his orchestra, which was traveling to the coast by train, into the baggage car, where they used their own equipment to broadcast Bach. "Oh Tempo! Oh Mores!" she punned, "What will he do next?"

During the late 1930s, Mabel was obsessed with the fear that she was losing her creativity as she verged on old age. She projected her fears onto Stokowski, who was younger, when she wrote that he was in the "dangerous" period of middle age during which he could either collapse or experience a "final birth" of full maturity. Stokowski rightly noted Mabel's implication that he might not work any more and asked her not to publish the essay, even though she qualified her statement by suggesting he had yet to make "his most original, significant and creative contribution to life, to music and to culture." Mabel obviously hoped that part of the contribution would flow from his time spent in Taos, but nothing more came of his interest in Pueblo culture. In the fall of 1937 and 1938, however, he brought with him to Taos a companion who created a far greater stir than his own presence. The arrival of Greta Garbo, with whom he was having an affair, caused the local papers to worry (and rejoice) about the prospect of traffic jams created by the hordes of tourists to follow in her wake.[44]

The most cordial relationship that Mabel established with a writer during the 1930s was with Thornton Wilder. Although he never wrote about Taos, he relied on Mabel as a respected friend who helped him through a crisis period in his life. Wilder had achieved early fame with his novel *The Bridge of San Luis Rey,* which won the Pulitzer Prize in 1927. He was a very popular playwright who also earned a great deal of money working on Hollywood scripts. Among the eastern critical establishment, however, he was considered a sentimental, middle-brow writer of not much substance.

Slight of stature and ascetic in nature, Wilder proved to be one of Mabel's most charming correspondents and devoted friends. Her relationship with him was, in fact, very much like the one she had maintained with Carl Van Vechten in her salon period. Thornton wrote to her as a cavalier to his lady, seeking the protection of her "humorous and disciplinary eye." Like Van Vechten, he was a good friend of Gertrude Stein's, whom he visited whenever he was in Paris. Both men appreciated Mabel and Gertrude for similar qualities: their robust interest in life and gossip, their astute observations about human nature, and their maternalism. On May 30, 1934, Wilder poured out his dissatisfactions with the criticisms of his writing: "I have read hundreds of reviews about my work and not one has ever said a keen, useful nourishing thing about it: where marks the borderline between strong feeling and sentimentality, earnest persuasion and didacticism?" He asked for Mabel's help in coming to terms with questions that no one else had been able to answer for him. While he promised not to spend time in Taos in "nail-biting introspection," he would "not conceal from you that I also look to you as a bracing analyst—of wonderful and rich resources."[45]

Wilder also provided Mabel with emotional and critical support. He looked forward eagerly to his visits, "not only because you are as brainy, good looking, and vital as can be, but because I am tremendously fond of you." He most enjoyed the afternoon drives they often took together in the "aw-ful loneliness of Taos Valley" during which they shared "*aperçus*" about their mutual friends. After the "breadth and clarity" of his visit to Los Gallos in the fall of 1934, he boasted that her "little Thornton" had stood up to Witter Bynner at a dinner party, where he was reading the latest of his nasty satires of the local literati (Mabel presumably included). Wilder informed him "that the portrait of the portraitist that emerges from the portrait is even more unlovely than the sitter." In December of that year, when he finished reading *Winter in Taos*, he wrote her that she had accomplished her goal of making Taos "a tremendous pilgrimage place. Your book breathes everything that the ten million (20?) urban apartment . . . dwellers know in their dreams that they lack."[46]

Winter in Taos

Wilder's response to *Winter in Taos* was shared by Willa Cather and many of Mabel's other friends, as well as by most critics who reviewed it and found it a delightful book. It is, indeed, her finest literary work, the one that comes closest to sustaining the richly integrated sense of self and environment, form and content, that she hoped the writers she brought to celebrate Taos would achieve. Reading it, one glimpses the regenerate vision that was sometimes hers.

Mabel offers her readers a chance to enjoy the cycle of recurrent ecstasy, intermittent hopelessness, and calm in a land that seems secured from most disease and disaster, where the senses and psyche are continually nourished, and where they can believe in the potential for men and women to escape the ill effects of insufficient work, family, and social lives—and begin again. The inspiration and design of her narrative grew out of her observations of the ritualized life cycle of the Pueblos. It reflects the intimate, organic relationship among human, nature, and cosmos the Pueblos experience, although the book's style and symbolic allusiveness derive from Western cultural traditions.

271

Mabel structured her narrative around the seasons, centering herself in what the Tiwa call the Time of Staying Still, the interregnum between Mother Earth's death and rebirth when the emergence of human life from the underworld is acknowledged.[47] The book progresses from the morning through the evening of one winter day, during which Mabel interweaves memories that are keyed to other seasons of the year.

As befits an exile from modern technology (or at least those aspects she felt interfered with her emotional and physical health), Mabel has turned back to the ways of her grandmother in order "to enjoy my storerooms full of the fruit of the earth."[48] As she lovingly details the cornucopia of fruits, vegetables, and meats that fills her larder, we cannot help but acknowledge the appetizing abundance and self-sufficiency of a life that seems to thrive outside the temporal affairs of ordinary mortals. Her ice chests are heaped with her own slaughter animals; her granaries with wheat and oats from her fields; her fruit bins with apples, quinces, cantaloupes, watermelons; her root cellar is brimming with home-grown potatoes, carrots, pumpkins, beets, and turnips; her shelves filled with jam preserves, pickles, apple butter, fruit chips, and marmalades all made in her kitchen.

In the winter, there are long rides in the cold snow, the taste of the piñon needles hung with icicles, the sun so bright the eyes ache. The sensuous contrast of the indoor and outdoor worlds of winter that Mabel creates is striking: "When we shake off the snow and go in the house, there is a warm smell of the narcissus and hyacinths that bloom all winter there, and of freesia and jonquils in vases, lovely in the firelight, with hot tea and cinnamon toast. But not more lovely than the cold, odorless world of ice and snow, where the piñon, cedar and sage are pungent with the magical oils they draw from the deep, living earth."[49]

Mabel's evocation of winter is followed by a paean to the arrival of spring in Taos Valley. The stark landscape, the violent cold and vividly contrasting colors, the light that is at times searingly blinding or lividly grey, are transformed almost magically one evening as both earth and sky open in a voluptuous awakening:

> Everything looks larger in this warm flood; it expands houses, horses, and even hearts. It is still a darkling twilight, but it is fuller and more fluid, for the tight winter sky is suffused with moisture and thin pink clouds float airily across the dusky broken dome. Like cold eyes that have forgotten the warmth of tears, the winter sky feels the sweet melancholy of renewal, and the ability to pour itself out with ease and ecstasy.[50]

Mabel creates a vivid sense of the affinity between the natural and human world that strongly suggests Pueblo gestation myths about the

Jean Toomer in Taos, c. 1935. (Photo by Marjorie Content Toomer.)

All photographs are courtesy of the Beinecke Library, Yale University, unless otherwise indicated.

Head of Mabel Dodge Luhan, by Jo Davidson, date unknown.

Portrait of Mabel Dodge Luhan, by John Young-Hunter, early 1930s. Collection of the Harwood Foundation of the University of New Mexico, Taos.

Carl Van Vechten and Mabel Luhan, 1934. (Courtesy of the estate of Carl Van Vechten, Joseph Solomon, executor.)

Georgia O'Keeffe, c. 1931. (Photo by Paul Strand.)

276

Andrew Dasburg, 1932. (Photo by Will Connell, courtesy of the Museum of New Mexico).

Mabel Luhan, Frieda Lawrence, and Dorothy Brett, 1930s.

emergence of man, whose ascent from the underworld is described in terms of the growth of other life forms from darkness to light. In the pueblo, the young Indian men help to restore the balance of nature, whose efforts to generate new life in the spring have resulted in disequilibrium: "The boys and young men give back power and speed to life . . . they run in relays, putting forth every particle of energy they can summon up . . . they tear along the track lightly but with incredible swiftness, and they are giving back to earth and sun what they have received. In due time they will harvest it again, in wheat and corn, and fruit. The everlasting exchange goes on—between man and earth, one and inseparable, but infinitely divisible."[51]

When Mabel sees the tall twisters of yellow dust that move across the land in May, she wonders whether it was not just such a column that led the Israelis "toward the Promised Land." After a rainstorm, the earth is redolent with the odors of paradise as God's covenant with his chosen people is renewed in the sky: "In the desert behind the house, every sagebrush is washed clean and a heavenly smell comes out of the damp, assuaged earth. The rainbow embraces us. We are between its horns, that sprout, one in the Pueblo, and the other in the cañon. Walk and walk and walk, in the lovely lightened air, breathing deep, with a high heart."[52]

The disequilibrium of her inner world, keyed to that of spring in Taos, is adjusted just as naturally by the very different rhythms of summer. Mabel's prose expands to meet its fullness and ease. Where spring had been fierce and gentle by turns, as unpredictable as an adolescent, summer is ripeness and peace:

> The grass is cool under one's fingers in the night, and lying on a serape one can comb the soft, crisp blades; talk is intermittent and unfocused at such hours . . . and time slides by unheeded, sleepily, and perhaps a little sadly, perhaps a little wistfully, with a tinge of undefined desire, the night is so beautiful, so fair, and unpartaken.[53]

Summer is a luxurious submission to indolence; fall, a quickening of impulses, a world of orderliness, and after the gathering of the harvest, of relaxation. The fruit falls to the ground in "magnificent abundance," while the "air is sweet with a fruity smell. . . . The desert behind the house turns yellow with fall flowers, and in dry years there are big clumps of purple asters growing wild everywhere. The autumn colors here are purple and yellow and there seems to be more of an overflow of blossoming and burgeoning than at any other season, like a last fling of life before the sleepy winter months." The odors of autumn are less subtle than those of summer, but they still set the tone of daily living:

On a crisp morning in October when the hills are veiled soft with smoke   279 from burning leaves, it is delicious to ride up to the cedars and get an armful of branches covered with blueberries. . . . The sweet wholesome fragrance penetrates every part of the house, refreshing the air, and it has a curious effect of composing the life and nerves of everyone, and establishing a feeling of order and clarity for the whole day.[54]

Accepting the seasonal cycle brings balm to psychic distemper. Where Mabel once felt a sharp pain at autumn's ending, she has now learned to feel pleasure in her submission to the season. Yet when Mabel's attention is finally brought back to the winter day around which she has woven her memories, she feels the pain of her solitude keenly. As the night lengthens, her sense of isolation and anxiety increase. She listens intently to the howling of the coyotes, whose hunger has driven them down from the hills. As she had once lived in the "now" of the summer's bliss, she is unable to imagine a future different from her unendurable present.

Mabel is delivered from the bondage of her loneliness and fear when Tony appears at midnight. She tells him she was frightened of the night and the brewing storm, and he takes her to the window to show her the moon shining on the still landscape. At this moment, the warmth of the only human love that sustained her binds Mabel, her land, and her home. Tony's presence assuages the tensions of her polarized nature, vividly objectified in the shadow and light beyond her window: "Sure enough, it was shining, and the desert was spread out so clear and visible that I could see the shadow of the whole house, a dark reflection of itself upon the snow."[55]

As *Commonweal* recognized in its review, the sensibility which created *Winter in Taos* was "poised and wholesome." Within the almost constantly illumined time span of her book, at least, the paradise that Mabel had been seeking was regained:

One lives from month to month all the year round, forgetting the future and what it will be like; then when it comes, with icicles and iris, sheaves of corn or violets in the shade, one's eternal recognition meets it with the same wonder and surprise. There is nothing so new in all eternity as this old earth, reborn every day like ourselves, and never twice the same. . . ."[56]

Unfortunately for Mabel, the balance that she was able to achieve in her book she was not able to maintain in her life. Two years later, after the completion of her final volume of memoirs, she felt as if there was nothing so old and unrenewable "in all eternity" as herself.

Decline

In January 1937, when Mabel was undergoing her late-life crisis, Thornton Wilder offered her his tempered theory of Christian optimism. Urging her to bury her negative feelings, he argued this "not from evasion of the tragic background of life, nor evasion of [*sic*] sad fact that 20th century man has lost an idea-system in which he had justification and dignity. But from a conviction that the Positive still lies about us in sufficient fragments to live by."[57]

During the winter, however, Mabel found very few of Wilder's fragments of the positive lying about her. She was almost sixty and suffering from the strains of an emotional collapse more severe than any she had endured during her trials with D. H. Lawrence. The intensity of her crisis was understandable, given the circumstances of the preceding seven years. Mabel had lost Lawrence, the man who was central to her literary gospel; alienated Collier, the man who tried to but could not revolutionize Indian affairs; and failed to replace either of them in her life. She had undertaken and accomplished a tremendous task with the publication of her memoirs, but neither the sales figures nor the critical reception seemed to justify the effort. The "great souls" who came to visit her in Taos in the 1930s seemed much more interested in her and the pleasant sanctuary offered by her estate than in promoting Taos or the Pueblo Indians.

Mabel's fear for her own retreat from creativity was also clearly connected to the general "retreat" in Taos from its 1920s prominence as a center that attracted some of the finest and most innovative writers and artists. In some important respects, that retreat was more felt than real, since there were vital signs which pointed to the writer and artist colonies at both Santa Fe and Taos as still experiencing their "golden age."

By the early 1930s the literati of both Santa Fe and Taos were beginning to build an establishment. The University of New Mexico funded the *New Mexico Quarterly* in 1931, which was dedicated to the publication of regional literature. At the same time Witter Bynner, Alice Corbin, Peggy Church, and Haniel Long established the Rydal Press on the firm conviction that "regional publishing would foster the growth of American literature." The December 1933 issue of *Poetry* was devoted to southwestern writers, who still had a national audience. In 1934, after the death of Mary Austin, the *Saturday Review* devoted an entire issue to her work. In the same year, the National Little Theater Movement came to Taos with the formation of the Taos Players.[58]

But by the mid-1930s, "something was clearly wrong in Santa Fe and Taos, both in print and life." Mary Austin had continued to write with optimism about her life in New Mexico in the early 1930s, but even she had begun to doubt by 1929 whether "the great 'fructifying' culture which was to come into being of itself" was actually taking shape. Her compatriots continued to praise their life "away from the beaten path," but they also began "to suspect that serious and long-lasting critical acclaim was eluding most of them." This "development of a strong concept of 'spirit of place,' and a stress upon the 'mystique' of Taos grew during the

281

1930s" to the point where "some New Mexican writers finally came to plead for the reverse, for their state to 'become less a part of the Southwest and more a part of the world.'"[59]

The retreat could be felt among the painters as well, though to a lesser degree. Throughout the 1930s, the national and international reputations established by the artists who had come since the postwar era drew new artists who shared the continuing recognition given through showings and prizes at prestigious eastern galleries. Both Taos and Santa Fe maintained their eclecticism, as regionalist schools flourished alongside the academic traditionalists and abstractionists. Emil Bisttram and Raymond Jonson started a transcendental movement in 1938, and Thomas Benrimo brought surrealism to Taos in 1939. New schools of art were formed in both colonies that supported Anglo, Hispanic, and Indian artists and craftsmen, who also benefited from subsidies granted through the Federal Art Project of the WPA.[60]

During the 1920s, the artist leaders of the Santa Fe and Taos colonies had been ahead of their times in some respects. They had learned from the best European modernist masters, but turned their attention away from Europe to focus on native scenes, arguing for an art inspired by and rooted in regional landscape and culture. With some exceptions, that pioneering spirit had diminished as many of them "remained immune to many of the more heated artistic contests of the 30s decade."[61] Furthermore, the founders of the colonies had fled an urban, industrial America and a mass society in which many depression artists took renewed interest. Taos and Santa Fe seemed increasingly divorced from the "real" world of the city, factory, and rural poverty that compelled proletarian realists like Grant Wood, Edward Hopper, and Ben Shahn.

The most important factor in the decline of both the writer and artist colonies, however, was the depression itself. It cut into book and painting sales, decreased the tourist trade, and thus limited the ability of artists to support themselves through their own work. In spite of the formation of guilds and cooperatives and the grants received through federal subsidies, many permanent and temporary artists left the colonies between 1930 and 1940.

While new artists and writers continued to arrive and settle in Santa Fe and Taos through the 1930s, few established themselves who had the stature and innovative vision of the founding mothers and fathers and the best of the 1920s visitors. As a founding mother, Mabel felt a profound sense of public, as well as personal, failure. Her malaise brought A. A. Brill out to visit in the fall of 1937.

Brill convinced Mabel to return to New York to work with him again. Just before she left Taos to join him, he summarized for her the compounding factors that had precipitated her latest mental crisis:

> You do not imagine for a moment that I had no cause for talking to you
> about psychic suicide. . . . The foundation of the hospital, your fight
> with your old friend, John C., the completion of your works—all these
> represented a consummation [*sic*] of a task that was almost titanic. I
> might say that your works, including the one that is coming out [ETD],
> represented your whole life's work, and like the sensitive creature that
> you are, you were ready to give up.[62]

Sick of writing autobiography, she hoped Brill would "open her up" to
other forms, but she doubted whether she had the energy or ability to
accomplish anything of significance in the future. Not only was it clear
that Taos was not going to become the "center" of America, but it seemed
unlikely that she would achieve status, let along immortality, as a writer.

During her crisis, Mabel wrote a moving letter to Andrew Dasburg
who, along with suffering from Addison's disease, was also experiencing
serious doubts about his abilities as an artist. Mabel reminded him of a
painting that Thornton Wilder had purchased from him two years before,
which described

> his own temporary predicament . . . the most perfect picture of middle-
> aged cessation & the end of usefulness of energy. That old freight-train
> fading, side tracked, no longer moving . . . drying up, abandoned! . . .
> But when there is enough sap & energy left, enough of the divine urge
> to go on—then that rare thing happens that I saw yesterday [when she
> viewed a mural Dasburg had recently completed], & the artist triumphs
> over the man & the beautiful rebirth takes place—where he arrived at a
> real maturity. I really believe that the mature work of an artist only
> comes if he survives the terrible pause of his energy in the middle
> years. . . . If it is true that "life begins at forty" it is more true that
> great art begins at fifty. . . . Your best work is being done . . . & is
> still ahead of you, and to end up with a thought of myself (of course!)
> that if you have done it, why can't I also![63]

With Brill's help, and her own seemingly endless store of resilient
energy and optimism, Mabel rallied. After a couple of months, she decided
that she was ready to take New York City by storm. Once again, as she
had in 1913, she hoped to create a home that could serve as a place for
intellectual discussion and cultural exchange, although her goals this time
reflected her sense that what New York City now needed most was an
"anchorage" for lonely men and women who felt no sense of intellectual
or social community because of the city's size and increasing impersonality.
She was also concerned about young, married, upper-middle-class women
who were bored and restless but did not want to "interfere" with their
husbands' work lives. During the winter, Mabel began to write what she

hoped would become a continuing series of "Conversation Pieces" on prominent men and women in the arts and in business. When her interviewees discovered her remarkable ability at recall, however, and blue-penciled all "the interesting bits," she "got discouraged and gave up the idea." Mabel's plans were greeted by the press with banner headlines. The *Buffalo Courier-Express* hailed the return to civilization of the "authoress, traveller and brilliant observer of human nature." The *New York Post* quoted her as saying that she was considering dividing her future life between Taos and New York.[64]

While in New York, Mabel wrote an open letter to the *New York Times* that indicated her renewed interest in the intersection of social and cultural issues. She pleaded for closer cooperation between artists and architects based on her assessment of how some Taos artists had been helped to feel less isolated from "the human situation" by getting federal commissions to paint murals on public buildings. Calling for an art that was both socially conscious and communal, she spoke of artists returning "to the guild idea on a new level. Architects, painters, engineers, writers, scientists are not too many elements in a cooperative group to make a new world."[65]

On the same day that Mabel's letter appeared in the *Times,* May 22, 1938, Spud Johnson announced her triumphant return to Taos for the summer in the *New Mexico Sentinel:* "Mabel Luhan Gets 'Socialized' But Won't Stop Writing Books." Luhan was going to open the "Big House" after having lived for the last few years in one of the smaller homes on her estate. "Everything suddenly opened up," she told Spud about her "metamorphosis." On July 3, Spud promised a "Big Four Star Weekend" at Luhan's with Brill, José Limon, Rep. J. J. Dempsey, and Robinson Jeffers. That summer, the "Sphynx of Taos Desert" was interviewed by Elizabeth Shepley Sargeant for the *Saturday Review.* Sargeant's Luhan still reigned supreme—both in the desert and over the national cultural landscape. She described her as "one of the most conspicuous, most publicized and discussed of American women" who ran off to New York and Washington every so often to get "re-charged" by contact with the latest young men, newest music, books, and plays. Mabel had attracted artists, writers, activists, and movie stars to "come out and . . . record the birth of a new American culture, stemming from the contact of Indian and white," by feeding them generously, housing them, and encouraging their work. Thus she "drew promising converts to the Southwest into her net of faith and words."[66]

By the summer of 1938, the public Mabel seemed restored to her former glory. But the private Mabel harbored the discontent of one who had not yet come to terms with the losses and disappointments she had suffered over the decade. Since the summer of 1930, she had drawn

Robinson and Una Jeffers yearly from their stone tower in Carmel with "her net of faith and words." No sooner had Lawrence died than Mabel determined Jeffers would take his place. For eight years she worked on him and waited. When he failed to speak Taos to the world, she helped to direct a scenario that almost ended in the death of his wife. Three years later, Mabel achieved her final fictional avatar when Myron Brinig sent her to a spectacular death in his roman à clef, *All of Their Lives* (1941).

American Gothic:
Mabel Dodge Luhan
and the Robinson Jefferses

Well, Jeffers, that is all I have to tell you about Lawrence in Taos. I
called him there, but he did not want to do what I called him to
do. . . . Perhaps you are the one who will, after all, do what I
wanted him to do: give a voice to this speechless land. Something
interfered with Lorenzo's chance to do that. Perhaps it was because
there was too much wilfullness and passion and egotism surrounding
him here. The irony of it is that if there is a greater freedom and
purity in my wish now, that the life here may become articulate, and
that you will be the channel through which it shall speak, it is
Lorenzo who released me from my insistent self-will and brought me to
the happy immolation that has in it no false desire. You are a clear
channel and I think I am become myself a clear one, now, too.[1]

In the spring of 1930, Mabel met Robinson Jeffers in Carmel, California. She immediately recognized him as Lawrence's heir. Where Lawrence had failed, Jeffers might succeed in making Taos known as the center of spiritual redemption in the West. Mabel chose as Lawrence's successor a man who had lived most of his adult life in the self-chosen exile of a "Tower Beyond Tragedy," the stone house that he built at the tip of the Monterey peninsula. He lived there with his two sons and his wife, Una, who guarded him and their privacy with a fierce possessiveness.

Jeffers was born in Pennsylvania in 1887. His father, a learned theologian and professor of classics, taught him Greek at the age of five. Steeped in classical literature, he spent much time traveling in Europe with his family while he was growing up. By 1911 he was determined to devote his life to poetry and was able to do so thanks to a small legacy left him by a cousin. In 1913, after she divorced her first husband, he married Una, with whom he had been in love since 1905. In 1914, they moved to Carmel, where they lived for the rest of their lives. Jeffers established his reputation—one of the most controversial of the early twentieth century—in 1924, with his publication of *Tamar and Other Poems*. Each year thereafter he produced at least one more volume. In 1930, when Mabel met him, he was at the height of his fame. He had a wide readership and extraordinary critical acclaim. Jeffers's admirers, Mabel among them, sanctified him as America's greatest living poet.

To get D. H. Lawrence to come to Taos, Mabel had willed him there from her solar plexus: "Before I went to sleep at night, I drew myself all in to the core of my being where there is a live, plangent force lying passive." Luring Jeffers away from his stone fortress would require a more cerebral technique: she would "seduce" him with a book. Mabel was staying in Carmel when she received the telegram informing her of Lawrence's death. Abandoning her memoirs for the time being, she told Una that she was only able to write *for* someone. With Lawrence now dead, Robin would take over and play an even more important role than his precedessor. Before completing the draft of her biography of Lawrence, which she dedicated to Jeffers, she wrote Una and Robin and asked them a question. Would the reader of *Lorenzo* remember that she had said Lawrence was like John the Baptist crying in the wilderness? Should she bring the phrase in again "where I say *he* couldn't do the thing to do here—that he only prepared the way—& that now maybe Robin will be the one to do it?"[2]

In her review of *Lorenzo in Taos* for the *Carmelite,* Una Jeffers recounted how she and her husband succumbed to the bait while the Luhans were visiting in Carmel. Mabel wrote each morning and in the evening gave the pages to Una and Robin to read. They read "those freshly typed pages, and began to forget that when we returned from Ireland a few months before, we had resolved never to leave Tor House again. Clear and magical the image she made of her remote pastoral land. . . ."[3]

Mabel did not rely on her book alone. Spud Johnson outlined her tactical maneuvers in "abducting" Carmel's poet laureate to Taos in his admiring article for the *Carmelite* entitled, "She Did It!" Spud described how her initial "urges and insistences" were met "by the blank wall" of Jeffers's insistence that he did not intend to stray from Tor House for years, if ever. But Mabel's "subtle campaign of Taos publicity" combined with an invitation that the two Jeffers boys spend their vacation in Taos proved irresistible in "undermining the studied pattern of their ordered lives. . . ." As Mabel well understood, even after so brief an encounter with them, such "fond parents" could not "disappoint their children after they had been completely 'sold' on the idea and were looking forward to it expectantly."[4]

Why did Mabel choose Robinson Jeffers as Lawrence's heir? She never explained her choice, but her reasons are implicit in everything she wrote to, for, or about him. Despite his vastly different temperament and character, Mabel was not wrong in seeing a kinship between the reclusive Jeffers and the peripetatic Lorenzo. Given Jeffers's aesthetic theories and philosophy, her choice of him was thoroughly comprehensible, even if it was just as thoroughly mistaken.

A major theme in both writers' works was the primary theme of Mabel's memoirs: that the solipsistic ego of Western man had denied love (what Jeffers called "falling in love outward") and had turned to power for its satisfaction. For Jeffers, as well as for Lawrence, the "original sin" was mental consciousness, what he called man's "distinction" but hardly our "advantage," since this form of awareness cuts us off from nature and makes us turn inward toward self-love and the will-to-power. Jeffers deplored the substitution of material goods for spiritual growth and the raping of the sacramental beauty of the landscape. As a poet of the apocalypse, he yearned for the holocaustal destruction that would have to precede the creation of a new world.

Jeffers shared Lawrence's belief in the regenerative power of symbolic language. What Mabel wrote of Lawrence in her review of *The Plumed Serpent* could be applied with equal justice to Robin. Jeffers's touch upon the "dying world" was "the last break up of dissolution." He had chosen for himself the task that Mabel said Lawrence had chosen for the American writer—to "burn the world to the ground so that a new flower might come up from the roots" that would replace "the egotistic robot of machine man."[5]

As was true of Lawrence's pre-American essays, there are hints in Jeffers's 1920s poetry of the Indians as unavenged spirits, trying to take back their own, possibly carrying the seeds of renewal. Tamar is not allowed knowledge of her past that she needs for self-transcendence until she appeases the Indian ghosts of the coast by allowing them to violate her body. In the "Torch-Bearer's Race," the dead tribes that the white man hunted are spoken of as unavenged ghosts whose hunger is simple in contrast with the white man's "complications and desires." In *Roan Stallion,* the Indian woman California is allowed to "know" the shining power of the godhead, while the Indian woman Maruca, in *The Women at Point Sur,* believes that the child she has conceived with the Reverend Barclay will be the savior of mankind.

Jeffers expressed his admiration for Lawrence's missionary zeal in the preface he wrote to Lawrence's posthumous book of poetry, *Fire.* In calling Lawrence "the last Protestant," however, he concluded that his was a faith that held its energies but had "lost its direction," because he retained his belief in the power of human life to renew itself.[6] He was, to use a phrase of William James's, "tender-minded" where Jeffers was "tough-minded." If Lawrence was the last Protestant, Jeffers was more like the first of his Calvinist forebears.

Jeffers held an unswerving distrust of all human schemes and a passionate, all-embracing love for divine beauty that encompassed horror and pain as its modes of discovery. Lawrence would have recoiled from Jeffers's philosophic doctrine of "Inhumanism" just as he finally recoiled from the erotic surrender of himself to the blind, impersonal energies of the New Mexican landscape. Yet he and Jeffers had begun at very much the same point in their early messianism. In the prewar period Jeffers celebrated the "new world" he had discovered in Carmel at the same time Lawrence was looking toward the American West in the hopes that it would offer a new beginning in the rising cycle of history. What New Mexico came to be for Lawrence, Carmel had already become for Jeffers: the most important outside experience to affect his life and art. There he found a people living amidst an unspoiled landscape as they did in earliest literature: "Here was life purged of its ephemeral accretions . . . contemporary life that was also permanent life . . . unencumbered by the mass of poetically irrelevant details and complexities that make a civilization."[7] Because of his vision of the world as being in a perpetually dynamic state of flux, he longed as much as, if not more than, Mabel and Lawrence for rootedness, for permanent things. Tor House became the literal and symbolic expression of his desire.

In spite of his disillusionment with man's essentially corrupt and violent nature, Jeffers's "surge to annihilation" was coupled with "a faith in messianic restitution." In seeing him as a potential Messiah, Mabel was not placing on him a burden he had not already undertaken himself. He envisioned himself a sacrificial Christ, whose healing message was ignored by a decadent civilization. By identifying with God's "victimhood," he hoped to teach others how to achieve "cosmic selflessness."[8]

Mabel understood Jeffers's motivation and explored his aesthetic, in both its private and public dimensions, in a very sensitive and perceptive portrait she wrote in 1933. Probably no one except Una understood as well as she how Robin tried to use his art to purchase immunity to the tragedies of human life:

> Experiencing the human tragedy consciously and voluntarily, and building it into solid blocks of poetry, is an atonement for his own three; but it is more than that. It is for all—for any of us. No one can read Robin's poetry and be just the same afterwards. One could be saved from those sins and sorrows by reading of them as he writes. Bringing into consciousness and clear understanding, the distracting terrors and troubles of life, he dissipates them. What a task for one man![9]

Before learning of Lawrence's death in April of 1930, Mabel had asked Jeffers to send Lawrence a few of his books and to write a personal inscription, because she felt they would have liked and understood each other. She was right that Jeffers chose well when he inscribed one of the volumes he sent Lawrence with these famous lines:

> This coast is crying out for tragedy. . . .
> . . . I said in my heart,
> "Better invent than suffer: imagine victims,
> Lest your own flesh be chosen the agonist."[10]

The Christ-like figure who offers redemption to mankind and security for his loved ones is only one strain in Jeffers's poetry that attracted Mabel to him. He also shared her distate for the flaws and limitations of the human flesh. Jeffers often used an incest motif to express this self-disgust. In *The Women at Point Sur,* April is seduced by her father, then hallucinates that she is her dead brother and must kill her father in revenge. In *Tamar,* David is presented as a falsely pious weakling who easily succumbs to his daughter's seduction. In *Cawdor,* the father kills his son in the mistaken belief that he has seduced his wife. For Jeffers the only erotic union that is not doomed is one in which he imagines the ecstasy of achieving identity with the godhead that resides in nature. His character Orestes says of this union: "I and my loved are one; no desire/but fulfilled; no passion but peace,/The pure flame and the white, fierier than any passion; no/time but splendid eternity."[11]

Although women represent the worst perversions of human lust in his poetry, they also (though not always in the same character) hunger for a transcendence of their human limitations. Their desire for transcendence adds a tragically heroic dimension to their inability to find men capable of answering to the elemental vitality of their life force. In fact, it is this inability that often turns them destructive (as is true of many of Lawrence's women characters). Like Lawrence, Jeffers embodied the anathema of self-consciousness at its most aggressive and lustful in his female characters.

A good part of Mabel's attraction to Una was based on the fact that Una was the inspiration of Jeffers's heroines. But she was also more than that. Like Frieda she has been credited with turning her husband from a minor poet into a major artist. Mabel understood that Una was indispensable to both Robin's life and work and knew that unless she captured her devotion, she would never have access to Robin. Una, however, succeeded where Mabel felt that Frieda failed by helping Robin achieve the "Fatherhood" Lawrence had only aspired to.

Robin's character contained an ideal paradox for Mabel. There was never any doubt in her mind that he was all male (as there was about Lawrence). Yet in his relationship with Una, he was the passive receptor and she, the aggressive huntress who stormed the Carmel coast gathering stories to feed his imagination. She was "his lifeline in the deep sea of human suffering." The double immunity they afforded one another was, to Mabel, a marvel, a perfect integration of life and art. Mabel's description of the Jefferses' family life reads like an abrogation of human nature. Donnan and Garth are examples of children who are growing to maturity without having to hate their parents. Una has made their lives so interesting that they would rather be home than anywhere. There is never any envy among any of them, and "there is no end to the giving amongst them all."[12] They had, in fact, everything that Mabel lacked when she was growing up, and everything that her own son lacked.

Like Frieda, Una treated her marriage as a sacred trust, a work of art continually in the making. She would brook no interference from other women who hoped to get their hands on Robin to see what they could do for him: "Knowing no one could take Robin's love away from her, was not enough for her realistic knowledge of human nature. She knew and knows their structure has the fragility that requires daily, hourly, creating. It is not something that, once made, will endure forever." Mabel had discovered the weak stones in the Jefferses' tower—Robin's emotional vulnerability and Una's need for dominion over the empire of his body and soul:

> Of course the psychologists are uncertain about Robin's complete
> abnegation, his absolute surrender to Una. He is apparently utterly
> selfless, has no personal wishes, is content to let her will rule them
> all. . . .
>
> [Yet] there is something that contracts the heart in the completion and
> the beauty of this life, removed from everything commonplace or sordid,
> *seemingly so safe* from disaster or accident.[13] (Italics mine.)

In five more years, she would use this knowledge in the most destructive way possible. But at the time she wrote her 1933 portrait, she was all admiration. Where Frieda's possessiveness had driven Mabel wild, she marveled at Una's far more exclusive bond. Una had, after all, possessed her man as completely as Mabel ever could have dreamed of possessing a man of creative genius. And, unlike Frieda, she was anything but hostile to consciousness.

Una was a highly intelligent and educated woman who throve on intellectual discussions, which she had more than enough opportunity for once she joined Mabel's circle of friends. The fact that the Jefferses spent more time in Taos than anywhere else in the world outside Carmel was mainly due to Una's strong attachment to Mabel. After her first visit to Taos, she wrote a friend that Mabel was the "most interesting woman" that she had met in years, that she had done all she could to make their trip enjoyable, and that Robin was much inspired by the visit. Una loved the stimulation and excitement that continually swirled about Mabel. Una was a woman of "insatiable vanity," and Mabel gave her all the "appreciation and praise" that she needed to feed it.[14]

Una was one more wife of a famous artist who was captivated by Mabel's 291 independence of spirit. She was most enthusiastic about her dedication of *Lorenzo* to Robin (and relished the intimate glimpses of the Lawrence ménage Mabel continually gave her. Frieda would later have a similar opportunity to learn about the Jefferses). Una was so taken with the biography that she did everything in her power to get it a good critical reception. In fact, she played in a small way for Mabel the same role that Mabel had tried to play for Gertrude Stein when she was working to help her to establish her reputation. Una sent a copy of the book to Virginia Woolf and wrote Mabel that everyone was reading it, a process she was aiding by lending her copy to everyone she knew and egging on many more to buy it. [15]

When friends berated the Jefferses for their association with Mabel, Una was quick to quash ugly rumors (apparently hinting of sexual irregularities). She sent Mabel a copy of one letter in which she had defended her. She told her friend that she resented anyone suggesting that her and Robin's relationship was so tenuous that it could not "remain intact even surrounded by a battalion of Mabels." She and Mabel had been intimate friends for three years during which Una had never ceased respecting and loving her. The Mabel that she and Robin knew was always generous and considerate, besides creating an energetic "whirlwind" about her that Una found irresistible. [16]

The vortex of mental and physical energy that attracted Una to Mabel had subtleties far beyond the understanding of Una's open and forthright personality. Mabel was bent on succeeding with Jeffers where she had failed with Lawrence. Her previous experience had taught her to behave with much more caution and propriety. One has only to reread *Lorenzo in Taos* and keep in mind the audience of one to whom it was directed to see her intentions. Throughout *Lorenzo,* Mabel presented herself in the mold of the archetypal destroying female that Jeffers dramatized in his epic poetry. She might have been consciously imitating "Tamar," a poem that dwelt upon the narcissistic self-centeredness of a heroine who ultimately transcended her own ego through the immolation of herself and her family. Even Lawrence is represented as a Jeffersian character, driven by an inner daimon that "cares nothing for systems, but only for life." But unlike Orestes (and Jeffers) he was destroyed before he could reach the serene heights of Jeffers's transhumanity. [17]

Mabel accentuated her she-wolf qualities in *Lorenzo.* She read the implication in Jeffers's poetry that "only certain superior individuals nurtured on violence, yet attuned to nature's glorious beauty, could hope . . . to prove worthy of their existence." Thus she outlined for him the evolution of her birth into higher forms of life: in Buffalo, she wrote, her lower sex center had awakened; in Italy, "the emotional, nervous, aesthetic center at the solar plexus"; in New York, the intellectual center had been awakened. And, finally, in Taos, "Tony had gradually awakened my dormant heart. . . ." Yet because her communication with Tony was silent, she was still filled with highly explosive Dionysian energy: "My total ego needed to pass off into words, else the accumulation of energy-carrying impressions, which made me like a Leyden jar charged to the brim, would destroy either me or my environment."[18]

Because Lawrence had been unable to pass off enough of the "overload," Mabel had written *Lorenzo*. At the end of the book, she makes clear that the she-wolf has been transformed into a dove, who has achieved the marriage of "peace with pain" that Jeffers felt was the most one could accomplish on earth. She is ready to represent Taos, the "dawn of the world," to the true Messiah.

The "clear channel" that Mabel claimed to have become for Jeffers was, of course, as muddied with desire to serve his genius and have him serve hers as her relationship with Lawrence had been. But this time she was much more careful about how she directed her campaign. She always addressed and saw the Jefferses "en famille." Throughout the 1930s, Mabel's letters were importunate about her love and need of the Jeffers family: Why don't they come? When are they coming? When will they return? When they were low on money, she sent them fare, even at times when she was having financial difficulties. Her pleas and flattery were enough to move mountains, even if Una had not been the type of woman who craved this attention.

Mabel also tried to trade houses with Una's first husband, who lived next to the Jefferses, so that she could "grow old along with you all!" She invited Robin to come and "do" the Mexicans, the Indians, and the Penitentes. Una shared Mabel's eagerness to have Robin turn his tragic imagination upon the landscape of Taos. In a letter of February 4, 1932, she wrote Mabel that although Robin had written nothing of length about New Mexico, "it will come. The period of gestation in him is longer than in an elephant." She concluded with a view of their relationship that is reminiscent of Frieda's apotheosis of Mabel, Lawrence, and herself: "Of you and Robin and myself, I have a realization of complete beings, real little cosmoses stepping about."[19]

From the very first, Mabel worked diligently to provide Jeffers with new seed plots for his poetry. As he wrote of her to one of his friends, she filled his eyes and ears to capacity with the sights and sounds of the landscape and the Indians. But her contributions went beyond guided tours. Like Una, she wished to gather morsels of the world's sins and sorrows to feed his imagination. Her first contribution, in 1930, was a detailed account of a gruesome murder trial that was taking place in Taos. The murder had involved the mutilation of George Manby (the English eccentric who thought that she and Maurice were German spies). The alleged killer was a strikingly beautiful woman who had been Manby's mistress and who was carried to trial each day in the arms of her Hispanic lover. Mabel's description of Carmen, the defendant, reads like a portrait of one of Jeffers's amoral heroines:

> The women of the past must have been like this—it is foolish to call her a "criminal type. . . ." She has all the hard firmness of one who has not yet become complicated by emotions & qualms . . . not yet—as we call it—civilized.[20]

But there was a far more compelling drama that Mabel had to offer, one that had to do with the Lawrences.

From the moment Frieda returned from Italy to Taos with her lover, Angelo Ravagli, Mabel kept Una posted on her every activity and statement, even going so far as to make copies of Frieda's letters and sending them to the Jefferses. Mabel wanted Una to know Frieda as intimately as she did so that she would recognize her as an intellectual inferior ("My *dear!*" she wrote Una in 1935, "I cannot *tell* you how absolutely empty, banal, & completely ridiculous [Frieda's book] is. What shall we do about it?")[21] Frieda and Una did become friends, however, and the Jefferses were one of the few couples in Carmel who warmly welcomed her when she came there with Ravagli.

Mabel's first portrait of Frieda after her return from Italy was richly comic. On June 3, 1931 she wrote Una that

> she talks of him [Lawrence] all the time & weeps & then laughs, & is all rosy & wrinkled & fuzzy haired & moist, with bright green pinpoints of light in her mad little eyes with their chiffoné eyelids. We are all glad they are here—it's so lively & amusing. . . .
>
> Frieda says: "Its such a *vonerful* country—where you arrive with a man & nobody says a *vord* (!!!) but I couldn't come *alone! I* am the kind of voman who must *have* a man!"

Frieda told Mabel that when she passed through menopause, Lawrence had wept that "some splendor was passing away from the earth." She claimed that she was still unwell and even asked Mabel if it were possible for her to have a baby, at age fifty-two.[22]

This was the "jolly sequel" to the harrowing events surrounding Lawrence's death, which were preceded and precipitated by Frieda's affair with Angelo. Frieda had met him in late 1925 and became his lover a year later, at about the time she revealed to friends that Lawrence had become sexually impotent. During the winter of 1930, Barbara Barr, Frieda's daughter by her first marriage, visited the Lawrences and was there at the time Lawrence died. Barbara believed that Lawrence was still in the house after his death and insisted on leaving the door of his room open so that his spirit could pass back and forth.

Meanwhile, John Middleton Murry came to offer his condolences, which were so persuasive that Frieda and he had sexual intercourse. When a friend informed Barbara about her mother's affair with Ravagli and her submission to Murry, the shock precipitated psychotic hysteria. Barbara had grown up her whole life listening to her father's family condemn Frieda as a woman steeped in sin, and Frieda certainly seems to have had no moral qualms about her behavior. She attempted, moreover, to cure Barby by encouraging a young Italian boy to come to the house and have intercourse with her, an experiment she repeated a number of times. When they heard of this, Frieda's horrified sisters insisted that Barby be sent back to England, where she seems to have recovered. [23]

Mabel learned many more lurid details from Frieda, and she revealed them to Una in three lengthy letters that she wrote her during June and July 1931. The most important revelation Frieda made was that Lawrence had "gotten" *Lady Chatterley's Lover* from her affair with Angelo. As Mabel dramatically recounted it:

"From you and Angellino!!!??"
"Yes!"
"Had it been going on long & Lorenzo got it intuitively?"
"*Yes!!* He just got it out of the air! & what I lovvve in Angellino is he's such a Man! When Lorenzo was moving to the San—I was going to see my mother & I thought I could go running by his garrison & see him & wrote him that—but he answered 'no if Lorenzo is going to a sanitarium he must be very sick & you must stay near him!'—Wasn't that *noble?*"

Mabel wanted to be sure that the Jefferses knew Frieda had "no sense of *personal* responsibility!" So she added the details about Murry's seduction. She also elaborated on Barby's reaction to Lawrence's death, a reaction that in Mabel's telling verges on necrophilia. In case the Jefferses did not notice how the material she was sending them paralleled Robin's, Mabel prefaced her story by saying that it "quite equals the terrible old Greek tragedys [*sic*]." [24]

Frieda apparently told Mabel that Barby was passionately in love with Lawrence. After his death, she lay in his bed and refused to eat. When she finally broke down from the strain of the events that surrounded her, she tore off her clothes, crawled naked on the floors, and destroyed everything in the house. At one point she almost killed Frieda. After Frieda brought in the Italian workingman, Barby began to sexually assault other men including, so Frieda thought, her brother Monty. In case the Jefferses had not gotten the point that Frieda out-Tamared Tamar, Mabel clinched it for them: "She's perfectly irresponsible—inhuman—rather like dynamite!" [25] Seeing the potential for her own future use in the materials she sent them, she asked Una to save them for a sequel she might write to *Lorenzo*.

She never did. Nor did Robinson Jeffers need to use her material. He had long ago discovered the almost limitless debauchery of which the human animal was capable in the war that destroyed all ideals, except those to be found in the rugged and flawless beauty of the Carmel coast. To Jeffers, Mabel's stories must have seemed merely contemporary versions of timeless archetypes. For the same reason, Taos could never become for Jeffers what Mabel hoped that it would, although he enjoyed his visits and had a great deal of admiration for his hostess. In June 1935, he wrote to Louis Untermeyer that Taos was lovely: "probably you have been here, or have read Mabel Luhan's 'Winter in Taos,' which describes it beautifully." In July he wrote Arthur Ficke that Taos was "very delightful. One can hardly even pretend to work in this warm golden sunshine.—I don't see how Mabel Luhan manages to write so much so well. . . ."[26]

Jeffers was stimulated by his visits "to consider the relationship of modern man to his primitive origins," but his conclusions were very different from Lawrence's more hopeful ones. He wrote only one poem that was directly inspired by his visits, entitled "New Mexican Mountain." In it, he noted the pathos of the young Pueblo Indians who were unable to match the power of the old ways, while American tourists looked on their ritual dances with hunger, unable to find enough religion in them to feed themselves:

> People from cities, anxious to be human again. Poor show how
>   they suck you empty! The Indians are emptied,
> And certainly there was never religion enough, nor beauty nor
>   poetry here . . . to fill Americans.

> Only the drum is confident, it thinks the world has not changed.
>   Apparently only myself and the strong
> Tribal drum, and the rockhead of Taos mountain, remember
>   that civilization is a transient sickness.[27]

Jeffers was not interested in primitive peoples. He was interested in man's primal passions as a source of creativity and discovery. Yet Mabel had good reason to believe that Jeffers would identify with the Pueblo Indians' reverence for natural life, their balanced view of the reciprocal relationship between man and nature, and their lack of self-centeredness. Why, then, did he reject them? His poem makes it obvious that he felt he was witnessing a decline in the purity and purpose of their ethos as Western ways encroached on them, but there may have been a more important reason.

The Pueblo creed was not harsh enough for Jeffers. His God was the one who spoke in *Job* out of the whirlwind, demanding worship and praise even as he damned man to torture and destruction. His God was not interested in family or clan loyalties, but in the total devotion of the individual's unquestioned worship. In spite of Jeffers's belief in the necessity of order and rational control of passion (evinced in his life-style and in his conservative politics), it is the Dionysian outbreak of violence at its most ecstatic that consumed his poetic energies: the tearing and rending and burning of human flesh, the destruction of the human family as the incestuous source of self-love—these are the requisites for the illumination and acceptance of the divine tragedy that is life.

By late 1932, Mabel seems to have come to a partial realization that Jeffers might not write her Gospel. After 1932, her letters focus mainly on her psychological and physical health, on her relationship with her son, and on her efforts to come to terms with her own writing. She rarely mentions Robin's poems, but when she does, it is always with the highest praise. She never ceased to believe that they contained the "farthest range" of anyone living or dead. Perhaps Mabel adopted Una's caveat that Jeffers's gestation period was longer than an elephant's, or perhaps she recognized that if she pushed harder, she would turn him away altogether. The friendship flourished throughout the mid-1930s. The Jefferses visited every summer but one, from 1933 through 1938, while Mabel spent a good part of the winters during these years in Carmel. There she was one of a flourishing colony of writers, artists, and intellectuals that included Sinclair Lewis, Lincoln Steffens, Langston Hughes, John and Molly O'Shea, Edward Weston, and John Steinbeck.

The O'Sheas, who were known as "royal dispensers of hospitality,' gave elaborate picnic luncheons at the bottom of the high cliff which jutted out at the end of their peninsula. On one occasion Mabel, Dorothy Thompson, the Jefferses, and Sinclair Lewis were in attendance. Ella Young recalled that

> everyone had to descend about a hundred steps cut in the rocks. Arrived, one might be on a desert island. No sound of a motor-horn, no glimpse of a roadway or of a house. A sound of the sea makes itself felt, the sea advancing in great waves and churning among the rocks. Far off, on Lobos magnificently thrust upon the horizon, there is the barking of sea lions.
>
> Sinclair Lewis, a slender figure with contumacious red hair and an ironic smile, comes down those steps long after everyone else. He is in a holiday mood and catching sight of me declares that he is going to say a poem in my honour. He makes one on the spot, and follows it with another for good measure, proceeding thereafter to burlesque himself and mimic sundry Americans while his hosts urge him to be seated and fall to on viands, plentiful enough and rare enough to tempt a Roman epicure.
>
> It is a gay party, as gay as the sunshine, as gay as the coloured stripes

on the awning, as light of heart as the circling sea-swallows. Sinclair Lewis is raying out the wittiest and most fantastic remarks. John O'Shea replies in kind. Lincoln Steffens is even more dazzling. So lightning-quick is thrust and riposte in this rapier play of wit that I find myself bewildered by it. Una Jeffers, at the other end of the table, is telling amusing anecdotes. Tony, tired of it all, is standing on a rock. He stands majestic in a scarlet serape. The sea curls in waves behind him, sapphire-blue except where churning foam transfigures it to chalcedony. Molly O'Shea, beautiful and gracious, is smiling and spreading that atmosphere of joyousness that makes her so renowned a hostess.[28]

After 1935, Jeffers began to show the effects of the decline of his writing power, which was accompanied by his declining reputation.[29] In the 1920s, his narrative and dramatic poetry was praised for its depth and originality; in the 1930s it came in for increasing criticism by both the New Critics and the Marxists (the latter found his philosophy perverse and defeatist). Mabel tried to help. She wrote to an agent she knew in Hollywood to place his works and at one point hoped to have a movie made from his poem *The Loving Shepherdess,* with Greta Garbo in the lead.

By 1937, Jeffers was suffering from a severe depression caused by his inability to write. Una urged him to accept Mabel's invitation to return to Taos the following summer in the hope that it would "stimulate his exhausted imagination."[30] Having just come through her own mental crisis that was partly a result of writer's block, Mabel could be expected to be highly sympathetic.

By spring of 1938, Mabel wrote Una that she had been "excavated" and "extroverted" by Brill. She was both "re-converted" to her love of people and now able to write. She looked forward eagerly to the Jefferses' visit. But Mabel's behavior to the Jefferses that summer verged on the pathological. Jeffers' depression and sterility combined with Mabel's psychological problems to precipitate the near-tragic scenario.

Mabel convinced herself that Una was at the root of Robin's inability to write and that what he needed was to be recharged sexually. Once again, she felt called upon to save a great artist from his wife. She could not service him herself, but she had at her disposal a young, attractive, and emotionally desperate young woman who could serve as surrogate. Hildegarde Nathan had fled to Mabel's after her husband came home with his mistress and announced they would all live together in a ménage à trois.

According to Mabel, Hildegarde informed her that while Jeffers loved his wife, he could not stand his life. She seemed as eager as Mabel to help out. Mabel more than encouraged their affair; she tried to get Tony to help by asking him to drive them to a rendezvous where they could have some privacy, which he refused to do. When Una discovered the affair, she took Jeffers's .32 caliber automatic, went up to Mabel's bathroom, and tried to shoot herself through the heart.[31] Fortunately, she missed.

Mabel's reaction to Una's attempted suicide was blood chilling. She was annoyed because her "guest" put her in the awkward position of creating a scandal for which she would be blamed. When Robin reminded her that she too had tried suicide twice in despair of love, she replied that was something one did in one's twenties and not in one's fifties.

While there is nothing that excuses Mabel's behavior in this affair, there is much to explain it. It is clear that she felt the Jefferses had failed her profoundly—Robin because he did not become her prophet, Una because she was Robin's "eyes and ears." She had pursued them indefatigably for seven years, and nothing had come of it. Their failure was, of course, hers, one more to add to the list of unfulfilled hopes.

The sense of betrayal that Mabel felt was complicated by the place the Jefferses held in her emotional life. She was not, it turns out, merely avenging her sense of failure on them, but on her parents and her son as well, through them. The portrait that Mabel drew of the Jefferses makes much of this clear. Written at the end of the summer, it could have been titled, "The Fall of the House of Jeffers." The ideal American family she had eulogized in 1933 now lives in a hell of hate and distrust. The once-generous, all-sacrificing mother has become the possessive shrew whose sons seek to escape her suffocating attempts to dominate them.

Una has become jealous of whatever "flow" has developed between Robin and Mabel. When she sees them discussing a book written by an Indian philosopher, she breaks out in racist tirades against the inferior and indecent black man. She admits to Mabel one evening that the abuse between her and Robin is not just verbal. When she was riding with him in the desert, he told her something that made her believe he would kill her. So she leapt at his jugular and clawed until she drew blood. After Robin presumably has sex with Hildegarde, he tells her that he has been reborn and given back his life. Hildegarde conveys the message to Mabel, who tells us that this knowledge destroyed her previous conception of the Jefferses' happiness. Una's compulsion to be everything to Robin—provider, mother, lover, muse—has proven an unhealthy mania.

Mabel's tale bears more than an uncanny relationship to her biography of Frieda and Lawrence. The fact that she despised her father and believed him responsible for her own frigidity helps to explain her trying to find fathers in men like Lawrence and Jeffers as well as her urge to punish them. This pattern was most evident in her relationship with the Jefferses. Her anger was like that of a young child who has discovered that her "perfect" parents are flawed human beings, that the love and security they symbolized can no longer be counted on with assurance.[32] Her identification of them with her own parents is revealed in her description of Una's immediate reaction after she shot herself. Mabel says her only anxiety was for her dog and who would care for it if she died. This scene reads like a haunting refrain from Mabel's own childhood. In *Background* she spoke of the love and affection her parents lavished on their dogs while they were totally indifferent to her. It also recalls a statement of hers in *Lorenzo* when she speaks of the love she gives to her dog as a sign of her inability to love people.

Mabel projected onto Una the traits of her own personality disorder (which is not to say that Una did not exhibit some of them). Thus she gives Una's relationship with her sons all the elements of her own destructive relationship with John Evans. Throughout the 1930s, Mabel wrote Una detailed analyses of John's shortcomings. He had divorced his first wife, Alice, in 1932, and married the novelist Claire Evans in 1933. John's relationship with Mabel, as evidenced in the poetry that he wrote her in the 1920s, was tinged with the erotic. Mabel descried his effeminacy to Una, which she believed was based on an unhealthy Oedipal attachment. But her letters leave the very uncomfortable impression that she encouraged the attachment even while deploring it.

The situation was complicated by the fact that John had chosen Una and Robin as surrogate parents. In fact, he visited Carmel during the time when Mabel and they were friends. Not only did he admire Robin greatly, but he is the only known imitator of his poetry. His first two novels borrowed heavily from Jeffers's themes, the second one including the theme of incest.[33]

All of these factors combined to make the situation that faced Mabel irresistible to her worst impulses. Robin and Una became *her* materials. She would play with them, godlike, in her own laboratory, using the tenets of Jeffers's own aesthetic to guide her. Jeffers had always viewed the work of the poet as analogous to that of the scientist. The poet puts the human atom under intense pressure, he explained, to see what comes of the explosion. "These explosions may cause the disintegration or death of the individuals concerned; but they will also cause the release of human energy, accompanied by flashes of illumination." As he wrote to a friend, "I think one of the most common intentions in tragic stories from the Oedipus down, is to build up a strain for the sake of the explosion of the release,—like winding up a ballista."[34]

Mabel adapted the credo of her final mentor well. She would up the "ballista" of Una's volatile emotions until they burst, while she stood apart, Olympian, unmoved by the passions she unleashed. Thus she obtained a rather perverse psychic release from her own inner torments. Mabel did not let the lesson of her "play" go unheeded. A few months after the Jefferses departed, she lectured Una on the benefits of the affair. It was her possessiveness that had crushed Robin, Mabel wrote her in February 1939. She should have allowed him to enjoy his woman friend for a while if he needed it.

Una was understandably hurt and mystified by Mabel's response to her attempted suicide. The gentleness of her replies make Mabel's attitude even worse by comparison. She wrote in March 1939 that if such an incident had occurred to Mabel in her home she would have felt devastating pity and tenderness that a beloved friend who was so avid for life should try to end her own. Una's capacity for love and forgiveness was rewarded, ironically, in the denouement of these events. Through experiencing such intense pain, and releasing such explosive emotions, Robin and she were able to transcend their selfishness and reestablish the basis of their love.

Una wrote Mabel about the outcome of their "fortunate fall." She and Robin had examined their past life and discovered its excellence. Her sons had paid her the greatest devotion, while their close friends, sensing something amiss, encompassed them with affection. Mabel's Jeffersian "plot" had worked, as Robin made clear in a hand-written note to Una's letter, which assured Mabel that they were at least as happy as Una averred. He was able to write again, and the days weren't long enough.

One other person's reaction to this episode must be acknowledged. It would seem too absurd to be possible, but Frieda Lawrence, whom Mabel kept posted every step of the way, sided with Mabel's view of the affair. After reading Mabel's second portrait of the Jefferses, she wrote that her advice to Una about being "broader" in her attitude toward what happened was "splendid." Unfortunately, Frieda seemed to sigh, Una was just not able to see that the reason for the Jefferses' newfound happiness was the young woman with whom Jeffers had made love.[35]

Love and Death in the American Novel:
Myron Brinig's
All of Their Lives

By now it must be apparent that Mabel Dodge Luhan has been imagined dead in a greater variety of ways than any other woman in American literary history. She has been disposed of by gang rape and suicide, had her heart torn out in an Indian sacrificial ritual, been squeezed to death by a snake and blinded by a vulture. By her own hand, in *Water of Life,* she froze to death on a mountain top. None of these deaths, however, matches her apocalyptic finale in Myron Brinig's *All of Their Lives,* in which she is struck dead by a stroke of heaven-sent lightning as she gallops furiously across the most precipitous mountain peak in New Mexico.

Myron Brinig, a Jewish novelist born in 1896, grew up in Butte, Montana and wrote realistic fiction about the miners, labor organizers, farmers, and businessmen who populated communities not far from the pioneering stage. When he first visited Taos, in the early 1930s, he was living in New York City and was spoken of by critics as one of America's leading young writers. Brinig was one of the several homosexual artists whom Mabel attracted—he might have said trapped—into her coterie. Their relationship began very much as hers and Bynner's did. Mabel wrote of his first visit with her in 1934 with friendship and affection.

Mabel admired Brinig's work and hired him to edit her memoirs for possible serialization in *Cosmopolitan.* Myron read the unedited manuscript, which impressed him as much as it had Lawrence. On October 3, 1934, he wrote her how upset he was that her memoirs had been expurgated because, as a whole, they represented "one of the most damning arraignments of modern white society in literature." A year later, he wrote of his utter amazement at how well known she was. Most people he met felt that she was "a legendary person living on some legendary planet" whom they imagined as "a woman who lies in wait like a lioness waiting to spring on any celebrity who may pass her way. A woman who kidnapped an Indian to be different. A woman who kidnapped Lawrence and proceeded to seduce him.[1]

Over the next year, Brinig's amazement turned to anger, as he joined those who viewed Mabel as a cross between a headhunter and a Venus flytrap. Mabel's opinion of Brinig had changed as well, although they maintained an on-and-off friendship for several years after. In 1934, Mabel was already writing to Una Jeffers about his being one of the "unformed" human beings who symbolized the degeneration of the racial impulse to survive.[2] Some of the reasons for Mabel's disgust are made clear in an unpublished short story that she wrote about him in 1935.

"Derision Is Easy" is an existentialist nightmare about a group of people who sit in a "cavernous library" where they drink themselves into a stupor of living death. Bored with themselves and their lives, they play a game called "Truth," the point of which seems to be to destroy each other verbally by stripping off their social masks. Mabel's description of it, which she says is Brinig's invention, indicates that he was a master of the game she often played. Myron is presented as a Hawthornesque Paul Pry who delights in a voyeuristic penetration of the hidden corners of people's lives. He pares them down to their vulnerable inner selves in order to find material for his art.

It is interesting that Mabel presents herself in this story as a woman whose lifework has far more worth than the perverted inversions of life exemplified in the works of artists like Myron:

> She was rather proud of her achievement along this line, for unlike Myron and other writers, she was always busy with herself. Not in any mere masturbatory sense, for that would not have satisfied her, as it might the literary type, for whom it would have appeared a practical outlet.
>
> No, she was busy making Mabel. Obversely from Myron, she wrote books so she could live deeper and understand herself better. By so doing, she thought, she could amount to something.
>
> "This is the planet of achievement," she repeated. "If I don't make something of myself, who will?" Resolutely she stripped herself of illusion after illusion in her effort to find the Fact? The world became an onion to her industrious observation. . . .[3]

As Brinig came to realize, Mabel was equally adept at "peeling" others in order to get to the core that would help her know and use them, just as she was interested in having herself "peeled" by writers like Myron so they could shape her into a work of art. The famous Hollywood clothes designer Adrian drew a portrait of Mabel a year later that makes a striking counterpart to the one Mabel did of Myron. Adrian's Mabel ensnares the "writhing great and near great" into her home in order to get them to reveal their most intimate secrets, which she then uses as grist for her literary mill:

> First, she sets her bowl of honey before you. This is a frank EGO with
> no shame. You are charmed by a disarming grace and you sip at the
> bowl, and *your* EGO is petted and inflated gently. You find strange
> courage . . . a courage to unbare the secret places of your soul. . . . She
> walks further into your consciousness and places a sweeter bowl before
> you. Then she retreats and gives you time to appreciate this good and
> deep friendship. . . . This friendship built upon a peep-show of the
> emotions . . . like children examining their organs together, and
> assuring themselves that they are normal and alike. For every peep at
> your soul, she gives you one of hers, and in time . . . you *Want* to tell
> the innermost upheavals. Then, after Mabel has gorged on this mental
> nourishment, she withdraws to tabulate, to file and put aside for
> digestion later. . . . And then in a few months she opens her bowels
> and with joyous spasm empties herself of this congested mass of
> impressions and you find it has not been in vain—at least for Mabel. . . .[4]

Brinig's fictional surrogate for Mabel in *All of Their Lives* reveals both her honey and her venom, although Mabel felt there was too much emphasis on the latter. She told Hutchins Hapgood that the novel was written "by a dear friend" who had loved her well but gotten angry at her: "toward the end of his 500 pages he got over it but the book remains *terrible*— so *stupid. Wait* till you see it." Mabel was right about Myron, but unfair in her estimation of the novel, which one critic described as a flawed *Vanity Fair.*[5] Although it has stylistic and structural weaknesses, it is a rich and detailed account of Mabel's life from her adolescence through her "death."

Florence Gresham, the heroine, is a fascinating character, partly because of the accuracy with which Brinig approaches his model. To authenticate his portrait, he rewrites and quotes extensively from "her" memoirs, citing page numbers and paragraphs. In some places, he stays so close to Mabel's style and content that it is difficult to know who is speaking. (The fact that he read her unedited manuscript makes his use of those aspects of her life she did not publish all the more intriguing.) But the portrait is also interesting from the standpoint of the distortions his model underwent in order to serve his view of twentieth-century American woman and her relationship to the development of America.[6]

Florence represents one half of the sexual and ethical dualism that is endemic to male American fiction from the early nineteenth century onward. *All of Their Lives* is the story of the dark lady and the fair lady who "were two halves of a whole woman, yet neither was whole by herself."[7] Florence is the daughter of a prosperous and influential businessman and a proper Victorian mother. She is brunette, bursting with sensual vitality, aggressive, magnetic, and irresistible to men of markedly different tastes and temperaments. Dora Lattimer, her unidentical psychic twin, is the daughter of a nymphomaniac mother. She is a blond, asexual virgin, a "fairy child" who suppresses her sexuality and her emotional life in order to serve the poor and needy. Ethical, refined, and introverted, she knows only the passions of despair and longing, and the pain of a love-hate relationship with Florence.

Lawrence had traced Mabel's life back to colonial times in his manuscript, in order to represent her as a pure-bred strain in America's psychic genealogy. Brinig locates her in Maritan, a town in the Midwest which "was an integral part of the heart and center of the American landscape, its mystery and endless wonder."[8] Lydia Gresham is a stock Victorian mother, forbiddingly severe, a pillar of clichéd piety against whom almost any child worth her salt would want to rebel. Victor Gresham is the ideal pioneer entrepreneur; a hard taskmaster, but honest, good-humored, philanthropic, and, where his only child is concerned, indulgent to a fault. No man in Florence's generation is able to match him. Brinig makes the primary motivation of her life her desire to find a man who can take her father's place.

Brinig conventionalizes Mabel's childhood in other ways in order to lay the groundwork for her role as a modern femme fatale. Florence has none of Mabel's early girlhood lesbian experiences, nor does she hanker after *la vie intérieure*. Her adolescence is spent purely in the pursuit of men. Nevertheless, her motivation in this pursuit is very like Mabel's. After she had almost broken up the marriage of a young doctor, she tells her father that she often finds herself behaving with "calculated meanness" when she means to be good. "But the worst of it is, I get a thrill out of it. I'm terribly impressed with my own power."[9]

Florence comes to maturity at a time when the small-town community is presumably suffering from the deterioration of character caused by the passing of the frontier. On the heels of the all-purpose pioneer woman came the late-nineteenth-century American terror: the woman with money in her pocket, time on her hands, and an itch to rob men of their sexual birthright. Florence is her fleshly incarnation:

> The pioneer women were dead or exhausted; but their daughters were
> very much alive, filled with impudence and audacity. They were taking
> the power away from the men, not in a crude outward way, but subtly

305

and from within. . . . Women formed the country's taste in art, literature and music. . . . They were changing the morals of a nation from a tempestuous, frontier hoodlumism to a censored, policed decency. The first half of the nineteenth century had belonged to the men, but the latter half and the early twentieth century were the sole property of the ladies, at least in America, *And Florence Gresham even now {at 17} was a portent of all these women.* With her tremendous vitality, her courage, her conceit, there was no stopping her, she was on the way. She was neither good nor evil; such qualities did not exist for her.[10] (Italics mine.)

Florence's mother represents the feminization of American culture, the morally pure and upright matriarch whom Gresham marries to provide himself with a solid wall of respectability while he climbs his way up a very ungenteel ladder of success. Florence represents the leisured class of inherited wealth for whom "such qualities do not exist." She is the spoiled darling of the indulged upper classes of the nation.

It is crucial to Florence's character (as it was to Mabel's) that she is a transitional figure, a liberated woman who has inherited the *male* pioneering spirit. A product of Victorianism, she cannot conquer the world in her own right, but she can conquer men and, because of her financial independence and mobility, rule the world through them. Florence has a man's hunger for achievement and experience. And there is nothing more dangerous in the eyes of the men who wrote about Mabel than an indulged woman, uprooted from the traditional roles of wife, mother, or Muse, who takes it into her head to meddle with the affairs of men.

Like his predecessors, Brinig identifies the New Woman with the unleashing of uncontrollable forces, irrationally blaming her for the upheavals created by a male-inspired and male-devised economy and technology. Florence is very much the sister of Sybil Monde in her role as the link between the "old" energy and the "new." The old energy had been used by men to carve a civilization from the wilderness; the new was usurped by machines and implements of warfare that destroyed men. Thus Florence is often identified with sources of energy that are blinding, destructive, or cataclysmic. One of her lovers thinks of her as "one of the rare beings of the earth, willful, selfish, stubborn, brave, malicious, witty, and so filled with self-importance that only an earthquake, a flood, or a stroke of lightning would defeat her—some great natural upheaval beyond man's control."[11] Having control over the fictive Mabel, if not the real one, Brinig makes sure that he fulfills his own prophecy.

Brinig makes his theory of the female dynamo explicit in a central passage in the novel. Florence's father is dying and she has come back to be with him in between husbands. On his deathbed he makes a speech in which he tries to show Florence that woman is the motivator of man's activity. When he graciously informs her that his wife was the reason for all that he had done, Brinig undercuts his self-deluding hypocrisy by revealing to us that he has a mistress and that he obviously married his wife for reasons of social propriety. Yet Gresham's dying speech seems very much in keeping with Brinig's dominant perspective in the novel.

> You know, Florrie, the female generates all the force in the world. She's the dynamo in human relations. It isn't the man. All he can do is set the darn thing to going, turn on the switch. Then, when the dynamo starts revolving and whirring, the man's work is finished. There's nothing for the poor duffer to do. Look at me, I'm finished. Without your mother I'd have never bothered to do all these things, investments, building, mills, railways, God knows what. I'd just have drifted pleasantly along. [12]

Brinig's ambivalence about modern women in general, and about his heroine in particular, is the primary cause of the novel's flaws. The *Saturday Review* critic who compared the novel to *Vanity Fair* recognized one aspect of this when he commented that the book "almost achieves an epic sweep but that he gives everything away and leaves very little to the imagination of the reader.[13] In spite of Florence's likeness to Becky Sharp, the novel too often lacks the richness of Thackeray's social fabric (an achievement for which Brinig had been complimented in previous works). Mabel was right about his anger, which takes the form of outbursts in which he attempts to assassinate the character of his heroine. These authorial intrusions are clearly a result of conflicting feelings about Mabel, which Brinig was trying to work out within the confines of the novel.

Because Brinig's fictional persona takes on several roles—narrator, critic, admirer, judge, and executioner—he often contradicts his portrayal of Florence. She is never so terrible or magnificent a personage as he claims in his analyses of her. In fact, she is, with a few major exceptions, a much more likable, intelligent, and attractive character than Brinig says she is. She is given the best lines of dialogue in the novel, although he tells us that she was inept at conversation and verbally banal. She is certainly much more interesting and alive than the morally superior Dora, "the Mother of all sorrow and the patron saint of the poor," who longs for the vitality of the bitch-goddess Florence: "There it was, the whirring dynamo, the life force, whereas she was merely the passive spectator, the virgin."[14]

Florence is allied with the isolated American hero who searches for a "father" to provide him with an identity and some metaphysical structure to counteract his antinomian spirit. It is ironic, to say the least, that the very quality Brinig praises in the male pioneer—his ultimate commitment to himself and his independence of spirit—is the quality that makes Mabel so dreadful in his eyes: "Throughout her *Autobiography,* Florence is falling in love with this or that man, but she is never so carried away that she can not think of her 'place in the world,' a young woman from the plains born to rule and bring light and understanding to her fellow men and women."[15]

From her earliest years, Florence demonstrates a sense of mission. Brinig tells us she believed she was going to be a great personage, that she aligned herself with a string of female rulers and heroines: Cleopatra, Mary Queen of Scots, Joan of Arc, and Queen Elizabeth. She writes to her friend Valerie from Paris that her generation needs a spokeswoman, implying that it will be she. After having been sexually accosted by a male servant and an Italian painter, she observes to Valerie, "Why these Europeans pick on me as their salvation, I don't know! Maybe I'm the symbol of America, to which every *decent* European wants to go at some time or another!"[16]

After a triumphant stay in Italy, during which she managed to captivate D'Annunzio, Debussy, and Proust, Florence returns to New York City, bent on capturing the dawning revolutionary age. Like Edith Dale she seems psychologically impervious to pain and self-doubt. She meets her match, however, in Dan Swift (John Reed). Ego-driven and as strong-willed as she, he could never be ensnared for long: he was "a man who looked on love as though it were a ham sandwich quickly eaten and digested, so that he might have time to rush to something more important." Florence responds to his hit-and-run lovemaking: "Every time I kiss you I feel that I'm kissing the American Federation of Labor, the Industrial Workers of the World, and the Amalgamated Clothing Workers of America!"[17]

In his rendition of Mabel's love affair with Maurice Sterne, Brinig departs from his source. Florence's interest in Leon Jardelle (Maurice) was based on her desire to control his artistic career. Brinig's entirely imaginary description of Florence's trip to her prospective in-laws for Yom Kippur dinner is the most vividly realized put-down of Florence in the novel. Beside their zest for life and their Jewish family pride in their playwright son and his Einstein of a kid brother, even Florence's magnetism pales: "The brilliance and pure selfishness of this family, their closeness to one another, suffocated her. Florence had never come up against anything like this. They had been through so much on every conceivable plane that even a personality as striking as Florence's meant little to them."[18]

Leon's attempt to turn her into a Jewish princess is given equal weight with Florence's shoddy production of his play as an explanation for the downfall of their marriage. Although the play is a fiasco, Florence triumphs when she goes on stage, and in a voice more "arresting and colorful" than any actress, demands courtesy of the irritated audience. More than this, she is given justification for leaving Jardelle. She tells him that she cannot fit his orthodox notion of a wife as a homebody, to be fed and flowered, that she had expected him to understand that they were both free individuals.

As Mabel suggested, Brinig seems to have gotten over his anger toward her by the end of his novel. In the Jardelle section and in the last segment, where she meets Brinig's surrogate D. H. Lawrence, Florence emerges as a much more sympathetic character. He obviously took many of the cues for his character of Laurence Cooper from Mabel's biography. That Mabel's greatest challenge and failure is made the climax and end of Florence's life may well have been due to his reading of Mabel's *Water of Life*.

Tired and disillusioned with a world at war, Florence travels to New Mexico on her way to Carmel, California. Brinig takes a final jab at her when he says that she now found all white men just "so much trash" and had decided that none of her husbands or lovers had "been fit to tie her shoelaces. They did not know a great woman when they saw one." Florence jumps the train at Lamy, just as Mabel did, and decides to live her life with the earth as her companion. She discovers Ramos (Taos) and after three days purchases land there and begins building her house.[19]

Laurence Cooper is a frail, red-headed American novelist who has come to Ramos for his health. A sensitive and intense man who had been overprotected by a mother he worshipped, he had published two novels that had received critical acclaim. In Ramos he meets Dora, now a visiting nurse who worked with the poor Indians and Spanish in the area. They are both lonely spirits who were "seeking a new restoration of hope and health in a wilderness country." Dora falls in love with him even though she realizes that "the man was obviously for no woman on this earth. He was too brilliant, too ill to fit into any human scheme. . . ."[20]

What Brinig writes of Laurence's first reaction to Florence was true of all the artists Mabel attracted. Highly flattered by her praise and enthusiasm for his work, Laurence succumbs because "one does not meet a woman like Florence every day; and when she is pleasant and seems interested in you and your work, that is unquestionably something to be happy about." At last Laurence has found "an extremely intelligent woman" who recognized his "true value" and confirmed his belief that he was one of the few, great living writers. At their first meeting they talk like intimate lovers.[21]

Although it seems that Florence has all the advantages over Dora, Laurence is emotionally committed to neither woman. He takes advantage of Florence's hospitality when she offers him her home, and he allows her to speak of her love without revealing his own feelings. Too deeply self-involved to fall in love with any woman, he is quite willing to accept "their kindness and attentions." Yet there is a deep bond between him and Florence in their shared pursuit of a structure of belief that would anchor their wandering spirits. In prophesying Florence's ultimate failure, Laurence reveals a fundamental truth about both Mabel Luhan and his own original:

> You're not anything, you know. . . . Yet I think many men must have
> found brightness in your spirit and soul even if you have not found

these things in men. . . . Men have found brightness in your spirit, but no salvation. . . . One could speak to you for days on end, analyze you into doom, and you would still be the woman on horseback, riding away, searching for an impossible consummation with dreams.[22]

Dora sees their kinship. Just before Florence takes her final trip up the mountain, she notes the same wildness in Laurence's eyes that she has seen in Florence's and wonders if Florence has at last found the man for whom she's been seeking.

When they approach the top of the mountain range, where the weather has turned to severe thunder and lightning storms, Brinig begins to translate Florence into a force of nature: "Now Florence Gresham and nature were pulling together in some awful unison, their tryst far away and unknown." They press on to a narrow ridge that is 13,000 feet above sea level with a sheer drop of 200 feet on either side. Their Indian guide tells them it's too dangerous to cross and Laurence accedes. When Florence asks him if he's really not going, "there was a terrible, agonized sorrow in that question." As she plunges forward on her horse, she seems to evoke the wrath of some primitive and vengeful god. Only a supernatural force can neutralize her unleashed fury: "and then a bolt of lightning reached down and stabbed her and the horse out of sight. The earth and the sky seemed to explode in an endless white fire, and in that fire she was consumed."[23]

Florence's death has the cathartic effect of a Greek tragedy in which she plays the role of the scapegoat god. First Dora is released with wild elation at the lifting of an oppressive, lifelong burden. Then the weather clears, and nature is purged of its own violence. When Florence is carried back to Ramos, her dead body shows "a strange nobility and peace." Dora tells Laurence, "I loved her . . . I loved that woman." This was the last, and perhaps the most fitting, tribute paid to the spirit of a woman who had dominated the aesthetic imaginations of artists on two continents for almost thirty years.[24]

Chapter 9

Epilogue

*Up on the Hill down the river . . . earnest scientists labor on the
contraption that may put an end to all these vestigial survivals. It is
sometimes difficult to put this fact out of mind in the Pueblo, in the
miraculous springs, in the many lovely places hidden away in New
Mexico. All one can do now is say to oneself: "We have had it
anyway." That is wonderful after all.*[1]

Mabel returned to New York City in the winter of 1939 with a burst
of renewed enthusiasm for the salon she had hoped to establish the previous
winter. Over the year, her plans had expanded beyond creating an "anchorage" for lonely men and women. With the outbreak of World War
II, Mabel was responding to her sense that the world was in "a time of
transition, changing patterns," which she talked of exploring with some
of the same élan that she had brought to her pre–World War I "at-homes."
As she told a reporter for the *New York World-Telegram,* "I'd like these
evenings to bring results. I'm not interested in politics. I wish we didn't
have to hear such words as Communism and Fascism. World federation
is the thing to think about. It's in the air, as a forward step to world
peace."[2] Just as she had some twenty-seven years before, Mabel opened
her salon in the first week of the new year—January 1940—one block
from where she had established the original, on One Fifth Avenue.

Writing to her old friend Max Eastman on January 5, Mabel invited
him to come to the first evening, which was devoted to the subject of
civil liberties and featured Roger Baldwin, the founder and leader of the
American Civil Liberties Union. Feeling herself very much cut off from
contemporary political and social issues, she appealed to Max to suggest
ideas for future sessions that would be "relevant to the times." As in earlier

days, crowds of people stormed her doors, particularly on the evening
Thornton Wilder attempted to elucidate eight pages of James Joyce's
Finnegan's Wake.[3]

Mabel had hoped to hold the salon through the spring of 1940, but
it doesn't seem to have lasted for more than a few weeks. While she had
hoped to find herself once again at the center of national life, she was too
out of touch with national and world events in 1940 to have much of an
impact. As a *Time* magazine reporter condescendingly implied of "Mabel's
Comeback," the "spry, 60-year-old, brown-eyed grandmother from Taos,
N.M., with long greying bangs, horn-rimmed glasses, [and] a thirst for
new experiences" didn't have much to offer the new generation of young
people she hoped to attract: "Her main interests today are science, psychology, religion. Radicalism, believes Mabel, is 'old hat.'"[4] For most of
the rest of her life, Mabel turned her attention to New Mexico and to
Indian affairs.

In April 1940, Mabel traveled with Tony to Mexico, where he had
been appointed a delegate to the First Inter-American Conference on
Indian Life, sponsored by the United States and twenty Latin American
republics. The conference was one of Collier's last and most important
initiatives as commissioner of Indian affairs, although, like his dream of
the Red Atlantis, its potential was vitiated by the increasingly conservative
political climate in the U.S.[5] For the Luhans, the conference was also
their last major involvement in Indian affairs beyond the local level. When
America entered World War II in 1941, many of the Taos Indians entered
the U.S. Army. After the war was over, a major concern of the tribal
elders, shared by their Anglo neighbors, was how the returning veterans
would be reintegrated into tribal life.

In the year that World War II ended, Mabel completed a novel which
centered on Taos as a place where Indian, Mexican, and Anglo "veterans"
of a war-torn world could find peace and prosperity through communal
enterprise. Here, and in her other postwar writings, she continued to
describe New Mexico as Shangri-la. Unlike Collier, who was urging the
West to turn to the Pueblos as a model for a postwar sociopolitical order
"predictive of a future world" that was neither "totalitarian" or "ravenous-
capitalist,"[6] the key metaphor in Mabel's postwar vision was "refuge."
Taos was now a place to *escape to* for individuals in search of physical and
spiritual regeneration. The shift can first be seen in her unpublished novel,
Let's Get Away Together (1945), her least successful fictional work.

Johnny Carruthers, the novel's protagonist, is a wealthy, naive, and
unhappy boy who suffers from a virulent case of arrested development.
Totally unconnected to people or to his outer environment, he is seeking
some path in life that will arouse his sense of wonder. His first mature
insight comes when his grandfather puts him to work on Wall Street.
Finding this center of American economic life to be rather like the zoo

at feeding time, he decides to quit this life in order to discover something "real." He joins the army at the outbreak of the war and meets some Indians at his boot camp. When they tell him how they live close to the land and in tune with nature, Johnny feels defrauded. In the meantime, he meets the sister of an army pal, with whom he falls in love and whom he marries after the war. They go to the Southwest and live happily ever after, far from war, politicians, and the social system in which he grew up.

Johnny finds what he is looking for in Taos. It stood out "like the mirage of an ancient lamasary at the base of some lofty Himalayan range."[7] When his wife tells him it looks "holy," Johnny remarks that what he is looking for is some place that is "unearthly, quiet, and good." The Indian he befriended at boot camp fortuitously appears on the scene to help out the naive easterners who do not have the slightest idea of how to survive in paradise on their own.

When Johnny and his friends buy a ranch on Lobo Mountain, Jerry (the Indian) shows them how to care for it and themselves. He then goes back to his Indian duties, which he tells Johnny are taking care of the world and of life. He teaches Johnny, as Tony taught Mabel, how to feel love. When Johnny visits Jerry's family, he is moved by their communal way of life and realizes how cut off he has been all his life. He sees that what holds them together is their religion, which does not consist of church-going, but is interwoven in everything they do—living, breathing, and eating.

A Mexican man that Johnny meets suggests that they go into trade by beginning a cooperative. Johnny and his wife begin by selling their wedding gifts. The Indian, the Anglo, and the Mexican form what Johnny calls The "New World Co-op," which Johnny claims to be "the End or maybe the Beginning!" One presumes that within twenty-five years, Johnny found himself a paterfamilias to the flower children who came to New Mexico in the 1960s because of a similar disaffiliation with the social, economic, and political life during the Vietnam War.[8]

Mabel traveled to New York with Tony in March 1945, to meet the novel's potential publishers, Smith & Durrell. Their decision not to publish her novel may well have been due less to its poor literary quality than to the fact that there was not much of an audience for her theme in an America that had regained its capitalist might and was experiencing the first winds of the Cold War. Her book, like herself, seemed an anachronism, as the coverage of her visit by the *New Yorker* made clear. The reporter who interviewed her "polished up a couple of durable aphorisms" for "the ritual visit," which consisted of his quoting her statements about the most foolish part of the novel's plot. Turning to "topical matters," Mabel was quoted on how the war had taken away all the artists, most of the cooks, and left her with the option of taking two Japanese from a nearby relocation camp. Had she done so, her "lawless" fellow citizens informed her, they would be killed. "I sometimes think," Mabel sighed, "there'll never be a servant class again."[9]

The *New Yorker's* portrait of Mabel as a fussy, class-conscious matron, writing silly novels in the outback of America certainly had some truth to it. But it did not take notice of her more serious writings, which were now published only in local newspapers and regional journals. If anything, the dropping of the atomic bomb on Hiroshima and Nagasaki, and the beginning of the nuclear arms race that threatened the apocalypse she had envisioned since the early 1920s, made her message more interesting, and urgent.

Mabel was aware of the extraordinary irony that Los Alamos was the site for the design of the atomic bomb. Some seventy miles to the west of Taos pueblo, it was the home of America's foremost physicists and engineers, a think tank and laboratory that had at its disposal the most sophisticated minds and advanced equipment in the world, all hard at work on the creation of the most destructive weapon in human history. J. Robert Oppenheimer, who owned a cabin in the Jemez Mountains and had been a frequent visitor to northern New Mexico in the 1930s, responded to the landscape with some of the same passion as Mabel and her artist friends. When he convinced the army to choose Los Alamos as the secret site for the Manhattan Project, he saw beyond the immediate goal, envisioning a "Utopian colony for physicists, a society . . . 'where theoretical ideas and experimental finds could affect each other.'" Aside from the hubris they both shared, one could not imagine two utopias, physically so close and spiritually so distant as Oppenheimer's and Mabel Luhan's. Frank Waters noted the incongruity when he wrote in *The Masked Gods,*

> Perhaps in no other comparable area on earth are condensed so many contradictions, or manifested so clearly the opposite polarities of all life. The oldest forms of life discovered in this hemisphere, the newest agent of mass death. The oldest cities in America and the newest. The Sun Temple of Mesa Verde and the nuclear fission laboratories of the Pajarito Plateau. The Indian drum and the atom smasher.[10]

Waters dramatized these contradictions by merging his memories of a picnic he went on with Mabel, Frieda Lawrence, Brett, and some Indian friends in the Rito de los Frijoles (some ten miles from Los Alamos) with his impressions of the day on which the first atomic bomb was tested. Climbing past the ancient cliff dwellings of the Anasazi in the early morning hours, they arrived among the cottonwoods on the high piñon slopes overlooking the Rio Grande Valley. While their steaks broiled on the fire and the Indians fished for trout, Frank, Mabel, Frieda, and Brett talked of times past. Tony tapped softly on his drum. An eagle circled high in the blue sky above them. Suddenly, it shot out of sight as a tremor shook the mountains. In Water's imagined re-creation:

> The peaks seemed jarred out of their sockets. The brown plain below ripples like a blanket. The whole earth and we upon it, the moaning trees, the weeping stream, the crying stones, shudder with a nameless fear, a black foreboding. It is over instantly. An hallucination. Nothing has happened. Yet something has. It is July 16, 1945. The first atomic bomb has been exploded on the desolate White Sands to the south. It is the end . . . of an era. The Four Corners, America, the whole world has been set on the threshold of the Atomic Age.[11]

Mabel's first published postwar article poignantly acknowledged the New Age that had begun. "Holiday From Science?" begins by describing the "magical state of New Mexico" as a retreat from civilization's most recent holocaust. Only the Indians, Mabel tells us, understand how to live reciprocally and nondestructively with nature and each other. They are still taking care of a world the white man ruins, still shining with a "radiance and living splendor we others, we outsiders, yearn toward. . . ."

The returning Indian veterans had informed their elders that while they had seen many lovely countries in their travels, they had seen no happy men and "no true earth love" in the men of the outside world. When one Indian was told that Indians did not "get anywhere" because they did not seem to want anything, he replied that they already had everything that was important—the sun and moon and earth: "We saw everything all smashed up by the white man's ideas. So we decided our way is the best in the whole world for us. We will stay and protect it." While we have learned to conquer certain diseases through science, Mabel notes, we have created occupational debilitations that are the "result of our industrious nerves." The cure for all this resides in New Mexico where there are medicinal springs that attract people from all over the country: "All in all wilderness is paradise enow in this state." But Mabel ends her article in an elegaic tone. The latest snake to enter paradise is one neither she nor anyone else has any power to remove, the "contraption," as she calls the atomic bomb created in Los Alamos. "For the end, perhaps, we will accept the old adjuration, to absent ourselves from felicity—*awhile.*"[12]

Mabel was not yet, however, ready to seek her brave new world in an afterlife. In 1947, she published *Taos and Its Artists,* one of her last two retrospective tributes to the men and women who celebrated the land she loved. The works she reproduced spoke eloquently of the remarkable fertility of imagination that the Taos landscape had inspired over the course of the twentieth century. Mabel gives credit to Phillips and Blumenschein for making Taos "the best known and most significant art center of America," although she had more to do with its cultural reputation and its attractiveness to so many of America's finest painters, who broadened the perspective of local artists and encompassed a variety of modernist schools.

In her introduction, Mabel paid her greatest tribute to the land that called them all:

> This is the provocative landscape that stirs the emotions. Tender and strong, sometimes darkening dramatically, the half-circle of mountains surrounds the somnolent desert and embraces the oasis that is named Taos, a name whose origin remains unknown.
>
> . . . In this high valley there is not a day that does not evoke the emotion of poesy, compounded as the surroundings are of beauty and terror, sun and shadow. . . .
>
> This place has attracted artists for . . . years, a fabulous honeycomb, irresistible and nourishing.[13]

In keeping with her 1940s retrenchment theories, Mabel speaks of Taos as a home for artists who have been assailed by "the dislocated outside world." But she still wanted the outside world to know about it, for she wrote to Sonya Levien and asked her to find a Hollywood contact who might be willing to make a motion picture based on her book.

In spite of her continuing public relations efforts, and her attempts to maintain her pristine image of the Taos Indians and Taos, Mabel was not blind to the changes that were taking place in the wake of the depression and World War II. Writing for *El Crepusculo,* a local newspaper, in 1949, she asked, "Can't we let the Indians find their own way home?" Mabel insisted that the veterans eventually returned to the fold because "they are part of something greater than themselves." But she had to admit to the divisiveness that existed between the conservative tribal elders and some of the young Taos veterans.[14]

Younger members of the tribe wanted to try their hand at business enterprise and argued for bringing plumbing, electricity, gas stoves, and other modern conveniences into the pueblo. Mabel, of course, argued that modernization would mean the end of the life and beauty, as well as the spirituality of the tribe. While the elders were on her side, some of the youth felt differently. One cannot help but sympathize with the anger of one young Taos Indian who took Mabel to task in the newspaper for preaching primitivism while enjoying the advantages of electricity and plumbing in her comfortable hacienda.

In another article she wrote for *El Crepusculo* that year, "Taos—Unrevisited," Mabel bemoaned the unsightly evidences of Taos's transformation into a modern American town. When people visited, she averred, "They come and wangle their way through the cluttered highway outside town,

Mabel Luhan and Thornton Wilder, c. 1935.

Myron Brinig, Los Gallos, c. 1934.

1936

Una Jeffers, Mabel Luhan, Robinson Jeffers.

Hawk Tower and Tor House, residence of Robinson and Una Jeffers.

319

On the beach in front of Tor House; seated on the left of the table are Tony Luhan, Mabel Luhan, and Lincoln Steffens. Also present are Dorothy Thompson, Sinclair Lewis, Ella Young, Molly O'Shea, and her husband, mid-1930s.

Mabel and Tony Luhan, Big House, Los Gallos, 1949.

Painting by Ernest Blumenschein, *Ourselves and Taos Neighbors*. (Courtesy of the Stark Museum, Orange, Texas.) Seated left to right: Bert Phillips, Mrs. Burt Harwood, Helen Blumenschein. Standing left to right: Oscar Berninghaus, Dr. Light, Leon Gaspard, Walter Ufer, Victor Higgins (partially hidden), Mrs. Lucille Couse, D. H. Lawrence, Mrs. Ward Lockwood (partially hidden), Mrs. Blumenschein, two unidentified men, Mabel Luhan, Mary Austin, Tony Luhan, Ernest Blumenschein.

past the dump where the tin cans shine in the sun and the blown papers are caught in the barbed-wire fences . . . past the service stations and the used car collections, the farm-machinery lined up for sale, and on into the plaza." The peaceful and serene haven that Taos was has given way to "business—busyness—a lot of activity, ending in nothing"—the kind of life, that is, that one could find "in almost any state of the union." She wistfully imagines Lawrence, "if he should unfortunately awaken from his long sleep, coming into our neon lighted village any night of the week. How he would turn away and hasten back to his dreams!"[15]

In the late 1940s, Mabel sometimes spoke of leaving Taos for good, but in 1948 she built a new house just outside the boundaries of her estate, where she lived for the rest of her life. This was her eighth and last Taos house. It followed a seventh she had built a few years previous in Embudo, at the junction of the Rio Grande and Embudo rivers, some 2,000 feet below Taos, where she and Tony spent many weekends as a relief from the high altitude of Taos. Her last house, like Los Gallos, was created "in such a way that space flow is continuous. . . . Sunlight streams into all of the rooms and the windows are just the right size." The smaller scale of Mabel's living space reflected the smaller scale of her life and aspirations, as did her hairstyle and mode of dress. Her photographs in the late 1940s and early 1950s reveal a sedate matron, with short, waved gray hair, dressed in conservative skirts and blouses.[16]

Although Mabel had been all but forgotten by the national media, she was still an honored resident of her state and region. As a tribute to her importance to the cultural life of the Southwest, the *New Mexico Quarterly* invited her in 1951 to edit and contribute to an issue devoted to "Taos and Individualism." The journal's editor noted that "Mabel Dodge Luhan has become, through the years, more or less of a 'legend' not only in the Southwest, but in the East and Europe. . . ."[17]

Although Mabel's own essay, "Paso por Aqui!" is primarily retrospective, one hears echoes of her once utopian vision. "Those were the days!" she begins, remembering Lawrence's statement that Taos was one of the "magnetic centres of the earth." Mabel would have us believe that the influence was not dead, for "the great visitors and the magical earth had created together an influence" which set up a chain reaction that still continues. Taos, she says, is still the center of a creative spirit that radiates across the nation. The spirit seems to have its vengeful side as well, since Mabel intimates that some of those, like Lawrence, who left it behind "began to die quite soon."[18]

With justifiable pride and some exaggeration, Mabel recounts the many artists who came, responded, and were marked indelibly by the spirit of place: Willa Cather, who found the materials for her best-loved book there; Leopold Stokowski, who tried to invent a machine that could capture Indian music; Thornton Wilder, whom Mabel says may have learned there "that all people are just people and so wrote of Caesar and his wife as of the people next door"; Robert Edmond Jones who found new forms for his stage designs; and, last of all, Robinson Jeffers, who was "even more starkly stripped of half and half realities down to bedrock."

Mabel seems, however, to be totally unaware of the irony in her statement that these famous men and women were drawn to Taos as "the last outpost of individualism." She had, after all, spent her thirty years there celebrating the communality of the tribal will. Yet here she acknowledges that the greatness of the spirit of place can be attributed to its allowance of the utmost diversity of feeling and thinking. Her own individuality had, of course, never given way to anyone else's and only rarely to the community's will.

For Mabel and those whom she "called" to Taos, life *beside* the pueblo had always been just that. In spite of her adoration of the Indian way of life, in spite of the inspiration the Indians and the landscape provided her and countless others, none of them ever chose what Mabel called the key to the white man's salvation. It was their very individuality that led to the feuds, explosive passions, and cultural fertility for which Taos became famous. For an artist like Lawrence, it was the tension that existed between the white Western ego structure, the highly ritualized tribal will, and the inhuman landscape that induced the works of art which made Taos, and Mabel, "a living symbol."

In the postwar era, Mabel was still very much a living symbol in New Mexico. Claire Morrill, who owned a bookstore in Taos and knew Mabel during the last twenty years of her life, remembered vividly both the contributions Mabel made and the image that she held in her community. In *A Taos Mosaic,* she admitted to Mabel's idiosyncratic and sometimes crudely egotistical behavior, but she focused on a side of Mabel rarely heard in Taos gossip: the hospital she gave, the thousands of dollars worth of books she donated to the Harwood Foundation, the "unwavering personal concern" for townspeople who were sick or in trouble. From the time she came to Taos and opened her store, Morrill and her partner were continually bombarded by visitors who showed an intense interest in Mabel and what she had found in Taos "that others might find." Many men and women wanted to establish contact with her because she seemed to have found what they were looking for.

Morrill says that even in the 1950s public interest did not flag in Mabel's "image as that of a young, wealthy, sophisticated woman who abruptly abandoned a monumentally successful career in Florence and New York as socialite and arts patron, retreated to this primitive village high in the Sangre de Cristo Mountains, married a blanket Indian, and apparently found what she was searching for in sufficient degree to hold her here for the rest of her life." Mabel's unwelcome sign to tourists was necessary for her own self-protection: "Had there been in Mabel Dodge

Luhan any of the teacher, any of the prophet, certainly any of the charlatan, she could have gathered about her in Taos a veritable cult." Morrill questions whether Mabel ever did find the truth she was seeking among the unknown gods of Taos. Morrill's answer to this seems just and adequate. Mabel may not have found the ultimate truth, but "she had, at least, found something truly good, and she knew it. I think one would have to say that she had, in quite a matter-of-fact way, acknowledged the wonder."[19]

The last twenty years of Mabel's life were a time of personal as well as public reckoning and reconciliation. In 1947, she wrote her last "secret" document about the painful side of her life with Tony. "Statue of Liberty" was a brutally honest portrayal of how "we have injured each other—torn each other apart, inhibited each other and removed, one from the other, the legitimate satisfactions of our so different *mores;* and what is left . . . is the necessary consolation of each other's continued presence, for I believe neither of us can remain on this earth without the other." Because they had made one another so unhappy, they had to believe in the "cosmic" purpose of their union: "We cannot bear it unless we are together in our strange, bleak separation from each other."[20]

But the sense of separateness and the impatience and resentment of Tony that surged through Mabel at intervals throughout their marriage did not accurately describe the main tenor of their last years together. Brett remembers that as Mabel aged she would get more and more frantic when Tony was late or absent too long, often tearing about the countryside looking for him or phoning everyone she knew in Santa Fe who might have seen him. Each supported the other through a series of ailments, Mabel adroitly seeing that Tony consented to much-needed goiter and cataract operations; Tony helping Mabel out through her bouts in her last years with hypertension, cataracts that left her nearly blind, and senility which, in the mid-1950s, sometimes left her unaware of his identity. The Luhans for a while both drank excessively. In the early 1950s, Collier returned to Taos and was saddened to hear about both Mabel's and Tony's dependence on alcohol. In 1954, Brett wrote to Mabel's grandchild, Bonnie Evans, assuring her that Mabel and Tony were "on the wagon," and Mabel in the midst of dictating a book.[21]

Bonnie was Mabel's favorite grandchild, the child of John Evans and his second wife, Claire Spencer. Among all those who knew Mabel in the last two decades of her life, hers are the most vivid and insightful memories. Bonnie favored Mabel in her looks as well as in her attitudes and behavior, which were unconventional, like "Ganny Mabel's," as she called her.

Bonnie visited Mabel on and off during the summers from the time she was a young teenager in 1942 and her father was working for the BIA in Albuquerque. She felt an immediate rapport with Tony, whom she remembers combing and wrapping her hair with the wool ties that he used in his own braids. She was impressed by his gentleness and calm, and a patience she was not used to from the adults that surrounded her. "He told me a story about the gods in the mountains and as he spoke to me he pointed to the mountains with his hand with a slow sweeping motion." Like her grandmother, she felt that he was "alive on the inside." Bonnie loved staying with them in Taos and became part of the settled routine of Mabel's and Tony's life in the 1940s. To her child's eye, they seemed a little like royalty. On the long afternoon drives the Luhans always took in the country, they would start at the plaza, where Tony honked his horn outside the grocery, and the manager ran out to take their order for a few pieces of fruit. Whomever they called on seemed expected to come outdoors in response to Tony's horn. Mabel also had a period each day when she held court. "Every day many came, Anglos, Spanish, nuns, Indians, artists."[22]

Mabel entertained a great deal in the 1940s, although there was no one new of great note whom she brought in to her circle. Rowena Myers, wife of Mabel's friend the artist Ralph Myers, remembers parties each fall to which she invited 300 guests, Long John Dunn and other locals as well as the visiting social and literary elite.[23] Bonnie admired the way Mabel socialized on a grand scale and surrounded herself with beauty that was fully pleasing to all the senses:

The ceilings in the Big House were layered with sweet grasses. She burned incense, she had servants go through the whole house twice a day burning cedar branches. . . . She used wonderful scented soaps, powders and perfumes. Years after she died certain rooms in the Big House still smelled like her. It was a light, sweet, clean smell. She had been raised a Victorian and to some extent that atmosphere of lavish propriety still existed around her.

Bonnie also acknowledged the "spoiled, self-indulgent, self-centered prima donna" whose impatience was evidenced in the way she would hold a piece of her skirt in her right hand and whip it back and forth when she stood still. "She kept things stirred up around her constantly. Tony was barely mobile but she was never still." Like a Persian cat, "she loved to recline on soft day beds reading piles of books. Her meanness was similar to that of a cat's. She would tire of someone and drop them with the same speed a cat would a suddenly dead mouse." Boredom was her greatest enemy. *"Well,* that's enough of *that,"* she could say at any time—during a visit or a dinner party—and dismiss her guest or leave the room. If someone were sitting in too comfortable a chair for too long, Mabel would drive them out of it. She had, in some ways, remained "a little girl through her whole life, whose temper was very much of the 'I'm not going to play in your yard' variety. I think she was wholly absorbed in herself; it was as if she were always saying, 'Well, here I am. Let's get something going!'"

But Bonnie found Mabel's self-directed energy liberating as well. She learned from her grandmother's independence and her courage and from the always resilient enthusiasm for living that Mabel shared with Brett and Frieda: "Tony taught me that there are mysteries in the world but she taught me to trust myself and keep on going forward with my eyes wide open." Mabel let nothing stand in her way and "more than that did not believe that anything really did exist that could stand in her way." In spite of her very traditional notions about women, Bonnie recognized, being a woman had never been an obstacle for Mabel. This was partly due, of course, to the fact that she "never had to worry about making a living or having a career."

In "The Statute of Liberty" Mabel had compared emancipated white women to the bronze figure in New York harbor who she believed symbolized their will-to-power to rule over men and the country. Yet throughout her life that had been exactly her own way. Yet Bonnie feels, with some justice, that she made a contribution to the liberation of women during her lifetime: "When it comes down to it, she did just about as she pleased her entire life and the sky did not fall in on her. . . . She is not seen, at this time, as a feminist heroine. When I knew her she was more than equal to anyone I ever saw her in relation to."

In the late 1940s and early 1950s Mabel made peace with her chief rivals: Frieda and Brett. The three Muses never ceased gossiping and quarreling with one another, but they also could not do without one another. All of Frieda's letters to Mabel from the late 1930s until her death in 1951 are filled with concern about Mabel's health, compliments on her vitality, and admissions of her importance. Mabel's letters are equally friendly, if not as effusive. She had a great deal to do with helping to keep Angelo Ravagli from being deported in 1939, when immigration officials learned he was living in America in an illicit relationship. In 1943, Frieda wrote that she and Mabel had at last "come through to a rare understanding." Just before her death, Frieda summed up what she felt their relationship had finally become: "I cared for you when we first met, then there was all that friction—but now I have come through of myself and you to rock bottom and I love you—sincerely and for always—it took a long time, but worth it {sic}."[24] There is a tender irony in the phrase Frieda chose, for it was the one with which Lawrence had entitled his book of love poetry that came out of his first stormy passion for Frieda, *Look, We Have Come Through.*

More than Frieda, Brett had continued to come in for her share of buffeting in the postwar era. But no matter how rough Mabel was—giving her a house and then taking it away, inviting her to luncheons that were Brett's main nourishment in the early 1950s when she was quite poor, and then not inviting her—Brett was always "delightfully impervious" to Mabel's insults, and they remained friends until Mabel's death. Even Witter Bynner, her Santa Fe rival for so many years, conceded reconciliation, under comic circumstances, as might be expected.

Both he and Mabel were invited to Thanksgiving dinner, in 1950, at the home of Millicent Rogers, one of the art patronesses and hostesses of Taos. This Thanksgiving she had managed to capture one of Hollywood's leading actresses—Moira Shearer, who had just completed *Red Shoes* and was on her way out to Hollywood to make *Hans Christian Anderson* with Danny Kaye. Rogers also invited several Indians, and other local notables, besides Bynner and Mabel to dinner. She even imported black butlers from her Virginia "plantation," who served the buffet in white gloves and livery. By the time Bynner arrived, the "Indians were pretty well *smashed* and the scene was something out of Hogarth's 'Rake's Progress.'" Bynner thought that Mabel had refused to come to the party, but Millicent informed him that she was "holding court *alone* in the ante-room." He apparently decided that their antagonism had gone on long enough and went out to greet her. They had a long talk and "made up." He then convinced Mabel to come in and join the party. According to the friend of Bynner's who recounted this story, Mabel had clearly, by the end of the evening, lost her title to "Queen of the Mountain."[25]

But Mabel had not been dethroned, as Bynner acknowledged when he invited her to the May 1955 production of *Cake* in Taos. The royal confrontation was eagerly anticipated by local residents, and all the tickets were sold out. Mabel never showed, later informing Bynner that she wanted him to be the "star" for the evening and didn't wish to steal the limelight, which she no doubt managed to do by making her absence felt. One month later, Bynner wrote his last letter to her, a gently ironic commentary on their past relationship. He thanked her for a cigarette case she had sent him along with a note that he told Spud was "mildly flirtatious." "And this time," he graciously wrote Mabel, "let's continue the flirting." Two years earlier, Thornton Wilder had assured a hesitant Winfield Townley Scott that it was safe to visit his seventy-four-year-old friend. "I'll give you a letter to Mabel if you like," he offered when he heard the poet was considering a trip to New Mexico (where he settled). "Those fires are pretty well banked now."[26]

When Bonnie returned to Taos after a three-year absence, in the summer of 1953, she felt how much her grandmother had aged. Mabel's and Tony's lives had become strictly routined. They rose early, breakfasted, took a drive, ate lunch, napped, had visitors, drinks, dinner, and bed. Bonnie was disturbed by how greatly Mabel had slowed down, although she had obviously still not lost her spunk.

When Mabel went to California to have a cataract operation, she was

supposed to lie still for several days afterwards. The night after the operation, she sat up, not knowing where she was. When the nurse attempted
to push her back down in bed, "Mabel socked her a good one and the
operation had to be re-done." Bonnie remembered one afternoon during
her summer visit in 1953 that a representative of the Kit Carson Park
Foundation came to visit Mabel with "wonderful news." The board of
directors had just voted her "the wonderful honor of being buried in the
Kit Carson Cemetery nice and close to Kit Carson. My grandmother was
so appalled that she didn't say anything for a while—then she got up
and walked across the room and stood in front of the woman's chair, her
hands on her hips. 'I think I want you to leave,' she said glaring at her."
The woman then reached out and grabbed Mabel's leg, exclaiming how
strong it was for her age. Mabel called her lawyer and then told Bonnie
she would not be buried there under any circumstances. "I hate Kit
Carson."

Mabel, however, was no more consistent in her seventies than she had
been in her twenties. Not long after, she agreed to be buried there after
all, perhaps at Tony's request, since he asked Rowena Myers if there were
room in her plot for Mabel to be buried next to Ralph. Mabel wrote to
Carl Van Vechten of the irony of her lying beneath the shadow of a man
who spent part of his life killing Indians, but she did not explain her
decision.[27] By this time Mabel's contradictory nature was complicated by
her increasing senility. She wore big, thick glasses and was confused and
disoriented much of the time. At times, she didn't know Tony. "Who is
that Indian?" she would ask. "Get him out of here." Tony would sit quietly
and hold her hand. "That don't matter," he told Bonnie. "I take care of
her." Most pitiful were the nights that Mabel wandered through her house
in Taos, a little girl, frightened and alone, thinking that she was lost in
her parent's home in Buffalo.

Mabel had several strokes in the late 1950s, and after many stays in
the hospital, John and Claire moved to Taos to be with her. She died on
August 18, 1962, of a coronary thrombosis. Brett wrote to Bonnie, who
had been unable to attend, about the funeral:

> I wonder if anyone has described to you the extraordinary fitness and
> beauty of Mabel's funeral . . . for some obscure reason, Mabel's was not
> grim. Even the service in the Church . . . was so simple and clearcut,
> that there was no female hysteria, nor to me sadness. The amazing
> beauty lay in the Cemetery, the Kit Carson Cemetery, under the large
> Cottonwood trees. The heavy greens, flashing, sunlight, was so peaceful
> and happy. The grave was in a corner, along the fences stood large
> sheaves of gladiolas, scarlet, orange, yellow white, perfectly lovely. Four
> sisters in pure white stood watching. On the polished mahony [*sic*] coffin
> lay a sheaf of shining Gladiolas. . . . It was so perfect, so Mabelish. . . .
> I felt she was where she would want to be, in a shady garden.[28]

Bonnie has noted that Mabel's wealth was not just in her money: "she was truly rich, as a tapestry or a landscape can be. . . . She was able to create a physical and emotional arena in which people found the energy to act." This was true, even in death. Brett was inspired by the beauty of her burial to paint it—a lovely work, redolent of the life-force Mabel had incarnated. Tony died a year later. After Mabel's death, he became "suddenly old and crumpled." He was taken from his house and buried immediately by his family in the Indian graveyard that lies within the walls of the church ruins at Taos pueblo. A year later, John Collier gave them both a warm tribute in his autobiography, *From Every Zenith:* "Now I want to record that in their separate and their joined lives there has been beauty, generosity, naiveté, human goodness, and a luminousness whose dying sundown gleam is around them still."[29]

Notes

All journal articles are given full citations in Notes; primary and secondary texts used as sources are given full citations in Bibliography.

Abbreviations

ASC: Alfred Stieglitz Collection, Beinecke Library, Yale University
CVVC: Carl Van Vechten Collection, Beinecke Library, Yale University
DBC: Dorothy Brett Collection, Beinecke Library, Yale University
DHLC-Texas: D. H. Lawrence Collection, Humanities Research Center, University of Texas, Austin
DHLC-Bancroft: D. H. Lawrence Collection, Bancroft Library, Stanford University
FLC: Frieda Lawrence Collection, Humanities Research Center, University of Texas, Austin
HC: Neith Boyce and Hutchins Hapgood Collection, Beinecke Library, Yale University
HLC: Sonya Levien and Carl Hovey Collection, Huntington Library, San Marino, California
JC: Una and Robinson Jeffers Collection, Bancroft Library, Stanford University
JCC: John Collier Collection, Yale University Library, Yale University

JRC: John Reed Collection, Houghton Library, Harvard University
JTC: Jean Toomer Collection, Fisk University Library, Nashville
MAC: Mary Austin Collection, Huntington Library, San Marino, California
MDLC: Mabel Dodge Luhan Collection, Beinecke Library, Yale University
    Sb: Scrapbooks in Luhan collection, Vols. 1–17
    I.M.: Vols. 5–7; 9–10; 13–14 of "Intimate Memories" are typed copies of
    letters. All other letters cited are originals in Luhan Collection that are filed
    alphabetically by author.
MEC: Max Eastman Collection, Lilly Library, University of Indiana
SJC: Spud Johnson Collection, Humanities Research Center, University of Texas,
    Austin
SC: Leo and Gertrude Stein Collection, Beinecke Library, Yale University
TWC: Thomas Wolfe Collection, Houghton Library, Harvard University
WBC: Witter Bynner Collection, Houghton Library, Harvard University

Introduction

1. Simone de Beauvoir, *The Second Sex*, p. 671.
2. Quoted in untitled newspaper article, n.d., Sb, vol. 17, MDLC.
3. Beauvoir, pp. 669, 671.
4. Martin Green, *The von Richthofen Sisters*, p. 250; Beauvoir, p. 535. See also p. 599: "Many women fully convinced of their superiority are incapable . . . of making it manifest to the world; their ambition will then be to use as intermediary some man whom they can impress with their merits. Such a woman . . . turns to men who possess influence and fame in the hope of identifying herself with them as inspiration, muse, Egeria. Mabel Dodge Luhan offers a striking example in her relations with Lawrence."
5. Virginia Woolf, *A Room of One's Own*, p. 35.
6. Carol Smith-Rosenberg, "The Hysterical Woman: Sex Roles and Role Conflict in 19th-Century America," *Social Research* 39, no. 4 (1972): 656 (652–78).
7. Patricia M. Spacks, *The Female Imagination*, p. 226; June Sochen, *The New Woman*, pp. 34–45.
8. Woolf, pp. 44–45.
9. See Christopher Lasch, "Mabel Dodge Luhan: Sex as Politics," in his *The New Radicalism in America*, pp. 104–40. Lasch offers some important insights into the nature of Mabel's sexual politics.
10. See Karen Horney, *The Neurotic Personality of Our Time*, Chap. 10. Horney attributes the genesis of those aspects of neurosis induced by cultural factors to contradictions within Anglo-American civilization. The "neurotic personality" she discusses bears striking resemblances to Mabel's persona in her four-volume autobiography, *Intimate Memories*. Mabel knew Horney's work. She sent her a copy of her book *Winter in Taos* (1935) and made arrangements to meet Horney in New York City in the winter of 1938.
11. Mabel Dodge Luhan, *"The Plumed Serpent," Laughing Horse* 13 (April 1926): 23–24 (23–29); Spacks, p. 193. See also Susan Gilbert and Sandra Gubar, *The Madwoman in the Attic,* Chap. 1. Gilbert and Gubar discuss the debilitation experienced by women writers who have been subject to the metaphors of "literary

paternity" that are all-pervasive in Western civilization. "In all these aesthetics the poet, like God the Father, is a paternalistic ruler of the fictive world he has created" (p. 5).

12. The unedited manuscripts of Mabel's memoirs are under restriction. See Donald Gallup, "The Mabel Dodge Luhan Papers," *Yale University Library Gazette* 37, no. 3 (1963): 97–105. Gallup, who was curator of the Beinecke's American literature collection at the time, noted that her papers constitute "an invaluable record of the period as seen by a woman of a superior order of intelligence and understanding, gifted with an extraordinary memory and a natural talent for self-expression" (p. 100).

13. Lasch, p. 107; Emily Hahn, *Mabel.*

Chapter 1

1. Luhan, *Background,* pp. 121–23. Hereafter cited as *B.*

2. D. H. Lawrence to Luhan, April 12, 1926. Quoted in Luhan, *Lorenzo in Taos,* p. 296. Mabel referred to herself as a "twentieth century type" in a letter she wrote about her memoirs to Hutchins Hapgood, 5 November (?), HC.

3. *B,* pp. 119–21. According to Jane Fletcher Fiske, author of *Thomas Cooke of Rhode Island,* Mabel had a line to the Mayflower, through the Soules, who married into the Cooke family. I am grateful to Ms. Fiske for correcting my genealogical information on the Cooke family.

4. See H. Katherine Smith, "Ganson Street Named for Congressman," *Buffalo Courier Express* (September 11, 1933), p. 2.

5. See Elwin H. Powell, "The Location of Anomie: A Culture Case Study of Urbanization: Buffalo, New York, 1810–1910," *Design of Discord,* pp. 60–65.

6. Powell, p. 66.

7. "The City of Buffalo," *New England Magazine* (April 1893): 257 (243–57). See also Olga Lindberg, *Buffalo in the Gilded Age,* and Powell, pp. 69–70.

8. See Hazel Martin, "Joseph Ellicott's Yesterday," *Buffalo Courier Express* (September 17, 1975): 25–30.

9. *B,* pp. 3, 5. See Powell, pp. 67–68. Although Mabel's estimate is partly a projection of her own family situation, Powell has noted its validity in his analysis of the increasing sense of alienation and discontent he discovered in the writings of upper-class Buffalonians in the late nineteenth century.

10. See Mary Swan, "Work of Author Depicts City's Early Social Life," *Buffalo Courier Express* (March 16, 1933): 8.

11. *B,* p. 26.

12. *B,* p. 23. Hutchins Hapgood questioned Mabel's description of her father as portrayed in her memoirs when he wrote to Miriam Hapgood Bright, his daughter, that Mabel's feelings about her father were different when he knew her than they appear in her book. "Her choice of details is highly selective." Evidently referring to Mabel's implications in *B* that her mother had lovers, Hapgood also commented on her "intensely problematical inferences about her mother." Hutchins Hapgood to Miriam Hapgood Bright, n.d. Copy of letter provided to me by Miriam Hapgood DeWitt.

13. See Lasch, pp. 109–13. "Beyond the chaos in the Ganson family, beyond the erosion of parental authority, one also senses the erosion of society itself,"

Lasch notes about Mabel's memoirs. See also G. William Domhoff, *The Higher Circles,* p. 36, where he discusses how the factors of nurses, governesses, the spiral of private schools, clubs, and exclusive social sets give the children of the rich a distinct sense of separateness from their middle-class and working-class peers.

14. *B,* pp. 73, 21. There are interesting parallels between *Background* and Edith Wharton's *A Backward Glance,* published one year later; see particularly Chap. 3, where Wharton discusses her childhood.

15. *B,* pp. 21, 42.

16. *B,* p. 189.

17. *B,* p. 29.

18. *B,* p. 265.

19. Smith-Rosenberg, p. 677. See also Horney, pp. 117–18, where she discusses this behavior in adults who have been emotionally deprived as children, and Gilbert and Gubar, p. 251, where they discuss the experience of "orphanhood" in nineteenth-century English women writers. *B,* pp. 200–201.

20. *B,* p. 223.

21. *B,* p. 211.

22. *B,* p. 238.

23. Quotations taken from "Affinities," Book of Poetic Quotations, July 1896, DHLC-Texas.

24. *B,* p. 249.

25. *B,* p. 259.

26. *B,* pp. 259, 265. In her autobiographical novel, *Water of Life* (1938, unpublished typescript, MDLC), Mabel symbolized the Kwannon-like role she herself played for twentieth-century artists in a figurine given to her heroine by one of her husbands.

27. *B,* p. 264.

28. *B,* p. 282.

29. *B,* pp. 145–46.

30. *B,* pp. 289–90.

31. Luhan, *European Experiences,* p. 21. Hereafter cited as *EE.* Ironically, Mabel did eventually become a columnist for Brisbane's paper. See Chap. 4.

32. *EE,* p. 7.

33. *EE,* pp. 16–17.

34. *EE,* p. 26.

35. *EE,* pp. 31, 28.

36. *EE,* p. 29.

37. *EE,* p. 34.

38. *EE,* pp. 36–38.

39. *EE,* pp. 46–48. The ecstasy of Mabel's self-surrender recalls Horney's discussion of modern men's and women's desperate search to escape isolation through submission to transcendental experiences. Whether they submit to mysticism, to another person, or to some generalized fate, Horney tells us, satisfaction comes from the weakening or extinction of the self. Horney, pp. 210–3.

40. *EE,* pp. 50–51.

41. The love affair is not discussed in Mabel's published memoirs. The doubt-

ful paternity of John Evans is mentioned in a letter of Jaime de Angulo to Luhan, n.d., MDLC.

42. *EE*, p. 55.
43. See Hahn, p. 23.

Chapter 2

1. *EE*, p. 59.
2. *EE*, pp. 62, 74.
3. *EE*, p. 77.
4. *EE*, p. 88.
5. *EE*, p. 84.
6. Luhan to Leo Stein, November 30, 1935, SC.
7. *EE*, p. 81.
8. *EE*, pp. 95, 97.
9. *EE*, p. 148.
10. See Walter Pater, *Studies in the History of the Renaissance.*
11. Meryle Secrest, *Being Berenson*, pp. 69–70, 111–12.
12. *EE*, pp. 34–35.
13. *EE*, pp. 203–4.
14. Enrico Barfucci, "Villa Curonia," *Florence and Tuscany* (May–June 1951): 10 (10–11, 18–19).
15. *EE*, pp. 136–37.
16. *EE*, pp. 150, 152.
17. *EE*, pp. 162–63.
18. *EE*, pp. 157–59.
19. *EE*, pp. 158, 147.
20. *EE*, p. 184.
21. Barfucci, p. 10.
22. *EE*, pp. 173, 347.
23. *EE*, p. 356.
24. *EE*, p. 244.
25. *EE*, p. 366.
26. See Mabel Dodge, "The Eye of the Beholder," *The Masses* (October 1917): 10–11.
27. See Muriel Draper, *Music at Midnight*, p. 159. Muriel later became a famous salon hostess in London. Befriended by Henry James and Oscar Wilde, she gained fame for her wit and high spirits.
28. *EE*, p. 197.
29. *EE*, p. 106.
30. *EE*, p. 126.
31. *EE*, p. 205.
32. *EE*, pp. 236–38.
33. Spacks, p. 253; *EE*, pp. 256–58.
34. *EE*, pp. 445, 259, 430.
35. *EE*, p. 445.

Steins

1. *EE,* pp. 324, 327.
2. Alfred Barr, Jr. has said that at this time Leo was "possibly the most discerning connoisseur and collector of twentieth century painting in the world." Barr's statement is quoted in Aline B. Saarinen, "The Steins in Paris,"*American Scholar* (August 1958), quoted in Richard Bridgman, *Gertrude Stein in Pieces,* p. 107. *EE,* pp. 321–22.
3. Gertrude Stein had published *Three Lives* in 1910 through a vanity press because she was unable to place any of her works with a reputable publisher at this time.
4. John Malcolm Brinnin, *The Third Rose,* p. 168; *EE,* p. 325.
5. Dodge to Gertrude Stein [April? 1911], in Donald Gallup, *Flowers of Friendship,* p. 52.
6. Leo Stein, *Journey into the Self,* pp. 195, 319. I have pieced Leo's theory together from fragments of his journal writings and letters.
7. Leo Stein, pp. 311, 315. Elements of Leo's theories can be found throughout his correspondence with Mabel.
8. Bridgman, p. 26.
9. Charles Feidelson, *Symbolism and American Literature,* pp. 17–18. Gertrude had, of course, been influenced by William James, who was her teacher at Radcliffe. He introduced her to his then revolutionary theories of consciousness as a dialectical process between the stream of experience and the human will. From him she first learned to think of the mind not as a passive recipient of sense impressions or a receptacle of fixed ideas but as an active shaper of an always unfinished universe. Brinnin, p. 95.
10. See Quentin Anderson, *The Imperial Self,* pp. ix–x. Gertrude Stein, "Portraits and Repetition," *Writings and Lectures,* p. 27.
11. James Mellow, *Charmed Circle,* p. 27.
12. Stein, "Portraits and Repetition," pp. 98–99.
13. Leo Stein to Mabel Weeks, February 7, 1913, in Stein, *Journey,* p. 53; Arnold Ronnëbeck, "Gertrude Was Always Giggling," *Books Abroad* (Winter 1948), quoted in Bridgman, p. 120.
14. Michael Hoffman, *The Development of Abstractionism in the Writings of Gertrude Stein,* p. 168.
15. Bridgman explains Gertrude's bursting forth into new forms in terms of her alliance with Alice, her response to the innovations of the Parisian avant-garde, and her trip to Spain in 1911. Yet Mabel's sensitive and enthusiastic response to Stein's *Making of Americans* may also have contributed to the renewed self-confidence that gave Stein impetus for her experimentation. In June 1911, after Stein's first visit to the villa, Mabel wrote her, "*Why* are there not more *real* people like you in the world? . . . I am *longing* for your book to get born! It will probably be a moral earthquake to me, as the other was quite a shock." Letter [June? 1911] in Gallup, p. 53. Bridgman and Mellow have both pointed out that Gertrude needed and responded enthusiastically to such praise.
16. Stein's portrait of Mabel is excerpted in *EE,* pp. 328–31.
17. Mellow, p. 207.
18. Dodge to Gertrude Stein, after a visit of October 1912, SC.

19. Gertrude Stein, *Picasso* (1938), quoted in Donald Sutherland, *Gertrude Stein,* p. 85.
20. Dodge to Gertrude Stein [November 1912], Gallup, pp. 65–66.

Jacques-Émile Blanche

1. *EE,* p. 406.
2. *EE,* p. 405. Mabel quoted in Jacques-Émile Blanche, *Portraits of a Lifetime,* p. 271.
3. Blanche, p. 272.
4. Blanche, *Aymeris,* pp. 331–32, 339. The sections from the novel from which I quote were translated by Ellen Denaro. Hereafter cited as *A.*
5. *A,* p. 340.
6. *A,* p. 335.
7. Henry Adams, "The Dynamo and the Virgin," *The Education of Henry Adams,* p. 384.
8. Blanche, *Portraits,* p. 274.
9. *A,* p. 342.
10. Draper, *Music at Midnight,* p. 10.
11. *EE,* pp. 447, 453.
12. *EE,* pp. 452, 451.

Chapter 3

1. Luhan, *Movers and Shakers,* p. 3. Hereafter cited as *MS.*
2. *MS,* pp. 18–21.
3. See Frederick Lewis Allen, *The Big Change,* pp. 55–56. Allen presents the traditional view of Progressivism as a broad-ranging reform movement. More recent studies have focused on the conservative nature of much Progressive reform; e.g., James Weinstein, *The Corporate Ideal in the Liberal State 1900–1918.* See also Gabriel Kolko, *The Triumph of Conservatism,* who views most Progressives as interested in the "rationalization of business and industrial conditions . . . on the assumption that the general welfare of the community could be served by satisfying the concrete needs of business" (pp. 2–3). Other historians have argued that the diversity of programs, interests, and values makes it impossible to speak of a "Progressive Movement" in any coherent sense. See Peter G. Filene, "An Obituary for 'the Progressive Movement,'" *American Quarterly* 22 (1970): 20–34.
4. Van Wyck Brooks, *The Confident Years,* p. 475. See also, Albert Parry, *Garrets and Pretenders,* Chaps. 21 and 22.
5. *MS,* p. 39. John Diggins, *The American Left in the Twentieth Century,* Chap. 4, "The Lyrical Left." See also Allen Churchill, *The Improper Bohemians,* p. 59.
6. Walter Lippmann, *Drift and Mastery,* p. 16; Lasch, pp. xiv–xv. See also Diggins, pp. 23–24. Diggins qualifies Lasch's generalization by pointing out that "some of the leading intellectuals of the Lyrical Left of 1913 neither broke with their parents nor rebelled against their familial heritage. Floyd Dell, Max Eastman, and John Reed had the fondest memories of their parents and family upbringing."

7. *MS*, pp. 173–75. See Diggins, p. 23, where he notes that "on such issues as racism, nationalism, culture, religion, and sex," the Lyrical Left was often in "another world" from the working classes with whom they aligned themselves.

8. Daniel Aaron, *Writers on the Left*, pp. 7–8. See also Parry, pp. 270–72.

9. Nathan Hale, Jr., *Freud and the Americans*, pp. 13, 140–41, 216, and passim. See also John R. Seeley, *The Americanization of the Unconscious*, Chap. 1.

10. Walt Whitman, "Song of the Open Road," *Complete Poetry and Selected Prose of Walt Whitman*, edited by James E. Miller, Jr. (Boston: Houghton Mifflin, 1959), p. 112.

11. Luhan, "Magnetism," unpublished typescript, "Poems," MDLC.

12. See J. Christopher Herod, *Mistress to an Age: The Life of Madame de Staël*.

13. *MS*, p. 72; William Innes Homer, *Alfred Stieglitz and the American Avant-Garde*, p. 175. See also Waldo Frank, ed., *America and Alfred Stieglitz*.

14. *MS*, pp. 36–37.

15. Dodge, "The International Exhibition of Modern Art," *Buffalo Courier Express* (n.d.), Sb vol. 10; Meyer Schapiro, "Rebellion in Art," in Daniel Aaron, *America in Crisis*, pp. 211, 221, 223.

16. *MS*, pp. 36, 26.

17. Dodge to Gertrude Stein, January 24, 1913. Donald Gallup, *Flowers*, pp. 71–72.

18. Dodge to Gertrude Stein, January 27 [1913], SC; Edwin Dodge to Mabel Dodge, n.d., MDLC.

19. Leo Stein, *Journey*, p. 50.

20. *MS*, pp. 75–76.

21. *MS*, pp. 76, 75. Van Vechten believed that Evans's book, *Sonnets from the Patagonian*, 1913 (in which two poems about Mabel are published) was inspired by Mabel and by Gertrude's portrait of her. See "Origins of the 'Sonnets from the Patagonian,'" n.d., among Luhan–Van Vechten correspondence, MDLC.

22. Quoted in *MS*, pp. 24–29. Mellow, p. 209. Mellow discusses how much Mabel did to establish Stein's reputation in America. Gertrude was initially very pleased with Mabel's efforts to publicize her and place her works. She soon began to wonder, however, as Leo said, "which was the more important, the bear or the one leading the bear" (*MS*, p. 38). James Mellow treats the cooling off of their friendship comprehensively, attributing much of it to Gertrude's "bad faith" (pp. 214–15). Mabel believed that the cooling off had to do with Gertrude's erotic interest in her at the time she was writing her portrait at the villa, an interest that Alice Toklas did her best to temper by alienating her from Mabel. See *EE*, p. 333. Mabel continued her correspondence with Gertrude through the 1930s, attempting reconciliations with her on her own and through the intercession of various friends, but to no avail. For Mabel's role in spreading some of the new theories of the European avant-garde on her return to New York, see Linda Henderson, "Mabel Dodge, Gertrude Stein, and Max Weber: A Four-Dimensional Trio," *Arts* 57, no. 1 (1982): 106–11.

23. Quoted in *MS*, pp. 94–95.

24. Hutchins Hapgood, *A Victorian in the Modern World*, p. 348.

25. Quoted in *MS*, p. 60.

26. Mabel Dodge, "The Mirror," in Jonathan Green, *Camera Work*, pp. 287–88. The poem is dated July 1914.

27. *MS,* p. 80.
28. Lincoln Steffens, *The Autobiography of Lincoln Steffens,* p. 655. See also Max Eastman, *Enjoyment of Living,* p. 523, and Margaret Sanger, *Margaret Sanger,* pp. 72–74.
29. *MS,* pp. 83–84.
30. *MS,* pp. 39, 83.
31. Quoted in *MS,* p. 82.
32. *MS,* p. 93.
33. Frederick Hoffman, *The 20s,* pp. 392–93.
34. *MS,* p. 90.
35. Andrew Dasburg to Grace Johnson, June 2, 1914. Copy provided to me by Alfred Dasburg.
36. Robert M. Crunden, *From Self to Society,* pp. 1–4.
37. Steffens, p. 655.
38. *MS,* p. 150. Frederick Hoffman, *Freudianism and the Literary Mind,* pp. 56–57.
39. Steffens, p. 656.
40. Upton Sinclair, *Money Writes!,* p. 59. Letters of O'Brien, Collier, Sinclair, and others from this period can be found in MDLC and in *MS,* pp. 151–64 and passim.
41. See Judith Schwarz, *Radical Feminists of Heterodoxy.*
42. Irving Howe, "To *The Masses*—With Love and Envy," in *Echoes of Revolt,* p. 23. Reed's policy statement is quoted in *Echoes,* p. 29. See also Aaron, *Writers on The Left,* pp. 18–26, for discussion of *The Masses.*
43. *MS,* p. 188.
44. See William D. Haywood, *Bill Haywood's Book,* pp. 261–63, for a description of the pageant. Unfortunately, the committee was left with a deficit, and the first flush of press enthusiasm faded with the news of financial failure. For a recent positive appraisal of the pageant, see Steve Golin, "The Paterson Pageant: Success or Failure?," *Socialist Review* 13, no. 3 (1983): 45–78.
45. Hutchins Hapgood, "A Promoter of Spirit," "Articles About Mabel Dodge Luhan," vol. 2, MDLC. As supportive as Hapgood was of his wife's writing career, he was strongly ambivalent about women's roles relative to men's. See discussion in "Dialogue of Hutchins and Neith Boyce Hapgood," unpublished typescript, in HC, where Neith points out to him that while he claims to participate gladly in the liberation of women, he still wants women to function as the mysterious "other" who inspires men's creativity.
46. *MS,* pp. 146, 166.
47. *MS,* pp. 164–65.
48. June Sochen, *The New Woman,* pp. 75–76.
49. Sochen, pp. 127–30. See also "Dialogue of Hutchins and Neith," which expresses Neith's as well as Hutch's ambivalence about women's roles. Also, William L. O'Neill, *Everyone Was Brave,* Chap. 9. O'Neill provides an interesting analysis of how the "liberation" of female sexuality ultimately served the rebirth of domesticity in the 1920s.
50. *MS,* p. 71.
51. See Lasch, p. 118. See also William L. O'Neill, *Divorce in the Progressive*

Era, p. 164, where, in speaking of the Village radicals, he says, "For others, like Mabel Dodge, sex *was* the new world." *MS*, p. 71.

52. See Green, *The Von Richthofen Sisters*, p. 10. He discusses the *liebensphilosophie* in Germany in 1912, where Frieda Weekley was learning its principles from her lover and Freud's radical disciple, Otto Gross.

53. Edward Carpenter, *Love's Coming of Age*, pp. 40–41.

54. *MS*, p. 205.

55. The definition of nympholepsy is Curtis Cate's in *George Sand: A Biography*, Chap. 27; Robert Rosenstone, *Romantic Revolutionary*, p. 136; Floyd Dell is quoted in Rosenstone, p. 6.

56. Rosenstone, Chap. 6.

57. Rosenstone, p. 96.

58. Walter Lippmann is quoted in Rosenstone, p. 6.

59. Quoted in *MS*, p. 213.

60. *MS*, p. 71.

61. John Reed to Edward Hunt, June 27, 1913 and July 20, ?, JRC.

62. Dodge to Gertrude Stein [1913], SC.

63. Arthur Rubenstein, *My Young Years*, pp. 414–15.

64. *MS*, p. 234.

65. See Granville Hicks, *John Reed*, p. 111. Mabel does not mention this episode in *MS*.

66. Dodge to Neith Boyce Hapgood, n.d., HC.

67. Lasch, p. 108.

68. Dodge to John Collier, n.d., vol. 9, I.M., MDLC.

69. Quoted in Rosenstone, p. 151.

70. Quoted in *MS*, p. 110.

71. *MS*, pp. 114, 151–52.

72. *MS*, p. 251.

73. Andrew Dasburg to Dodge, January 11, ?, vol. 6, I.M., MDLC. Interview with Dasburg, May 1977. See also Van Deren Coke, *Andrew Dasburg*, p. 30.

74. See Alexander Brook, "Andrew Dasburg," *Arts* 6 (1924): 20 (19–26). Brook claims that the "first pictures that brought him to public notice were his interpretations of Mabel Dodge, purely abstract products with little success at organization . . ."; "Post-Futurist Picture, You Look At It Upside-Down, Right-Side Up, Or Sideways," *New York World*, February 8, 1914, Sb vol. 13; *MS*, p. 251.

76. Mary Heaton Vorse to Catherine Huntington, January 23, 1962, as quoted in Robert K. Sarlós, *Jig Cook and the Provincetown Playhouse: Theatre in Ferment* (Amherst: University of Massachusetts Press, 1982), p. 15.

77. *MS*, p. 289.

78. Carl Van Vechten, *Sacred and Profane Memories*, pp. 93, 118–20. In her journal, "August, 1914" (unpublished typescript, HC), Neith describes Mabel's attitude during this period as confident and cheerful.

79. Mabel Dodge, "The Secret of War," *The Masses* (November 1914): 13–16.

80. Elizabeth Glendower Evans to Dodge, February 21, 1915, vol. 10, I.M., MDLC.

81. Mabel Dodge, "We Women Want to Stop War," n.d., in vol. 10, I.M.

82. *MS,* pp. 298, 309.
83. *MS,* p. 301; Rosenstone, p. 210.
84. Rosenstone, p. 213.
85. Quoted in *MS,* pp. 384–85.
86. These postcards, in MDLC, are all that remain of Reed's correspondence, which Mabel says she burned at Maurice Sterne's insistence.
87. Neith Boyce, "Constancy," n.d., unpublished typescript, HC. There are four versions of the play; two are incomplete, and one is set in Italy and treats the theme comically. In the first performance, Neith played Moira, and Jo O'Brien played Rex.
88. Quoted in Richard O'Connor, *The Lost Revolutionary,* p. 213.
89. Andrew Dasburg wrote of this to Mabel Dodge, n.d., vol. 14, I.M., MDLC. He had a brief affair with Louise before she went to Russia; *MS,* p. 422.

Carl Van Vechten

1. *MS,* p. 16.
2. *Carl Van Vechten,* Oral History Research Office, p. 147. See Edward Leuders, *Carl Van Vechten,* p. 26; also Bruce Kellner, *Carl Van Vechten and the Irreverent Decades,* p. 63. Kellner speaks of Mabel's "profound influence" on Van Vechten.
3. Van Vechten's essay on Stein was actually the first piece published on her in the United States. Most of his article was based on the interview he had with Mabel, who later provided him with a letter of introduction to Stein.
4. Van Vechten, "Some 'Literary Ladies' I Have Known," *Yale University Library Gazette* 26, no. 3 (1952): 105 (97–116).
5. *MS,* p. 41.
6. Van Vechten to Dodge, September 14, 1913, vol. 9, I.M., MDLC. Dodge to Van Vechten, n.d., CVVC.
7. Fania Marinoff to Dodge [1913], vol. 9, I.M., MDLC.
8. One of Mabel's clippings from a 1923 New York newspaper shows a cartoon of Edith Dale subtitled, "The new fiction is truth." In a second cartoon, several people are sitting around a table asking who Edith Dale is. One answers "Mabel Dodge." The reporter quotes the Chicago paper that described her as "the most peculiar common denominator that society, literature, art and radical revolutionists ever found in New York and in Europe," n.d., Sb vol. 17, MDLC.
9. Kellner, pp. 143, 131. *Peter Whiffle* was one of the best-selling novels of the 1920s.
10. Quoted in Kellner, p. 106. See Van Vechten, "The Later Work of Herman Melville," *Excavations,* p. 73. Van Vechten wrote that his primary interest in Melville was in his autobiographical rendering of his inner torments. He delighted in the sardonic wit Melville applied to the nineteenth-century bourgeoisie. He said of *Pierre* that it is "a magnificent and witty jumble of all the current philosophies" for which Melville was lynched by the "one hundred percent Americans" of his day (p. 87).
11. Van Vechten, *Peter Whiffle,* p. 119. Hereafter cited as *PW.*
12. *PW,* p. 122.
13. *PW,* pp. 124, 126, 141.
14. *PW,* pp. 178–80. See Edward Leuders, *Carl Van Vechten,* p. 71. Leuders points out that the speech was taken verbatim from a letter she sent Carl. He wrote her that the letter provided him with the resolution of the novel.

15. *PW,* pp. 185–86.
16. *PW,* pp. 244–45.
17. Sterne (?) to Van Vechten, n.d., CVVC. There is substantial evidence to suggest that Mabel was also the primary model for the heroine of Van Vechten's next novel, *The Blind Bow-Boy* (1923). Campaspe Lorillard is another sophisticate who initiates an ingenue into the world of upper-class bohemian life. It is a much more diminished world than Edith Dale's, where the sole business of life is cheapened pleasure (female sexuality has been reduced to the snuggling of Hollywood flappers).

Max Eastman

1. *MS,* p. 346.
2. Milton Cantor, *Max Eastman,* pp. 17–19, 33. See also Eastman, *Enjoyment of Living,* p. 527.
3. Quoted in Cantor, p. 115.
4. Quoted in *MS,* p. 435; also Eastman to Dodge [1914], vol. 9, I.M., MDLC.
5. Cantor, p. 34; Eastman, p. 523.
6. Quoted in Cantor, p. 36.
7. Cantor, p. 39; Joseph Freeman quoted in Aaron, *Writers on the Left,* p. 12.
8. Eastman, *Venture,* p. 6. Hereafter cited as *V.*
9. *V,* pp. 44, 24–25.
10. *V,* pp. 66–68.
11. *V,* pp. 27–28.
12. *V,* p. 62.
13. *V,* pp. 94–96.
14. *V,* p. 268.
15. *V,* p. 277.
16. *V,* pp. 282–83.

Chapter 4

1. *MS,* pp. 344, 303.
2. *MS,* pp. 319–20.
3. *MS,* p. 328.
4. Quoted in *MS,* p. 331.
5. *MS,* p. 336.
6. *MS,* p. 307.
7. "A Perspective of the Elizabeth Duncan School," "Articles About Mabel Dodge Luhan's Family and Friends," MDLC.
8. *MS,* p. 347.
9. *MS,* p. 371.
10. *MS,* p. 347. Arnold Hughes, n.t., *Vanity Fair* (May 1915), in "Articles About Mabel Dodge Luhan," MDLC.
11. *MS,* p. 466.
12. Maurice Sterne, *Shadow and Light,* pp. 112, xxiv. Hereafter cited as *SL.*

In 1933, Sterne was given the first retrospective exhibition of an American artist by the Museum of Modern Art in New York.

13. *SL,* p. 61.
14. *SL,* p. 82.
15. *MS,* p. 365.
16. *MS,* p. 369.
17. *MS,* p. 391.
18. Quoted in "The Monumental Simplicity in the Pictorial Art of Maurice Sterne," *Current Opinion* (December 1915), Sb vol. 15, MDLC.
19. Maurice Sterne to Dodge, February 17, ?; Sterne to Dodge, March 23, 1916, vol. 10, I.M., MDLC.
20. Quoted in *MS,* pp. 411–12.
21. *MS,* p. 482.
22. Hale, p. 225. William James discusses the "Mind-cure movement" in his *Varieties of Religious Experience,* pp. 87–89.
23. Hale, pp. 140, 93.
24. Hale, Chap. 9.
25. John Collier to Dodge, May 13, ?, vol. 6, I.M., MDLC.
26. Fritz Wittels, "Brill—the Pioneer," *Psychoanalytic Review* 35, no. 4 (1948): 397 (394–402).
27. Quoted in *MS,* p. 445.
28. *MS,* pp. 446, 467.
29. Donald Meyer, *The Positive Thinkers,* p. 98.
30. Meyer, p. 64. Sterne to Will Levington Comfort, 1921, vol. 14, I.M., MDLC.
31. Hapgood, *A Victorian,* p. 348.
32. See Charles Bradon, *These Also Believe,* Chap. 4.
33. Letters from the Unity School to Mabel are in vol. 7, I.M., MDLC.
34. Nina Bull to Sterne, n.d., MDLC.
35. Dodge to Sterne, July 18, 1916. Sterne to Dodge, August 10, ?, vol. 10, I.M., MDLC.
36. Quoted in *MS,* pp. 493, 482–83.
37. "A Quarrel," *The Masses* (September 1916): 8.
38. "The Parting," *The Masses* (October 1916): 16–17.
39. R. D. Laing, *The Divided Self,* pp. 42–43, 52–53.
40. Laing, pp. 54–58.
41. See Paula Fass, "A. A. Brill—Pioneer and Prophet," p. 2; see also Hale, p. 394, and A. A. Brill, "The Introduction and Development of Freud's Work in the United States," *American Journal of Sociology* 45 (1939): 318–25.
42. Fass, p. 33.
43. Fass, p. 43. As Fass points out, Brill's interpretations of Freud were often simplified and superficial.
44. Brill, *Basic Principles of Psychoanalysis,* p. 28.
45. Sigmund Freud, "'Civilized' Sexual Morality and Modern Nervousness" (1908), *Sexuality and the Psychology of Love,* p. 32.
46. See Hale, pp. 397–403, for a discussion of the popularization of psychoanalysis between 1900 and 1918; also, Hoffman, *Freudianism,* Chap. 2.
47. Mabel's first article appeared on August 13, 1917, and her last on February

8, 1918. My excerpts are taken from the editorial pages of the *Washington Times* and from her newspaper clippings in Sb vol. 17, MDLC. Most of her articles were headlined "Mabel Dodge Writes on (or About). . . ." See Spacks's discussion of Mary MacLane, in *The Female Imagination,* pp. 173, 177.

48. *SL,* p. 129.

49. *MS,* pp. 534–35.

Chapter 5

1. Luhan, *Edge of Taos Desert,* p. 298. Hereafter cited as *ETD.*

2. Luhan, *Lorenzo in Taos,* p. 3; John Young-Hunter, *Reviewing the Years,* p. 86.

3. *ETD,* p. 6.

4. Brooks, pp. 368–70; Hoffmann, *The 20s,* p. 330.

5. See Kay Aiken Reeve, *Santa Fe and Taos.* See also Arrell Morgan Gibson, *The Santa Fe and Taos Colonies.* Gibson has compiled much useful data about the two colonies, but his book suffers from errors of fact and interpretation. See also Lois Rudnick, "Mabel Dodge Luhan and the Myth of the Southwest," *Southwest Review* 68, no. 3 (1983): 205–21. For an illuminating study of Anglo writers' use of Indian materials, see Michael Castro, *Interpreting the Indian.*

6. D. H. Lawrence, "New Mexico," *Phoenix,* p. 142.

7. Quoted in *SL,* pp. 136, 134.

8. *SL,* p. 134.

9. *ETD,* p. 16.

10. Marta Weigle and Kyle Fiore, *Santa Fe and Taos,* p. 9. Weigle and Fiore survey the writers who settled in New Mexico during the 1920s and 1930s.

11. Andrew Dasburg to Grace Johnson, January 13, 1918, quoted in Coke, *Dasburg,* p. 47. See also Young-Hunter for a description of the journey he made the same year, pp. 83–86.

12. *ETD,* p. 59.

13. *ETD,* p. 32; *SL,* p. 137.

14. *ETD,* p. 77.

15. *ETD,* p. 130.

16. Mabel Sterne to Neith Hapgood, April 21 [1918], HC.

17. See Edward Dozier, *The Pueblo Indians of North America,* pp. 179–200; Ruth Benedict, "The Pueblos of New Mexico," *Patterns of Culture,* pp. 122–23, and pp. 79, 105 for description of personality characteristics; Alfonso Ortiz, ed., *The Tewa World* and *New Perspectives on the Pueblos.* Ortiz's *The Tewa World* is the most recent in-depth study of the Pueblo group that is closest to the Tiwa. There hasn't been a full-length study of the Tiwa since Elsie Clews Parsons, *Taos Pueblo* (1936), which is limited in its usefulness. The best brief accounts of the Taos Indians' social and political structures are Alan Beals and Bernard Siegel, "The Background of Conflict in Taos," *Divisiveness and Social Conflict,* and John Bodine, "Taos Pueblo," *Handbook of North American Indians,* vol. 9, *The Southwest,* pp. 255–67.

18. Thompson and Joseph, *The Hopi Way,* quoted in Dozier, p. 211 is explanatory of the Pueblo way as well; Ortiz, *The Tewa,* p. 98.

19. *ETD*, pp. 62–63.

20. Quoted in Frank Waters, *The Masked Gods*, p. 357. The Pueblos were not, of course, androgynous. The Tiwa maintained a bilateral kinship system in which there was relative social equality between men and women, but women played a subordinate role in the religious life of the community and had no formal role in its political life. Parsons noted that Taos was particularly male-dominated and found evidence there of "personal vanity and group conceit" (p. 117). She also had "heard expressions of self-assertiveness and boastfulness in Taos politics that I feel would never be made in any other pueblo" (p. 5).

21. This ceremony is described in Waters, *The Masked Gods*, p. 357.

22. *ETD*, p. 94.

23. *ETD*, p. 219.

24. *ETD*, p. 177.

25. *ETD*, p. 66–67.

26. Luhan, "An Intimation," 1929, unpublished typescript, pp. 1–2, MDLC.

27. *ETD*, pp. 331–32.

28. Quoted in *SL*, p. 157.

29. Mabel changed the *j* in Luhan to *h* because it was so often mispronounced by her friends. Tony adopted the spelling as well. At Mabel's insistence he gave up his leadership of the peyote cult at Taos pueblo. Mabel's aversion to the drug stemmed from a peyote party she gave one evening at her 23 Fifth Avenue apartment with a few friends, one of whom became totally disoriented and was lost for a while on the streets of New York. Mabel was frightened by the drug's power and by the remoteness she felt in Tony when she thought he was using it. On Tony's position in the pueblo, see Waters, p. 124.

30. Bainbridge Bunting, "Residence of Mabel Dodge Luhan," *New Mexico Architect* (September–October 1961): n.p. Bunting states that Mabel's architectural work is deserving of serious study.

31. Agnesa Lufkin, "A Rare Place: Mabel Dodge Luhan's Taos Estate," *El Palacio* 86, no. 91 (Spring 1980): 29–35. See *ETD*, pp. 292–94 for a description of the development of the estate.

32. *ETD*, p. 66.

33. See Claire Morrill, *A Taos Mosaic*, p. 58. The tribal members who were discovered to be informants were punished.

34. Luhan, "An Intimation," p. 11.

35. Luhan, "An Intimation," pp. 13–15. These quotes from the story are corroborated by Mrs. Dudley's letters to Mabel, April 16, and May 29, 1919 in vol. 6, I.M., MDLC.

36. See Annette Kolodny, *The Land Before Her*, Chap. 4, where she discusses Anglo-American women who gave up their families to live with Indians on eighteenth- and nineteenth-century frontiers.

37. Sterne to Arthur Brisbane, April 20 [1918], vol. 6, I.M., MDLC.

38. Luhan, *Taos and Its Artists*, p. 11.

39. In an interview she gave some years later, Mabel claimed that she was lured to the Southwest by the paintings of Irving Couse, one of the members of the Taos Art Society, noted for his romanticized portraits of Indians. See "Why Bohemia's Queen Married an Indian Chief," *Pittsburgh Post* (n.d.), Sb vol. 17, MDLC.

40. On the Taos Society, see Morrill, p. 98 and Van Deren Coke, *Santa Fe and Taos,* p. 69. Andrew Dasburg to Grace Johnson, January 14, 1918, quoted in Coke, *Dasburg,* p. 47.

41. Coke, *Dasburg,* p. 54.

42. Dasburg to Sterne, 1920, vol. 6, I.M., MDLC. Not all artists grew more conservative under the influence of the landscape. Raymond Jonson and Emil Bisttram moved toward greater abstractionism. See Reeve, pp. 9–10.

43. Quoted in Luhan, *Taos and Its Artists,* p. 21. See Coke, *Taos and Santa Fe,* pp. 51–52, where Coke quotes Hartley's biographer, Elizabeth McCausland, on his post-1920 works.

44. Elida Sims, n.t., *New York Times Book Review* (December 25, 1921), Sb vol. 17, MDLC.

45. Mary Austin, *Earth Horizon,* p. 330. For biographical information on Mary Austin, see T. M. Pearce, *Mary Hunter Austin,* and Augusta Fink, *I—Mary: A Biography of Mary Austin.*

46. See Austin, *The Arrow Maker.*

47. Austin, p. 347. Austin first arrived in Santa Fe in the fall of 1918. She finished work on her novel, *No. 26 Jayne Street,* while staying at Mabel's.

48. She is described by Erna Fergusson in *New Mexico,* p. 371. Austin, pp. 354–55. See Fink, pp. 215–16, 224–25, on how helpful Mabel was to her during two periods of crisis in the early 1920s.

49. See Pearce, pp. 54–55; also Fergusson, pp. 366–75, who speaks of the beneficial as well as the less attractive aspects of this renewed interest in native handicrafts. Fergusson notes that it also brought with it economic exploitation of the Spanish and Indian populations by artists and entrepreneurs, who bought at low prices and then drove prices up. The publicity that the artists and writers helped to foster also brought some of the crasser forms of tourism and commercialized art that they deplored. In the 1920s, the Santa Fe Railroad began pushing ads for Santa Fe and Taos. Austin, Bynner, and Henderson, in fact, wrote publicity pieces for the railroad. During the same period, Harvey tour guides began to take tourists on trips to "quaint" towns and pueblos. For a critical view of the effects of Anglo patronage on Indian art and artists, see J. J. Brody, *Indian Painters and White Patrons.*

50. Austin, *Land of Journey's Ending,* p. 442.

51. See Vine Deloria, Jr., *Custer Died for Your Sins,* p. 54.

52. Collier, *The Indians of the Americas,* p. 20.

53. Kenneth Philp, *John Collier's Crusade for Indian Reform,* pp. 11–12. Philp notes Collier also shared some of the elitism of Progressive social engineers. He had great difficulty establishing primary group communities in immigrant neighborhoods because of the variety of nationalities and had a tendency, when his goals were thwarted, to "abandon democratic goals and impose coercive measures to secure his reforms"—a trait that would create problems for him, especially after he became commissioner of Indian affairs. See also Lawrence C. Kelly, *The Assault on Assimilation,* Chap. 2. *MS,* p. 323.

54. See Kelly on Collier's work in California, pp. 106–10. Collier, p. 25.

55. Collier to Mabel Sterne, May 14, 1921, MDLC.

56. Collier, p. 22.

57. Quoted in Dozier, p. 105.

58. The Brookings Institution Report is discussed in Allen, *The Big Change,* p. 144. For Collier's investigation, see Philp, pp. 44–45.

59. For a full discussion of the doctor case but no clear resolution, see Hahn, pp. 128–31. On Shevky's findings, see Kelly, p. 120. Hahn discusses Mabel's contracting syphilis, p. 173. The most common treatment for syphilis at the time was Salversan 606 (arsenic). If the disease was caught in its early stages and the patient received weekly injections for a period of eighteen months, it was curable.

60. See Philp, pp. 28–54, and Kelly, Chaps. 5–7 for excellent background information on federal Indian policy and on the land issues involved in the Bursum Bill.

61. Collier, "The Red Atlantis," *Survey* (October 1, 1922): 18. Larry Kelly, "John Collier and the 'Discovery of the American Indian,'" paper presented at the Biennial American Studies Association Convention, November 1, 1981, Memphis.

62. See Clarke Chambers, *Seed Time of Reform.* Chambers discusses the continuity and growth of social welfare activities in the 1920s by prewar Progressives but does not mention the campaign for Indian reform.

63. See Dozier, p. 211, who has described the campaign as "unparalleled in the annals of American Indian affairs."

64. See *The Indian Speaks,* MDLC.

65. "An Appeal by the Indians of New Mexico to the People of the United States," *The Indian Speaks.*

66. Sterne to Collier, November 21, 1922?, JCC; Collier to Sterne, November 26, 1922, MDLC.

67. Sterne to Stella Atwood, November 21, 1922, JCC.

68. Sterne to Mary Austin, December 1922?, in T. M. Pearce, *Literary America,* p. 171. Luhan's letters to Austin are in MAC.

69. See Philp, pp. 44–53; Kelly, *Assault,* pp. 253–63.

70. See Kelly, *Assault,* pp. 275 and 411. The prime mover against Mabel was Ralph Twitchell, a lawyer for the BIA who "despised Mabel's 'bohemian' conduct and her influence at Taos."

71. John Evans to Luhan [1923]. Mabel rarely discussed her income, except to note when she was in financial straits.

72. "Why Bohemia's Queen Married an Indian Chief"; "Mabel's Amazing Marriage to Tony," *Denver Post,* August 7, 1932, Sb vol. 11, MDLC.

73. Collier used this phrase to describe Mabel's "call to Taos" in *Indians,* p. 3.

74. Luhan, "The Door of the Spirit," *Laughing Horse* 9 (December 1923): n.p. A story in a similar vein is "Southwest," published in the *Dial* (December 1925): 477–84. It is a slice of life that depicts with gentle humor one aspect of the relationship between Hispanics and Indians in New Mexico. Luhan, "From the Source," *Laughing Horse* 11 (September 1924): n.p.

75. Luhan, "A Bridge Between Cultures," *Theatre Arts Monthly* 9, no. 5 (1925): 297–301.

76. Robert Edmond Jones to Luhan [1923], MDLC.

77. After his return from Europe, Jones was less sanguine about his recovery and thought he had perhaps been plunged into a deeper emotional abyss by

Mabel's insistence he see Jung. Mabel had apparently "crowed" about getting Jones to go and he wrote her to express the hope that the rumors he had heard to that effect weren't true.

78. Jaime de Angulo to Luhan, January 16, 1925, MDLC.

79. Carl Jung, *Memories, Dreams, Reflections,* pp. 247–52.

80. Carl Jung, *Man and His Symbols,* p. 76.

81. See Philp, pp. 54–64.

82. Luhan to H. L. Mencken, May 21, 1925, typed copy, JCC.

83. Edith Lewis, *Willa Cather Living,* pp. 139–43.

84. Willa Cather, *Death Comes for the Archbishop,* p. 132. On Cather's response to Mabel's marriage, see Elizabeth Shepley Sargeant, *Willa Cather,* p. 206.

85. Cather, p. 95. See Judith Fryer, "Cather's Felicitous Space," *Prairie Schooner* (Summer 1981): 185–98, on the Southwest as spatial metaphor in Cather's works. Lewis, p. 143.

86. For Cather's attitude toward Indian affairs, see Sargeant, p. 206. See Willa Cather to Luhan, August 1925, MDLC. Cather, *Death,* p. 275.

87. Luhan, *Lorenzo,* p. 270.

Chapter 6

1. Luhan, *Lorenzo,* p. 270. Hereafter cited as *LT.*

2. See Frieda Lawrence, *The Memoirs and Correspondence,* p. 250. Frieda wrote to Mabel [in 1935?]: "You never cared for anybody and you never will, that is your Tragedy. Do you know what a shock it was to find you wanted to steal Lorenzo's ashes?" See also p. 136. In her fictional fragments "Last Chapter" and "Friends," Frieda says that R. and S. (Mabel and Brett) wanted to take the ashes and have them scattered. On the day of the ceremony Frieda says she received a note from R: "But when you are dead I shall have my way and the ashes will be scattered." Robert Lucas, *Frieda Lawrence,* pp. 269–70, gives the fullest account. There is also an undated letter of Mabel's to Frieda in FLC, in which Mabel says, "I despair of ever convincing you that you have nothing to blame me for beyond the willingness I had to help in the disposal of L's ashes. Every single other thing you have accused me of doing & saying was from others! You can imagine my indignation! Why should I have been made the scapegoat? Never mind—whoever was the origin hurt you & dismayed you & frightened you." See Harry T. Moore, *The Intelligent Heart,* pp. 301, 441; Bynner, *Journey with Genius,* p. 348. Most Lawrence critics are contemptuous of Mabel and do their best to dismiss or downplay her influence on and relationship with Lawrence. See Lasch, *The New Radicalism,* pp. 134–39; Lucas, pp. 186–87; Moore, p. 296.

3. See Knud Merrild, *A Poet and Two Painters,* pp. 239–40. Merrild quotes Lawrence's fantasy of murdering Mabel with a knife.

4. *LT,* p. 66.

5. See Green, *The von Richthofen Sisters,* pp. 54, 85, 249–50; also p. 134, where Green states that to Lawrence Mabel "seemed like a sister."

6. Erich Neumann, *The Great Mother,* pp. 12, 16–17; Luhan, "The Lawrence I Knew," *Carmelite* (March 6, 1930): 3.

7. *LT,* p. 70.

8. See James Cowan, *D. H. Lawrence's American Journey*, pp. 1–3, 11, 126.

9. D. H. Lawrence, "America, Listen to Your Own," *Phoenix*, p. 90. See Graham Hough, *The Dark Sun*, p. 118; also Armin Arnold, *Lawrence and America*, p. 131.

10. Quoted in *LT*, pp. 13, 18, 48.

11. Smith Ely Jelliffe to Sterne, December 3, 1921; February 2, 1923, MDLC.

12. *LT*, p. 36.

13. Mabel's poem was published in *Palms* 2, no. 5 (1923): 136–38. In the 1930s, Mabel expanded on this idea in an essay where she compared postmenopausal women to Prometheus and argued that a woman's life could be "more full and intense than before, creative in new ways unguessed during the child bearing period." Yet even here she qualified the freedom she allows women by insisting their main work is the "comforting and strengthening of men." See Luhan, "Change of Life," 1938, unpublished typescript, MDLC.

14. Lawrence's poem was published posthumously in *Fire and Other Poems*. On p. x there is a note by Frieda in which she says, "I believe Mabel Luhan had sent him a poem of the same title and then he wrote his own 'Change of Life.'" Lawrence wrote his poem sometime in 1927 or 1928, but there are intimations of the attitudes expressed in it throughout his earlier work in the 1920s.

15. *LT*, pp. 37, 61. Luhan to Una Jeffers, 1938, JC.

16. Luhan to Leo Stein, December 27, 1924?. Three months before, Mabel had written to Carl Van Vechten (postmark September 24, 1924) that he had "outworn the primary sexual symbols as the means to expression. . . . You know very well that while we do never get away from *sex* that we *do* get away from its elementary aspects. . . . If you have grown up to the sublimation of love as a glandular demonstration, or a spiritual enlargement of consciousness, why then oh why in verbal forms do you remain so collegiate?" CVVC. Mabel was able to see Frieda's side of things at times, especially the hunger left in her by the abandonment of her children. When Lawrence forbade Frieda to write to her children, Mabel wrote for her.

17. *LT*, p. 37.

18. Joseph Foster, *D. H. Lawrence in Taos*, p. 268.

19. Frieda Lawrence, *Not I But the Wind*, pp. 135, 137.

20. Frieda Lawrence to Sterne, 1922, MDLC; Frieda Lawrence, *Memoirs and Correspondences*, pp. 134–35. Frieda took Mabel very seriously as both a rival and fellow Muse.

21. *LT*, p. 67.

22. Sterne to Leo Stein, fragment, 1924?. Internal evidence suggests the date of the letter is more likely 1922.

23. L. D. Clark, *Dark Night of the Body*, p. 23.

24. ["November of the year 1916"]. The manuscript is included in the Lawrence notebook titled "Cavelleria Rusticana," DHLC-Bancroft. Hereafter cited as *CR*. A description and summary of the manuscript is given in E. W. Tedlock, *The Frieda Lawrence Collection of D. H. Lawrence Manuscripts*, pp. 50–53.

25. *CR*, p. 7.

26. *CR*, p. 2.

27. *CR*, p. 5.

28. *CR*, p. 2.

29. Lawrence, "Certain Americans and an Englishman," *New York Times Magazine* (December 24, 1922): 3, 9. Lawrence to Harriet Monroe, September 23, 1922, in Lawrence, *The Collected Letters of D. H. Lawrence*, vol. 2, p. 718.

30. Lawrence to Bessie Freeman, October 31?, 1922, *Letters*, p. 728.

31. *LT*, p. 87.

32. *LT*, pp. 69–70.

33. Lawrence to Baroness Von Richthofen, December 5, 1922. Quoted in Frieda Lawrence, *Not I But the Wind*, pp. 158–59; quoted in Merrild, p. 45.

34. *LT*, p. 120.

35. See Foster, pp. 35–36; 39–40.

36. See Armin Arnold, ed., *The Symbolic Meaning*, pp. 6, 82, 218. According to Arnold, Lawrence only slightly revised his essays for those he wrote second versions of in England, but "radically revised them in version 3." Arnold attributes many of the flaws in the final version to Lawrence's responses to Mabel. In comparing the versions, I have found Mabel's influence more pervasive and not as negative as Arnold. In spite of Lawrence's maniacal outbursts, the final version gained in rhythmic and critical intensity.

37. Lawrence, *Studies in Classic American Literature*, pp. 93, 95, 33. Hereafter cited as *SCAL*.

38. *SCAL*, pp. 70, 72.

39. *SCAL*, pp. 83, 88.

40. *SCAL*, pp. viii, 6–7.

41. *SCAL*, p. 4; *LT*, p. 98; Frieda Lawrence to Luhan, April 28, 1930, MDLC.

42. *LT*, pp. 118–19; Lawrence to Spud Johnson, October 18, 1923, *Letters*, p. 758.

43. *LT*, pp. 131–32, 135.

44. *LT*, pp. 123–25. "False Start" was published in *The Turquoise Trail*, p. 93.

45. *LT*, pp. 125–26.

46. Luhan to Leo Stein, early? 1924?, SC.

47. *LT*, p. 136; Luhan to Van Vechten, n.d., CVVC.

48. Luhan, "The Ballad of a Bad Girl," *Laughing Horse* 10 (May 1924): n.p.

49. Interview with Dorothy Brett, May 1977.

50. Brett, "Autobiography: My Long and Beautiful Journey," *South Dakota Review* 5, no. 2 (Summer 1967): 37–38 (11–71); also Brett, *Lawrence and Brett: A Friendship*, p. 49.

51. *LT*, pp. 178–79, 267.

52. *LT*, p. 227. Brett, *Lawrence*, p. 109. See also Lasch, p. 134.

53. Lawrence, *Not I But the Wind*, p. 69; *LT*, p. 219.

54. *LT*, pp. 235–36.

55. *LT*, pp. 275–76.

56. *LT*, p. 278; Luhan to Leo Stein, December 27, 1924?, SC.

57. See Arnold, *Lawrence*, p. 139, where he says that Mabel appears as Mrs. Witt. I believe that Lawrence split Mabel's characteristics between mother and daughter, giving Mrs. Witt Mabel's "old" self and Lou, her potential self. Lawrence, *St. Mawr*, pp. 9, 96. Hereafter cited as *SM*.

58. *SM*, pp. 96–97, 95.

59. *LT,* p. 247.

60. David Cavitch, *D. H. Lawrence and the New World,* p. 163.

61. Frieda Lawrence to Luhan, July 3, 1930, MDLC. See Arnold, *Lawrence,* p. 139, who states that the story is "another picture of Mabel finally submitting to the gods"; also Cowan, p. 77, who says the story represents the essentials of the monomyth, the purpose of which is the rebirth of the world through the woman's sacrifice. Mabel may have provided Lawrence with the seed plot for the story when she took him to a cave above Arroyo Seco and described to him a psychic experience she had undergone there once when she was possessed by ghostlike voices from the aboriginal past.

62. *LT,* p. 238; Lawrence, "The Woman Who Rode Away," *Short Stories,* vol. 2, p. 552. Hereafter cited as *WWRA.*

63. *WWRA,* p. 569. See Kate Millett, *Sexual Politics,* p. 292, on the subject of the woman's death. Lawrence wrote one further death-dealing story about Mabel that was published in 1928, "None of That," *Short Stories,* vol. 3, pp. 701–21. It is a brutally sadistic and degrading story of an American woman, Ethel Cane, who is obsessed with overcoming her lust for a seedy toreador. He, in turn, fulfills his fantasy of abusing white women by having her gang raped.

64. Frieda Lawrence to Luhan, 1932, MDLC.

65. Lawrence, *The Plumed Serpent,* p. 150. Hereafter cited as *PS.* In October 1923, Lawrence had written to Mabel, "your marriage with Tony may even yet be the rounding of a great curve; since certainly he doesn't merely draw you back, but himself advances perhaps more than you advance, into the essential onwards." Quoted in *LT,* p. 119.

66. *LT,* pp. 120–21.

67. Mabel returned Lawrence's compliment in a thinly disguised autobiographical novel that she wrote about their relationship, *Water of Life,* 1938, unpublished typescript, MDLC. The novel is the story of a powerful and mysterious woman named Gaza (Mabel), who achieves her strength from a Kore-like relationship with nature. Destructive of men and incapable of giving love, she is redeemed from an impersonal earth goddess into a loving woman. Her redemption comes from her relationship with a brilliant, neurotic artist named Gendrin, who very much resembles Lawrence. Until she meets him, her energies are essentially antisocial. She is humanized only when she realizes the importance of relatedness among humans through her love for him. For a full discussion of Mabel's novel, see Lois P. Rudnick, "D. H. Lawrence's New World Heroine: Mabel Dodge Luhan," *D. H. Lawrence Review* 14, no. 1 (1981): 85–111.

68. Quoted in *LT,* pp. 120–21.

Chapter 7

1. Luhan, *Lorenzo,* pp. 234–35.

2. The private papers referred to are under restriction, although they were seen and quoted from extensively by Marcia Haubold in "Mabel Dodge Luhan." They are "The Statue of Liberty: A Story of Taboos" (1947) and "My Attitude in the Writing of Autobiography" (1933).

3. See Darwin Turner, *In a Minor Chord,* pp. 5–7, on Toomer's childhood.

Toomer's denial of his black heritage, which had so enriched the poetry and stories in *Cane,* and his adoption of Gurdjieff as his mentor, destroyed his career as a writer. He never sold another book after *Cane,* when he turned to writing didactic allegories and philosophical summaries of his ideas on race, art, and literature.

4. On Gurdjieff's teachings, see G. I. Gurdjieff, *Gurdjieff;* J. G. Bennett, *Gurdjieff;* Margaret Anderson, *The Unknowable Gurdjieff.*

5. See Bennett, p. 154, for a description of life at Fontainebleau Institute.

6. Toomer, "The Gurdjieff Experience," *The Wayward and the Seeking,* p. 130.

7. Luhan to Jean Toomer, n.d., JTC.

8. Luhan to Toomer, n.d., JTC.

9. Luhan to Toomer, n.d., JTC.

10. Toomer to Luhan, January 9 [1926], MDLC. See John Griffin, "Jean Toomer: American Writer," p. 350.

11. Toomer to Luhan, 1926, MDLC.

12. Luhan to Toomer, November 26, 1927, JTC; Toomer to Luhan, November 26, 1934, MDLC. There is one intriguing publication that is very likely connected to tensions surrounding Mabel's passion for Jean. In 1926, Langston Hughes published "A House in Taos," a poem which he admitted seemed very strange for him to have written during his "Blues" period. While Hughes claimed never to have heard of Mabel at the time he wrote the poem (for which he won a $150 prize in a poetry contest that year), his biographer suggests that it may well have been inspired by gossip he heard about Toomer and Mabel from Carl Van Vechten. The last verse, in particular, seems to deal with the racial triangle created by Mabel's marriage to Tony and her love for Jean:

> Touch our bodies, wind.
> Our bodies are separate, individual things.
> Touch our bodies, wind,
> But blow quickly
> Through the red, white, yellow skins
> Of our bodies
> To the terrible snarl,
> Not mine
> Not yours,
> Not hers,
> But all one snarl of souls.

Langston Hughes, *Selected Poems of Langston Hughes,* p. 95. When Hughes did meet Mabel in Carmel, in 1932, "she had no kind words for him" because of what she felt was the false image of her home that he created in his poem. See Faith Berry, *Langston Hughes: Before and Beyond Harlem,* pp. 82–83, 239.

13. Eya Fechin, "Fechin's Home in Taos," *Southwestern Art* 7, no. 1 (1978): 5–12. The house has been restored and is open as a historic landmark.

14. Luhan to Van Vechten, January 13 [1920], CVVC.

15. Luhan, "Twelfth Night," n.d., unpublished typescript, p. 3, MDLC.

16. Luhan, "Awa Tsireh," *Arts* 7, no. 6 (1927): 299 (298–300).

17. Alice Corbin Henderson, ed., *The Turquoise Trail,* p. ix.

18. See Philp, pp. 65–68.

19. Philp, pp. 75–77; 90–91.
20. Georgia O'Keeffe to Luhan, 1925, MDLC. See Laurie Lisle, *Portrait of an Artist,* p. 93.
21. See Lisle, p. 109.
22. Luhan, "The Art of Georgia O'Keeffe," n.d., unpublished typescript, pp. 1–3, MDLC.
23. See Lisle, pp. 211–19.
24. Lisle, pp. 220–22. See Calvin Tomkins, "Profile," in Paul Strand, *Paul Strand,* p. 15. Tomkins comments that Strand felt Mabel was "domineering, destructive, and rather silly in her self-appointed role as the doyenne of Taos" and quotes him as saying that he had not "the slightest interest in photographing her." Strand did photograph Mabel, however, and returned to visit in 1930 and 1931.
25. Luhan, "Georgia O'Keeffe in Taos," *Creative Arts* 8, no. 6 (1931): 407 (407–10).
26. Ansel Adams, *Images,* n.p.
27. Weston J. Naef, "Afterword," *Taos Pueblo,* n.p. *Taos Pueblo* was Adams's second published book of photographs. It included one of his portraits of Tony Luhan. Adams obviously felt his power and his dignity, which he emphasized through the photo's angle and lighting.
28. John Marin, *John Marin,* p. 65.
29. John Marin to Alfred Stieglitz, 1928?, in *Selected Writings of John Marin,* p. 127. Marin was living in Cliffside, New Jersey and had painted in Maine, Massachusetts, and New Hampshire; MacKinley Helm, *John Marin,* pp. 64–65.
30. Ella Young, *Flowering Dusk,* p. 259; Marin to Paul Strand, September 30, 1930, in *Selected Writings,* pp. 136–37.
31. Interview with Miriam Hapgood DeWitt, March 1983.
32. O'Keeffe to Luhan, n.d., MDLC.
33. Luhan to Stieglitz, August 7, 1929, ASC.
34. Luhan to Stieglitz, July 20, 1929, ASC.
35. Lisle, p. 223. Luhan to Dorothy Brett, n.d., DBC. The complicated love relationships that swirled about Mabel came full circle when Georgia, in 1932, carried on a passionate correspondence with Jean Toomer. See Lisle, pp. 223, 265–67.
36. Bonnie Evans to Lois Rudnick, April 15, 1982.
37. "Profiles," *New Yorker* (March 4, 1974): 52 (40–57). Dorothy Brett said much the same thing in "Autobiography," p. 16: "All through the years that I was close to Mabel, I never knew her to win against Tony. If Tony wanted to do something or go anywhere, nothing Mabel said or did changed or prevented him from doing it. Quietly, with no talk or argument or fuss, he announced what he wanted to do, and did it."

Witter Bynner

1. James Kraft, "Introduction," *Prose Pieces,* p. xiv; Witter Bynner, "The Story of the Spectric School of Poetry," *Prose Pieces,* pp. 314–18.

2. See entry on "History of Taoism," *Encyclopedia Britannica,* vol. 17, 15th ed., 1974, pp. 1044–49.

3. See Luhan, *Taos and Its Artists,* p. 111.

4. Bynner, "A City of Change," *Prose Pieces,* pp. 45–46; Bynner, "The Persistence of Poetry," p. 380. Bynner argues for the appreciation of Indian poetry on the grounds that it avoids the narrow esoteric appeal of modern American and European verse and thus comes closer to fulfilling the purpose of poetry as a guide to life that speaks to ordinary men and women.

5. Bynner, "Pueblo Dances," *Prose Pieces,* p. 380. This piece was originally published as publicity for the Atchison, Topeka, and Santa Fe Railroad in 1928.

6. Witter Bynner to M. A., July 6, 1922 and July 18, 1922. Copies of these letters were provided to me by James Kraft. I am indebted to Mr. Kraft for biographical information as well. Bynner, "New Mexico Portrait of Mabel Sterne," Sb vol. 11, MDLC. The poem was published in the July 1923 issue of the *Bookman,* pp. 509–10.

7. Luhan to Spud Johnson, n.d., SJC. Mabel claimed not to have known they were under contract to one another. She wrote Spud that she had offered to pay him to work for her and Lawrence only on the condition that his leaving Bynner would not be unethical.

8. Bynner to D. H. Lawrence, 1926, quoted in Bynner, *Journey with Genius,* p. 336. Mabel's poem, "Ballad of a Bad Girl," may well have provided him with his donnée. See Chap. 6.

9. Mabel had always prided herself on her ability to inspire artistic breakthroughs into more revolutionary art forms. In this case it certainly seems that her life and personality encouraged Bynner to anticipate a form of drama that had not yet been invented. James Kraft has informed me that none of Bynner's other plays, published between 1910 and 1917, are remotely like *Cake* in form or content.

10. Bynner, *Cake,* p. 14. Hereafter cited as *C. Cake* was performed in Pasadena (1927), Santa Fe (1929), and Cambridge, Massachusetts (1930). It received excellent reviews.

11. *C,* pp. 32, 50.

12. *C,* pp. 79–80. It is fascinating to contemplate this version of Mabel next to the portraits by Van Vechten and Eastman published during the same decade that celebrate her embodiment of some of the best impulses of the cultural life of the nation during the prewar era.

13. *C,* p. 91.

14. *C,* pp. 153–58.

15. *C,* p. 92.

16. See H. R. Hays, *The Dangerous Sex.* Quoted in Bynner, *Journey,* p. 336.

17. James Kraft to Lois Rudnick, March 2, 1976. In 1935, Bynner reinforced his earlier portrait of Mabel in "gourmande," *guest book,* p. 32:

> Though she is fed and surfeited and fat,
> She does her best to drink a waterfall—
> Not that she wants the water for a minute,
> But she thinks she had better be round it than be in it.

18. Luhan, "An Intimation," p. 18.

19. Lawrence to Luhan, May 28, 1927, *Letters,* pp. 981–82.
20. Quoted in Luhan, *Lorenzo,* pp. 351–52.
21. Frieda Lawrence to Luhan, July 3, 1930, MDLC.

Chapter 8

1. Luhan to Hapgood, November 5, ?, HC, on the writing of *Intimate Memories.*
2. Quoted in the *Rocky Mountain News* (April 14, 1935), Sb vol. 11, MDLC.
3. "Back From Utopia," *Saturday Evening Post* (July 6, 1929); *Washington, D.C. News* (August 18, 1934); *Town and Country,* n.d.; Henry McBride, "Exhibition of New Mexico Paintings Holds Interest," *North Carolina Observer,* May 5, 1935; James Gray, *St. Paul Minnesota Dispatch,* August 16, 1934. Newspaper clippings in Sb vol. 11, MDLC.
4. Spud Johnson, "People Talked About," *Carmel Pine Cone* (n.d.), Sb vol. 11, MDLC.
5. Luhan, "Taos—A Eulogy," *Creative Arts* 9, no. 4 (1931): 294 (289–95).
6. For clippings of Mabel's 1930s articles, see Sb vols. 11 and 12.
7. Brett, "Autobiography," p. 41; see Hahn, p. 188. Alice Rossin, John Evans's first wife, says that Mabel began writing her memoirs while the Lawrences were still in Taos and that she read parts to them. But Mabel's and Lawrence's letters indicate that she did not start writing until after the Lawrences left.
8. Brill, *Basic Principles,* p. 8; also Luhan to Leo Stein, October 23, 1925?, where she explains that her memoirs will record "no more or less content than the moment held. It is what the analysts call 'abreaction' in writing."
9. *LT,* p. 296; Lawrence to Luhan, December 5, 1927, DHLC-Texas.
10. Luhan to Leo Stein, November 30, 1935?, SC.
11. Luhan, "My Attitude in the Writing of Autobiography," quoted in Haubold, p. 110.
12. See Jane Nelson, *Mabel Dodge Luhan,* pp. 25–26, where she discusses the influence of confessional and epic forms on the writing of *Intimate Memories.* See also William C. Spengemann and L. R. Lundquist, "Autobiography and the American Myth," *American Quarterly* 17, no. 3 (1965): 501–19.
13. Frederick Lewis Allen, *Since Yesterday,* pp. 202–8. See Mabel Major and T. M. Pearce, *Southwest Heritage,* pp. 121–35. See also Weigle, p. 52, who says that the most successful FWP project in New Mexico was the gathering and translation of Hispanic folklore.
14. See Diggins, pp. 111, 118–20, where he discusses the important differences between the pre–World War I and depression generations of radicals. The Greenwich Village group had, on the whole, been small-town heirs of a native radicalism that encompassed the individualism of Thoreau and the cosmic collectivism of Whitman, as well as Marxist ideas. The 1930s radicals were primarily of working-class and European origin. They tended to turn away from American intellectual traditions for their ideology and look to the Soviet Union for "a new social ethic."
15. Herbert Gorman, "A Young Girl in the Stuffy Nineties: Mabel Dodge Luhan's Memoirs Give an Indelible Picture of the Genteel Era," *New York Times* (March 23, 1933). The *New York Times* listed *Background* as a best seller in April

1933. All reviews and letters from friends are in Sb vol. 1, MDLC. *Background* sold 2,699 copies according to the records of Harcourt, Brace, Jovanovich.

16. Louis Kronenberger, *New York Times Book Review* (October 20, 1935). The *San Francisco Chronicle* listed it as a best seller during the week of October 6. All reviews and letters are in Sb vol. 2, MDLC. *European Experiences* sold 3,022 copies; Luhan to Leo Stein, November 30, 1935?, MDLC.

17. Malcolm Cowley, "Fable for Russian Children," *New Republic* (November 25, 1936): 122; Granville Hicks, "Portrait of a Patroness," *New Masses* (November 24, 1936); Floyd Dell, "The Scent and Flavor of a Lost Young World," *New York Herald Tribune* (November 22, 1936). All reviews and letters in Sb vol. 8, MDLC. *Movers and Shakers* sold 2,968 copies.

18. Luhan to Neith Hapgood, n.d., HC.

19. *ETD*, p. 301.

20. Clifton Fadiman, *New Yorker*, n.d.; "Mabel Dodge Luhan is Saint in Latest Memoir," *Dallas Morning News* (September 6, 1937). All reviews and letters in Sb vol. 9, MDLC. *Edge of Taos Desert* sold 3,660 copies.

21. Ansel Adams to Luhan, December 6, 1937; Adams to Rudnick, February 8, 1984, noted: "Mabel . . . did represent something very important in the arts and letters of her time. She did have peculiar and unexpected capability [sic] to insult, confuse and reject people—even old friends. But such was secondary to her creative contributions."

22. Cornelia Otis Skinner, "A Brief Digest of the Intimate Memoirs of Mabel Fudge Hulan," *Dithers and Jitters*, pp. 3–7.

23. Michael Gold, "Mabel Luhan's Slums," *New Masses* (Sept. 1, 1936): 11–13.

24. See Lawrence C. Kelly, "Choosing the New Deal Indian Commissioner: Ickes vs. Collier," *New Mexico Historical Review* 49 (1974): 269–88. Kelly notes that Collier was instrumental in helping to get Ickes appointed, in part because he was opposed to having Ickes as Indian commissioner. Mabel fully supported Collier's appointment and sent Tony to Washington to testify in his behalf.

25. See Philp, pp. 118–20, 140.

26. Philp, pp. 120–26.

27. Quoted in Luhan, *Winter in Taos*, pp. 219–21.

28. See Philp, Chap. 8; also Deloria for description and positive assessment of the IRA, pp. 44, 146. According to Philp, Collier became an early target for anti–New Deal sentiment both because of his own radical visions and his support of Roosevelt's court-packing. Most of the IRA and Collier's reforms were undone in the post–World War II era.

29. Luhan to Collier, December 15, 1934; Luhan to Harold Ickes, December 1934, JCC.

30. See Philp, pp. 193–95.

31. See the *New York Times* (May 12, 1936) in JCC. Luhan to Collier, March 10, 1937; Collier quoted in Philp, p. 196.

32. See Omer Stewart, "Taos Factionalism," paper presented at the Ethnohistory Society Meeting, Colorado Springs, 1981.

33. See Philp, pp. 196–97, 211.

34. Malvina Hoffman, *Heads and Tails*, p. 385. Hoffman gives a lovely description of the dance at Mabel's house and of the spring dedication at Taos pueblo, pp. 390–96.

35. Sonya Levien to Luhan, n.d. Mabel's letters to Sonya Levien and Carl

Hovey in LHC. *The Taoseño* (November 14, 1940), Sb vol. 12, MDLC.

36. Thomas Wolfe, *Of Time and the River*, p. 157.

37. Luhan to Thomas Wolfe, May 16, ?, TWC.

38. Wolfe to Luhan, July 8, 1935, TWC.

39. See Andrew Turnbull, *Thomas Wolfe*, pp. 221–23.

40. See Paul Turok, "A Life of Conviction, Controversy, and Courage," *Ovation* (April 1982): 12–14; also David Ewen, *Dictators of the Baton*, Chap. 1.

41. Leopold Stokowski to Luhan, November 23, 1931; [1932]; January 3, 1932; August 1932, MDLC.

42. Tony Luhan to Stokowski, n.d., MDLC.

43. Brett, "Autobiography," p. 54. Brett painted a striking portrait of Stokowski.

44. Luhan, "Bach in the Baggage Car," May 1936, unpublished typescript, MDLC. Media coverage of the Stokowski-Garbo affair and trips to Taos can be found in Sb vol. 12, MDLC.

45. Thornton Wilder to Luhan, August 29, 1933; May 19, 1934, MDLC.

46. Thornton Wilder to Luhan, April 8, 1936; October 7, 1934; December 6, 1934; February 25, 1935. The portraits Wilder refers to very likely included Bynner's poem "gourmande."

47. See Waters, *Masked Gods*, p. 192.

48. Luhan, *Winter in Taos*, pp. 26–28. Hereafter cited as *WT. Winter in Taos* sold 2,614 copies and was reviewed favorably by the *New York Times, San Francisco Chronicle, Washington Post*, and *Commonweal*. Reviews and letters are in Sb vol. 3, MDLC.

49. *WT*, p. 70.

50. *WT*, pp. 108–9.

51. *WT*, p. 125.

52. *WT*, p. 129.

53. *WT*, pp. 154–55.

54. *WT*, pp. 226–28.

55. *WT*, p. 237.

56. *WT*, p. 110.

57. Wilder to Luhan, January 17, 1937, MDLC.

58. See Weigle and Fiore, pp. 38–41.

59. See Weigle and Fiore, pp. 44–45; Cecil Robinson, *Mexico and the Hispanic Southwest in American Literature*, Chap. 11; Charles Eldredge, *Ward Lockwood*, p. 37.

60. See Gibson, pp. 60–66; 75–79; 99–100; 161–73.

61. Eldredge, p. 37.

62. A. A. Brill to Luhan, September 2, 1937, MDLC.

63. Quoted in Coke, *Dasburg*, pp. 97–98.

64. Quoted in untitled newspaper articles, n.d., Sb vol. 15. "Mabel Dodge is Back Looking for City Studio," *New York Post* (February 24, 1938), Sb vol. 16; *Buffalo Courier-Express* (April 3, 1938), Sb vol. 15, MDLC. Mabel did two interviews for *Cosmopolitan*, one with William Bendix, head of the Bendix Corporation, and one with the architect, William Lescaze.

65. Luhan, *New York Times* (May 22, 1938), Sb vol. 15, MDLC. At the same time, however, Mabel's increasing skepticism about the possibilities of political and social change can be seen in a huge tome that she completed in 1938, titled "On Human Relations." Intended as a lay guide to psychoanalysis, the work

combined Freudian psychology with New Thought sentimentalism, much like the Hearst articles she wrote in 1917. Here, however, she specifically speaks out against the attempt to solve human ills by such means as the redistribution of wealth and advocates individual therapy as the sole means. Mabel hoped to get her manuscript serialized in *Cosmopolitan*. Unpublished typescript, MDLC.

66. Spud Johnson, "Mabel Luhan Gets 'Socialized' But Won't Stop Writing Books," *New Mexico Sentinel* (May 22, 1938), Sb vol. 15, MDLC. Elizabeth Shepley Sargeant, "Sphynx of the Taos Desert," *Saturday Review* 19 (1938): 14–15.

Jeffers

1. *LT,* pp. 280–81.
2. *LT,* p. 35. Luhan to Una Jeffers, n.d., JC.
3. Una Jeffers, "Strange Idyl," *Carmelite* (March 3, 1932): 9.
4. Spud Johnson, "She Did It!," *Carmelite* (May 29, 1930): 11.
5. Luhan, *"Plumed Serpent,"* p. 24.
6. Lawrence, *Fire*, p. x.
7. Quoted in Radcliffe Squires, *The Loyalties of Robinson Jeffers*, p. 16.
8. Squires, p. 63; Robert Brophy, *Robinson Jeffers*, pp. 277–78.
9. Luhan, *Una and Robin*, pp. 10–11. Hereafter cited as *UR*.
10. Quoted in *LT,* p. 3.
11. Robinson Jeffers, "The Tower Beyond Tragedy," *Roan Stallion, Tamar, and Other Poems*, p. 82.
12. *UR*, p. 29.
13. *UR*, pp. 31, 34.
14. See *UR*, p. 3; Una is quoted in Melba Barnett, *The Stone Mason of Tor House*, pp. 138, 171. See also Lawrence Clark Powell, *Robinson Jeffers*, p. 28. Powell credits Una with shoring up Jeffers's life and keeping him from going the way of Poe and Verlaine: "She is to him now simultaneously friend, mother, and guardian of his gift." But he also notes her less pleasant attributes, which Mabel would bring out in full force in her second portrait of the Jefferses: that she was "jealous, violent, ambitious, snobbish, and reactionary." See also Edith Greenan, *Of Una Jeffers*. Greenan, who was married to Una's first husband, wrote this essay in great admiration, but also pointed out that Una was capable of "rages and mad bursts of temper." Robin called her his "little savage" (pp. 7–8).
15. Una's reaction was colored by her unqualified admiration for Mabel. More significant was the response of A. R. Orage, editor of the *New English Weekly*, to her work, since he had often been critical of her. On July 30, 1933, he wrote that while the English were saying they hated *Lorenzo,* "privately they feel it is the only book on Lawrence written with his own fearlessness. I got this from the Carswell stable!" Orage to Luhan, Sb vol. 5, MDLC.
16. Una Jeffers to Luhan, n.d., Sb vol. 5, MDLC.
17. *LT,* pp. 14–15, 170.
18. *LT,* p. 65.
19. Luhan to Una Jeffers, July 19 (1930?); May 13 (1931?), JC. There are

over 300 letters to the Jefferses from Mabel in this collection. Una Jeffers to Luhan, February 4, 1932, Sb vol. 5, MDLC.

20. Luhan to Una Jeffers (1930?), JC.

21. Luhan to Una Jeffers, January 18, ?, JC.

22. Luhan to Una Jeffers, June 3, 1931, JC.

23. See Lucas, *Frieda Lawrence,* for description, pp. 218, 230, 238, 254–56.

24. Luhan to Una Jeffers, July 2, 1931; July 15, 1931, JC.

25. Luhan to Una Jeffers, July 15, 1931, JC.

26. Robinson Jeffers to Louis Untermeyer, June 17, 1935, in Robinson Jeffers, *Selected Letters,* pp. 227, 230. Jeffers's biographers regret the visits and say they were taxing. While Jeffers always preferred Carmel and did not find the hot, dry summers of Taos conducive to work, his letters indicate that he enjoyed his visits.

27. Squires, p. 113; Jeffers, *Selected Poetry,* p. 363.

28. Young, *Flowering Dusk,* pp. 300–301. See also Brett, "Autobiography," pp. 33–34 for a description of trips to Carmel to see the Jefferses.

29. See Frederick Carpenter, *Robinson Jeffers,* pp. 57–58. Carpenter points out that Jeffers's inspiration was depleted in the decade between 1935 and 1945 and that the characters in his poems during this time seem increasingly like case histories in abnormal psychology.

30. Jeffers, *Selected Letters,* p. 258.

31. The story I relay comes primarily from Mabel's version of "Una and Robin," part 2, MDLC, which is under restriction and may not be quoted from. See also Barnett, p. 171, who treats the situation rather flippantly, laying it to Una's self-dramatization: "Knowing Una, I am quite sure that she created a scene violent enough for the guests to be aware of her emotions. This was followed by Una's shooting herself. Her story was that she had removed a gun from a shelf in the bathroom to clean it; that someone entered the house, and it startled her and the gun accidently exploded; and that she had no intention of killing herself." Robert Brophy lays the blame squarely on Mabel (Brophy to Rudnick, June 26, 1974): "Mabel . . . evidently set up a seduction scene between Jeffers and the young wife of a Yale University Press editor. She brought Una in at the proper time and Una shot herself. . . . This story comes in four or five versions."

32. See letter of Luhan to Una Jeffers, October 22 (1935): "I adore your perfect mechanism, all in running order, up to the mark, & adequate. You make me feel I may be mistaken in thinking our race is running down like an old clock whose works are worn out," JC.

33. John Evans dedicated his second novel, a badly written book about incest and homosexuality, to Jeffers. According to Squires, Evans was the only writer who ever attempted to imitate Jeffers.

34. Carpenter, p. 137; Robinson Jeffers to Carpenter, March 31, 1932, *Selected Letters,* p. 196.

35. Frieda Lawrence to Luhan, n.d., MDLC.

Brinig

1. Interview with Miriam DeWitt, March 1983. The story was told to Mrs. DeWitt by Sally Bolk Davis.

1. Myron Brinig to Luhan, October 3, 1934?; November 4, 1935, MDLC.
2. Luhan to Una Jeffers, January 18, ? (in 1935 folder). In another letter to Una (1936?), Mabel described Myron's obviously strong and contradictory feelings about her. Having gotten drunk at a party Mabel gave, Myron attacked her for hating her race and picked on Tony. Finally, he leaned over and muttered: "Oh, I've said some dreadful things. . . . Mabel is wonderful. Mabel is magical in a way. If I could love women I'd love Mabel," JC.
3. Luhan, "Derision Is Easy," c. 1935, unpublished typescript, pp. 4–5, MDLC.
4. Adrian, "A Bird's Eye View of Mabel," September 1936; typed copy that Mabel sent to Una Jeffers is in JC. Mabel published an article, "Gowns by Adrian," in *Town and Country* 91, no. 4 (1936): 70–71, 114–20. On p. 71, she said of their first meeting: "for we took a good look at each other and decided we would not have to weed each other out. We are both practiced weeders! If someone turns out to be not quite so authentic as he or she gave promise of being, that one is done up in a neat bundle and returned, marked 'empty.'"
5. Luhan to Hapgood, August 5, ?, HC. The *New Mexico Quarterly* 5 (1941): 382, noted that Mabel was the central character in the novel; Richard Cordell, "Becky Sharp, 1941," *Saturday Review* 24, no. 10 (1941): 10.
6. A reviewer for the *New York Times* called it "a fictionalized version of Jung's psychological types.'" *New York Times Book Review* (July 6, 1941): 4.
7. Myron Brinig, *All of Their Lives*, p. 384. Hereafter cited as *ATL*. See Leslie A. Fiedler, *Love and Death in the American Novel*, for an analysis of this classic theme.
8. *ATL*, p. 6.
9. *ATL*, p. 158.
10. *ATL*, p. 79.
11. *ATL*, p. 257.
12. *ATL*, p. 418.
13. Cordell, p. 10.
14. *ATL*, p. 377.
15. *ATL*, p. 184.
16. *ATL*, p. 339.
17. *ATL*, pp. 372–73.
18. *ATL*, p. 407.
19. *ATL*, p. 456.
20. *ATL*, p. 451.
21. *ATL*, p. 471.
22. *ATL*, pp. 484–85.
23. *ATL*, p. 517.
24. *ATL*, p. 518.

Chapter 9

1. Luhan, "Holiday From Science?," *Southwest Review* 31 (1946): 224 (221–24).

2. Sally MacDougall, "1918 Salon Revived by Mabel Dodge," *New York World-Telegram* (January 5, 1940), Sb vol. 14, MDLC.

3. Luhan to Eastman, January 5, ?, MEC.

4. "Mabel's Comeback," *Time Magazine* (January 22, 1940), Sb vol. 14, MDLC.

5. See Philp, pp. 206–8.

6. Collier, *On the Gleaming Way,* p. 29.

7. Luhan, *Let's Get Away Together,* 1945, unpublished typescript, p. 324, MDLC.

8. Mabel's estate was purchased by Dennis Hopper in the early 1970s. He discovered it when he was on location making "Easy Rider," and he kept it, for the few years he owned it, as an artists' commune.

9. "The Chicken Pull," *New Yorker* (May 5, 1945), Sb vol. 14, MDLC.

10. Quoted in Weigle and Fiore, p. 75; Waters, p. 445.

11. Waters, pp. 432–33.

12. Luhan, "Holiday From Science?," pp. 221–24.

13. Luhan, *Taos and Its Artists,* p. 11.

14. Luhan, "Can't We Let the Indians Find Their Own Way Home?," *El Crepusculo* (May 26, 1949), Sb vol. 14, MDLC.

15. Luhan, "Taos—Unrevisited," *El Crepusculo* (June 16, 1949), Sb vol. 14, MDLC.

16. Bonnie Evans remembers her grandmother speaking of moving away from Taos in the late 1940s. Mabel rented a room in Ralph Myers's studio early in the 1950s in order to sell some of her antiques. "Mabel Dodge Luhan Builds New House," *Taos Star* (October 21, 1948), Sb vol. 14, MDLC.

17. Luhan, ed., "Taos and Individualism," *New Mexico Quarterly* 21, no. 2 (1951): 134.

18. Luhan, "Paso Por Aqui!," pp. 137–38 (137–46).

19. Morrill, p. 114.

20. Luhan, *Statue of Liberty,* quoted in Haubald, p. 67.

21. Dorothy Brett to Bonnie Evans, November 7, 1954. Copy provided me by Bonnie Evans.

22. All information from Bonnie Evans in Evans to Rudnick, April 15, 1982.

23. Interview with Rowena Myers, July 5, 1980.

24. Frieda Lawrence to Luhan, n.d., MDLC.

25. Mirandi Levy to James Kraft, November 17, 1974. Copy provided to me by Kraft. Mrs. Levy was a strong partisan of Bynner's who disliked Mabel.

26. Bynner to Luhan, June 1955, WBC, quoted in Scott Donalson, *Poet in America,* p. 252.

27. Bonnie Evans remembers Mabel saying that she wished to be buried in the garden of her estate. Bonnie says that John Evans was opposed to this because he felt "the house would be harder to sell" if Mabel were buried in the garden. Rowena Meyers suggested that Mabel's decision may have been due to the fact that the Carson Cemetery was the only decent one in Taos. Mabel left an estate (real and personal) of $194,724.02 net value.

28. Brett to Evans, August 18, 1962. Copy provided me by Bonnie Evans.

29. Collier, *From Every Zenith,* p. 106.

Bibliography

Aaron, Daniel, ed. *America in Crisis: Fourteen Crucial Episodes in American History.* New York: Alfred A. Knopf, 1952.

———. *Writers on the Left: Episodes in American Literary Communism.* New York: Harcourt, Brace and World, 1961.

Adams, Ansel. *Images, 1923–1971.* Edited by L. DeCock. Boston: New York Graphic Society, 1974.

Adams, Henry. *The Education of Henry Adams.* New York: Modern Library, 1931 (1918).

Allen, Frederick Lewis. *The Big Change: America Transforms Itself, 1900–1950.* New York: Harper and Brothers, 1952.

———. *Since Yesterday: The 1930s in America.* New York: Harper and Row, 1968 (1939).

Anderson, Margaret. *The Unknowable Gurdjieff.* New York: Weiser, 1962.

Anderson, Quentin. *The Imperial Self: An Essay in American Literary and Cultural History.* New York: Vintage Books, 1972 (1971).

Arnold, Armin. *D. H. Lawrence and America.* London: Linden Press, 1958.

———, ed. *The Symbolic Meaning: The Uncollected Versions of "Studies in Classic American Literature."* New York: Viking Press, 1962.

Austin, Mary. *The Arrow Maker.* New York: Duffield, 1911.

———. *Earth Horizon.* Boston: Houghton Mifflin, 1932.

———. *Land of Journey's Ending.* Tucson: University of Arizona Press, 1983 (facsimile of 1924 edition).

―――. *Taos Pueblo.* Boston: New York Graphic Society, 1977 (facsimile of 1930 Grabhorn Press edition).

Barnett, Melba. *The Stone Mason of Tor House.* Los Angeles: Ward Ritchie Press, 1966.

Beals, Alan, and Siegel, Bernard. *Divisiveness and Social Conflict.* Palo Alto: Stanford University Press, 1966.

Beauvoir, Simone de. *The Second Sex.* New York: Bantam Books, 1961 (1949).

Benedict, Ruth. *Patterns of Culture.* Boston: Houghton Mifflin, 1934.

Bennett, John G. *Gurdjieff: Making a New World.* London: Turnstone Books, 1973.

Berry, Faith. *Langston Hughes: Before and Beyond Harlem.* Westport, Conn.: Lawrence Hill, 1983.

Birnbaum, Martin. *Introductions.* New York: F. Sherman Fairchild, 1919.

Blanche, Jacques-Émile. *Aymeris.* Paris: Librairie Plan, 1923.

―――. *Portraits of a Lifetime.* Edited and translated by Walter Clement. New York: Coward-McCann, 1938.

Braden, Charles S. *These Also Believe: A Study of Modern American Cults and Minority Religious Movements.* New York: Macmillan, 1951.

Brett, Dorothy. *Lawrence and Brett: A Friendship.* Philadelphia: J. B. Lippincott, 1933.

Bridgman, Richard. *Gertrude Stein in Pieces.* Oxford: Oxford University Press, 1970.

Brill, A. A. *Basic Principles of Psychoanalysis.* New York: Pocket Books, 1960 (1921).

Brinig, Myron. *All of Their Lives.* New York: Farrar and Rhinehart, 1941.

Brinnin, John Malcolm. *The Third Rose: Gertrude Stein and Her World.* Boston: Little, Brown, 1959.

Brody, J. J. *Indian Painters and White Patrons.* Albuquerque: University of New Mexico Press, 1971.

Brooks, Van Wyck. *The Confident Years, 1885–1915.* New York: E. P. Dutton, 1952.

Brophy, Robert J. *Robinson Jeffers: Myth, Ritual, and Symbol in His Narrative Poems.* Cleveland: Case Western Reserve University Press, 1973.

Brown, Milton S. *American Painting From the Armory Show to the Depression.* Princeton: Princeton University Press, 1970 (1955).

Bynner, Witter. *Cake, An indulgence.* New York: Alfred A. Knopf, 1926.

―――. *guest book.* New York: Alfred A. Knopf, 1935.

―――. *Journey with Genius: Recollections and Reflections Concerning the D. H. Lawrences.* New York: John Day, 1951.

―――. *Prose Pieces.* Edited by James Kraft. New York: Farrar, Straus, Giroux, 1979.

Campbell, Joseph. *The Hero With A Thousand Faces.* 2d edition. Princeton: Princeton University Press, 1972 (1968).

Cantor, Milton. *Max Eastman.* New York: Twayne Publishers, 1970.

Carpenter, Edward. *Love's Coming-of-Age: A Series of Papers on the Relations of the Sexes.* Manchester, England: Labour Press, 1896.

Carpenter, Frederick. *Robinson Jeffers.* New York: Twayne Publishers, 1962.

Castro, Michael. *Interpreting the Indian: Twentieth-Century Poets and the Native American.* Albuquerque: University of New Mexico Press, 1983.

Cate, Curtis. *George Sand: A Biography.* Boston: Houghton Mifflin, 1975.

Cather, Willa. *Death Comes for the Archbishop.* New York: Vintage Books, 1971 (1927).

Cavitch, David. *D. H. Lawrence and the New World.* Oxford: Oxford University Press, 1971 (1969).

Chambers, Clarke. *Seed Time of Reform: American Social Service and Social Action, 1918–1933.* Minneapolis: University of Minnesota Press, 1963.

Churchill, Allen. *The Improper Bohemians: The Re-Creation of Greenwich Village in Its Heyday.* New York: E. P. Dutton, 1959.

Clark, L. D. *The Dark Night of the Body: D. H. Lawrence's "The Plumed Serpent."* Austin: University of Texas Press, 1964.

Coffin, Arthur. *Robinson Jeffers: Poet of Inhumanism.* Madison: University of Wisconsin Press, 1971.

Coke, Van Deren. *Andrew Dasburg.* Albuquerque: University of New Mexico Press, 1979.

———. *Taos and Santa Fe: The Artist's Environment: 1882–1942.* Albuquerque: University of New Mexico Press, 1963.

John Collier. *From Every Zenith.* Denver: Sage Books, 1963.

———. *The Indians of the Americas.* New York: W. W. Norton, 1947.

———. *On the Gleaming Way: Navajos, Eastern Pueblos, Zunis, Hopis, Apaches, and Their Land.* Chicago: Sage Books, 1962 (1949).

Cowan, James C. *D. H. Lawrence's American Journey: A Study In Literature and Myth.* Cleveland: Case Western Reserve University Press, 1970.

Crunden, Robert M. *From Self to Society, 1919–1941.* Englewood Cliffs: Prentice-Hall, 1972.

Deloria, Vine, Jr. *Custer Died For Your Sins: An Indian Manifesto.* New York: Avon Books, 1970 (1969).

Diggins, John P. *The American Left in the Twentieth Century.* New York: Harcourt, Brace, Jovanovich, 1973.

Domhoff, G. William. *The Higher Circles: The Governing Class in America.* New York: Random House, 1970.

Donalson, Scott. *Poet in America: Winfield Townley Scott.* Austin: University of Texas Press, 1972.

Dozier, Edward. *The Pueblo Indians of North America.* New York: Holt, Rhinehart, and Winston, 1970.

Draper, Muriel. *Music at Midnight.* New York: Harper and Brothers, 1929.

Eastman, Max. *The Enjoyment of Living.* New York: Harper and Brothers, 1948.

———. *Venture.* New York: Boni and Liveright, 1927.

Eldredge, Charles. *Ward Lockwood: 1894–1963.* Lawrence: University of Kansas Museum of Art, 1974.

Ewen, David. *Dictators of the Baton.* New York: Ziff-Davis, 1943.

Fass, Paula. "A. A. Brill—Pioneer and Prophet." Master's thesis, Columbia University, 1969.

Feidelson, Charles Jr. *Symbolism and American Literature.* Chicago: University of Chicago Press, 1951.

Fergusson, Erna. *New Mexico: A Pageant of Three Peoples.* New York: Alfred A. Knopf, 1951.

————. *Our Southwest.* New York: Alfred A. Knopf, 1940.

Fiedler, Leslie A. *Love and Death in the American Novel.* Rev. ed. New York: Dell, 1966.

Fink, Augusta. *I—Mary: A Biography of Mary Austin.* Tucson: University of Arizona Press, 1983.

Foster, Joseph. *D. H. Lawrence in Taos.* Albuquerque: University of New Mexico Press, 1972.

Frank, Waldo, ed. *America and Alfred Stieglitz.* New York: Literary Guild, 1934.

Freud, Sigmund. *Sexuality and the Psychology of Love.* New York: Collier Books, 1963.

Gallup, Donald, ed. *Flowers of Friendship: Letters Written to Gertrude Stein.* New York: Alfred A. Knopf, 1953.

Gibson, Arrell M. *Santa Fe and Taos Colonies: Age of the Muses, 1900–1942.* Norman: University of Oklahoma Press, 1983.

Gilbert, Sandra M., and Susan Gubar. *The Madwoman in the Attic: The Woman Writer and the Nineteenth Century Literary Imagination.* New Haven: Yale University Press, 1979.

Graves, Robert. *The White Goddess: A Historical Grammar of Poetic Myth.* New York: Farrar, Straus, Giroux, 1966 (1948).

Gray, Cleve, ed. *John Marin.* New York: Holt, Rhinehart, and Winston, 1970.

Green, Jonathan, ed. *Camera Work: A Critical Anthology.* New York: Aperture, 1973.

Green, Martin. *The von Richthofen Sisters: The Triumphant and the Tragic Modes of Love.* New York: Basic Books, 1974.

Greenan, Edith. *Of Una Jeffers.* Los Angeles: Ward Ritchie Press, 1939.

Griffin, John. "Jean Toomer: American Writer." Ph.D. diss., University of South Carolina, 1976.

Gurdjieff, G. I. *Gurdjieff: Views From the Real World: Early Talks of Gurdjieff.* London: Routledge and Kegan Paul, 1973.

Hahn, Emily. *Mabel: A Biography of Mabel Dodge Luhan.* Boston: Houghton Mifflin, 1977.

Hale, Nathan G., Jr. *Freud and the Americans: The Beginnings of Psychoanalysis in the United States, 1876–1917.* New York: Oxford University Press, 1971.

Hapgood, Hutchins. *A Victorian in the Modern World.* New York: Harcourt, Brace and World, 1939.

Haubold, Marcia. "Mabel Dodge Luhan: An Historical Study of an American Individual and Her Social Environment." Master's thesis, University of Iowa, 1965.

Hays, H. R. *The Dangerous Sex: The Myth of Feminine Evil.* New York: Pocket Books, 1966 (1964).

Haywood, William D. *Bill Haywood's Book: The Autobiography of William D. Haywood.* New York: International Publishers, 1929.

Helm, MacKinley. *John Marin.* Boston: Pellegrini and Cudahy, 1948.

Henderson, Alice Corbin, ed. *The Turquoise Trail.* Boston: Houghton Mifflin, 1928.

Herod, J. Christopher. *Mistress To an Age: The Life of Madame de Stäel*. New York: Time, 1958.

Hicks, Granville. *John Reed: The Making of a Revolutionary*. New York: Macmillan, 1936.

Hoffman, Frederick J. *The 20s: American Writing in the Post War Decade*. Rev. ed. New York: Free Press, 1965.

———. *Freudianism and the Literary Mind*. 2d ed. Baton Rouge: Louisiana State University Press, 1967.

Hoffman, Malvina. *Heads and Tales*. New York: Charles Scribner's Sons, 1943.

Hoffman, Michael. *The Development of Abstractionism in the Writings of Gertrude Stein*. Philadelphia: University of Pennsylvania Press, 1965.

Homer, William I. *Alfred Stieglitz and the American Avant-Garde*. Boston: New York Graphic Society, 1977.

Horney, Karen. *The Neurotic Personality of Our Time*. New York: W. W. Norton, 1937.

Hough, Graham. *The Dark Sun: A Study of D. H. Lawrence*. London: Duckworth, 1956.

Hughes, Langston. *Selected Poems of Langston Hughes*. New York: Alfred A. Knopf, 1969.

Jeffers, Robinson. *Roan Stallion, Tamar, and Other Poems*. New York: Boni and Liveright, 1925.

———. *Selected Poetry of Robinson Jeffers*. New York: Random House, 1938.

———. *Selected Letters of Robinson Jeffers, 1897–1962*. Edited by Ann Ridgeway. Baltimore: Johns Hopkins University Press, 1968.

James, William. *The Varieties of Religious Experience: A Study in Human Nature*. New York: New American Library, 1958 (1902).

Jung, Carl G. *Man and his Symbols*. New York: Dell, 1968 (1964).

———. *Memories, Dreams, Reflections*. Edited by Aniela Jaffe. New York: Pantheon Books, 1965.

Kaplan, Justin. *Lincoln Steffens: A Biography*. New York: Simon and Schuster, 1974.

Kellner, Bruce. *Carl Van Vechten and the Irreverent Decades*. Norman: University of Oklahoma Press, 1968.

Kelly, Lawrence C. *The Assault On Assimilation: John Collier and the Origins of Indian Policy Reform*. Albuquerque: University of New Mexico Press, 1983.

Kolko, Gabriel. *The Triumph of Conservatism: A Reinterpretation of American History*. Chicago: Quadrangle, 1967 (1963).

Kolodny, Annette. *The Land Before Her: Fantasy and Experience of the American Frontiers, 1630–1860*. Chapel Hill: University of North Carolina Press, 1984.

Laing, R. D. *The Divided Self: An Existential Study in Sanity and Madness*. Baltimore: Penguin Books, 1965 (1960).

Lasch, Christopher. *The New Radicalism in America (1889–1963): The Intellectual as a Social Type*. New York: Vintage Books, 1967 (1965).

Lawrence, D. H. *The Collected Letters of D. H. Lawrence*, vol. 2. Edited by Harry T. Moore. New York: Viking Press, 1962.

———. *The Complete Short Stories*, vols. 2 and 3. New York: Viking Press, 1961.

———. *Fire and Other Poems*. Grabhorn Press, 1940.

————. *Phoenix: The Posthumous Papers of D. H. Lawrence (1936).* New York: Viking Press, 1972.

————. *The Plumed Serpent.* New York: Vintage Books, 1959 (1927).

————. *St. Mawr and The Man Who Died.* New York: Vintage Books, 1953.

————. *Studies in Classic American Literature.* New York: Viking Press, 1964 (1923).

Lawrence, Frieda. *Frieda Lawrence: The Memoirs and Correspondence.* Edited by E. W. Tedlock, Jr. New York: Alfred A. Knopf, 1964.

————. *Not I But the Wind.* New York: Viking Press, 1934.

Leuders, Edward. *Carl Van Vechten.* New York: Twayne Publishers, 1965.

Lewis, Edith. *Willa Cather Living: A Personal Record.* New York: Alfred A. Knopf, 1953.

Lindberg, Olga. *Buffalo in the Gilded Age: Adventures in Western New York History,* vol. 24. Buffalo: Buffalo and Erie County Historical Society, 1977.

Lippmann, Walter. *Drift and Mastery.* Englewood Cliffs: Prentice-Hall, 1961 (1914).

Lisle, Laurie. *Portrait of An Artist: A Biography of Georgia O'Keeffe.* New York: Pocket Books, 1981 (1980).

Lucas, Robert. *Frieda Lawrence: The Story of Frieda von Richthofen and D. H. Lawrence.* New York: Viking Press, 1972.

Luhan, Mabel Dodge. *Intimate Memories: Background.* New York: Harcourt, Brace and Company, 1933.

————. *European Experiences: Volume Two of Intimate Memories.* New York: Harcourt, Brace and Company, 1935.

————. *Movers and Shakers: Volume Three of Intimate Memories.* New York: Harcourt, Brace and Company, 1936.

————. *Edge of Taos Desert: An Escape to Reality: Volume Four of Intimate Memories.* New York: Harcourt, Brace and Company, 1937.

————. *Lorenzo in Taos.* New York: Alfred A. Knopf, 1932.

————. *Winter in Taos.* New York: Harcourt, Brace and Company, 1935.

————. *Taos and Its Artists.* New York: Duell, Sloan, and Pierce, 1947.

————: *Una and Robin.* Edited by Mark Schorer. Berkeley: Friends of the Bancroft Library, University of California, 1976.

Major, Mabel, and T. M. Pearce. *Southwest Heritage: A Literary History with Bibliography.* Albuquerque: University of New Mexico Press, 1972.

Marin, John. *Letters of John Marin.* Edited by Herbert Seligmann. Boston: private printing for An American Place, 1931.

————. *Selected Writings of John Marin.* Edited by Dorothy Norman. Boston: Pelegrini and Cudahy, 1949.

————. *John Marin.* New York: Holt, Rinehart, and Winston, 1971.

Mellow, James R. *Charmed Circle: Gertrude Stein & Company.* New York: Avon Books, 1975 (1974).

Merrild, Knud. *A Poet and Two Painters.* London: George Routledge, 1938.

Meyer, Donald. *The Positive Thinkers: A Study of the American Quest for Health, Wealth, and Personal Power from Mary Baker Eddy to Norman Vincent Peale.* New York: Anchor Books, 1966 (1965).

Millett, Kate. *Sexual Politics.* New York: Avon Books, 1971 (1969).

Moore, Harry T. *The Intelligent Heart: The Story of D. H. Lawrence.* New York: Farrar, Straus, Giroux, 1954.

Morrill, Claire. *A Taos Mosaic: Portrait of a New Mexico Village.* Albuquerque: University of New Mexico Press, 1973.

Nelson, Jane. *Mabel Dodge Luhan.* Western Writer's Series, No. 55. Boise: Boise State University Press, 1982.

Neumann, Erich. *The Great Mother: An Analysis of the Archetype.* 2d ed. Princeton: Princeton University Press, 1972 (1963).

O'Connor, Richard, and Dale Walker. *The Lost Revolutionary: A Biography of John Reed.* New York: Harcourt, Brace and World, 1967.

O'Neill, William L. *Divorce in the Progressive Era.* New Haven: Yale University Press, 1967.

————, ed. *Echoes of Revolt: The Masses, 1911–1917.* Chicago: Quadrangle Books, 1966.

————. *Everyone Was Brave: A History of Feminism in America.* Chicago: Quadrangle Books, 1969.

Ortiz, Alfonso, ed. *New Perspectives on the Pueblos.* Albuquerque: University of New Mexico Press, 1972.

————. *Southwest.* Vol. 9, *Handbook of North American Indians.* Washington, D.C.: Smithsonian, 1979.

————. *The Tewa World.* Chicago: University of Chicago Press, 1969.

Parry, Albert. *Garrets and Pretenders: A History of Bohemianism in America, 1885–1915.* New York: Dover Press, 1960 (1933).

Parsons, Elsie Clews. *Taos Pueblo.* Menasha, Wisc.: George Banta, 1936.

Pater, Walter. *Studies in the History of the Renaissance.* London: Macmillan, 1873.

Pearce, T. M. *Alice Corbin Henderson.* Austin: Steck-Vaughn, 1969.

————. *Mary Hunter Austin.* New York: Twayne Publishers, 1965.

Philp, Kenneth R. *John Collier's Crusade for Indian Reform, 1920–1945.* Tucson: University of Arizona Press, 1977.

Powell, Elwin. *Design of Discord: Studies in Anomie.* New York: Oxford University Press, 1970.

Powell, Lawrence C. *Robinson Jeffers: The Man and His Work.* Pasadena: San Pasqual Press, 1940.

Reeve, Kay Aiken. *Santa Fe and Taos, 1898–1942: An American Cultural Center.* Southwestern Studies, No. 67. El Paso: Texas Western Press, 1982.

Robinson, Cecil. *Mexico and the Hispanic Southwest in American Literature.* Tucson: University of Arizona Press, 1977.

Rosenstone, Robert A. *Romantic Revolutionary: A Biography of John Reed.* New York: Alfred A. Knopf, 1975.

Rubenstein, Arthur. *My Young Years.* New York: Alfred A. Knopf, 1973.

Sanger, Margaret. *Margaret Sanger: An Autobiography.* New York: W. W. Norton, 1938.

Sargeant, Elizabeth S. *Willa Cather: A Memoir.* Omaha: University of Nebraska Press, 1953.

Schwarz, Judith. *Radical Feminists of Heterodoxy: Greenwich Village 1912–1940.* Lebanon, N.H.: New Victoria Publishers, 1982.

Secrest, Meryl. *Being Berenson.* New York: Holt, Rinehart, and Winston, 1979.

Seeley, John R. *The Americanization of The Unconscious*. Philadelphia: J. B. Lippincott, 1967.

Sinclair, Upton. *Money Writes!* New York: Charles Boni, 1927.

Skinner, Cornelia Otis. *Dithers and Jitters*. New York: Dodd, Mead, 1938.

Sochen, June. *The New Woman: Feminism in Greenwich Village, 1910–1920*. New York: Quadrangle Books, 1972.

Spacks, Patricia M. *The Female Imagination*. New York: Alfred A. Knopf, 1975.

Squires, Radcliffe. *The Loyalties of Robinson Jeffers*. Ann Arbor: University of Michigan Press, 1956.

Steffens, Lincoln. *The Autobiography of Lincoln Steffens*, vol. 2. New York: Harcourt, Brace and World, 1958 (1931).

Stein, Gertrude. *Writings and Lectures, 1911–1945*. Edited by Patricia Meyerowitz. London: Owen, 1967.

Stein, Leo. *Journey Into the Self: Being the Letters, Papers, and Journals of Leo Stein*. Edited by Edmund Fuller. New York: Crown Publishers, 1950.

Sterne, Maurice. *Shadow and Light: The Life, Friends, and Opinions of Maurice Sterne*. Edited by Charles Mayerson. New York: Harcourt, Brace and World, 1965.

Strand, Paul. *Paul Strand: Sixty Years of Photographs*. Millerton, N.Y.: Aperture, 1976.

Sutherland, Donald. *Gertrude Stein: A Biography of Her Work*. New Haven: Yale University Press, 1951.

Tedlock, E. W., Jr. *The Frieda Lawrence Collection of D. H. Lawrence Manuscripts: A Descriptive Bibliography*. Albuquerque: University of New Mexico Press, 1948.

Toomer, Jean. *The Wayward and the Seeking: A Collection of Writings by Jean Toomer*. Edited by Darwin Turner. Washington, D.C.: Howard University Press, 1980.

Turnbull, Andrew. *Thomas Wolfe*. New York: Charles Scribner's Sons, 1968.

Turner, Darwin. *In A Minor Chord: Three Afro-American Writers and Their Search for Identity*. Carbondale: Southern Illinois University Press, 1971.

Van Vechten, Carl. *Peter Whiffle: His Life and Works*. New York: Alfred A. Knopf, 1922.

———. *The Blind Bow-Boy*. New York: Alfred A. Knopf, 1923.

———. *Excavations*. New York: Alfred A. Knopf, 1926.

———. *Sacred and Profane Memories*. New York: Alfred A. Knopf, 1932.

———. *Carl Van Vechten*. Oral History Research Office. New York: Columbia University, 1960.

Vorse, Mary Heaton. *A Footnote to Folly: Reminiscences*. New York: Farrar and Rhinehart, 1935.

Waters, Frank. *Masked Gods: Navajo and Pueblo Ceremonialism*. New York: Ballantine Books, 1960 (1950).

Weigle, Marta, and Fiore, Kyle. *Santa Fe and Taos: The Writer's Era, 1916–1941*. Santa Fe: Ancient City Press, 1982.

Weinstein, James. *The Corporate Ideal in the Liberal State, 1900–1918*. Boston: Beacon Press, 1969 (1968).

Wharton, Edith. *A Backward Glance*. New York: Appleton-Century, 1934.

Whitman, Walt. *Complete Poetry and Selected Prose of Walt Whitman*. Edited by James Miller. Boston: Houghton Mifflin, 1959.

Wolfe, Thomas. *Of Time and the River.* New York: Charles Scribner's Sons, 1935.

Woolf, Virginia. *A Room of One's Own.* New York: Harcourt, Brace and World, 1957 (1929).

Young, Ella. *Flowering Dusk: Things Remembered Accurately and Inaccurately.* New York: Longmans, Green, 1945.

Young-Hunter, John. *Reviewing the Years.* New York: Crown, 1962.

Index

Note: References to Mabel Dodge Luhan within entries are given as M. D. L.

Index

Lawrence, 195; and Indian and Spanish crafts, 170–71; and Indian affairs, 312; and Indian art, 171; and Indian culture, 142; and Indian life-style, 154; and intellectuals, 253, 258, 265–70; interview with, by Elizabeth Shepley Sargeant, 284; and Isadora Duncan, 122; and Jacques-Émile Blanche, 42; and Jean Toomer, 227–28; and John Collier, 125, 130, 173–74, 264–65; and Leopold Stokowski, 268–70; and Leo Stein, 42, 43; and Leo Stein's approach to art, 43; *Lorenzo in Taos,* 287, 292–93; and Malvina Hoffman, 266; marriage to Edwin Dodge, 30; marriage to Karl Evans, 24–25; marriage to Maurice Sterne, 141; marriage to Tony Luhan, 182; and Mary Austin, 170; medical treatment by Bernard Sachs, 130; memoirs, 219, 253–59; memories of childhood, 15–19; and mind cure, 132–35; movie script, 269; as Muse, 90; and New Mexico, 144–45, 323–24; and New Thought, 132–35; and New Woman, 89, 90; and New York, 225–26; in New York, 59, 60, 284; 1904 trip to Europe, 26, 29; 1912 trip to U.S., 57; old age, 328, 329; parents' relationship, 6, 17; in Paris, 101; "The Parting," 136; and Paterson Strike Pageant, 93; and Paul Draper, 41; personality, 48, 217–18, 225–26, 299–300; philosophical aspirations, 73; philosophy, 71; photograph of, by Gertrude Kasebier, 124; poem about, by Witter Bynner, 244; poem to D. H. Lawrence, 195–96, 220; poetry inspired by D. H. Lawrence, 212–13; and politics, 72–73; popular image of, 251–52; portrait of, by Jack Young-Hunter, 253; portrait of, by Mary Foote, 76; portrait of, by Nicolai Fechin, 230; portraits of, by Jacques-Émile Blanche, 52–53; portraits of, by Maurice Sterne, 127–28; pregnancy, 25; proposed project with Craig Gordon, 38; proposed project with Muriel Draper, 38; psychic experience concerning Indians, 142; psychological problems, 16–19, 21, 23, 30, 31, 41–42, 69, 88–89, 129–39, 234–35; psychological problems of, and those of

Leo and Gertrude Stein, 45; and Pueblo crusade, 175–83, 186–87; and Pueblo culture, 149–52, 183–84; "A Quarrel," 135–36; and relationship between Witter Bynner and Spud Johnson, 244; relationships with men during late adolescence, 21; relationship with Bobby Jones, 84–85, 184–85; relationship with Carl Van Vechten, 108–9; relationship with D. H. Lawrence, 189, 191–96 passim, 199, 201–2, 211–14, 216–17, 219–24, 249; relationship with Dorothy Brett, 215–16, 235, 327–28; relationship with Edwin Dodge, 30–31; relationship with father, 6, 24; relationship with Frieda Lawrence, 196–97, 198, 215–16, 294, 327; relationship with Grandfather Cook, 1; relationship with Hutchins Hapgood, 133; relationship with John Reed, 91–106, 121; relationship with Karl Evans, 25; relationship with Maurice Sterne, 125–29, 133–36, 141–42; relationship with Max Eastman, 115–16; relationship with mother, 6, 15; relationship with Myron Brinig, 302, 303; relationship with parents, 17; relationship with Robinson Jeffers, 286–88, 290–94, 297, 298–99; relationship with Seward Cary, 23; relationship with son, 57, 300; relationship with Thornton Wilder, 270–71, 280–81; relationship with Tony Luhan, 152–55, 158, 218–19, 225–26, 228–29, 231–32, 238–39, 240–41, 325, 329; relationship with Una Jeffers, 291–92, 294, 299; relationship with Uncle Carlos, 21–22; relationship with Violet Shillito, 20–21; relationship with Witter Bynner, 244–45, 248, 328; report of John Reed's last words, 106; review of *I, Mary MacLane,* 139–40; salon, 74, 75–76, 83–84, 311–12; and Santa Fe, 145–46; "The Secret of War," 101–2; self-portrayals, 248, 292–93; separation from Edwin Dodge, 60; separation from Maurice Sterne, 154–55; sexual awakening, 25; and sexuality, 90, 196; short stories, 135–36; and Sigmund Freud's ideas, 139; social background, 3–6; social

379